Big Data Analytics in Cybersecurity

Data Analytics Applications

Series Editor: Jay Liebowitz

PUBLISHED

Actionable Intelligence for Healthcare
by Jay Liebowitz, Amanda Dawson
ISBN: 978-1-4987-6665-4

Data Analytics Applications in Latin America and Emerging Economies
by Eduardo Rodriguez
ISBN: 978-1-4987-6276-2

Sport Business Analytics: Using Data to Increase Revenue and Improve Operational Efficiency
by C. Keith Harrison, Scott Bukstein
ISBN: 978-1-4987-6126-0

Big Data and Analytics Applications in Government: Current Practices and Future Opportunities
by Gregory Richards
ISBN: 978-1-4987-6434-6

Data Analytics Applications in Education
by Jan Vanthienen and Kristoff De Witte
ISBN: 978-1-4987-6927-3

Big Data Analytics in Cybersecurity
by Onur Savas and Julia Deng
ISBN: 978-1-4987-7212-9

FORTHCOMING

Data Analytics Applications in Law
by Edward J. Walters
ISBN: 978-1-4987-6665-4

Data Analytics for Marketing and CRM
by Jie Cheng
ISBN: 978-1-4987-6424-7

Data Analytics in Institutional Trading
by Henri Waelbroeck
ISBN: 978-1-4987-7138-2

Big Data Analytics in Cybersecurity

Edited by
Onur Savas
Julia Deng

CRC Press
Taylor & Francis Group
Boca Raton London New York

CRC Press is an imprint of the
Taylor & Francis Group, an **informa** business
AN AUERBACH BOOK

CRC Press
Taylor & Francis Group
6000 Broken Sound Parkway NW, Suite 300
Boca Raton, FL 33487-2742

First issued in paperback 2021

Printed on acid-free paper

ISBN-13: 978-1-4987-7212-9 (hbk)
ISBN-13: 978-1-03-209636-0 (pbk)

Visit the Taylor & Francis Web site at
http://www.taylorandfrancis.com

and the CRC Press Web site at
http://www.crcpress.com

Contents

SECTION II BIG DATA IN EMERGING CYBERSECURITY DOMAINS

SECTION III TOOLS AND DATASETS FOR CYBERSECURITY

Preface

Cybersecurity is the protection of information systems, both hardware and software, from the theft, unauthorized access, and disclosure, as well as intentional or accidental harm. It protects all segments pertaining to the Internet, from networks themselves to the information transmitted over the network and stored in databases, to various applications, and to devices that control equipment operations via network connections. With the emergence of new advanced technologies such as cloud, mobile computing, fog computing, and the Internet of Things (IoT), the Internet has become and will be more ubiquitous. While this ubiquity makes our lives easier, it creates unprecedented challenges for cybersecurity. Nowadays it seems that not a day goes by without a new story on the topic of cybersecurity, either a security incident on information leakage, or an abuse of an emerging technology such as autonomous car hacking, or the software we have been using for years is now deemed to be dangerous because of the newly found security vulnerabilities.

So, why can't these cyberattacks be stopped? Well, the answer is very complicated, partially because of the dependency on legacy systems, human errors, or simply not paying attention to security aspects. In addition, the changing and increasing complex threat landscape makes traditional cybersecurity mechanisms inadequate and ineffective. Big data is further making the situation worse, and presents additional challenges to cybersecurity. For an example, the IoT will generate a staggering 400 zettabytes (ZB) of data a year by 2018, according to a report from Cisco. Self-driving cars will soon create significantly more data than people—3 billion people's worth of data, according to Intel. The averagely driven car will churn out 4000 GB of data per day, and that is just for one hour of driving a day.

Big data analytics, as an emerging analytical technology, offers the capability to collect, store, process, and visualize BIG data; therefore, applying big data analytics in cybersecurity becomes critical and a new trend. By exploiting data from the networks and computers, analysts can discover useful information from data using analytic techniques and processes. Then the decision makers can make more informative decisions by taking advantage of the analysis, including what actions need to be performed, and improvement recommendations to policies, guidelines, procedures, tools, and other aspects of the network processes.

This book provides a comprehensive coverage of a wide range of complementary topics in cybersecurity. The topics include but are not limited to network forensics, threat analysis, vulnerability assessment, visualization, and cyber training. In addition, emerging security domains such as the IoT, cloud computing, fog computing, mobile computing, and the cyber-social networks are studied. The target audience of this book includes both starters and more experienced security professionals. Readers with data analytics but no cybersecurity or IT experience, or readers with cybersecurity but no data analytics experience will hopefully find the book informative.

The book consists of 14 chapters, organized into three parts, namely "Applying Big Data into Different Cybersecurity Aspects," "Big Data in Emerging Cybersecurity Domains," and "Tools and Datasets for Cybersecurity." The first part includes Chapters 1–7, focusing on how big data analytics can be used in different cybersecurity aspects. The second part includes Chapters 8–12, discussing big data challenges and solutions in emerging cybersecurity domains, and the last part, Chapters 13 and 14, present the tools and datasets for cybersecurity research. The authors are experts in their respective domains, and are from academia, government labs, and the industry.

Chapter 1, "The Power of Big Data in Cybersecurity," is written by Song Luo, Malek Ben Salem, from Accenture Technology Labs, and Yan Zhai from E8 Security Inc. This chapter introduces big data analytics and highlights the needs and importance of applying big data analytics in cybersecurity to fight against the evolving threat landscape. It also describes the typical usage of big data security analytics including its solution domains, architecture, typical use cases, and the challenges. Big data analytics, as an emerging analytical technology, offers the capability to collect, store, process, and visualize big data, which are so large or complex that traditional data processing applications are inadequate to deal with. Cybersecurity, at the same time, is experiencing the big data challenge due to the rapidly growing complexity of networks (e.g., virtualization, smart devices, wireless connections, Internet of Things, etc.) and increasing sophisticated threats (e.g., malware, multistage, advanced persistent threats [APTs], etc.). Accordingly, this chapter discusses how big data analytics technology brings in its advantages, and applying big data analytics in cybersecurity is essential to cope with emerging threats.

Chapter 2, "Big Data Analytics for Network Forensics," is written by scientists Yi Cheng, Tung Thanh Nguyen, Hui Zeng, and Julia Deng from Intelligent Automation, Inc. Network forensics plays a key role in network management and cybersecurity analysis. Recently, it is facing the new challenge of big data. Big data analytics has shown its promise of unearthing important insights from large amounts of data that were previously impossible to find, which attracts the attention of researchers in network forensics, and a number of efforts have been initiated. This chapter provides an overview on how to apply big data technologies into network forensics. It first describes the terms and process of network forensics, presents current practice and their limitations, and then discusses design considerations and some experiences of applying big data analysis for network forensics.

Chapter 3, "Dynamic Analytics-Driven Assessment of Vulnerabilities and Exploitation," is written by U.S. Army Research Lab scientists Hasan Cam and Akhilomen Oniha, and MIT Lincoln Laboratory scientists Magnus Ljungberg and Alexia Schulz. This chapter presents vulnerability assessment, one of the essential cybersecurity functions and requirements, and highlights how big data analytics could potentially leverage vulnerability assessment and causality analysis of vulnerability exploitation in the detection of intrusion and vulnerabilities so that cyber analysts can investigate alerts and vulnerabilities more effectively and faster. The authors present novel models and data analytics approaches to dynamically building and analyzing relationships, dependencies, and causality reasoning among the detected vulnerabilities, intrusion detection alerts, and measurements. This chapter also describes a detailed description of building an exemplary scalable data analytics system to implement the proposed model and approaches by enriching, tagging, and indexing the data of all observations and measurements, vulnerabilities, detection, and monitoring.

Chapter 4, "Root Cause Analysis for Cybersecurity," is written by Amin Kharraz and Professor Engin Kirda of Northwestern University. Recent years have seen the rise of many classes of cyber attacks ranging from ransomware to advanced persistent threats (APTs), which pose severe risks to companies and enterprises. While static detection and signature-based tools are still useful in detecting already observed threats, they lag behind in detecting such sophisticated attacks where adversaries are adaptable and can evade defenses. This chapter intends to explain how to analyze the nature of current multidimensional attacks, and how to identify the root causes of such security incidents. The chapter also elaborates on how to incorporate the acquired intelligence to minimize the impact of complex threats and perform rapid incident response.

Chapter 5, "Data Visualization for Cyber Security," is written by Professor Lane Harrison of Worcester Polytechnic Institute. This chapter is motivated by the fact that data visualization is an indispensable means for analysis and communication, particularly in cyber security. Promising techniques and systems for cyber data visualization have emerged in the past decade, with applications ranging from threat and vulnerability analysis to forensics and network traffic monitoring. In this chapter, the author revisits several of these milestones. Beyond recounting the past, however, the author uncovers and illustrates the emerging themes in new and ongoing cyber data visualization research. The need for principled approaches toward combining the strengths of the human perceptual system is also explored with analytical techniques like anomaly detection, for example, as well as the increasingly urgent challenge of combatting suboptimal visualization designs—designs that waste both analyst time and organization resources.

Chapter 6, "Cybersecurity Training," is written by cognitive psychologist Bob Pokorny of Intelligent Automation, Inc. This chapter presents training approaches incorporating principles that are not commonly incorporated into training programs, but should be applied when constructing training for cybersecurity. It should help you understand that training is more than (1) providing information that the organization expects staff to apply; (2) assuming that new cybersecurity staff who recently received degrees or certificates in cybersecurity will know what is required; or (3) requiring cybersecurity personnel to read about new threats.

Chapter 7, "Machine Unlearning: Repairing Learning Models in Adversarial Environments," is written by Professor Yinzhi Cao of Lehigh University. Motivated by the fact that today's systems produce a rapidly exploding amount of data, and the data further derives more data, this forms a complex data propagation network that we call the data's lineage. There are many reasons that users want systems to forget certain data including its lineage for privacy, security, and usability reasons. In this chapter, the author introduces a new concept machine unlearning, or simply unlearning, capable of forgetting certain data and their lineages in learning models completely and quickly. The chapter presents a general, efficient unlearning approach by transforming learning algorithms used by a system into a summation form.

Chapter 8, "Big Data Analytics for Mobile App Security," is written by Professor Doina Caragea of Kansas State University, and Professor Xinming Ou of the University of South Florida. This chapter describes mobile app security analysis, one of the new emerging cybersecurity issues with rapidly increasing requirements introduced by the predominant use of mobile devices in people's daily lives, and discusses how big data techniques such as machine learning (ML) can be leveraged for analyzing mobile applications such as Android for security problems, in particular malware detection. This chapter also demonstrates the impact of some challenges on some existing machine learning-based approaches, and is particularly written to encourage the practice of employing a better evaluation strategy and better designs of future machine learning-based approaches for Android malware detection.

Chapter 9, "Security, Privacy, and Trust in Cloud Computing," is written by Ruiwen Li, Songjie Cai, and Professor Yuhong Liu Ruiwen Li, and Songjie Cai of Santa Clara University, and Professor Yan (Lindsay) Sun of the University of Rhode Island. Cloud computing is revolutionizing the cyberspace by enabling convenient, on-demand network access to a large shared pool of configurable computing resources (e.g., networks, servers, storage, applications, and services) that can be rapidly provisioned and released. While cloud computing is gaining popularity, diverse security, privacy, and trust issues are emerging, which hinders the rapid adoption of this new computing paradigm. This chapter introduces important concepts, models, key technologies, and unique characteristics of cloud computing, which helps readers better understand the fundamental reasons for current security, privacy, and trust issues in cloud computing. Furthermore, critical security, privacy and trust challenges, and the corresponding state-of-the-art solutions are categorized and discussed in detail, and followed by future research directions.

Chapter 10, "Cybersecurity in Internet of Things (IoT)," is written by Wenlin Han and Professor Yang Xiao of the University of Alabama. This chapter introduces the IoT as one of the most rapidly expanding cybersecurity domains, and presents the big data challenges faced by IoT, as well as various security requirements and issues in IoT. IoT is a giant network containing various applications and systems with heterogeneous devices, data sources, protocols, data formats, and so on. Thus, the data in IoT is extremely heterogeneous and big, and this poses heterogeneous big data security and management problems. This chapter describes current solutions and also outlines how big data analytics can address security issues in IoT when facing big data.

Chapter 11, "Big Data Analytics for Security in Fog Computing," is written by Shanhe Yi and Professor Qun Li of the College of William and Mary. Fog computing is a new computing paradigm that can provide elastic resources at the edge of the Internet to enable many new applications and services. This chapter discusses how big data analytics can come out of the cloud and into the fog, and how security problems in fog computing can be solved using big data analytics. The chapter also discusses the challenges and potential solutions of each problem and highlights some opportunities by surveying existing work in fog computing.

Chapter 12, "Analyzing Deviant Socio-Technical Behaviors using Social Network Analysis and Cyber Forensics-Based Methodologies," is written by Samer Al-khateeb, Muhammad Hussain, and Professor Nitin Agarwal of the University of Arkansas at Little Rock. In today's information technology age, our thinking and behaviors are highly influenced by what we see online. However, misinformation is rampant. Deviant groups use social media (e.g., Facebook) to coordinate cyber campaigns to achieve strategic goals, influence mass thinking, and steer behaviors or perspectives about an event. The chapter employs computational social network analysis and cyber forensics informed methodologies to study information competitors who seek to take the initiative and the strategic message away from the main event in order to further their own agenda (via misleading, deception, etc.).

Chapter 13, "Security Tools for Cybersecurity," is written by Matthew Matchen of Braxton-Grant Technologies. This chapter takes a purely practical approach to cybersecurity. When people are prepared to apply cybersecurity ideas and theory to practical applications in the real world, they equip themselves with tools to better enable the successful outcome of their efforts. However, choosing the right tools has always been a challenge. The focus of this chapter is to identify functional areas in which cybersecurity tools are available and to list examples in each area to demonstrate how tools are better suited to provide insight in one area over the other.

Chapter 14, "Data and Research Initiatives for Cybersecurity," is written by the editors of this book. We have been motivated by the fact that big data based cybersecurity analytics is a data-centric approach. Its ultimate goal is to utilize available technology solutions to make sense of the wealth of relevant cyber data and turning it into actionable insights that can be used to improve the current practices of network operators and administrators. Hence, this chapter aims at introducing relevant data sources for cybersecurity analysis, such as benchmark datasets for cybersecurity evaluation and testing, and certain research repositories where real world cybersecurity datasets, tools, models, and methodologies can be found to support research and development among cybersecurity researchers. In addition, some insights are added for the future directions on data sharing for big data based cybersecurity analysis.

About the Editors

Dr. Onur Savas is a data scientist at Intelligent Automation, Inc. (IAI), Rockville, MD. As a data scientist, he performs research and development (R&D), leads a team of data scientists, software engineers, and programmers, and contributes to IAI's increasing portfolio of products. He has more than 10 years of R&D expertise in the areas of networks and security, social media, distributed algorithms, sensors, and statistics. His recent work focuses on all aspects of big data analytics and cloud computing with applications to network management, cybersecurity, and social networks. Dr. Savas has a PhD in electrical and computer engineering from Boston University, Boston, MA, and is the author of numerous publications in leading journals and conferences. At IAI, he has been the recipient of various R&D contracts from DARPA, ONR, ARL, AFRL, CTTSO, NASA, and other federal agencies. His work at IAI has contributed to the development and commercialization of IAI's social media analytics tool Scraawl® (www.scraawl.com).

Dr. Julia Deng is a principal scientist and Sr. Director of Network and Security Group at Intelligent Automation, Inc. (IAI), Rockville, MD. She leads a team of more than 40 scientists and engineers, and during her tenure at IAI, she has been instrumental in growing IAI's research portfolio in networks and cybersecurity. In her role as a principal investigator and principal scientist, she initiated and directed numerous R&D programs in the areas of airborne networks, cybersecurity, network management, wireless networks, trusted computing, embedded system, cognitive radio networks, big data analytics, and cloud computing. Dr. Deng has a PhD from the University of Cincinnati, Cincinnati, OH, and has published over 30 papers in leading international journals and conference proceedings.

Contributors

Nitin Agarwal
University of Arkansas at Little Rock
Little Rock, Arkansas

Samer Al-khateeb
University of Arkansas at Little Rock
Little Rock, Arkansas

Songjie Cai
Santa Clara University
Santa Clara, California

Hasan Cam
U.S. Army Research Lab
Adelphi, Maryland

Yinzhi Cao
Lehigh University
Bethlehem, Pennsylvania

Doina Caragea
Kansas State University
Manhattan, Kansas

Yi Cheng
Intelligent Automation, Inc.
Rockville, Maryland

Julia Deng
Intelligent Automation, Inc.
Rockville, Maryland

Wenlin Han
University of Alabama
Tuscaloosa, Alabama

Lane Harrison
Worcester Polytechnic Institute
Worcester, Massachusetts

Muhammad Hussain
University of Arkansas at Little Rock
Little Rock, Arkansas

Amin Kharraz
Northwestern University
Boston, Massachusetts

Engin Kirda
Northwestern University
Boston, Massachusetts

Qun Li
College of William and Mary
Williamsburg, Virginia

Ruiwen Li
Santa Clara University
Santa Clara, California

Yuhong Liu
Santa Clara University
Santa Clara, California

Magnus Ljungberg
MIT Lincoln Laboratory
Lexington, Massachusetts

Song Luo
Accenture Technology Labs
Washington, DC

Matthew Matchen
Braxton-Grant Technologies
Elkridge, Maryland

Tung Thanh Nguyen
Intelligent Automation, Inc.
Rockville, Maryland

Akhilomen Oniha
U.S. Army Research Lab
Adelphi, Maryland

Xinming Ou
University of South Florida
Tampa, Florida

Bob Pokorny
Intelligent Automation, Inc.
Rockville, Maryland

Malek Ben Salem
Accenture Technology Labs
Washington, DC

Onur Savas
Intelligent Automation, Inc.
Rockville, Maryland

Alexia Schulz
MIT Lincoln Laboratory
Lexington, Massachusetts

Yan (Lindsay) Sun
University of Rhode Island
Kingston, Rhode Island

Yang Xiao
University of Alabama
Tuscaloosa, Alabama

Shanhe Yi
College of William and Mary
Williamsburg, Virginia

Hui Zeng
Intelligent Automation, Inc.
Rockville, Maryland

Yan Zhai
E8 Security Inc.
Redwood City, California

I

APPLYING BIG DATA INTO DIFFERENT CYBERSECURITY ASPECTS

Chapter 1

The Power of Big Data in Cybersecurity

Song Luo, Malek Ben Salem, and Yan Zhai

Contents

This chapter introduces big data analytics and highlights the needs and importance of applying big data analytics in cybersecurity to fight against the evolving threat landscape. It also describes the typical usage of big data security analytics including its solution domains, architecture, typical use cases, and the challenges. Big data analytics, as an emerging analytical technology, offers the capability to collect, store, process, and visualize big data, which are so large or complex that traditional data processing applications are inadequate to deal with them. Cybersecurity, at the same time, is experiencing the big data challenge due to the rapidly growing complexity of networks (e.g., virtualization, smart devices, wireless connections, Internet of Things, etc.) and increasing sophisticated threats (e.g., malware, multi-stage, advanced persistent threats [APTs], etc.). Accordingly, traditional cybersecurity tools become ineffective and inadequate in addressing these challenges and big data analytics technology brings in its advantages, and applying big data analytics in cybersecurity becomes critical and a new trend.

1.1 Introduction to Big Data Analytics

1.1.1 What Is Big Data Analytics?

Big data is a term applied to data sets whose size or type is beyond the ability of traditional relational databases to capture, manage, and process. As formally defined by Gartner [1], "Big data is high-volume, high-velocity and/or high-variety information assets that demand cost-effective, innovative forms of information processing that enable enhanced insight, decision making, and process automation." The characteristics of big data are often referred to as 3Vs: Volume, Velocity, and Variety. Big data analytics refers to the use of advanced analytic techniques on big data to uncover hidden patterns, unknown correlations, market trends, customer preferences and other useful business information. Advanced analytics techniques include text analytics, machine learning, predictive analytics, data mining, statistics, natural language processing, and so on. Analyzing big data allows analysts, researchers, and business users to make better and faster decisions using data that was previously inaccessible or unusable.

1.1.2 Differences between Traditional Analytics and Big Data Analytics

There is a big difference between big data analytics and handling a large amount of data in a traditional manner. While a traditional data warehouse mainly focuses more on structured data relying on relational databases, and may not be able to handle semistructured and unstructured data well, big data analytics offers key advantages of processing unstructured data using a nonrelational database. Furthermore, data warehouses may not be able to handle the processing demands posed by sets of big data that need to be updated frequently or even continually. Big data analytics is able to deal with them well by applying distributed storage and distributed in-memory processing.

1.1.2.1 Distributed Storage

"Volume" is the first "V" of Gartner's definition of big data. One key feature of big data is that it usually relies on distributed storage systems because the data is so massive (often at the petabyte or higher level) that it is impossible for a single node to store or process it. Big data also requires the storage system to scale up with future growth. Hyperscale computing environments, used by major big data companies such as Google, Facebook, and Apple, satisfy big data's storage requirements by constructing from a vast number of commodity servers with direct-attached storage (DAS).

Many big data practitioners build their hyberscale computing environments using Hadoop [2] clusters. Initiated by Google, Apache Hadoop is an open-source software framework for distributed storage and distributed processing of very large data sets on computer clusters built from commodity hardware. There are two key components in Hadoop:

- HDFS (Hadoop distributed file system): a distributed file system that stores data across multiple nodes
- MapReduce: a programming model that processes data in parallel across multiple nodes

Under MapReduce, queries are split and distributed across parallel nodes and processed in parallel (the Map step). The results are then gathered and delivered (the Reduce step). This approach takes advantage of data locality—nodes manipulating the data they have access to—to allow the dataset to be processed faster and more efficiently than it would be in conventional supercomputer architecture [3].

1.1.2.2 Support for Unstructured Data

Unstructured data is heterogeneous and variable in nature and comes in many formats, including text, document, image, video, and more. The following lists a few sources that generate unstructured data:

- Email and other forms of electronic communication
- Web-based content, including click streams and social media-related content
- Digitized audio and video
- Machine-generated data (RFID, GPS, sensor-generated data, log files, etc.) and the Internet of Things

Unstructured data is growing faster than structured data. According to a 2011 IDC study [4], it will account for 90% of all data created in the next decade. As a new, relatively untapped source of insight, unstructured data analytics can reveal important interrelationships that were previously difficult or impossible to determine.

However, relational database and technologies derived from it (e.g., data warehouses) cannot manage unstructured and semi-unstructured data well at large scale because the data lacks predefined schema. To handle the variety and complexity of unstructured data, databases are shifting from relational to nonrelational. NoSQL databases are broadly used in big data practice because they support dynamic schema design, offering the potential for increased flexibility, scalability, and customization compared to relational databases. They are designed with "big data" needs in mind and usually support distributed processing very well.

1.1.2.3 Fast Data Processing

Big data is not just big, it is also fast. Big data is sometimes created by a large number of constant streams, which typically send in the data records simultaneously, and in small sizes (order of kilobytes). Streaming data includes a wide variety of data such as click-stream data, financial transaction data, log files generated by mobile or web applications, sensor data from Internet of Things (IoT) devices, in-game player activity, and telemetry from connected devices. The benefit of big data analytics is limited if it cannot act on data as it arrives. Big data analytics has to consider velocity as well as volume and variety, which is a key difference between big data and a traditional data warehouse. The data warehouse, by contract, is usually more capable of analyzing historical data.

This streaming data needs to be processed sequentially and incrementally on a record-by-record basis or over sliding time windows, and used for a wide variety of analytics including correlations, aggregations, filtering, and sampling. Big data technology unlocks the value in fast data processing with new tools and methodologies. For example, Apache Storm [5] and Apache Kafka [6] are two popular stream processing systems. Originally developed by the engineering team at Twitter, Storm can reliably process unbounded streams of data at rates of millions of messages per second. Kafka, developed by the engineering team at LinkedIn, is a high-throughput distributed message queue system. Both streaming systems address the need of delivering fast data.

Neither traditional relational databases nor NoSQL databases are capable enough to process fast data. Traditional relational database is limited in performance, and NoSQL systems lack support for safe online transactions. However, in-memory NewSQL solutions can satisfy the needs for both performance and transactional complexity. NewSQL is a class of modern relational database management systems that seek to provide the same scalable performance of NoSQL systems for online transaction processing (OLTP) read-write workloads while still maintaining the ACID (Atomicity, Consistency, Isolation, Durability) guarantees of a traditional database system [7]. Some NewSQL systems are built with shared-nothing clustering. Workload is distributed among cluster nodes for performance. Data is replicated among cluster nodes for safety and availability. New nodes can be transparently added to the cluster in order to handle increasing workloads. The NewSQL systems provide both high performance and scalability in online transactional processes.

1.1.3 Big Data Ecosystem

There are many big data technologies and products available in the market, and the whole big data ecosystem can be divided generally into three categories: infrastructure, analytics, and applications, as shown in Figure 1.1.

- Infrastructure

  Infrastructure is the fundamental part of the big data technology. It stores, processes, and sometimes analyzes data. As discussed earlier, big data infrastructure is capable of handling both structured and unstructured data at large volumes and fast speed. It supports a vast variety of data, and makes it possible to run applications on systems with thousands of nodes, potentially

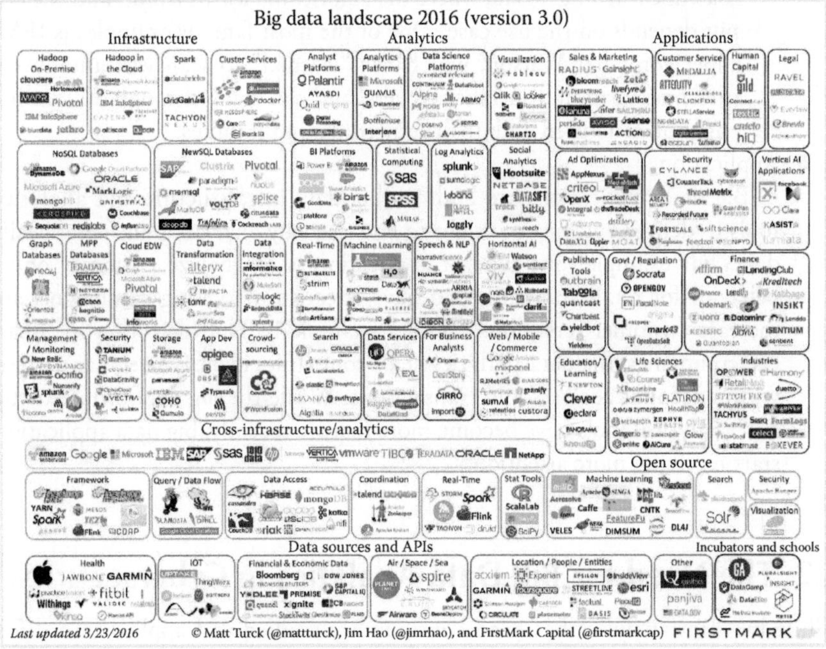

Figure 1.1 Big data landscape.

involving thousands of terabytes of data. Key infrastructural technologies include Hadoop, NoSQL, and massively parallel processing (MPP) databases.

- Analytics

  Analytical tools are designed with data analysis capabilities on the big data infrastructure. Some infrastructural technologies also incorporate data analysis, but specifically designed analytical tools are more common. Big data analytical tools can be further classified into the following sub-categories [8]:

  1. Analytics platforms: Integrate and analyze data to uncover new insights, and help companies make better-informed decisions. There is a particular focus on this field on latency, and delivering insights to end users in the timeliest manner possible.
  2. Visualization platforms: Specifically designed—as the name might suggest—for visualizing data; taking the raw data and presenting it in complex, multidimensional visual formats to illuminate the information.
  3. Business intelligence (BI) platforms: Used for integrating and analyzing data specifically for businesses. BI platforms analyze data from multiple sources to deliver services such as business intelligence reports, dashboards, and visualizations
  4. Machine learning: Also falls under this category, but is dissimilar to the others. Whereas the analytics platforms input processed data and output analytics or dashboards or visualizations to end users, the input of machine learning is data where the algorithm "learns from," and the output depends on the use case. One of the most famous examples is IBM's super computer Watson, which has "learned" to scan vast amounts of information to find specific answers, and can comb through 200 million pages of structured and unstructured data in minutes.

- Application

  Big data applications are built on big data infrastructure and analytical tools to deliver optimized insight to end-users by analyzing business specific data. For example, one type of application is to analyze customer online behavior for retail companies, to have effective marketing campaigns, and increase customer retention. Another example is fraud detection for financial companies. Big data analytics helps companies identify irregular patterns within account accesses and transactions. While the big data infrastructure and analytical tools have become more mature recently, big data applications start receiving more attention.

1.2 The Need for Big Data Analytics in Cybersecurity

While big data analytics has been continuously studied and applied into different business sectors, cybersecurity, at the same time, is experiencing the *big* data challenge due to the rapidly growing complexity of networks (e.g., virtualization, smart devices, wireless connections, IoT, etc.) and increasingly sophisticated threats (e.g., malware, multistage, APTs, etc.). It has been commonly believed that cybersecurity is one of the top (if not the most) critical areas where big data can be a barrier to understanding the true threat landscape.

1.2.1 Limitations of Traditional Security Mechanisms

The changing and increasing complex threat landscape makes traditional cybersecurity mechanisms inadequate and ineffective in protecting organizations and ensuring the continuity of their business in digital and connected context.

Many traditional security approaches, such as network-level and host-level firewalls, have typically focused on preventing attacks. They take perimeter-based defense techniques mimicking physical security approaches, which focus primarily on preventing access from the outside and on defense along the perimeter. More defense layers can be added around the most valuable assets in the network in order to implement a defense-in-depth strategy. However, as attacks become more advanced and sophisticated, organizations can no longer assume that they are exposed to external threats only, nor can they assume that their defense layers can effectively prevent all potential intrusions. Cyber defense efforts need to shift focus from prevention to attack detection and mitigation. Traditional prevention-based security approaches would then constitute only one piece of a much broader security strategy that includes detection methods and potentially automated incident response and recovery processes.

Traditional intrusion and malware detection solutions rely on known signatures and patterns to detect threats. They are facing the challenge of detecting new and never-before-seen attacks. More advanced detection techniques are seeking to effectively distinguish normal and abnormal situations, behaviors, and activities, either at the network traffic level or at the host activity level or at the user behavior level. Abnormal behaviors can further be used as the indicator of malicious activity for detecting never-before-seen attacks. A 2014 report from the security firm Enex TestLab [9] indicated that malware generation outpaced security advancements during the second half of 2014 to the point that in some of its monthly e-Threats automated malware tests, solutions from major security vendors were not able to detect any of the malware they were tested against.

Security information and event management (SIEM) solutions provide real-time monitoring and correlation of security events as well as log management and aggregation capabilities. By their very nature, these tools are used to confirm a suspected breach rather than proactively detecting it. More advanced security approaches are needed to monitor the behaviors of networks, systems, applications, and users in order to detect early signs of a breach before cyber attackers can cause any damages.

1.2.2 The Evolving Threat Landscape Requires New Security Approaches

New technologies, such as virtualization technologies, smartphones, IoT devices, and their accelerated pace of change are driving major security challenges for organizations. Similarly, the huge scale of organizations' software operations is adding to the complexity that cyber defenders have to deal with. Furthermore, the expanded attack surface and the increasingly sophisticated threat landscape pose the most significant challenges to traditional cyber security tools.

For example, the rapid growth of IoT connects a huge number of vulnerable devices to the Internet, therefore exponentially expands the attack surface for hackers. The IDC study of worldwide IoT market predicts that the installed base of IoT endpoints will grow from 9.7 billion in 2014 to more than 25.6 billion in 2019, hitting 30 billion in 2020 [10]. However, the fast growth of IoT also exponentially expands the attack surface for hackers. A recent study released by Hewlett Packard [11] showed that 70% of IoT devices contain serious vulnerabilities. The scale of IoT and the expanded attack surface make traditional network-based security controls unmanageable and unable to secure all communications generated by the connected devices. The convergence of information technology and operations technology driven by the IoT further complicates the task of network administrators.

As another example, advanced persistent threat (APT) has become a serious threat to business, but traditional detection methods are not effective defending against it. APT is characterized by being "advanced" in terms of using sophisticated malware to explore system vulnerabilities and being "persistent" in terms of using an external command and control system to continuously monitor and extract data from a specific target. Traditional security is not effective on APT because

- APT often uses zero-day vulnerabilities to compromise the target. Traditional signature-based defense does not work on those attacks.
- Malware used by APT usually initiates communication to the command and control server from inside, which makes perimeter-based defense ineffective.
- APT communications are often encrypted using SSL tunnels, which makes traditional IDS/firewall unable to inspect its contents.
- APT attacks usually hide in the network for a long time and operate in stealth mode. Traditional security, which lacks the ability to retain and correlate events from different sources over a long time, is not capable enough to detect them.

In short, new cybersecurity challenges make traditional security mechanisms less effective in many cases, especially when big data is involved.

1.2.3 Big Data Analytics Offers New Opportunities to Cybersecurity

Big data analytics offers the opportunity to collect, store, and process enormous cybersecurity data. This means that security analytics is no longer limited to analyzing alerts and logs generated by firewalls, proxy servers, IDSs, and web application firewalls (WAFs). Instead, security analysts can analyze a range of new datasets in a long time period that gives them more visibility into what's happening on their network. For example, they can analyze network flows and full packet captures for network traffic monitoring. They can use communication data (including email, voice, and social networking activity), user identity context data, as well as web application logs and file access logs for advanced user behavior analytics.

Furthermore, business process data, threat intelligence, and configuration information of the assets on the network can be used together for risk assessments. Malware information and external threat feeds (including blacklists and watchlists), GeoIP data, and system and audit trails may help with cyber investigations. The aggregation and correlation of these various types of data provides more context information that helps broaden situational awareness, minimize cyber risk, and improve incident response. New use cases are enabled through big data's capabilities to perform comprehensive analyses through distributed processing and with affordable storage and computational resources.

1.3 Applying Big Data Analytics in Cybersecurity

1.3.1 The Category of Current Solutions

Existing efforts of applying big data analytics into cybersecurity can be grouped into the following three major categories [12]:

- Enhance the accuracy and intelligence of existing security systems.

  Security analytics solutions in this category use ready-to-use analytics to make existing systems more intelligent and less noisy so that the most egregious events are highlighted and prioritized in queues, while alert volume is reduced. The big data aspect of this solution domain comes in a more advanced phase of deployment, where data and alerts from separate systems, e.g., data loss prevention (DLP), SIEM, identity and access management (IAM), or endpoint protection platform (EPP), are enriched with contextual information, combined and correlated using canned analytics. This gives an enterprise a more intelligent and holistic view of the security events in its organization.

- Combine data and correlated activities using custom or ad hoc analytics.
  Enterprises use big data analytics solutions or services to integrate internal and external data, structured as well as unstructured, and apply their own customized or ad hoc analytics against these big data sets to find security or fraud events.
- External cyber threat and fraud intelligence.
  Security analytics solutions apply big data analytics to external data on threats and bad actors, and, in some cases, combine external data with other relevant data sources, like supply chains, vendor ranking, and social media. Most vendors of these solutions also create and support communities of interest where threat intelligence and analytics are shared across customers. Vendors in this category actively find malicious activities and threats from the Internet, turn this information into actionable data such as IP addresses of known bad servers or malware signatures, and share with their customers.

1.3.2 Big Data Security Analytics Architecture

In general, a big data security analytics platform should have five core components as shown in Figure 1.2.

- A basic data storage platform to support long-term log data retention and batch processing jobs. There are a few offerings in the market that skip this layer and use a single NoSQL database to support all the data retention, investigation access, and analytics. However, considering all the available open-source applications in the Hadoop ecosystem, a Hadoop-based platform still gives a more economical, reliable, and flexible data solution for larger data sets.
- A data access layer with fast query response performance to support investigation queries and drill-downs. Because the data access inside Hadoop

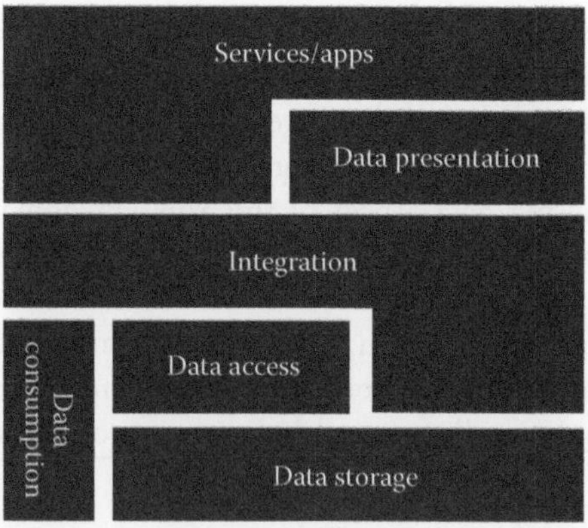

Figure 1.2 Big data security analytics architecture.

is batch-based, this layer is necessary to support analysts' investigations. This layer can be either a stand-alone massive parallel database (MPD) such as Vertica [13] and GreenPlum [14], and/or a NoSQL database like Solr [15], Cassandra [16], and Elasticsearch [17], and/or some integrated offerings such as Impala [18] and Spark [19] directly from popular Hadoop distributions.

- A data consumption layer to receive data from various data sources, either from the log sources directly, or through log concentrators such as syslog-ng, flow collectors, and SIEM tools.
- An integration layer that is composed of a collection of APIs to integrate with other security operational tools such as SIEM, eGRC, and ticketing systems. At the same time, a good API layer not only supports integration with other solutions, but also provides flexibility and cleaner design to internal analytical modules. As we expect that the amount of requirements and complexity of analytics will have tremendous growth in the next few years, API-based analytics-as-a-service architecture is highly recommended.
- In addition to the above four parts, an optional data presentation layer to allow users to consume the analytical results more efficiently and effectively. This usually means one or more visualization platforms to visualize both the high dimensional data and the relation graphs.
- Security analytics services and applications can be built on top of the integration layer and/or the data presentation layer, depending on if visualization is necessary to the user applications.

1.3.3 Use Cases

A use case is a set of solutions to solve a specific business challenge. It is important to understand that the challenge/requirement comes first, and then we engineer the solutions. When talking about cyber security analytics use cases, a common mistake is to start with the available data and think about what can be done with the data. Instead, an organization should start with the problems (threats) before looking up data, and then design a solution with the available data.

In the following we describe three use cases for big data security solutions: data retention/access, context enrichment, and anomaly detection. The first two cases are more straightforward and relatively easy to implement and measure. Hence, we are going to spend more time discussing the anomaly detection use case. But it should be noted that, in practice, the first two may probably generate better return on investments (ROI) for most organizations.

1.3.3.1 Data Retention/Access

By nature, the number 1 requirement a big data solution fulfills is data availability. The Hadoop-based architecture enables the storage of a large volume of data with high availability, and makes them relatively easy to access (compared to the tapes). Mapping into security operations, a basic requirement is that analysts need to access the security data and information for their daily operations. This includes providing managed access to raw logs and extracted metadata, advanced data filtering and query access, and visualization interfaces.

In practice, there are many factors to consider in requirements. Keep in mind that the Hadoop system does not provide the best query-response time. There are many other database systems that can be leveraged to provide faster query performance and serve as a data cache for analysts. However, there is additional cost, scalability concerns, and sometimes accuracy trade-offs to be considered with those systems.

The best way to approach this design problem is to start with the bare minimum requirements on data accesses and retention:

- What is the minimum retention period for various types of data?
- What is the minimum requirement on the query performance?
- How complex will the queries be?

From there, we will ask further questions such as: What's the preferred retention period for various data in the fast access platform? Is learning a new query language an option or are we stuck with SQL? After we identified the requirements, we can then survey the technology market to find the technology solution that can support those requirements, and design the proper architecture for the initiative.

1.3.3.2 Context Enrichment

Because the big data platform possesses so many different kinds of data from a vast number of sources, it is of great value to use heterogeneous data to enrich each other to provide additional contexts. The goal of such enrichments is to preload the security relevant data automatically so that analysts do not need to check those enriching data sources manually. Below are some examples of such enrichments:

1. Enriching IP-based data (e.g., firewall logs and net flows) with workstation host names from DHCP logs.
2. Enriching host-based data with user identities from IAM logs (e.g., Active Directory).
3. Enriching account-based data with human resource contexts (e.g., job roles, team members, supervisors).
4. Enriching proxy logs with the metadata of emails containing the links accessed.
5. Enriching internal network flow data with processes/services information from endpoint data.
6. Enriching internal findings with external threat intelligence (e.g., virustotal).
7. Enriching alert findings with historical similar alerts and their depositions.

Practitioners should note that the key performance constraint of data enrichment solutions is the underlying data parsing and linking jobs. Because this type of solution involves close interactions with human analysts, it is ideal to have a low latency here.

1.3.3.3 Anomaly Detection

Anomaly detection is a technology to detect malicious behaviors by comparing the current activities with learned "normal" profiles of the activities and entities, which can be user accounts, hosts, networks, or applications. As an intrusion detection technology, anomaly detection has been proposed and studied for over two decades, but it is still notorious for its low accuracy. Specifically, although it is capable of detecting some novel attack behaviors, it tends to give excessive amounts of false positives, which renders the technology impractical. However, now enterprises are revisiting the idea of implementing anomaly detection technologies as part of their security monitoring measures for two reasons:

- The threat of advanced persistent attacks (APT) has become significant to many organizations. Traditional signature-based monitoring is not effective against such attacks.
- The advance in big data technology enables organizations to profile entity behaviors over large volumes of data, long periods of time, and with high dimensions in modeling behaviors. This can greatly improve the accuracy of anomaly detection.

There are many possibilities when it comes to anomaly detection use cases. Based on the origin and target of the threats, anomaly detection use cases can be roughly grouped into the following categories:

1. External access anomalies, e.g., browsing activity monitoring.
2. Remote access anomalies, e.g., VPN access monitoring.
3. Lateral movement anomalies, e.g., internal resource access monitoring.
4. Endpoint anomalies, e.g., data at rest monitoring.
5. External-facing (web) service anomalies, e.g., early warning of Denial of Service (DoS) attacks.
6. Data movement anomalies, e.g., internal sensitive data tracking and data exfiltration.

An actual use case may be a combination of the aforementioned cases. For example, a model built to monitor the beaconing behaviors with user's web browsing activities may be combined with endpoint anomalies together to form a malware monitoring use case. An internal lateral movement model may be combined with a data exfiltration model to establish a data loss prevention monitoring case.

To establish those cases, data scientists need to first work with business owners to identify the control gaps where analytics needs to fill in, then work with engineers to identify the available data to build the models. When considering available data sets, one should always keep in mind that there are some great resources publicly available on the Internet, like geo-IP data that can be used to track remote access' source locations, whois info [20] and various threat intelligence data that can be cross-referenced to evaluate a remote site's credibility.

Here we briefly discuss two examples to showcase the key components of building an anomaly detection use case.

1.3.3.3.1 Example 1: Remote VPN Access Monitoring

1. Threat Scenario
    a. An unauthorized party stole (or is given) a user's credential to log onto company VPN remotely to get into company's internal network.
    b. Two users sharing the same VPN credential, which violates company's remote access policy.
2. Control Gaps: Currently, the only control over VPN is users' credentials. Once a user passes the authentication, there is no additional control.
3. Data Sources: VPN logs, user's office badging data, and Geo-IP data.
4. Data Exploration
    a. VPN logs contain timestamps, user ID, external source IP address, and the DHCP address assigned to the VPN connection.
    b. Badging data contains timestamps, employee ID, and the action (badging in and out).
    c. Geo-IP data here is a free MaxMind dataset—for more accuracy, a commercial dataset can also be used here. Further investigation shows that such dataset is reported to have an approximately 5% chance of being more than 1000 miles off from the actual location.
5. Features: External IP addresses are converted into geo-locations with the geo-IP data; VPN user IDs are mapped into the actual employee IDs.
6. Detection Model
    a. Measure the distance between user's last two accesses (e.g., badge-off office location and VPN logon, or between two VPN logons).
    b. Measure the elapsed time between those events.
    c. Derive the minimum travel speed of the user between the two accesses.
    d. Compare that to a pre-established max travel speed threshold (e.g., 400 miles/hour), and see if it exceeds that threshold.

7. Additional Improvements to the Model
   a. Inherent errors with geo-IP data: Such errors usually happen with large nationwide ISPs, especially with mobile connections. A whois check and whitelist from a training session usually minimizes such errors.
   b. For corporations with travel portals, which provides users' business travel agendas, such data can provide additional detection opportunities/accuracies.

1.3.3.3.2 Example 2: Abnormal Sensitive Data Gathering

1. Threat Scenario: A malicious insider or compromised account gathers sensitive data in preparation for exfiltration.
2. Control Gaps

   Although the enterprise does have a DLP solution deployed on endpoints and in the network, the coverage of the DLP is not complete. The most significant gaps are that the host DLP does not track the system level dependencies and hence has no control over transformed (compressed, encrypted) files. The network DLP is only deployed over email, http, and ftp channels. The inspection is not adequate for other protocols such as SSL or sftp. Hence, a behavior-based analytical model would be a great mitigation control here.
3. Data Sources: SQL audit log for customer info DB, internal netflows, inventory of file shares containing sensitive data.
4. Data Exploration
   a. SQL audit log contains a lot of noise yet provides great details on the queries and number of records returned.
   b. Internal NetfLow shows source/destination IP addresses, ports, and upload/download volumes.
   c. File share inventory is updated on a daily basis by a custom-built data scanner. It identifies the host name, IP address, share name of the file shares, the sensitivity of the data content, and the level of security controls over the share (publicly accessible or shared to specific users/groups).
5. Features
   a. Daily (potentially) sensitive data download volume—by accumulating the download volume through port 445 (windows fileshare) and 1433 (SQL) from fileshares/DBs hosting sensitive data.
   b. Number of sensitive data records downloaded—identified directly from SQL audit log.
6. Model: Profile users' daily sensitive data download volume and detect significant spikes with time series model.

7. Additional Improvements to the Model
    a. Identifying each user's peers based on their team/group/supervisor data can help identify the context of sensitive data usage of the peer group, which can be used to improve detection accuracy. That is, if a user's peer group is seen to download a lot of sensitive data on a regular basis, a spike on one user who happens to not use the data much is not as concerning as for a member whose group does not use sensitive data at all.
    b. Can be correlated with data exfiltration anomalies such as suspicious uploads to file sharing sites/uncategorized sites.
    c. Can be correlated with malware anomalies such as C2 beaconing behavior.
    d. Can be correlated with remote access anomalies as well.

1.4 Challenges to Big Data Analytics for Cybersecurity

Big data analytics, as a key enabling technology, brings its power into the cybersecurity domain. The best practices in industry and government have demonstrated, when used in a proper way, big data analytics will greatly enhance an organization's cybersecurity capability that is not feasible with traditional security mechanisms. While it is worth noting that applying big data analytics in the cybersecurity domain is still in its infancy stage, and facing some unique challenges that many data scientists from more "traditional" cybersecurity fields or other big data domains may not be aware of. In the following, we list these challenges and discuss how they affect the design and implementation of cybersecurity solutions using big data. They can also be considered as potential future directions of big data analytics for cybersecurity.

1. Lack of labeled data

    The way big data works is to learn from data and tell stories with data. However, the quantity of labeled data and quality of normal data can both pose big challenges to security analytics. The goal of doing cybersecurity analytics is to detect attacks, breaches, and compromises. However, such incidents are usually scarce for individual organizations. Even though there are a few government and commercial platforms for organizations to share intelligence about attacks and breaches, there is usually not enough details in the shared data. Except for a few very special problems (e.g., malware analysis), there is very limited labeled data for cybersecurity. In such a situation, traditional supervised learning techniques are not applicable. The learning will rely heavily on unsupervised learning and heuristics.
2. Data quality

    Among all the data available for cybersecurity analytics, an important type of data source is the alerts from various security tools such as IDS/IPS, firewalls, and proxies. Unfortunately, such security alert data is usually saturated with false alerts and missing detections on real attacks. New signatures and rules can also add significant hiccups to the alert streams. Such situations, together with false positives and negatives, should all be taken into consideration of analytics programs.

3. High complexity

   The complexity of large enterprise IT environments is usually extremely high. A typical such environment can involve hundreds of logical/physical zones, thousands of applications, tens of thousands of users, and hundreds of thousands of servers and workstations. The various activities, accesses, and connections happening among such a large collection of entities can be extremely complex. Because security threats take place all over, properly modeling and reducing such a high-dimensional problem is very difficult.
4. Dynamic environment

   The modern IT environments are highly dynamic and constantly changing. Models that work for one organization may not apply to another organization, or the same organization six months later. It is important to recognize this dynamic nature of IT environments in the analytics projects, and plan plenty of flexibility in analytics solutions in advance.
5. Keeping up with the evolving technologies

   Big data is a fast evolving technology field. New improvements or groundbreaking technologies are being developed every week. How to keep up with this technology revolution and make correct decisions on technology adoptions can be a million dollar question. This requires deep understanding of both data technologies and business requirements.
6. Operation

   Analytics is only one of the functions of big data cybersecurity programs. Usually, the program also needs to provide data retention and data accesses for security analysts and investigators. Hence, there will be a lot of operational requirements in data availability, promptness, accuracy, query performance, workflow integration, access control, and even disaster recovery for the data platform, data management, and the analytics models.
7. Privacy

   The era of big data raises the concern on privacy to a new level. By combining a vast number of data sources, analysts can gain unprecedented insight on user or customer behaviors. How to protect and control the exposure of user privacy while providing necessary information for cybersecurity operations is not a trivial problem. Data encryption, data masking, and access control technologies need to be carefully designed and integrated to achieve the proper protection according to an organization's requirements.
8. Regulation and compliance

   Big data also poses new challenges for organizations to meet regulation and compliance requirements. The challenges are mostly on the classification and protection of the data because combining multiple data sources could reveal additional hidden information that may be subject to higher classification. Due to this reason, in some highly regulated situations, it is difficult to apply big data analytics.

9. Data encryption

   We enjoy the benefit of having a lot of data and extracting useful information from it. But benefits come with responsibilities. Gathering and retaining data will impose the responsibility of protecting the data. In many situations, data needs to be encrypted during transfer and storage. However, when multiplied by the large volume of big data, this can mean significant performance and management overhead.

10. Disproportionate cost of false negative

    In traditional big data fields such as web advertising, the cost of false negatives is usually at an acceptable level and comparable to the cost of false positives. For example, losing a potential buyer will not cause much impact to a company's profit. However, in cybersecurity, the cost of a false negative is disproportionately high. Missing one attack will potentially lead to catastrophic loss and damage.

11. Intelligent adversaries

    Another unique challenge of cybersecurity analytics is that the subjects of investigation are usually not static "things." Big data cybersecurity deals with highly intelligent human opponents who will deliberately avoid detection and change strategies if they are aware of detection. It requires cybersecurity analytics to quickly adapt to new security threats and context, and adequately adjust its goals and procedures as needed.

References

1. http://www.gartner.com/it-glossary/big-data/.
2. https://en.wikipedia.org/wiki/Apache_Hadoop.
3. https://en.wikipedia.org/wiki/MapReduce.
4. IDC IView, "Extracting Value from Chaos" (June 2011).
5. http://hortonworks.com/apache/storm/.
6. http://hortonworks.com/apache/kafka/.
7. Aslett, Matthew (2011). "How Will The Database Incumbents Respond To NoSQL And NewSQL?". https://cs.brown.edu/courses/cs227/archives/2012/papers/newsql/aslett-newsql.pdf.
8. http://dataconomy.com/understanding-big-data-ecosystem/.
9. http://www.cso.com.au/article/563978/security-tools-missing-up-100-malware-ethreatz-testing-shows/.
10. IDC, Worldwide Internet of Things Forecast Update: 2015–2019, February 2016.
11. HP, Internet of things research study, 2015 report.
12. Gartner, "Reality check on big data analytics for cybersecurity and fraud," 2014.
13. https://my.vertica.com/get-started-vertica/architecture/.

14. http://greenplum.org/.
15. http://lucene.apache.org/solr/.
16. http://cassandra.apache.org/.
17. https://www.elastic.co/.
18. http://impala.incubator.apache.org/.
19. http://spark.apache.org/.
20. https://www.whois.net/.

Chapter 2

Big Data for Network Forensics

Yi Cheng, Tung Thanh Nguyen,
Hui Zeng, and Julia Deng

Contents

Network forensics plays a key role in network management and cyber security analysis. Recently, it is facing the new challenge of big data. Big data analytics has shown its promise of unearthing important insights from large amounts of data that were previously impossible to find, which attracts the attention of researchers in network forensics, and a number of efforts have been initiated. This chapter provides an overview on how to apply big data technologies into network forensics. It first describes the terms and process of network forensics, presents current practice and their limitations, and then discusses design considerations and some experiences of applying big data analysis for network forensics.

2.1 Introduction to Network Forensics

Digital forensics [1–4] commonly refers to the investigation of situations where there is computer-based (digital) or electronic evidence of a crime or suspicious behavior, but the crime or behavior may be of any type, quite possibly not otherwise involving computers. Network forensics [3,5–10], as one of its sub-branches, follows the same principles, but deals with network-based digital evidence. Network forensics is also closely associated with computer forensics (also known as cyber forensics). Traditionally, computer forensics has been associated with data on a computer's storage media, while network forensics has been associated with data passing through a network. With the rapid growth of the Internet, the scope of the two disciplines has expanded and has become more intertwined. Network forensics is leading to investigations of various data from both computer systems and networks in order to get a more accurate estimate of problems and make more informative decisions, and cyber forensics also goes beyond traditional computer systems and covers new emerging networking and computing paradigms, like mobile computing, Internet of Things (IoTs), social technical networks.

Generally speaking, network forensics is defined as the capture, recording, and analysis of network data in order to discover the source of security attacks or other problem incidents [8]. The essential part of network forensics is *data from the networks and computers*, and the objective is to discover useful information from data using *analytic techniques and processes*. Accordingly, network forensics sometimes simply refers to network data analysis, by emphasizing the data science aspect and weakening the necessary actions for preserving the integrity of data and evidences [3,8,9]. This chapter also follows the same principle, and uses network forensics and network analysis interchangeably.

Network forensics is critical to support security analysis as well as network management. For security analysis, it provides network- and system-level cyber data tracking, collection, processing, and analysis to support a set of security analysis needs, such as vulnerability assessment, intrusion/anomaly detection, risk analysis, information leakage, data theft, damage assessment, impact mitigation, and cyber situational awareness. For network management, it provides analytical information needed to help network operators or administrators better understand the status of an intended network, and quickly identify potential issues (e.g., faults, attacks, etc.) related to network/devices/services. By supporting configuration management, performance management, fault management, and security management, it ensures that the network itself does not become a bottleneck for network services and user applications.

Network forensics has been extensively studied over the last decade, and a significant number of techniques and tools have been developed. Recently, network forensics is facing the new challenge of big data. A typical enterprise network can generate terabytes of relevant data each day, including traffic packets, system logs and events, as well as other related data such as security alerts or reports that are generated by third-party network monitors or management tools. Network forensics is moving forward and updating the tools and techniques by taking advantage of vast amounts of data. Big data analytics has shown its promise of unearthing important insights from the sheer amount of data that were previously impossible to find; hence, it attracts the attention of researchers in network forensics and initiates a number of research and development efforts. However, for the moment, big data tools are immature and big data based network forensics is still in its early stage.

2.2 Network Forensics: Terms and Process

2.2.1 Terms

There are a couple of different but closely related terms. Sometimes these terms are used interchangeably in literature and also cause confusion.

- Network Security versus Network Forensics

  Network security is to secure down systems. It is most often concerned with monitoring, protecting, and defending networks from threats, such as illegal access, misuse, attackers, data theft, and malware outbreaks. Network forensics is to figure out exactly what happened when the network security failed. It is the process of investigating all possible evidence after an attack or crime has taken place [1]. While this means the two focus on different stages of network breaches ("before" and "after") with overlapping tasks (e.g., network monitoring) using its own methodology, both frequently operate from a shared knowledge and experience base. It is also worth noting that network security is commonly used as a much broader term, referring to almost any issues related to the network in public writing. In that sense, network forensics belongs to a part of network security.
- Network Forensics versus Anomaly Detection

  Network forensics uses a variety of analytic methods to understand and discover what happened in the network, what and who is the cause of network events, and potential suggestions to fix the issue. Anomaly detection refers to the process of pinpointing the anomalies in the network, so an analyst or network administrator can link these anomalies (also known as alerts) with other evidence for further analysis. It can be easily seen that anomaly detection is a part of network forensics, and its output alerts are commonly used as important inputs for network forensics.

2.2.2 Network Forensics Process

Network forensics is usually performed in the following four phases: data collection, data examination, data analysis, and visualization and reporting, as shown in Figure 2.1.

Figure 2.1 Cyber forensic process.

2.2.2.1 Phase 1: Data Collection

The first step in the forensic process is to identify potential sources of data and acquire data from them. During collection, data related to a specific network event is identified, captured, time stamped, labeled, and recorded.

2.2.2.2 Phase 2: Data Examination

After data has been collected, data examination examines the data, which includes assessing, identifying, extracting the relevant pieces of information from the collected data, and then performing a series of preprocessing (e.g., data enrichment, metadata generation, aggregation, etc.) to prepare data for analysis.

2.2.2.3 Phase 3: Data Analysis

Once the relevant information has been extracted, data analysis applies a selected set of methodical approaches to study the data. This step usually involves correlating data among multiple sources. For instance, the output of a network intrusion detection system (IDS) (e.g., Snort) may link a detected event to a specific host with an IP address. The system logs of the particular host may further link the event to a specific user account or a specific application. By correlating the data collected from IDS and system logs, data analysis may provide more useful information to understand the event better.

2.2.2.4 Phase 4: Visualization and Reporting

The final phase involves presenting and reporting the data, extracted information, and analysis results to end users (e.g., network operators, analysts, and/or administrators) using visual display and documents (e.g., email alerts, messages, reports, etc.). The results of the analysis may also include the actions performed, what other actions need to be performed, and improvement recommendations to policies, guidelines, procedures, tools, and other aspects of the forensic process.

Along with these steps, the cyber forensic process transforms raw data into evidence and presents it to network operators, analysts, and/or administrators to help them better understand the network and quickly identify and respond to various network issues.

2.3 Network Forensics: Current Practice

2.3.1 Data Sources for Network Forensics

Network forensics usually looks at a variety of data sources from different network layers in order to discover the source of security attacks or other problem incidents. Typical data types used in network forensics are listed as follows:

- **Full Packet Capture (PCAP):** Capture and record all network packets in full, including both header and payload. It usually takes up a lot of space. For example, a full packet capture of a saturated 1 Gbps link will yield 6TB for one day.
- **Flow data:** Records of *conversations* on the network. It only stores the packet header information such as time, duration, number of packets, total bytes, source IP, destination IP, and so on, but no payload. It usually saves a lot of space, compared with full packet capture; it is good for understanding how data flows in the network quickly, but also loses the packet details. NetFlow was developed by Cisco and is widely used for flow data collection and analysis. Information collected by NetFlow includes source and destination device and port, timestamps, number of bytes in the traffic flow, type of service data, and routing information. Other flow data are also available for network monitoring and forensics, such as sFlow [11], SNMP [12], and local traffic flow information collected by packet sniffers (e.g., snoop [13], tcpdump [14], and Wireshark [15]).
- **Logs:** A log file is a text file that contains a record of all actions, such as user access or data manipulation, that have been done on a computer, a website, or a program during a period of time, to serve as an audit trail or security measure [16]. Log files often contain messages about the system, including the kernel, services, and applications running on it. There are different log files for different information. For example, web servers maintain log files for every request made to the server. With the help of log file analysis tools, one can get a good idea of where visitors are coming from, how often they return, and how they navigate through a site. Through log files, system administrators can easily determine the websites that users accessed, know details about sending and receiving e-mails, downloading history, and so on.
- **Alerts:** An intrusion detection system (IDS) is designed to monitor all inbound and outbound network traffic or activity to identify suspicious patterns that may indicate a network attack, e.g., attempting to break into or compromise a system [17]. When an IDS identifies suspicious activities, alerts will be generated to provide timely information about the identified security issues, vulnerabilities, or exploits. An IDS specifically looks for suspicious activity and events that might be the result of a virus, worm, or hacker. This is done by looking for known intrusion signatures or attack signatures that characterize different worms or viruses and by tracking general variances which differ from regular system activity. The IDS is able to provide notification of only known attacks.

2.3.2 Most Popular Network Forensic Tools

There are many tools that can support network forensic analysis, from commercial or open-source communities. Some of the common network forensic analysis tools are listed as follows.

2.3.2.1 Packet Capture Tools

- **Tcpdump** [14]: A common packet analyzer that uses the libpcap library for low-level network sniffers. Tcpdump captures the TCP/IP and other packets being transmitted or received over a network. It works on Unix-like and other operating systems (OSs), such as Solaris, BSD, Mac OS X, HP-UX, and AIX. The port of tcpdump for Windows is WinDump, which uses the port of libcap (called WinPcap). Tcpdump runs on a standard command line and outputs to a common text file for further analysis. It uses a standard libpcap library as an application programming interface to capture the packets in the user level. Although all packet sniffers can examine the traffic in real-time, the processing overhead is also higher, so it might cause the packet to drop. As a result, it is recommended to output raw packets and do some analysis later. Due to the performance concern, tcpdump functions only as a traffic-capturing tool. It just captures the packets and saves them in a raw file. However, due to the peculiarity of tcpdump, there are many analysis tools built for it. For example, tcpdump2ascii [18] is a Perl script used to convert the output from tcpdump raw file to ASCII format. tcpshow [19] is a utility to print raw tcpdump output file in human readable form. tcptrace [20] is a free powerful analysis tool for tcpdump, which can produce different types of output, such as elapsed time, bytes/segments sent/received, round trip times, window advertisements, and throughput.
- **Wireshark** [15]: As a free packet sniffer, Wireshark provides a user-friendly interface with sorting and filtering features. Wireshark supports capturing packets from a live network and a saved capture file. The capture file format is libpcap format, just like that in tcpdump. Wireshark supports various kinds of operating systems, such as Linux, Solaris, FreeBSD, NetBSD, OpenBSD, Mac OS X, other Unix-like systems, and Windows. It can also assemble all the packets in a TCP conversation and show the ASCII (or EBCDIC, or hex) data in that conversation. Packet capturing is performed with the pcap library. Wireshark is a popular interactive network packet capture and protocol analysis tool, and can be used for network troubleshooting, analysis, and protocol development. It can provide in-depth inspection of hundreds of protocols and run on most existing platforms.
- **TShark** [21]: A network protocol analyzer that can capture packet data from a live network, or read packets from a previously saved capture file, either printing a decoded form of those packets to the standard output or writing the packets to a file. Similarly as tcpdump, TShark's native capture file format is the pcap format. Without any options set, TShark works much like tcpdump. It uses the pcap library to capture traffic from the first available network interface and displays a summary line on stdout for each received packet. TShark can detect, read, and write the same capture files that are supported by Wireshark. The input file doesn't need a specific filename extension; the

file format and an optional gzip compression will be automatically detected. Compressed file support uses (and therefore requires) the zlib library. If the zlib library is not present, TShark will compile, but will be unable to read compressed files.

- **RSA Netwitness** [22]: A network monitoring system that uses log data to detect and prevent cyber threats. RSA Netwitness comes in three parts: a Concentrator (a Linux-based network appliance), Decoder (a configurable network-recording appliance), and Investigator (an interactive threat analysis application). It can capture the packets traveling through the network over wired and wireless interfaces, generate an organized report for the users, and allow the user to implement the packets for risk assessment.

2.3.2.2 Flow Capture and Analysis Tools

- **NetFlow** [23]: An industry standard for traffic monitoring, supported by Cisco IOS, NXOS, Juniper routers, Enterasys Switches, and many others. NetFlow data can help analysts to understand who, what, when, where, and how the network traffic is flowing. NetFlow-based analyzers include Cisco IOS NetFlow [24], Ntop or ntopng [25], SolarWinds NetFlow Traffic Analyzer [26], and so on.
- **Cisco IOS NetFlow-based analyzer** [24]: A web-based bandwidth monitoring tool that uses Cisco NetFlow technology. It offers extensive support for monitoring Cisco-based environments such as routers, switches, WLCs, and Firewall in performing network traffic monitoring and security analytics. Specifically, it can provide traffic monitoring, network bandwidth monitoring, network troubleshooting, capacity planning, IP SLA monitoring, threshold-based alerting, application performance optimization, application performance optimization, and so on.
- **SolarWinds NetFlow Traffic Analyzer** [26]: An open source NetFlow analyzer that can monitor the network traffic by capturing flow data including NetFlow, J-Flow, IPFIX, and sFlow. It can identify the users, applications, or protocols that consume the most network bandwidth, map the traffic arriving/originated from designated ports, IPs, and protocols, perform class-based quality of service (CBQoS) monitoring, enable users to quickly drill-down into traffic on specific network elements, generate network traffic reports, and facilitate investigation of fault, performance, and configuration issues.
- **Ntop or ntopng** [25]: One of the most popular open source traffic analyzers, it is a web-based tool that can provide packet capture, traffic recording, network probe, and traffic analysis. Ntopng supports sFlow and IPFIX for flow-based analysis. It streams the flow data, provides high-speed web-based traffic analysis, and stores persistent traffic statistics in RRD format.

2.3.2.3 Intrusion Detection System

- **Snort** [27]: A free and open source network intrusion detection system (IDS), which has the ability to perform real-time traffic analysis and packet logging on Internet Protocol (IP) networks. Snort can perform protocol analysis, content searching, and matching. It can also be used to detect probes or attacks, such as OS fingerprinting attempts, common gateway interface, buffer overflows, server message block probes, and stealth port scans. Essentially, Snort can be configured in three main modes: sniffer, packet logger, and network intrusion detection. In sniffer mode, it can read network packets and display them on the console. In packet logger mode, it can log packets to the disk. In intrusion detection mode, it can monitor network traffic and analyze it against a rule set defined by the user. Snort can perform a specific action based on what has been identified.
- **Bro** [28]: An open source Unix-based network monitoring framework that can be used to build a network level IDS. Bro can also be used for collecting network measurements, conducting forensic investigations, traffic baselining, and more. Bro has been compared to tcpdump, Snort, netflow, and Perl (or any other scripting language) all in one. It is released under the BSD license. Bro can be conceptualized in two layers: (1) Bro Event Engine, which analyzes live or recorded network traffic or trace files to generate neutral events, and (2) Bro Policy Scripts, which analyze events to create action policies. Bro Event Engine generates events when "something" happens, triggered by the Bro process or something taking place on the network. Events are handled within Bro policy scripts. Bro uses common ports and dynamic protocol detection (signatures and behavioral analysis) to make a best guess at interpreting network protocols. Bro produces NetFlow-like output and application event information, and can read in data from external files such as blacklists.
- **OSSEC** [29]: A free, open source, host-based intrusion detection system (HIDS) that performs log analysis, integrity checking, Windows registry monitoring, rootkit detection, time-based alerting, and active response. OSSEC provides intrusion detection for most OSs, including Linux, OpenBSD, FreeBSD, OS X, Solaris, and Windows. OSSEC has a centralized, cross-platform architecture allowing multiple systems to be easily monitored and managed. OSSEC delivers alerts and logs to a centralized server where analysis and notification can occur even if the host system is taken offline or compromised. Another advantage of OSSEC's architecture is the ability to centrally manage agents from a single server. The installation of OSSEC is extremely light. As the installer is under 1 MB and the majority of analysis actually occurs on the server, very little CPU is consumed by OSSEC on the host. OSSEC also has the ability to send OS logs to the server for analysis and storage, which is particularly helpful on Windows machines that have no native or cross-platform logging mechanisms.

2.3.2.4 Network Monitoring and Management Tools

Over the last few decades, commercial tools have been developed for network traffic monitoring and analysis, including, but not limited to, Orion NPM portfolio [30] and Netcordia NetMRI [31]. Open-source tools are also available, such as OpenNMS [32], GNetWatch [33], GroundWork [34], and Nagios [35].

- **Orion NPM** [30] continuously monitors a network through ICMP, SNMP, and Syslog communication data. It stores gathered information in an SQL database and provides a user-friendly web console to view network status.
- **Netcordia NetMRI** [31] automates network change and configuration management (NCCM) by analyzing network configuration, syslog/events collected through SNMP and ICMP protocols, to provide daily actionable issues.
- **OpenNMS** [32] is an open-source enterprise network management platform, scaling to thousands of managed nodes from a single instance, to provide service availability management, performance data collection, event management and deduplication, and flexible notifications.
- **GNetWatch** [33] is an open source Java application that offers real-time graphical monitoring and analysis of network performance, using traffic generators and SNMP probes. It can monitor events (e.g., throughput) that change, for instance, every second and the user can see a dynamic graphical window.
- **GroundWork** [34] combines several open-source projects such as Nagios [35], Nmap, Sendpage, and MySQL, with custom dashboards in one software package, for monitoring Linux, Unix, and Windows platforms or devices.
- **Nagios** [35] is a powerful network monitoring tool that provides alerting, event handling, and reporting for critical systems, applications, and services. The Nagios Core contains the core monitoring engine and a basic web UI. On top of the Nagios Core, plugins are available or can be implemented to monitor services, applications, and performance metrics, as well as add-ons for data visualization, graphs, load distribution, and MySQL database support.

Besides the above tools for general traffic monitoring and analysis, many other tools are also designed specifically for network security analysis, using knowledge- or signature-based IDSs, or behavior-based anomaly detection technologies [36]. The former approaches mainly use *signatures* of well-known exploits and intrusions to identify attack traffic or activities [37], while the latter approaches [38] mainly compare current activities with predefined models of normal behaviors, and flag deviants as anomalies.

For instance, Gu, Zhang, and Lee [39] introduce an efficient anomaly detection method to identify centralized botnet command and control (C&C) channels, based on their spatial-temporal correlation. Binkley and Singh [40] and Goebel and Holz [41] combine an internet relay chat (IRC) mesh detection component with a TCP scan detection heuristic. Goebel and Holz [41] rely on IRC nickname matching to identify anomalies. Karasaridis, Rexroad, and Hoeflin [42] detect botnet controllers by flow aggregation and feature analysis. Livadas et al. [43], Strayer et al. [44], and Porras, Saidi, and Yegneswaran [45] utilize supervised machine learning to classify network packets in order to identify the C&C traffic of IRC-based botnets. Porras et al. [45] try to detect Storm bot by constructing its dialogue lifecycle model and identifying the traffic that matches this model. The BotMiner system classifies malware based on both malware activity patterns and C&C patterns [46]. TAMD detects infected hosts by finding those hosts that share common and unusual network communications [47]. Bailey et al. [48] use packet-level inspection, depending on network-based information, for protocol- and structure-independent botnet detection.

Machine-learning approaches are also developed for network security analysis [43,49]. For example, Bayesian network classifiers are used to distinguish between non-IRC traffic, botnet IRC traffic, and non-botnet IRC traffic [43]. Gianvecchio et al. [49] use an entropy classifier and a machine-learning classifier to detect chat bots. Statistical traffic anomaly detection techniques are also developed to identify botnet-like activities. For example, the exPose system uses statistical rule-mining techniques to extract significant communication patterns and identify temporally correlated flows such as worms [50]. Threshold random walk uses hypothesis testing to identify port scanners and Internet worms [51].

2.3.2.5 Limitations of Traditional Technologies

Note that current performance visibility obtained from existing network measurement or monitoring tools is only a fraction of what should be in today's networks. While there are many network monitoring and analysis tools from different vendors trying to address this need, existing tools have the following limitations:

- Most of them provide basic network performance monitoring and simple analysis, such as bandwidth usage, network throughput, and traffic categories, and leave complex network issues open or untouched.
- Typically associated with one specific type of network measurement tool/dataset. For example, SolarWinds NetFlow Traffic Analyzer takes the input from NetFlow and performs NetFlow-based traffic analysis. Little effort has been put into supporting the integration of multiple sources and types of measurement data for a better and higher level of data analysis.
- Although current tools and services are able to identify the existence of some failures and anomalies/attacks, detailed understanding and pinpointing the root cause of the failures/anomalies/attacks still remains an open problem.

- A large volume of network data are generated in real time, but only a small fraction of collected data (about 5%) is ever examined or analyzed, due to the lack of automated detection and analysis tools.

These critical issues impair network operators' ability to accurately and quickly gain understanding of network status and effectively maintain the network, resulting in increased cost and less effective network operations. In addition, for large-scale enterprise networks, traditional security analysis mechanisms are not efficient. For example, they cannot effectively detect distributed attacks (e.g., distributed denial of services), advanced persistent threats (APTs), malwares (e.g., worms, botnets), or zero-day attacks due to lack of efficient methods to process the large volume of data in a timely manner.

2.4 Applying Big Data Analysis for Network Forensics

Most traditional systems are deployed on a single server, which is not scalable. The main issue is that it cannot meet the extremely high demand of users in both processing power and data storage. For example, based on a report in 2011 [52], Google was running approximately 900,000 servers. There is simply no single server solution that can store and analyze the network data collected from them. Even in mid-size companies, with the decreasing cost of the computing devices, the network normally has several hundred nodes.

Besides scalability, there are many reasons that make big data solutions viable such as high availability, reliability, resistant to failure, and so on. With a single server solution, it essentially has a single point of failure. The service will be interrupted during maintenance, failure, or updating processes. The availability and ability to handle large datasets can be solved by developing and deploying the system in an HPC (distributed) environment. However, such a solution is not cost-effective (due to high CAPEX) and scalable. Big data solutions are essentially distributed services or systems deployed in a cloud environment. Thanks to the virtualization and distributed technologies in the cloud, the aforementioned issues can be addressed. But it comes with a price, too. First, as big data based solutions are new to most existing users, it takes time for them to learn, adapt, and use these new tools. In addition, the big data is still in its early and rapid developing stages, and a large number of software tools are available. It becomes very challenging for users to identify which tools are best suited for their situations/needs. Second, with big data, one simply needs more resources to store and process it. The data cannot be accommodated by a single server as in traditional situations anymore. Normally, when referring to big data, it implies a distributed system that presents its own challenges like synchronization, fault-tolerance, naming, data locality, and so on.

2.4.1 Available Big Data Software Tools

Big data analytics is important because it provides unprecedented opportunity to understand business, as well as to advance science/discovery and research. In our context (network forensics), the system can learn from or analyze the rich set of history data and try to prevent similar future attacks, raise reliable alerts (low false positives and false negatives) in (near) real-time. The large network dataset can also enable administrators to find/analyze the root cause of a failure. In general, there are many available software tools (not the network forensic analytics) to work with big data ranging from the programming model to resource manager to programming framework and applications. Some examples of such software and categories are listed as follows:

2.4.1.1 Programming Model: MapReduce [53]

MapReduce is a programming model and an associated implementation for processing and generating large data sets with a parallel, distributed algorithm on a cluster. A MapReduce program is composed of a Map and a Reduce method. The Map method performs filtering and sorting, and the Reduce method performs a summary operation. The MapReduce system orchestrates the processing by marshaling the distributed servers, running the various tasks in parallel, managing all communications and data transfers between the various parts of the system, and providing for redundancy and fault tolerance. MapReduce libraries have been written in many programming languages, with different levels of optimization. A popular open-source implementation that has support for distributed shuffles is part of Apache Hadoop.

2.4.1.2 Compute Engine: Spark [54], Hadoop [55]

Apache Spark is an open-source big data processing framework built around speed, ease of use, and sophisticated analytics. Compared to other big data and MapReduce technologies, such as Hadoop and Storm, Spark has several advantages. For example, it gives a comprehensive, unified framework to manage big data processing requirements with a variety of data sets and data sources. Spark enables applications in Hadoop clusters to run up to 100 times faster in memory and 10 times faster even when running on disk. Spark lets users quickly write applications in Java, Scala, or Python.

Apache Hadoop [55] is an open-source software framework used for distributed storage and processing of very large data sets. It consists of computer clusters built from commodity hardware. All the modules in Hadoop are designed with a fundamental assumption that hardware failures are a common occurrence and should be automatically handled by the framework. The core of Hadoop consists of a storage part, known as Hadoop Distributed File System (HDFS), and a MapReduce processing part. Hadoop splits files into large blocks and distributes them across nodes in a cluster. It then transfers packaged code into nodes to process the data in parallel. This approach takes advantage of data locality and allows the dataset to be processed faster and more efficiently than conventional supercomputer architecture.

2.4.1.3 Resource Manager: Yarn [56], Mesos [57]

Apache Hadoop Yarn is a cluster management technology. Yarn is one of the key features in the second-generation Hadoop 2 version of the Apache Software Foundation's open-source distributed processing framework. Originally described by Apache as a redesigned resource manager, Yarn is now characterized as a large-scale, distributed operating system for big data applications.

Apache Mesos [57] is an open-source cluster manager that was developed to provide efficient resource isolation and sharing across distributed applications or frameworks. It enables resource sharing in a fine-grained manner, improving cluster utilization. Mesos has been adopted by several large software companies, including Twitter, Airbnb, and Apple.

2.4.1.4 Stream Processing: Storm [58], Spark Streaming [54], Apache Flink [59], Beam [60]

Storm is a distributed stream processing computation framework. It uses custom created "spouts" and "bolts" to define information sources and manipulations to allow batch, distributed processing of streaming data [58]. A Storm application is designed as a "topology" in the shape of a directed acyclic graph (DAG) with spouts and bolts acting as the graph vertices. Edges on the graph are named streams and direct data from one node to another. This topology acts as a data transformation pipeline.

Spark Streaming [54] leverages Spark Core's fast scheduling capability to perform streaming analytics. It ingests data in mini-batches and performs resilient distributed dataset (RDD) transformations on those mini-batches of data. This design enables the same set of application code written for batch analytics to be used in streaming analytics, thus facilitating easy implementation of lambda architecture.

Apache Flink [59] is a community-driven open-source framework for distributed big data analytics, like Hadoop and Spark. The core of Flink is a distributed streaming dataflow engine written in Java and Scala. It aims to bridge the gap between MapReduce-like systems and shared-nothing parallel database systems.

Apache Beam [60] is an open-source unified programming model to define and execute data processing pipelines, including ETL, batch and stream (continuous) processing. Beam Pipelines are defined using one of the provided SDKs and executed in one of Beam's supported runners (distributed processing back-ends) including Apache Flink, Apache Spark, and Google Cloud Dataflow.

2.4.1.5 Real-Time In-Memory Processing: Apache Ignite [61], Hazelcast [62]

Apache Ignite is a high-performance, integrated and distributed in-memory platform for computing and transacting on large-scale data sets in real-time, orders of magnitude faster than possible with traditional disk-based or flash-based technologies [61]. In addition to Spark and Hadoop, Ignite integrates with a variety of other technologies and products. It is intended to simplify coupling of Apache Ignite and other technologies, used in your applications or services, in order to either perform a transition to Apache Ignite smoothly or to boost an existing solution by plugging Ignite into it.

Hazelcast [62] is an open-source in-memory data grid based on Java. In a Hazelcast grid, data is evenly distributed among the nodes of a computer cluster, allowing for horizontal scaling of processing and available storage. Backups are also distributed among nodes to protect against failure of any single node. Hazelcast provides central, predictable scaling of applications through in-memory access to the frequently used data and across an elastically scalable data grid. These techniques reduce the query load on databases and improve speed.

2.4.1.6 Fast SQL Analytics (OLAP): Apache Drill [63], Kylin [64]

Apache Drill is an open-source software framework that supports data-intensive distributed applications for interactive analysis of large-scale datasets [63]. Drill is able to scale to 10,000 servers or more and is able to process petabytes of data and trillions of records in seconds. Drill supports a variety of NoSQL databases and file systems, such as HBase, MongoDB, HDFS, MapR-FS, and local files. A single query can join data from multiple datastores. Drill's datastore-aware optimizer automatically restructures a query plan to leverage the datastore's internal processing capabilities. In addition, Drill supports data locality, so it is a good idea to colocate Drill and the datastore on the same nodes.

Apache Kylin [64] is an open-source distributed analytics engine designed to provide an SQL interface and multidimensional analysis (OLAP) on Hadoop supporting extremely large datasets. Originally developed by eBay, Apache Kylin is now a project of the Apache Software Foundation.

2.4.1.7 NOSQL (Non-Relational) Databases: HBase [65], Accumulo [66], MongoDB [67], Cassandra [68], Voldmort [69]

HBase is an open-source, non-relational, distributed database modeled after Google's BigTable [65]. It provides a fault-tolerant way of storing large quantities of sparse data. HBase features compression, in-memory operation, and Bloom filters on a per-column basis. HBase is a column-oriented key-value data store and has been idolized widely because of its lineage with Hadoop and HDFS. HBase runs on top of HDFS and is well-suited for faster read and write operations on large datasets with high throughput and low input/output latency.

Apache Accumulo [66] is a computer software project that developed a sorted, distributed key/value store based on the BigTable technology. It is a system built on top of Apache Hadoop, Apache ZooKeeper, and Apache Thrift. Written in Java, Accumulo has cell-level access labels and server-side programming mechanisms. Accumulo is one of the most popular NoSQL wide column stores according to the DB-Engines ranking, like Apache Cassandra and Hbase.

MongoDB [67] is a free and open-source cross-platform document-oriented database program. Classified as a NoSQL database program, MongoDB uses JSON-like documents with schemas. MongoDB is developed by MongoDB, Inc. and is free and open-source, published under a combination of the GNU Affero General Public License and the Apache License. Apache Cassandra [68] is a free and open-source distributed database management system designed to handle large amounts of data across many commodity servers, providing high availability with no single point of failure.

Cassandra offers robust support for clusters spanning multiple datacenters, with asynchronous masterless replication allowing low latency operations for all clients. Cassandra places a high value on performance and can achieve the highest throughput for the maximum number of nodes with the price of high write and read latencies.

Voldemort [69] is a distributed data store that is designed as a key-value store used by LinkedIn for high-scalability storage. It is neither an object database, nor a relational database. It does not try to satisfy arbitrary relations and the atomicity, consistency, isolation, and durability (ACID) properties, but rather is a big, distributed, fault-tolerant, persistent hash table. Compared with Voldemort, Cassandra, and Hbase, Voldemort has the lowest latency.

2.4.1.8 NOSQL Query Engine: Pheonix [70], Pig [71]

Apache Phoenix is an open-source, massively parallel, relational database engine supporting OLTP for Hadoop using Apache HBase as its backing store [70]. It provides a JDBC driver that hides the intricacies of the NoSQL store enabling users to create, delete, and alter SQL tables, views, indexes, and sequences; insert and delete rows singly and in bulk; and query data through SQL. Phoenix compiles queries and other statements into native NoSQL store APIs rather than using MapReduce enabling the building of low latency applications on top of NoSQL stores.

Apache Pig [71] is a high-level platform for creating programs that run on Apache Hadoop. The language for this platform is called Pig Latin. Pig can execute its Hadoop jobs in MapReduce, Apache Tez, or Apache Spark. Pig Latin abstracts the programming from the Java MapReduce idiom into a notation that makes MapReduce programming high level, similar to that of SQL for RDBMSs. Pig Latin can be extended using user defined functions (UDFs), which the user can write in Java, Python, JavaScript, Ruby, or Groovy, and then call directly from the language.

2.4.2 Design Considerations

In this section we provide ideas on how to select big data software tools suitable for a particular user's needs, or what should be considered when users want to design a new system. There are many decisions and selections that a big data adopter has to make before developing a beneficial application. Choosing open-source or proprietary solutions is such a popular example decision. In the open-source case, the pros are that it is free and can be adapted easily to user-specific cases by modifying the source-code directly. The cons are that open-source software often lacks support and is not well-documented. In the proprietary case, although the software is well supported, the user may have concerns about the cost and vendor lock-in.

Another important consideration is the high barrier to adopt new related technologies. For example, the system architect has to know many available technologies, the key differences among them (which tools are designed or used for which case), and keep updating it to make the right decision for designing the architecture for their software. In addition, many tools use not very popular languages such as Scala (Spark) and Clojure (Storm), making code modification more challenging.

To shed some light in this decision-making process, we will compare characteristics of top specific NoSQL databases and big data computing frameworks in terms of current popularity and derive decision diagrams to guide the selection of which database/computing framework to use. These two categories (database and computing) were selected to guide the design because they are key components of almost any big data based solutions.

2.4.2.1 NOSQL Databases

2.4.2.1.1 HBase/Accumulo

HBase and Accumulo are both column-oriented and schema-less databases [72,73]. They share similar architecture and are both best at handling multiple row queries and row scans. HBase and Accumulo support range query so if you want querying information based on ranges (e.g., finding all items in a particular price range), these databases may be your solution. In addition, Accumulo and HBase are built on top of HDFS. Therefore, they can be natively integrated into an existing Hadoop cluster.

Accumulo is far more scalable than MongoDB, and even HBase and Cassandra [74]. It is the only NoSQL database with cell-level security capabilities which allow a user to see different values as appropriate based on the row. Accumulo also has another unique feature called Iterator which is a prevailing server-side programming mechanism that enables a variety of real-time aggregations and analytics.

2.4.2.1.2 Cassandra

Cassandra is another column-oriented database that consistently outperforms popular NoSQL alternatives [75,76]. However, the high performance can be achieved only if the way the data will be queried is known clearly in advance at the database designing stage. When properly designed, Cassandra could be the fastest database in terms of the performance of write operations because it is carefully designed to effectively store the data on disk. As a result, it would be the correct choice for a database with a high volume of writes. For example, one can use Cassandra to store log data because it has a high volume of writes.

If the data is too big for MongoDB, Cassandra can be an excellent option. Besides performance, it can also support multi-datacenter replication which allows the system to survive regional outages. Although not originally designed to run natively on your Hadoop cluster, recently Cassandra has been integrated with MapReduce, Pig, and Hive. However, it does not have fine-grained security controls.

2.4.2.1.3 MongoDB

MongoDB is different from the previous databases because it is document-oriented. A relational column-oriented database may not be the best choice when the data fields to be stored vary between the different elements because there would be a lot of empty columns. Although it is not necessarily bad to have many empty columns, MongoDB provides a method to store only the necessary fields for the document. For example, this design would fit interview/questionnaire data where, depending on the answer of the current question (e.g., male/female), certain fields may become required (pregnant?) or which follow-up questions should be asked.

MongoDB is such a good easy-to-use document store that is widely selected as a replacement candidate for a SQL database due to its schema-less feature (like other NoSQL databases). However, it cannot scale to very large datasets (approximately more than 100 TB), does not work with your Hadoop cluster natively, and has just recently had fine-grained security controls [73,77].

The characteristic differences between MongoDB, Cassandra, HBase, and Accumulo are summarized in the decision diagram shown in Figure 2.2. It is noteworthy that by "data not too big," we mean the size of the dataset is less than 100 TB.

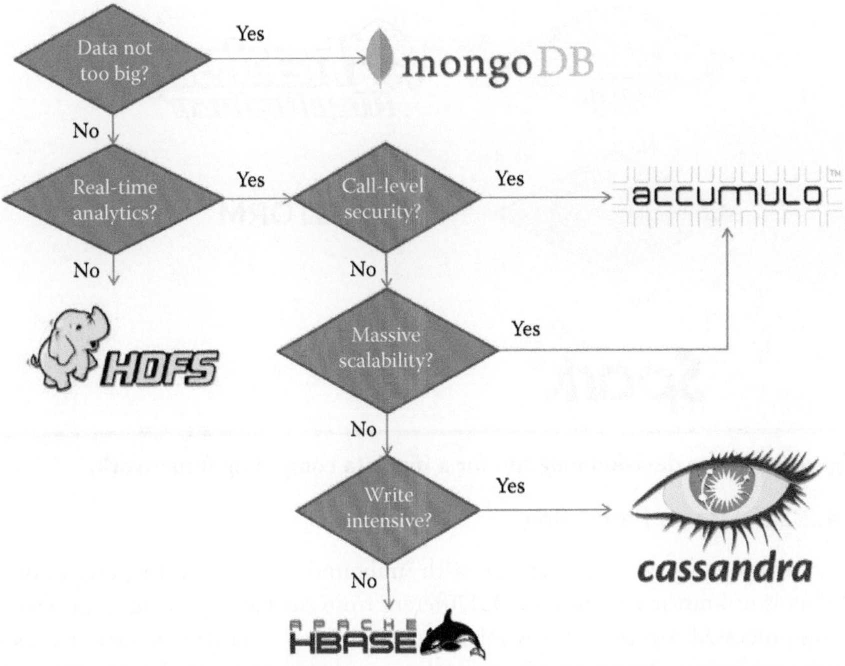

Figure 2.2 The decision diagram for big data storage.

2.4.2.2 Computing Frameworks

Unlike the NoSQL database, fortunately there are not many options for big data computing framework. Basically, there are two types of big data processing: batch processing and real-time processing.

2.4.2.2.1 Batch Processing

Batch processing often deals with an extremely large, bounded (a finite collection of data), and persistent (stored in permanent storage) dataset. The result is returned when the computation is complete (normally after a while). Batch processing is suitable for applications that need access to a whole set of records. The state of the dataset should be maintained for the duration of the computation. Batch processing systems are also well-suited for tasks that require very large volumes of data because they are developed with large quantities in mind. Therefore, they are often used with persistent historical data.

The trade-off for the ability of handling extremely large datasets is a longer computation time, which makes batch processing inappropriate for applications requiring a fast response.

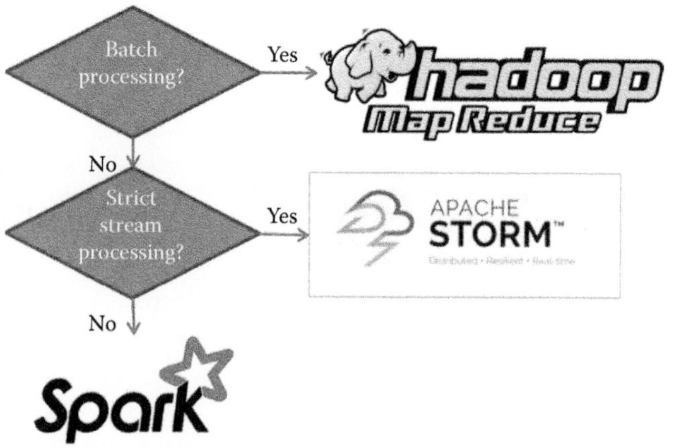

Figure 2.3 The decision diagram for a big data computing framework.

2.4.2.2.2 Stream Processing

Stream processing systems often deal with "unbounded" datasets. The total amount of data is unknown and unlimited. Different from the batch paradigm, instead of being processed together as a whole, each individual data item is executed as it enters the system. Processing is typically event-based and running forever until explicitly stopped. Results should be available shortly after the new data arrival because the data size is often small. Stream processing systems only execute one (strict stream processing) or very few (micro-batch processing) data items at a time, with minimal or no state being maintained between computations.

The stream processing model is well-suited for near real-time analytics, server or application error logging, and other time-based metrics where it is critical to respond to changes or spikes. It is also a good fit with data where trends over time are of interest. Hadoop with MapReduce is considered as a batch processing computing framework. It is suitable for back-end processing (data mining, data warehouse) on large datasets. Apache Storm or Samza belong to the real-time processing category. Apache Spark [54] or Flink can be thought of as hybrid types because they can mimic the real-time processing with their micro-batch processing. Figure 2.3 shows the decision diagram for a big data computing framework.

2.4.3 State-of-the-Art Big Data Based Cyber Analysis Solutions

2.4.3.1 Cisco OpenSOC [78,79]

OpenSOC is an open-source development project that is dedicated to providing an extensible and scalable advanced security analytics tool. It provides a big data security analytics framework designed to consume and monitor network

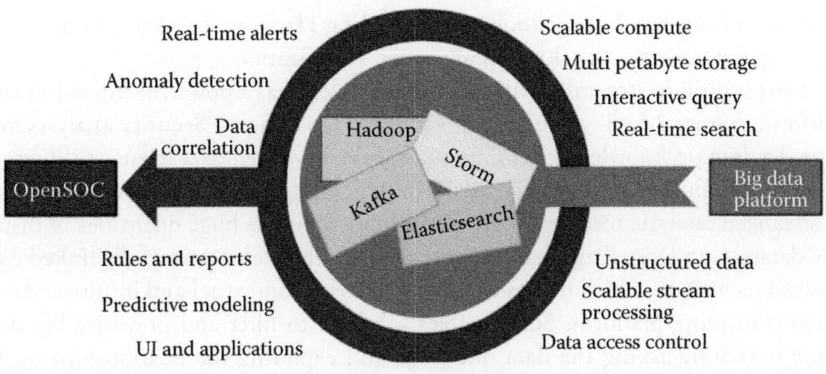

Figure 2.4 OpenSOC features. (From http://www.slideshare.net/JamesSirota/cisco-opensoc.)

traffic and machine exhaust data of a data center. OpenSOC is designed to be extensible and work at a massive scale. The framework provides the following capabilities:

- Extensible enrichment framework for any telemetry stream
- Anomaly detection and real-time rules-based alerts for any telemetry stream
- Hadoop-backed storage for telemetry stream with a customizable retention time
- Automated real-time indexing for telemetry streams backed by Elasticsearch
- Telemetry correlation and SQL query capability for data stored in Hadoop backed by Hive
- ODBC/JDBC compatibility and integration with existing analytics tools

OpenSOC is designed to scale up to consume millions of messages per second, enrich them, run them through anomaly detection algorithms, and issue real-time alerts. As shown in Figure 2.4, OpenSOC integrates numerous elements of the Hadoop ecosystem such as Storm, Kafka, and Elasticsearch. OpenSOC and provides a scalable platform incorporating capabilities such as full-packet capture indexing, storage, data enrichment, stream processing, batch processing, real-time search, and telemetry aggregation.

2.4.3.2 Sqrrl Enterprise [80]

Developed by Sqrrl Data, Inc., Sqrrl Enterprise aims to provide a security analytics solution for detecting and responding to advanced cyber threats. It lets organizations pinpoint and react to unusual activity by automatically uncovering hidden connections in the data. It also gives analysts a way to visually investigate these connections, so that they can understand the surrounding contexts and take actions.

Sqrrl is built on big data technologies, including Hadoop, link analysis, machine learning, data-centric security, and advanced visualization.

Sqrrl is built to streamline the hunting experience as a powerful threat hunting platform. Figure 2.5 shows the threat hunting loop of Sqrrl. Security analysts may have the domain knowledge to hunt, but not the advanced data science skill sets to directly manipulate and filter big data. Making sense of big data is not an easy task, so advanced analytic techniques are critical. Sqrrl ingests huge quantities of disparate datasets, and visualizes that data dynamically through a powerfully linked data analysis technique, which makes exploring the data contextual and intuitive. As an optimal hunting platform, Sqrrl enables a hunter to filter and prioritize big data while iteratively asking the data questions and exploring the relationships in the data. Sqrrl provides the scalability, visualization, and analytics that help analysts track down advanced threats via more advanced hunting techniques, turning data gatherers into data hunters. With Sqrrl, users can detect and respond to advanced data breaches, insider threats, and other hard-to-detect attacks.

In Sqrrl, hunting is an iterative process that is carried out in a loop to continuously look for adversaries hidden in vast datasets [80], and begins with a hypothesis. Sqrrl's threat hunting framework defines three types of hypotheses:

- **Intelligence-Driven:** Created from threat intelligence reports, threat intelligence feeds, malware analysis, and vulnerability scans.
- **Situational-Awareness Driven:** Crown jewel analysis, enterprise risk assessments, company- or employee-level trends.
- **Analytics-Driven:** Machine-learning and user and entity behavior analytics, used to develop aggregated risk scores that can also serve as hunting hypotheses.

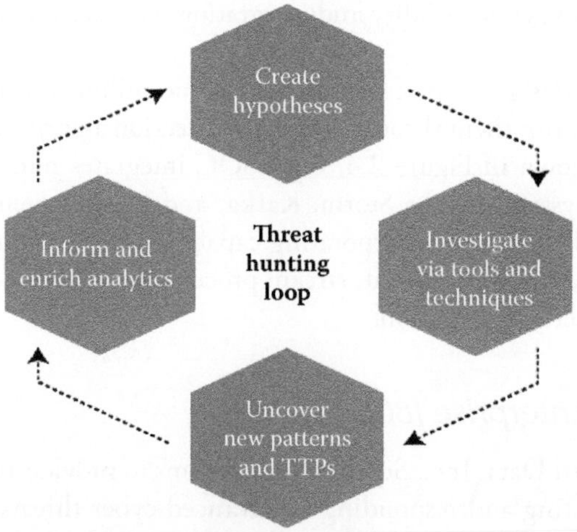

Figure 2.5 Sqrrl cyber threat hunting process. (From Sqrrl: Cyber Threat Hunting. https://sqrrl.com/solutions/cyber-threat-hunting/.)

The outcomes of hunting trips will be stored and used to enrich automated detection systems and analytics, as well as to form the foundation of future hunts. For big data analysis, an enterprise needs to store as much data as possible, such as flow data, proxy logs, host authentication attempts, IDS alerts, and even non-security focused information. In order to make sense of big data, advanced analytic techniques are critical. Sqrrl can ingest huge quantities of disparate datasets, and visualize that data dynamically through a powerfully linked data analysis capability to make exploring the data contextual and intuitive.

2.5 Our Experiences

In this section, we present our experiences in building a big data based network forensic solution, named Cerberus. Cerberus aims to help network operators and security analysts to better understand the network and discover issues and threats faster with less time and effort. It takes network data as input from a variety of data collectors (deployed at different network levels), interprets network performance and status, conducts analysis to detect and identify potential cybersecurity issues (e.g., attacks, anomalies, localizations, reasons), and presents analysis results to the network operators through the graphic interface. It supports both real-time and batch processing of data, and handles queries on history data and near real-time detection/statistics.

2.5.1 Software Architecture

The software architecture of Cerberus consists of big data storage, batch and streaming processing, web services, messaging, visualization, and user interface/analytics dashboard, as illustrated in Figure 2.6.

- **Message Queue:** Message Queue is responsible for efficiently transmitting network data into the cloud-based processing engine.
- **Stream Processing:** A stream processing engine is used to preprocess the data (i.e., convert the data format and dump data back to the database) or perform complex stream processing (e.g., event detection or certain real-time processing).
- **Big Data Database/Storage:** A database or storage is used to save the preprocessed data.
- **Web Services API:** A web services API is responsible for interacting with the backend system and providing data to the dashboard.
- **Application Data Database/Storage:** A database store is used by the user interface to store system data necessary for the web front-end application.
- **User Interface:** A user interface is provided to support user friendly visualization of analytics data.

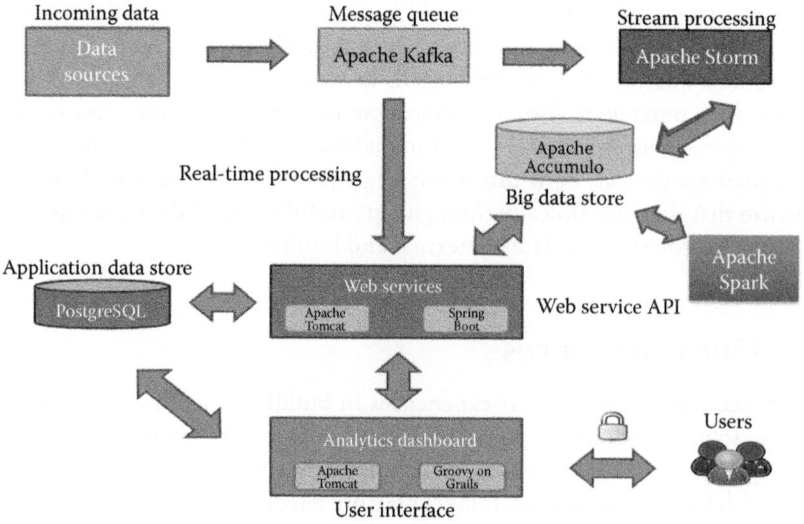

Figure 2.6 Illustrative software architecture of a cloud-based solution.

As discussed earlier, there are many decisions and selections we need to make for such a system. For each component, a particular supportive tool has been chosen to fulfill the design considerations and requirements:

- **Message Queue:** Apache Kafka [81] is chosen to support the message queue. Apache Kafka is a distributed messaging system, which supports high throughput and performs automatic load balancing.
- **Stream Processing:** Both Apache Storm [58] and Spark [54] are used to provide the distributed stream processing engine (aka a framework) for the system.
- **Big Data Database/Storage:** Apache Accumulo [66] is used as the backend database. Apache Accumulo is a distributed database management system implemented over Hadoop and Hadoop Distributed File System (HDFS). Apache Accumulo supports table-based databases and provides query interface over the tables.
- **Web Services API:** Spring Boot [82] is used on Apache Tomcat 7 [83] to provide an interface to the backed analytics data. Spring Boot is a way to get a spring framework application started faster with fewer configurations up front. It provides access to the features and components users need without forcing additional baggage. The Spring framework has a large user community with many avenues for support, and fits the need for real-time application using Accumulo.

- **Application Data Database/Storage:** The web application framework that provides UI features requires an SQL data store for its runtime processing. PostgreSQL is used for this purpose [84].
- **User Interface:** The web application framework called Grails [85] is used for the user interface also known as the "Analytics Dashboard."

2.5.2 Services Components

2.5.2.1 Data Processing Using Accumulo

Accumulo provides a set of flexible processing capabilities for a third party to develop additional data processing algorithms. Combining Accumulo with Hadoop [55] or other distributed processing frameworks, Accumulo can be further extended to process complex data processing algorithms. In this architecture, all persistent data (including network data) are stored in Accumulo. Hence, Accumulo plays a key role in our system design and implementation. Specifically, since we designed our system so that most of the analysis will be run at the server side to be able to support thin clients, we have developed many utility "iterators" in Accumulo to query data and boosting the analysis performance. The rowID of a table is designed carefully so that the data is distributed evenly among Accumulo hosts. This will leverage the aggregated bandwidth and parallelism to improve the query performance.

2.5.2.2 Log Service (Message System) Using Kafka

Kafka is a distributed, partitioned, replicated commit log service. It provides the functionality of a messaging system, but with a unique design. Kafka maintains feeds of messages in categories called *topics*. The processes that publish messages to a Kafka topic are *producers*. The processes that subscribe to topics and process the feed of published messages are called *consumers*. So, at a high level, producers send messages over the network to the Kafka cluster which in turn serves them up to consumers. Kafka is simply used as a buffer in our system between the sensors (producer) and data processing and analysis (consumer). Queuing systems are generally used to balance the data processing capacity and the data generating rate.

2.5.2.3 Stream Processing Engine Using Storm

Storm is only a real-time processing engine. Its users need to create jobs/topologies and submit them to the Storm framework to be executed. A Storm topology is similar to a MapReduce batch job. The difference is that a MapReduce batch job eventually finishes while a Storm topology runs forever. In this illustrative system, our team developed a Storm topology (consisting of a Kafka *spout* and an

Accumulo *bolt*) to process the data from Kafka and then feed them into Accumulo. Specifically, our storm topology can detect near-real-time anomalies and generate alerts for different types of network events and attacks. It can also connect to other data inputs, e.g., IDS, OpenVAS, http logs, to get as much information as possible to feed in the correlation engine to detect a variety of cyber threats and attacks.

2.5.3 Key Features

The key features of Cerberus include:

- **Integration of multiple data sources** for better and real-time cyber situation awareness. Cerberus supports the integration across different types of data at select points in the network, such as measurement data from network monitoring tools (e.g., NetFlow, sFlow), security alerts and logs from existing IDS (e.g., Snort), http/DNS logs on critical servers, SIEM data, and network configurations.
- **Targeting complex network issues:** Cerberus is targeting complex network issues. It not only identifies failures, but also pinpoints the root cause of the failures. To support that, it applies a scalable graph-based root-cause analysis, whose computation complexity is roughly linear to the total number of faults and symptoms, and hence achieves better scalability and computation efficiency.
- **Detecting stealthy and sophisticated attacks:** Cerberus is able to detect various types of security events from different data sources, and also correlate them to identify and understand more stealthy and sophisticated attacks.
- **Big data processing:** It uses the most advanced big data technologies to achieve scalable data storage and processing, including Kafka, Storm, Spark, Accumulo, Spring Boot, SQL/noSQL, and Grails.

2.6 Summary

This chapter provides an overview on how to apply big data technologies into network forensics, as network forensics plays a key role in today's enterprise network monitoring, management, and security analysis. Big data analytics has shown its promise of unearthing important insights from large amounts of data, and hence attracts attention from researchers and network analysts. In this chapter, we provided a brief introduction to network forensics, terms and processes, current solutions, and their limitations. We also discussed how to apply big data analysis for network forensics, and shared our experiences in building a big data based network forensics solution.

References

1. Computer and Digital Forensics Blog, Cyber Security and Digital Forensics: Two Sides of the Same Coin. http://computerforensicsblog.champlain.edu/2014/10/22/cyber-security-digital-forensics-two-sides-coin/ (visited October 10, 2016).
2. G. Kessler. Online Education in Computer and Digital Forensics, Proceedings of the 40th Hawaii International Conference on System Sciences, 2007.
3. G. M. Mohay. *Computer and Intrusion Forensics*, Artech House Inc, Boston, 2003.
4. G. Palmer. A Road Map for Digital Forensic Research, Report from DFRWS 2001, First Digital Forensic Research Workshop, Utica, NY, August 7–8, 2001, pp. 27–30.
5. T. Grance, S. Chevalier, K. Kent, and H. Dang. Guide to Computer and Network Data Analysis: Applying Forensic Techniques to Incident Response, NIST Special Publication 800-86, 2005.
6. K. Sisaat and D. Miyamoto. Source Address Validation Support for Network Forensics, Proceedings of the 1st Joint Workshop on Information Security, Sept. 2006.
7. Network Security and Cyber Security—What Is the Difference. https://www.ecpi.edu/blog/whats-difference-between-network-security-cyber-security.
8. http://searchsecurity.techtarget.com/definition/network-forensics.
9. S. Davidoff and J. Ham. *Network Forensics: Tracking Hackers Through Cyberspace*, Pearson Education, Inc. Prentice Hall, NJ, ISBN 9780132564717, 2012.
10. opensecuritytraining.info/NetworkForensics_files/NetworkForensics.pptx.
11. sFlow, Traffic Monitoring using sFlow, http://www.sflow.org/, 2003.
12. SNMP, https://en.wikipedia.org/wiki/Simple_Network_Management_Protocol.
13. Snoop, http://docs.sun.com/app/docs/doc/816-5166/6mbb1kqh9?a=view.
14. Tcpdump, http://www.tcpdump.org/.
15. Wireshark, http://www.wireshark.org/.
16. Log File, http://www.remosoftware.com/glossary/log-file.
17. Intrusion Detection System, https://en.wikipedia.org/wiki/Intrusion_detection_system.
18. tcpdump2ASCII, http://www.Linux.org/apps/AppId_2072.html.
19. tcpshow, Network Security Tools, http://www.tcpshow.org/.
20. tcptrace, http://jarok.cs.ohiou.edu/software/tcptrace/tcptrace.html.
21. tshark, https://www.wireshark.org/docs/man-pages/tshark.html.
22. RSA NetWitness suite, https://www.rsa.com/en-us/products/threat-detection-and-response.
23. Cisco IOS® NetFlow, http://www.cisco.com/go/netflow.
24. Cisco NetFlow Analyzer, http://www.cisco.com/c/en/us/products/ios-nx-os-software/ios-netflow/networking_solutions_products_genericcontent0900aecd805ff728.html.
25. Ntop, http://www.ntop.org/.
26. SolarWinds NetFlow Traffic Analyzer, http://www.solarwinds.com/netflow-traffic-analyzer.
27. M. Krishnamurthy et al., Introducing Intrusion Detection and Snort. In: *How to Cheat at Securing Linux*. Burlington, MA: Syngress Publishing, Inc., 2008.
28. Bro, https://en.wikipedia.org/wiki/Bro_(software).
29. OSSEC, https://en.wikipedia.org/wiki/OSSEC.
30. Orion NPM, http://www.solarwinds.com/products/orion/.
31. Netcordia NetMRI, http://www.netcordia.com/products/index.asp.
32. OpenNMS, http://www.opennms.org/.

33. GNetWatch, http://gnetwatch.sourceforge.net/.
34. GroundWork, http://www.groundworkopensource.com/.
35. Nagios, IT Infrastructure Monitoring, https://www.nagios.org/.
36. H. Debar. An Introduction to Intrusion Detection Systems. *Proc. of Connect*, 2000.
37. M. Roesch. The SNORT Network Intrusion Detection System. http://www.snort.org.
38. H. Javitz and A. Valdes. The SRI IDES Statistical Anomaly Detector. *Proc. of IEEE Symposium on Research in Security and Privacy*, 1991.
39. G. Gu, J. Zhang, and W. Lee. Botsniffer: Detecting Botnet Command and Control Channels in Network Traffic. *Proc. of NDSS'08*, 2008.
40. J. R. Binkley and S. Singh. An Algorithm for Anomaly-Based Botnet Detection. *Proc. of USENIX SRUTI Workshop*, pp. 43–48, 2006.
41. J. Goebel and T. Holz. Rishi: Identify Bot Contaminated Hosts by IRC Nickname Evaluation. In: *Hot Topics in Understanding Botnets (HotBots)*, Cambridge, MA, 2007.
42. A. Karasaridis, B. Rexroad, and D. Hoeflin. Wide-Scale Botnet Detection and Characterization. *Proc. of the 1st Conference on First Workshop on Hot Topics in Understanding Botnets*, 2007.
43. C. Livadas, R. Walsh, D. Lapsley, and W. T. Strayer. Using Machine Learning Techniques to Identify Botnet Traffic. *2nd IEEE LCN WoNS*, 2006.
44. W. T. Strayer, R. Walsh, C. Livadas, and D. Lapsley. Detecting Botnets with Tight Command and Control. *Proc. of the 31st IEEE Conference on LCN06*, 2006.
45. P. Porras, H. Saidi, and V. Yegneswaran. A Multi-Perspective Analysis of the Storm (Peacomm) Worm. Computer Science Laboratory, SRI International, Tech. Rep., 2007.
46. G. Gu, R. Perdisci, J. Zhang, and W. Lee. Botminer: Clustering Analysis of Network Traffic for Protocol- and Structure-Independent Botnet Detection. *Proc. of the 17th USENIX Security Symposium*, 2008.
47. T. F. Yen and M. K. Reiter. Traffic Aggregation for Malware Detection. In: Zamboni D. (eds) *Detection of Intrusions and Malware, and Vulnerability Assessment. (DIMVA).* Lecture Notes in Computer Science, vol 5137, Springer, Berlin, Heidelberg, 2008.
48. M. Bailey et al., Automated Classification and Analysis of Internet Malware. *Recent Advances in Intrusion Detection (RAID)*, 2007.
49. S. Gianvecchio, M. Xie, Z. Wu, and H. Wang. Measurement and Classification of Humans and Bots in Internet. *USENIX Security*, 2008.
50. S. Kandula, R. Chandra, and D. Katabi. What's Going On? Learning Communication Rules in Edge Networks. *Sigcomm*, 2008.
51. J. Jung, V. Paxson, A. Berger, and H. Balakrishnan. Fast Port Scan Detection Using Sequential Hypothesis Testing. *Proc. of the IEEE Symposium on Security and Privacy*, 2004.
52. http://www.datacenterknowledge.com/archives/2011/08/01/report-google-uses-about-900000-servers/.
53. MapReduce, https://en.wikipedia.org/wiki/MapReduce.
54. Apache Spark, https://spark.apache.org/.
55. Apache Hadoop, https://en.wikipedia.org/wiki/Apache_Hadoop.
56. Apache Haddop Yarn, http://searchdatamanagement.techtarget.com/definition/Apache-Hadoop-YARN-Yet-Another-Resource-Negotiator.
57. Apache Mesos, https://en.wikipedia.org/wiki/Apache_Mesos.

58. Apache Storm, https://en.wikipedia.org/wiki/Storm_(event_processor).
59. Apache Flink, https://en.wikipedia.org/wiki/Apache_Flink.
60. Apache Beam, https://en.wikipedia.org/wiki/Apache_Beam.
61. What Is Ignite, http://apacheignite.gridgain.org/.
62. Hazelcast, https://en.wikipedia.org/wiki/Hazelcast.
63. Apache Drill, https://en.wikipedia.org/wiki/Apache_Drill.
64. Apache Kylin, https://en.wikipedia.org/wiki/Apache_Kylin.
65. Apache HBase, https://en.wikipedia.org/wiki/Apache_HBase.
66. Apache Accumulo, https://en.wikipedia.org/wiki/Apache_Accumulo.
67. MongoDB, https://en.wikipedia.org/wiki/MongoDB.
68. Apache Cassandra, https://en.wikipedia.org/wiki/Apache_Cassandra.
69. Voldemort, https://en.wikipedia.org/wiki/Voldemort_(distributed_data_store).
70. Apache Phoenix, https://en.wikipedia.org/wiki/Apache_Phoenix.
71. Apache Pig, https://en.wikipedia.org/wiki/Pig_(programming_tool).
72. http://bigdata-guide.blogspot.com/2014/01/hbase-versus-cassandra-versus-accumulo.html.
73. http://www.ippon.tech/blog/use-cassandra-mongodb-hbase-accumulo-mysql.
74. https://sqrrl.com/how-to-choose-a-nosql-database/.
75. T. Rabl, S. Gómez-Villamor, M. Sadoghi, V. Muntés-Mulero, H.-A. Jacobsen, and S. Mankovskii. Solving big data challenges for enterprise application performance management. *Proc. VLDB Endow.* 5, 12 (August 2012), 1724–1735.
76. http://blog.markedup.com/2013/02/cassandra-hive-and-hadoop-how-we-picked-our-analytics-stack/.
77. https://kkovacs.eu/cassandra-vs-mongodb-vs-couchdb-vs-redis.
78. http://opensoc.github.io/.
79. http://www.slideshare.net/JamesSirota/cisco-opensoc.
80. Sqrrl, Cyber Threat Hunting. https://sqrrl.com/solutions/cyber-threat-hunting/.
81. Apache Kafka, http://kafka.apache.org/.
82. Spring Boot, http://projects.spring.io/spring-boot/.
83. Apache Tomcat 7, https://tomcat.apache.org/.
84. PostgreSQL, http://www.postgresql.org/.
85. Grails, https://grails.org/.

Chapter 3

Dynamic Analytics-Driven Assessment of Vulnerabilities and Exploitation

Hasan Cam, Magnus Ljungberg, Akhilomen Oniha, and Alexia Schulz

Contents

This chapter presents vulnerability assessment, one of the essential cybersecurity functions and requirements, and highlights how big data analytics could potentially leverage vulnerability assessment and causality analysis of vulnerability exploitation in the detection of intrusion and vulnerabilities so that cyber analysts can investigate alerts and vulnerabilities more effectively and faster. Vulnerability assessment has become a critical national need in support of mission operations by realistically assessing attacker access to existing vulnerabilities and improving the ability of mission leaders and planners to triage which system vulnerabilities present the highest risk to mission assurance. As the vulnerabilities and attack surface of assets grow in complexity and size, threat and malware also grow more pervasive, and cyber sensors generate more data to be analyzed. A holistic cybersecurity approach is thus necessary considering not only observation and detection of all events of attackers, intrusions, and vulnerabilities, but also analysis of their interactions, causality, and temporal and spatial orderings in real time.

In order to accurately assess exploit likelihood and impact of vulnerability exploitations in a cybersecurity environment, the interactions and causality reasoning of cybersecurity events and assets need to be analyzed in-depth with their context-specific services and parameters. However, it seems extremely difficult, if not impossible, to have all the required knowledge of cybersecurity events and activities within a network for assessing its cyber risk in real-time, primarily due to uncertainties or unexplained patterns of network traffic, incomplete or noisy attack measurements and observations, and insufficient information about vulnerabilities and cyber assets. Therefore, it is highly desirable to enhance and extract the quality information of all available cybersecurity data in order to maximize its utility.

This chapter presents novel models and data analytics approaches to dynamically building and analyzing relationships, dependencies, and causality reasoning among the detected vulnerabilities, intrusion detection alerts, and measurements. The resultant analysis leads to the detection of zero-day vulnerabilities and stealthy malware activities. In addition, it provides a more accurate dynamic risk assessment due to the available quantitative and qualitative knowledge on vulnerabilities and exploit likelihood. This chapter also describes a detailed description of building an exemplary scalable data analytics system to implement the proposed model and approaches by enriching, tagging, and indexing the data of all observations and measurements, vulnerabilities, detection, and monitoring.

3.1 Introduction

3.1.1 The Need and Challenges

Most sectors providing the underpinnings of modern society have come to critically rely on computers and computer networks to function properly. These sectors include public health, finance and banking, business and retail, media and telecommunications, and national defense, along with more fundamental critical infrastructure such as electrical power, water utilities, and food distribution. Our deep reliance on these sectors makes them particularly attractive targets for attacks [1]. Adversaries can leverage computer or network vulnerabilities to interfere with the proper functioning of American society [2–6].

Trusted networks are used by the Department of Defense (DoD), law enforcement and the intelligence community (LE/IC), as well as countless business and industrial enterprises (BIE) to provide access to critical information and services that are vital to accomplishing their respective missions. Collectively, we will refer to the DoD, LE/IC, and BIE as the trusted network user base (TNUB). Vulnerabilities on these trusted networks confer opportunity to adversaries of the TNUB to interfere with mission execution. Adversaries can leverage vulnerabilities to gain unauthorized access to the trusted network or to prevent authorized users from having access, either of which can negatively impact the missions of the TNUB. The motivation of adversaries to exploit vulnerabilities on a trusted network can be classified broadly according to five major categories: (1) Espionage and intelligence gathering, (2) denial of service, (3) data corruption and misinformation, (4) kinetic and cyber-physical effects, and (5) hijack of asset control. A specific vulnerability may enable one or more of these classes of adversary operations. The extent to which an adversary can leverage the vulnerability to interfere with mission success depends on (1) which of these five categories the vulnerability may enable and (2) the extent to which mission execution can withstand adversary activity in each category. Therefore, the inherent risk presented by a vulnerability is specific to each mission that is impacted.

A critical national need in support of TNUB missions is to augment the current capabilities of vulnerability assessment tools to realistically assess attacker access to existing vulnerabilities and to improve the ability of mission leaders and planners to triage which system vulnerabilities present the highest risk to mission assurance. This requires a dynamic approach to vulnerability assessment rather than a static approach because the attacker posture and vulnerability access as well as the way the trusted network is being leveraged to accomplish the mission are both subject to significant variability in time [1,7]. The inherent challenge to filling this national need is that the available data are constrained to a limited number of observable vantage points: vulnerabilities are collected at the host locations, and observations of network traffic are limited to a small number of centralized tap locations, whereas the non-local problem of the attacker access depends more globally on the network topology. It will be necessary to estimate the vulnerability and resulting mission risk on the basis of incomplete information, gathered from myriad sensor types deployed at strategic locations. There are several enabling technologies that will be critical for satisfying this national need, none of which is currently deployed or exists. First is technology to dynamically infer network topology and the interconnection of hosts. Second is the ability to use this information, in conjunction with existing scans and other observations such as network traffic capture, to assess the severity of a vulnerability in terms of its specific impact to a particular mission or set of missions. To this end, technology will also be needed to assess which assets each mission is leveraging as a function of time.

As the vulnerabilities and attack surface of assets grow in complexity and size, threats and malware also grow more pervasive, cyber sensors generate more data to be analyzed. Intrusions are often obfuscated to the extent that its traces and fingerprints are hidden within different types of data (e.g., intrusion detection system [IDS] alerts, firewall logs, reconnaissance scans, network traffic patterns, and other computer monitoring data) that are involved with a wide range of assets and time points. However, even a small organization's security operation center may end up dealing with an increasingly huge volume of daily data.

3.1.2 The Objective and Approach of This Chapter

Given the time constraints, service level agreements, and computational and storage resource constraints in the analysis of such data, we aim at first identifying and extracting high-quality data products describing cyber events from the raw data. The analysis and assessment of these high-quality data products can be performed more quickly and dynamically by requiring a smaller amount of time and computational resources. We address the questions of (1) how the raw data size of cyber events can be reduced significantly at close to real time and (2) what effective methods can be used to detect and analyze the noisy data of intrusion and vulnerability detections and exploitations. To this end, we undertake a holistic approach of considering the size and analysis of intrusion data, together with the analysis of vulnerability data and exploitations, by investigating how the cyber events and processes of intrusions and vulnerabilities are detected, cross-correlated, analyzed, and assessed.

In answering the two questions above, we present why data analytics, machine learning, and temporal causality analysis are considered essential components, and we show how they interactively function in very important roles. High-quality data products can be extracted from raw cyber data by pinpointing the specific assets and time instances involved with intrusions. We suggest using temporal causality analysis of main cyber sensor observations and events including intrusion alerts, vulnerabilities, attacker activities, firewall and HBSS log data, and network traffic. Our premise is that if we know what vulnerabilities exist in the system and how these vulnerabilities can be exploited by intrusion, then we can develop a causality analysis diagram for cyber events, vulnerabilities, intrusions, and observations of attacker activities. This causality analysis narrows down the cyber data to be searched and analyzed, leading to a significant reduction in size and scope from the raw cyber data. This results in faster data analysis, less computational resources, and potentially more accurate results. This chapter presents how data analytics could potentially leverage vulnerability assessment and causality analysis of vulnerability exploitation in the detection of intrusion and vulnerabilities so that cyber analysts can investigate alerts and vulnerabilities more effectively and faster.

The remainder of this chapter is organized as follows. Section 3.2 provides background information on vulnerability assessment, attribution, and exploitation, along with a use case. Section 3.3 presents the state-of-the-art vulnerability assessment tools, data sources, and analytics. Section 3.4 first provides comparison of some security information and event management (SIEM) tools and then presents our temporal and causality analysis to enhance the analysis and management of vulnerabilities, exploitations, and intrusion alerts. Concluding remarks are made in Section 3.5.

3.2 Vulnerability Assessment, Attribution, and Exploitation

This section presents basic background information on vulnerability assessment, scoring, and attributes and then discusses a use case on the identification of attribution and exploitation within a cyber analytics environment.

3.2.1 Vulnerability Assessment

In general, vulnerability refers to any weakness of information technology, assets, or cyber-physical or control systems that could be exploited to launch an attack by an adversary. Vulnerability identification, detection, and assessment are essential to cybersecurity, particularly risk assessment. Any combination of security penetration tests and auditing, ethical hacking, and vulnerability scanners may be used to detect vulnerabilities at various processing layers of information, communication, and operations of a system within a cybersecurity environment. Once vulnerabilities are identified, they are ranked with respect to severity and risk score. This helps determine the order in which the prioritized vulnerabilities are put through the patching or recovery process to mitigate system risk, while maintaining system functionality at an acceptable level. To develop a reasonable assessment for a vulnerability, its meaningful attributes should be determined and quantified dynamically by considering system and environmental conditions, as well as its relationship with other relevant vulnerabilities in the space and time domain.

The minimal software attributes of a vulnerability can be listed as authentication, access complexity, and access vector. The minimal impact factors that need to be taken into consideration in case of vulnerability exploitation are confidentiality impact, integrity impact, and availability impact. In general, an attack (e.g., a denial of service attack) can exploit a vulnerability at various network layers, including the physical layer (e.g., wireless jamming attack), the MAC layer (e.g., an attack forging address resolution protocol), the network and transport layers (e.g., an attack degrading the routing and delivery of information), and the application layer (e.g., an attack making intensive requests to overwhelm computer resources). A dynamic accurate assessment of detection capability, exploit likelihood, and exploitation impact associated with a vulnerability assists network defenders and decision makers in improving the assessment of situational awareness and risk of a system. Our approach to achieving such accurate assessment is to determine dynamically not only individual vulnerability attributes and characteristics, but also dependencies, interactions, and probabilistic correlations among vulnerabilities, and then to harness the power of big data analytics to determine correlations and temporal causality among vulnerabilities and cyber events. The vulnerability dependencies and correlations of assets can provide cues about the severity of their attack surface.

Given that zero-day vulnerabilities and exploits always exist, it is critical to have timely detection and control of vulnerabilities and attacks, along with timely recovery and patching of vulnerabilities. For controlling and limiting damage of vulnerability exploitations as well as providing mission assurance, the basic tasks include determining the following: criticality of assets (to a dynamically evolving mission landscape), infection and exploitation status of assets, the movement and propagation paths of exploits, exploitation likelihood, impact and spread of attacks, recognition of adversary strategies and activities, and mission assurance requirements. The common objective of all these tasks at a high level can be expressed as providing real-time detection, containment, and control of vulnerabilities and attacks over a cybersecurity environment that ideally supports at least the following five features: (1) use of end-to-end visibility and observability tools across an enterprise network system; (2) understanding the context and correlation of data, user, and adversary activities; (3) performing real-time analysis; (4) implementing an in-depth defense by monitoring networks and detecting compromised assets and attacker activities; and (5) reducing damage and dwell time of the attacker within the network [2]. The adverse impact of vulnerability exploitations should be minimized by controlling their spread and maintaining mission assurance of systems and operations.

The minimal software attributes of a vulnerability can be listed as authentication, access complexity, and access vector, as stated in the Common Vulnerability Scoring System (CVSS) [8–11]. CVSS indicates that the minimal impact factors to consider in case of a vulnerability exploitation are confidentiality impact, integrity impact, and availability impact. Although vulnerability scoring in CVSS and similar types of systems is carefully designed using expert knowledge, they are still inherently ad hoc in nature and possibly assign scores incorrectly to some vulnerabilities. Therefore, it is highly desirable that security evaluation of both individual and collective assets is conducted objectively and systematically [7]. CVSS provides a score for each new software vulnerability discovered that prioritizes the importance of the vulnerability. However, the existing methods and by-default standards such as CVSS do not take into consideration varying conditions in time, environmental factors, and collective behaviors of vulnerabilities and attack impacts, nor does it make unrealistic assumptions about cyber vulnerabilities, exploits, observations, and their models.

In the current CVSS, the base score is a function of access vector, access complexity, authentication, confidentiality impact, integrity impact, and availability impact, where only atomic attack (i.e., single-stage attack) is considered, and no damage on assets is included. In [7], we introduced both theoretical and experimental methods to enhance the assessment of vulnerabilities and vulnerability exploitations, starting initially with CVSS scores and Bayesian network of vulnerability dependencies, and then using Markov models for identifying the most probable exploited vulnerabilities.

One shortfall with vulnerability assessments as they exist today is that the level of criticality of the vulnerability is associated only with the vulnerability itself, but not with the exposure of that vulnerability to an attacker. A technological mechanism that could help address this shortfall is to cross-correlate the existence of a vulnerability with the occurrence of known signatures of adversary behavior. These signatures could be event logs on a system, or specific combinations of event logs that occur within a given timeframe, or they could be based on traffic patterns such as a sudden increase in outbound volume of data. The co-occurrence of the vulnerability with anomalies in system logs or traffic patterns is an indication that the criticality assessment of the vulnerability should be escalated. Furthermore, if the vulnerable host is buried deep inside several layers of security apparatus, it is important to be able to trace the traffic as it crosses through the various proxies and firewalls all the way to an attacker on the Internet, in order to assess the risk to the programs or missions being supported by the vulnerable host.

There are many shared challenges in traffic attribution and in discovering co-occurrence of vulnerability and system or traffic anomalies. The relevant data are often difficult to identify because the different tiers in the security apparatus collect disparate data from separate locations. Often there is minimal overlap in assets between separate datasets, and even datasets that include shared events and assets but are generated on different hosts can suffer arbitrary timing differences and latencies between associated observations. Network address translation further complicates valid cross-correlation by obfuscating the true start and endpoints of flow records.

Surmounting these challenges to improve vulnerability assessment requires a centralized data store, coupled with a process that aggregates data streams from multiple sensors, normalizes the data across the different sources to allow pivoting from data collected in one location to data collected in another, and labels the data with appropriate knowledge engineering to provide analysts ready access to the data coupled with discoverable knowledge about the provenance and contents of the data. Centralization of different data streams would enable automatable analytics to simultaneously process data collected in multiple locations.

Developing improved vulnerability assessment apparatus is likely to be an iterative process in which an analyst explores various correlations and patterns in the data, forms a hypothesis, tests the hypothesis by querying the data, develops a more robust signature for the attack mode under investigation, and automates the association of that attack mode with a known vulnerability using the signature and the data available in the data store. An example of a portion of this process, leveraging the Scalable Cyber Analytic Processing Environment (SCAPE) technology [6], is carried out at the U.S. Army Research Laboratory.

3.2.2 Use Case: Identification and Attribution of Vulnerability Exploitation

A computer network defense service provider (CNDSP) is an accredited organization responsible for delivering protection, detection, response, and sustainment services to its subscribers [12]. Such an organization typically assembles large datasets consisting of IDS alerts, firewall logs, reconnaissance scans, network traffic patterns, and other computer monitoring data. In this particular example, such CNDSP-collected data have been stored in an Accumulo database, which has been made available to an analyst for data exploration purposes via the SCAPE (formerly known as LLCySA [6]). This is illustrated as a big data cyber analytic system architecture in Figure 3.1.

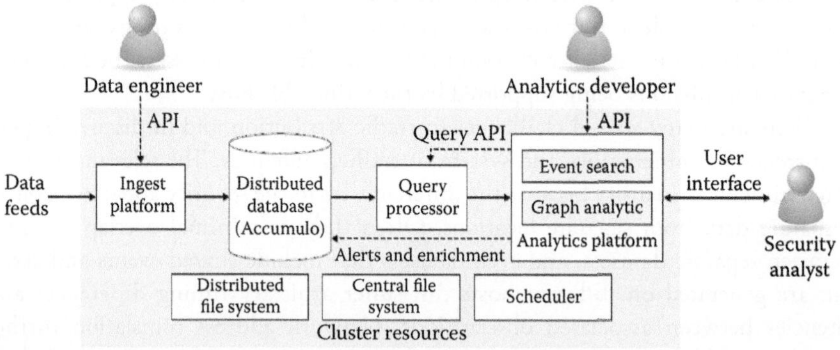

Figure 3.1 A big data cyber analytics framework. (From S.M. Sawyer, T.H. Yu, M.L. Hubbell, and B.D. O'Gwynn. *Lincoln Laboratory Journal,* 20(2), 67–76, 2014.)

The SCAPE environment provides knowledge engineering that allows an analyst to access the data without detailed *a priori* technical expertise regarding where data have been collected, which sensors have been deployed, or knowledge of the data storage format and schema. In this particular example, the goal is to identify an attack deep inside the DoD network and trace the net flows back to an attacker on the Internet. Host intrusion data are used to provide the initial tip. SCAPE is used to conduct an interactive investigation, pivoting between different relevant data sources to develop a hypothesis and confirm illicit activity. A simple aggregating analytic identifies a subset of hosts with the highest number of Host Intrusion Protection System (HIPS) alerts. Using SCAPE, the analyst pivots to the associated NetFlow data communicating with these hosts and identifies a suspicious flow revealing a late-night surge of server message block (SMB) activity for one of these Internet protocols (IPs). This process is depicted on the right-hand side of Figure 3.2, which also shows a plot of NetFlow activity associated with this time period. Comparison with the previous several days of traffic suggests that the volume of data exchange on December 11 is potentially atypical for the host in question.

The SCAPE environment provides an easy-access interface to multiple cyber data sources, allowing an analyst to quickly pivot from host intrusion protection events to NetFlow. The correlation of HIPS alerts with suspicious flow activity may imply that the assessment of the associated vulnerability should be escalated to a higher level of priority.

Closer inspection of the HIPS data on the host uncovered evidence in this time period of a possible SMB brute force attempt. The next step in this investigation would be to aggregate network address translation logs from the various firewall and proxy devices that intervene between this host and the remote host on the open Internet. Doing so would allow the analyst to determine the destination of the large outflux of data.

An analysis of this type could be used to improve an existing assessment of the vulnerability associated with this host, and others like it. Having discovered the specific signatures associated with a breach of this type, the co-occurrence of the

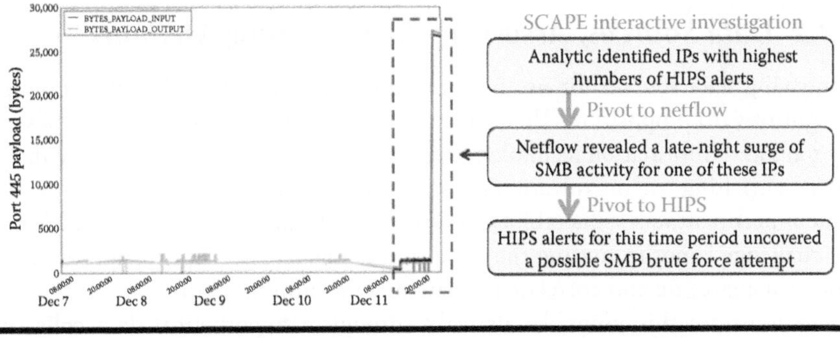

Figure 3.2 Sample SCAPE workflow and resulting graphic output.

existing vulnerability with significant HIPS activity or with significant changes in network traffic could be used to escalate the associated severity of the vulnerability, indicating that a higher priority should be designated to this host, because of indications of potential exposure to an adversarial entity.

3.3 State-of-the-Art Vulnerability Assessment Tools, Data Sources, and Analytics

3.3.1 Vulnerability Assessment Tools

Vulnerability is thought to be the intersection of three elements: a system susceptibility or flaw, attacker access to the flaw, and attacker capability to exploit the flaw [3]. Many vulnerability assessment tools exist, both in industry and within the TNUB, to detect the presence of such flaws. The tools typically leverage extensive databases of known software vulnerabilities and itemize the observed malware and other attacks that leverage each vulnerability to assess its severity. Network-based scanners perform credentialed or uncredentialed scans of endpoint hosts to enumerate open ports, identify which software is installed, and detect missing patches. Web application and database scanners check for flaws in data validation and other mechanisms for command injection or information leakage. Host-based scanners look for known problems, such as viruses, or faulty operating system configurations to identify security gaps. Collectively, these tools exhibit a weakness; the scan can identify a system flaw or susceptibility, and a database can estimate the attacker capability to exploit the flaw, but none of the tools is equipped to quantify the extent to which an attacker can access a flaw. The fundamental reason driving this weakness is that all current vulnerability assessment processes are inherently local to each host. Assessing attacker access to a flaw is inherently a non-local problem that involves not only the vulnerabilities on a given system, but also the vulnerabilities of systems that are connected to it on the network.

3.3.2 Data Sources, Assessment, and Parsing Methods

Identifying data sources for use in vulnerability assessment and exploitation is a straightforward proposition. There are literally hundreds, if not thousands, of security tools and information technology systems that generate data useful for enhancing or enriching an organization's situational awareness posture and providing content pertinent to a vulnerability assessment and exploitation exercise. However, the challenge is not in finding the data sources but rather adopting approaches or tools that aggregate and correlate the data in a meaningful manner.

To illustrate this point, let us walk through a hypothetical data collection exercise in preparation for a vulnerability assessment. For the sake of simplicity, consider three data sources in this example, although there could be dozens of data sources in an actual assessment. The first data source is Nessus, which is an industry-recognized vulnerability assessment scanning tool. Nessus is developed and maintained commercially by Tenable Network Security and provides a variety of features, including the following: network vulnerability scanning, application vulnerability scanning, device compliance assessment, and network host discovery.* The second data source is McAfee ePolicy Orchestrator (ePO), which is an industry-recognized, host-based security tool. The ePO is developed and maintained commercially by Intel Security and provides many features, including the following: host intrusion prevention, policy auditing, and anti-malware.† The third data source is Snort,‡ which is an open-source network intrusion detection and intrusion prevention tool. Martin Roesch developed Snort for public use and dissemination in 1998. Snort is freely available for download, and there are hundreds of thousands of community members that use, maintain, and contribute to the tool. Snort provides intrusion detection and prevention capabilities by means of network traffic analysis and packet capture.

These example tools all independently provide some degree of situational awareness. A naive approach toward vulnerability assessment would be to consider the output from each tool in isolation. So, Nessus output would be used for application vulnerability assessment, McAfee ePO would be used for host policy compliance assessment, and Snort would be used for exploitation detection and assessment. Although this approach may be straightforward to understand and easy to implement, there is no correlation occurring between the different data sources, leaving the potential for major holes in the analysis of vulnerability exploitation process.

As an illustrative example, imagine a scenario where a Snort subject matter expert named Samantha is providing intrusion detection analysis services to a small organization. During her shift, Samantha receives two alerts identifying unauthorized remote access attempts on two separate network segments: Alpha and Beta. Without consulting any additional information sources, how would Samantha assess which alert to investigate first? The alerts are identical (i.e., triggered by the same intrusion detection signature), so there is no clear way to gauge which subnet should be prioritized. Samantha could assess the alerts in a sequential manner based upon the time of notification and investigate subnet Alpha first. However, what if the software patches for the assets in subnet Alpha are all current, whereas in subnet Beta they are months old? Snort cannot detect this, but a vulnerability scanner such as Nessus can. Moreover, what if the assets in subnet Beta have not received updated anti-virus signatures in weeks, but subnet Alpha received the latest definitions the previous night. Again, Snort does not have visibility, but a host-based security system such as McAfee ePO does. Furthermore, what if the alerts have a causal relationship? Insights provided by other tools could establish such relationships and provide the

---

* http://www.tenable.com/products/nessus-vulnerability-scanner.

† http://www.mcafee.com/us/products/epolicy-orchestrator.aspx.

‡ https://www.snort.org/.

analyst with means to detect future attacks. The failure to establish even the most basic of associations between the various tools and data sources ultimately increases the risk of more vulnerability exploitations on Samantha's watch.

An improved approach is the analyst-to-analyst or ad hoc correlation of tools and sources. Some refer to this as the "swivel-chair" approach because it involves an analyst turning in her chair in order to request assistance from a colleague operating a different tool. The swivel-chair approach mitigates some of the concerns in our hypothetical scenario by Samantha engaging with her team of colleagues. The swivel-chair approach is an improvement over relying on a tool in isolation because diverse data increase the probability of making better-informed decisions. However, this approach suffers from its own drawbacks: namely, timeliness of information gathered and consistency of analysis. What questions will Samantha ask of her colleagues? Will her colleagues interpret her questions correctly? Will her colleagues be able to provide her with relevant responses within the same temporal domain as the alerts she is investigating? How long will it take for Samantha to receive responses from her colleagues? More importantly, if Samantha and her colleagues miss something critical, there is no digital record of the swivel-chair exchange, and no way to track which observations led the team to the direction they ultimately took in the investigation. Human fatigue may also play a role in increasing the risk of errors. In addition, different levels of education and experience will yield different analysis methodologies. As a result, manual or ad hoc correlation of data sources is also problematic and may not yield consistent and comprehensive results.

A more formal and analytic approach to vulnerability analysis may improve reliability and produce actionable results. This approach stages the various data sets to support a variety of interfaces and visual representations of the data. This approach also ensures that relationships established between the various data sets are stable with consistent and unique key values. The approach is also the basis for data analytics. Data analytics includes a conceptual data modeling process that needs to be applied to the various data sources. This process helps the understanding of underlying attributes of the individual datasets and the current schema of the individual datasets. The common attributes across the datasets serve to establish relationships between the data sources. In our example, all three data sources share IP address information. When modeling these data, keying on the IP address would be one method to allow for a comparison of the elements across the data sources. In addition, during the data modeling process, a common taxonomy or data dictionary for the data elements of interest should be established. The data dictionary is an important tool to establish proper relationships between entities in the different data sources. All three data sources have multiple references to IP addresses in their schema. McAfee ePO references IP in multiple ways, including the following: AnalyzerIPv4, SourceIPv4, TargetIPv4, and IPAddress. Nessus has several references, including the following: IPS, Host IP, Scanner IP, and IP. Snort also has several references, including the following: IPv4, IP Source, and IP Destination. Without a taxonomy defining the various IP elements across the data sources, establishing a relationship using McAfee SourceIPv4 and Snort IPv4 may yield incorrect results. Indeed, even though they are both IPv4 addresses, they do not necessarily represent the same node.

Once the data modeling process is complete, the data elements identified in the modeling phase need to be extracted and stored in a common data format. This phase consists of developing parsers to extract, transform, and load (ETL) the data. Multiple parsers may be required for each data source in order to account for different input formats. In our example, each of our tools has various output formats, including the following: XML, JSON, CSV, CEF, and PCAP. The parsing process involves extracting the data attributes of interest, tagging the attributes with metadata and taxonomic details, and outputting the data in a common format for efficient querying. In addition, unlike the swivel-chair approach, the analytics approach automates the majority of the steps after modeling the data. Automation ensures a consistent stream of correlated data is available to support a vulnerability event and affords a decision maker more time to take an appropriate course of action. In our example, all three tools have application programming interfaces (APIs) that allow for the programmatic extraction of data, in order to be used in other applications. Automating this approach would be as straightforward as reviewing the respective API documentation for each tool and writing scripts in order to extract the attributes of interest. The APIs generally support high-level programming languages (i.e., Python, Java, Perl, etc.). In addition, many of these software manufacturers and support communities already have preconfigured scripts that can be tweaked to fit most purposes.

3.4 Secure Management of Cyber Events Involved with Vulnerability and Exploitation

This section first describes the basics and comparison of three well-known SIEM tools. Then, to enhance the dynamic analysis and management of cyber events, we present the basic idea and method behind temporal causality analysis by addressing the structured query language (SQL) injection attack.

3.4.1 Comparison of Current SIEM Tools

SIEM tools are designed to correlate a variety of log events in order to enhance an organization's situational awareness. SIEM tools accomplish this by collecting log events from multiple data sources and across numerous hosts, leveraging a variety of analytical methods to establish relationships between disparate events, and, finally, providing security analysts a central console for managing and visualizing events in a unified manner.

Each SIEM product has features that set it apart from competing products; however, at a minimum, each SIEM must provide three basic capabilities: namely, a mechanism for data ingestion, a mechanism for event correlation/analysis, and a mechanism for reporting and visualization. Many SIEMs go further and offer additional capabilities such as native integration with common log and event generating tools, providing threat intelligence feeds, enhanced logging via deployable agents, and automatable response capabilities. SIEM tools are a critical part of every industry due to the sheer volume and velocity of events that organizations generate on a daily basis. It is literally impossible for a security analyst to review pages upon pages of log events from dozens of sources and expect to pinpoint threats and vulnerabilities with any reasonable degree of accuracy or timeliness. The usage of SIEM tools is not exclusive to activities in the vulnerability assessment or cybersecurity domain; however, these activities greatly benefit from the use of SIEMs for two major reasons:

1. First, SIEMs can detect anomalous events obfuscated by large volumes of benign traffic. By correlating events from a variety of sources, it becomes increasingly difficult for an attacker to hide actions that would not occur during "normal" business operations. Individual events in operating system logs, application logs, firewall logs, and directory service logs may seem innocuous, but through the lens of a SIEM, relationships that were once invisible become transparent. For example, take the following four events: (1) user downloads an email attachment on her workstation, (2) workstation makes domain name system (DNS) requests to several unknown domains, (3) workstation attempts the installation of an unsigned executable, (4) workstation experiences a spike in outbound network traffic over transition control protocol (TCP) port 443. Collected from different logging systems and assessed independently, these events may or may not raise red flags. However, upon correlation and investigation as one unified event in multiple stages, this activity could be deemed highly anomalous, potentially malicious, and warrant further investigation.
2. Second, SIEMs can enhance the efficacy of incident-handling practices. By automating the correlation and aggregation of cyber events, providing reports and descriptive statistics, and, in some instances, supporting automated responses, SIEMs can be thought of as a virtual incident response team that helps a security analyst prioritize what is noise or benign and what is suspicious or malicious. SIEMs use a variety of statistical and analytical methods to transform and relate events over long periods of time. For example, a low and slow data exfiltration event is difficult to detect because it occurs over an extended period of time (i.e., weeks, months, or longer), and only a small fraction of a target file is transferred during each session. A web log entry documenting a 10 MB http transfer to a public web server on any given day is uninteresting and quite common. On the other hand, a SIEM that correlates six months' worth of web logs and discovers a 10 MB http transfer each day to the same web server is quite interesting and suspicious!

	Correlation capabilities	Compatibility with common log formats	Threat intelligence	Scalability
OSSIM	Handful of community submitted correlating rules. Custom engine to create new and more complex rules.	Native support for a variety of logging formats including server logs, vulnerability assessment tools, and system monitoring tools.	Alien vault open threat exchange. Community of interest feeds, free and open source.	Limited to deployment on a single server.
HP ArcSight ESM	HP proprietary CORR-engine for optimized log and event correlation. Hundreds of out-of-the-box rules configured for perimeter and network security monitoring.	Smart connectors and flex connectors used to parse raw log/event data into ArcSight's common event format (CEF). Forwarding connectors used to export events from ESM to other tools in CEF format.	STIX/TAXII compliant threat intel providers, such as Verisign iDefense (requires a separate subscription) or HP Threat Central.	Highly scalable. Vertical scaling unnecessary supports clustered deployments.
Splunk	Search Processing Language (SPL) supports statistical and analytical correlation; manual correlation across universally indexed data based on temporal domain or field values. Automatic correlation of events with similar field values.	Handles raw log files with universal indexing. Automatically separates log stream into searchable events. Supports manual indexing for custom feeds.	Enterprise Security App for ingesting external threat feeds and correlating the indicators of compromise with existing events indexed in Splunk.	Highly scalable. Vertical scaling unnecessary supports clustered deployments.

Figure 3.3 Summary of SIEM tool comparison.

In this section, we discuss three SIEM tools: one open source, one traditional, and one non-traditional. We broadly focus on their strengths and weaknesses in five major areas: cost of adoption, correlation capabilities, compatibility with common logging sources, threat intelligence capabilities, and scalability. We did not include visualization capabilities as one of the criteria of comparison because the topic is highly subjective. Figure 3.3 summarizes our findings.

3.4.1.1 Open Source SIEM Tools

AlienVault Open Source Security Information and Event Management (OSSIM) is a community supported open source SIEM tool and the "lite" version of AlienVault's commercial SIEM: Unified Security Management (USM) [13–15]. The OSSIM project began in 2003 in Madrid, Spain, and it became the basis of the Alien Vault Company founded in 2007. Of the three tools presented in this chapter, OSSIM is the only one that is free to download and use without restriction. However, the cost of adoption is not free. Using and supporting OSSIM requires time and effort in reviewing documentation, posting questions on online forums, and researching functionality. OSSIM has an online threat intelligence portal called the Open Threat Exchange (OTX) that gathers daily threat events with indicators of compromise, referred to as pulses [15]. The portal is configured in a publish–subscribe fashion, so anyone in the community can publish pulses, and anyone in the community can subscribe to specific publishers and feeds of interest. Threat intelligence is an important but often understated aspect of the vulnerability assessment process. It is a critical component because these indicators act as a supplement for threats, and an organization should be on the watch for these indicators. For example, most threat intelligence services (including OTX) host a list of known bad IPs. This list can be used by a SIEM as a watch list, and any traffic originating or destined for one of these bad domains should immediately be flagged as suspicious.

OSSIM can natively parse and ingest a variety of common logging sources, including the following: Apache, IIS, OpenVAS, OSSEC, Nagios, Nessus, NMAP, Ntop, Snare, Snort, and Syslog. OSSIM leverages regular expressions to parse data, which allows for a custom parser to be written and extend its support to any data source that outputs in a text format. In addition, OSSIM comes equipped with a host IDS that can be deployed as an agent for collecting system and log events if no preferred collection tools are present in a given environment [13].

OSSIM performs correlation by relating events in a sequential and temporal fashion. OSSIM comes packaged with a handful of built-in directives for common cyber events such as brute-force attacks, DOS attacks, enumeration, fingerprinting scans, and so on. Beyond the handful of preconfigured templates, OSSIMs have a correlation engine that allows for the creation of custom directives. Figure 3.4 illustrates a logical sequence of events that could be built as a custom correlation directive in OSSIM to uncover a potential brute-force attack [14]. At each level, an alert can be sent to the appropriate parties indicating a potential threat. Furthermore, time

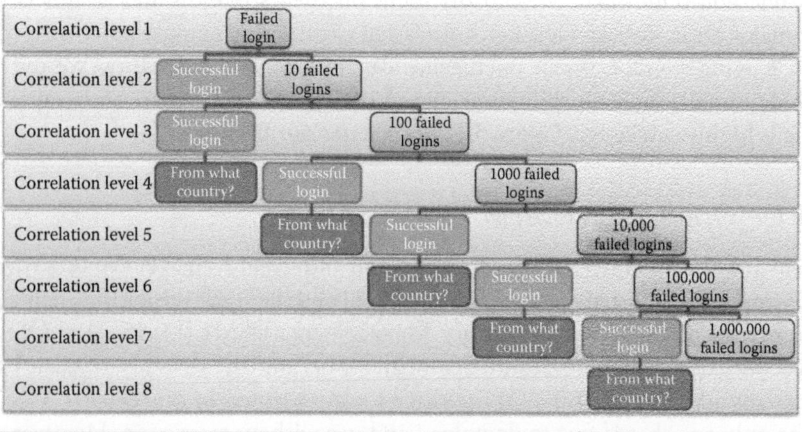

Figure 3.4 Example brute-force attack correlation logic.

can be introduced as an additional attribute of interest, so that if the failed logins are occurring at a particular frequency, a different alert or severity level can be triggered.

OSSIM is not an enterprise class SIEM and cannot scale beyond one host or server. If there is a need for a large deployment, OSSIM's commercial counterpart USM provides support for horizontal scaling (adding more servers instead of buying bigger servers) and may be a better choice. OSSIM is the least expensive USM license [13] that includes hundreds of professionally developed correlation directives and forensic logging capabilities not included in the open source version. OSSIM does not support integration with big data technologies such as Hadoop, nor does it natively support exporting of events to external relational databases. OSSIM supports basic authentication or integration into directory services such as LDAP or Active Directory. More information about OSSIM and a free download of its SIEM software (ISO format) can be found on its website [16].

3.4.1.2 Traditional SIEM Tool

ArcSight has been developing SIEM tools since 2000 and is one of the oldest players in the market. In 2010, Hewlett Packard (HP) acquired ArcSight USD [17] and extended its portfolio of services to include enterprise cybersecurity. Today, HP ArcSight Enterprise Security Management (ESM) [18–24] is arguably the most heavily adopted SIEM tool by commercial and government organizations alike. ESM takes a modular approach toward SIEM. The standalone configuration of ESM excels in the three basic requirements of a SIEM tool (i.e., ingest, correlation, and visualization). Additional features such as central log management and threat intelligence can be subscribed to and deployed separately, to further enhance the capabilities of ESM. The cost of the ESM software and professional support is not clear, and it appears to fluctuate based upon the deployment configuration, number of data sources, and volume of ingest.

ESM has hundreds of built-in features all configurable from the ESM graphical user interface. If configured properly, these built-in features can substantially increase the resolution of an incident handler and decrease its time of response. Some of the features include the following: (1) data enrichment with user, asset, or key-terrain information; (2) prioritization and normalization of events [5]; (3) "near-real time" correlation of data and threat intelligence; (4) data forensics and historical and trending analysis; (5) a vast library of predefined security use cases, compliance automation, and reporting tools, which are designed to minimize time spent on creating compliance content and custom reports; and (6) workflow automation, which generates alerts and escalates events based on elapsed time [18].

ESM is feature rich and, as a result, there is a steep learning curve. As seen from Figure 3.5, the ESM console is loaded with options, and it is arguably the least user-friendly interface. ESM protects its user console and data with authentication and

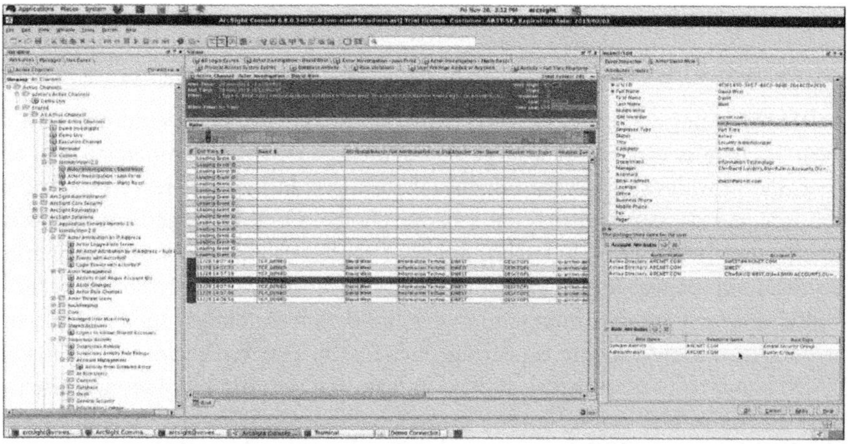

Figure 3.5 ArcSight ESM 6.8 console.

authorization via directory service (e.g., LDAP, Active Directory) integration and role-based access control.

For threat intelligence, ESM takes a standards-based approach and can receive feeds in the STIX or TAXII formats [25,26]. STIX stands for Structured Threat Information eXpression and TAXII stands for Trusted Automated eXchange of Indicator Information. Both standards are part of cybersecurity information sharing efforts led by the Department of Homeland Security. A list of threat intelligence providers that support STIX and TAXII can be found at https://stixproject.github.io/supporters/. In addition, HP provides a community intelligence portal "HP Threat Central" that hosts private security forums, threat databases, and anonymized indicators of compromise (IOC) [22].

Out-of-the-box, the ESM smart-connector natively supports the parsing, ingestion, and conversion of hundreds of industry-recognized technologies into ArcSight's Common Event Format standard. Some technology examples include the following: operating systems (Microsoft, Apple, Redhat Enterprise Linux, Oracle Solaris), anti-malware tools (Kaspersky, McAfee, Symantec, Trend Micro), application security (Bit-9, RSA, McAfee), network devices (Cisco, Juniper), and cloud (Amazon Web Service) [21].

In the event that the smart-connector does not support a particular feed, a custom feed can be written using the ESM flex-connector. The flex-connector framework is a software development kit (SDK) that enables the creation of a smart-connector tailored to the specific event data format [19].

ESM performs log correlation via the proprietary HP ArcSight's Correlation Optimized Retention and Retrieval (CORR) engine. The CORR engine is a flat file system optimized for read performance. According to the ArcSight team, it is 5 times more efficient at event correlation and 10 times more efficient at data storage [20] than the previous SQL-based correlation engine.

ESM has rule-based, statistical, or algorithmic correlation, as well as other methods that include relating different events to each other and events to contextual data. In addition, ESM has hundreds of preconfigured rules for advanced correlation and with the integration of threat intelligence sources, the correlation engine can quickly identify IOC [21]. A few example rules that are available out-of-the-box include the following: top attackers and internal targets, top infected systems, top alert sources and destinations, bandwidth usage trends, and login activity trends [22]. More information about HP ArcSight ESM can be found on its website [18].

3.4.1.3 Non-Traditional SIEM Tool

In 2002, Eric Swan and Rob Das [27–30] founded Splunk on the premise that it would serve as the Google (i.e., search engine) for enterprise log data. Splunk satisfies the basic requirements of a SIEM (i.e., data ingest, correlation, and visualization), but it is not a traditional SIEM. Traditional SIEMs often have a fixed schema of attributes that can be correlated against one another. Data are ingested and bucketed into those attributes and then correlation rules are applied to establish relationships and insights. Splunk was designed in a more flexible manner to ingest any type of log data, automatically index it, and extract searchable events. If Splunk's automatic indexing is off base, manual user intervention can be taken to tweak the indexing for a specific data source/type. Once the data are indexed and searchable, Splunk offers a variety of methods to interact with the data, including methods that support enterprise security use cases. Splunk initially offers its product for free via a 500 MB/day data-indexing license. However, 500 MB/day can quickly be consumed in minutes when multiple sources are being indexed. Splunk's cost model is based on the volume of raw and uncompressed data indexed per day. Similar to ESM and OSSIM, Splunk protects its user console and data stores with authentication and authorization via directory service integration and role-based access control.

Splunk includes an application for enterprise security [28] that supports ingestion of external threat feeds for correlation with log events. Splunk itself does not offer any threat intelligence feeds or host a threat intelligence portal. It relies on external feeds and can support both open source as well as subscription-based models. External threat intelligence feeds can be thought of as an additional data source that Splunk can automatically ingest, index, and create searchable events.

Splunk does not rely on predefined correlation rules. Splunk's approach toward event correlation is to provide the end user with a powerful search processing language (SPL) and present him or her with a unified, indexed, and searchable database of events. SPL is designed to transform statistical correlation methods into queries across the unified search database [29]. This pool of indexed data can also be searched in a manual fashion, and events can be correlated on the basis of time of occurrence or attribute of interest. Splunk can also perform automatic correlations based upon event attributes with similar values. An added advantage Splunk has over some of its competition is that if an export is available, Splunk can ingest and correlate events processed by other SIEM tools.

Splunk is highly scalable as illustrated in Figure 3.6 [30]. Depending upon the use case, all of the Splunk roles can run on a single host or run distributed across hundreds of hosts.

More information about Splunk and a 60-day free trial download of the Enterprise version of its software can be found on its website [31].

There are various documented reports that quantify the return on investment that SIEMs tools provide. HP commissioned one such investigation where they identified millions in time and monetary savings across a variety of organizations [24]. The majority of the savings appear to be the result of SIEMs tools transforming assessment work from a large team of analysts to a handful of specialists. For many industries, SIEM tools are the current answer to the question of how to enhance situational awareness and look at vulnerabilities from a holistic perspective. Unfortunately, many SIEM tools, including the three discussed in this chapter, suffer from drawbacks, resulting in a false sense of security.

The majority of SIEM tools such as OSSIM and ArcSight ESM rely heavily on rule-based correlation. As a result, these systems require frequent tuning in order to account for false positives and false negatives. As the volume of data increases, so do the false positives. As correlation rules are tuned to account for false positives, the number of false negatives increases. This is a known and often poorly addressed fact of SIEM and standalone security tools alike. Splunk's approach is a bit better than the traditional SIEM tool because it doesn't focus on predefined correlation rules. Giving the end user a language (e.g., SPL) with which to interact with the data is a step in the right direction. However, this approach is limited by how creative an analyst's queries are and how well the language can transform an analyst inquiry into queries across the data.

SIEM tools cook the data (e.g., preprocessing and normalizing) using a variety of methods that primarily support their predefined correlation capabilities. This approach works well to detect and mitigate known threats, but unknown threats

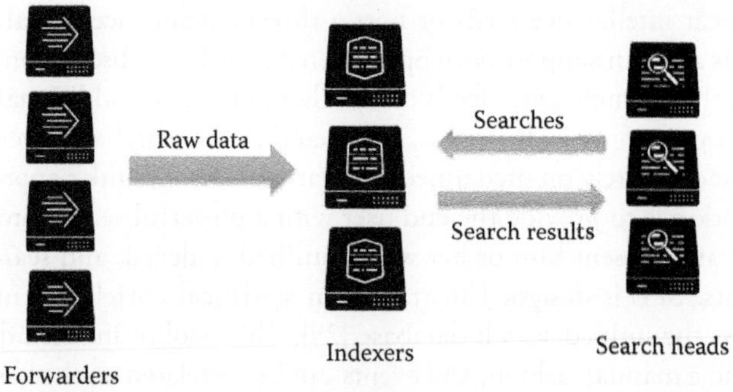

Figure 3.6 Splunk three-tier architecture.

are still a problem. Again, Splunk's approach is somewhat better in that it attempts to automatically index and make all the data searchable. The question is, however, how accurate is their automatic indexing? It is also convenient that Splunk's cost model is based upon volume of indexing.

Horizontal scaling for SIEM tools only slightly mitigates bandwidth and storage constraints. If there is a spike in volume or velocity of log data for a given organization, adding more nodes to enhance a SIEM tool's capacity and performance only works until the next spike occurs, not to mention the challenges of using SIEM tools in a decentralized model. For instance, if an enterprise is geographically dispersed between two continents, how will the logs from one site be transferred to the other site in order to be processed by a SIEM tool in a timely fashion? The answer is they will not be transferred. Each site will likely have its own SIEM tool infrastructure on premises with some mechanism to cross-correlate the data. This is not a trivial proposition. Some SIEM tool manufacturers have started offering "cloud"-based models to better support this use case, but it is not yet clear whether this approach is beneficial.

3.4.2 Temporal Causality Analysis for Enhancing Management of Cyber Events

This subsection introduces a novel temporal causality analysis for cyber events classified into five processes: namely, attacker, vulnerability detection and protection, intrusion detection, agility, and risk assessment. This temporal causality analysis differs from the current SIEM tools in that it provides vector-time, vulnerability-centric causality pairing graphs, and context-specific vulnerability-centric causality pairing graphs of events including agility and risk actions, which can also provide cues for the detection of zero-day vulnerabilities and attacks. With the help of timestamps of events, the vector-time concept that is imported from distributed systems [32] allows analysts to investigate the events in a temporal domain, even if time synchronization is not available among the hosts of a cybersecurity environment. In addition, this causality analysis can incorporate the human factor from the perspectives of user, defender, and adversary, although it is not included in this section due to space constraints.

To protect against malware detection and spread control are essential to maintaining the functionality or mission assurance of a system. The success of the protective measures depends on a number of factors, including the accuracy of IDS, the system's resilience against attacks, the strength of vulnerability patching and recovery, the level of situational awareness, and the correlation of sensor observations and measurements. It is highly desirable to perform real-time data analytics of cyber events, observations, and sensor measurements to discover interactions and characteristics of cyber events. In stealthy malware, the adversary aims to make the malware invisible and undetected to a cyber-defensive mechanism over a target network. To achieve this, the adversary gathers information on the state of defensive mechanisms. In addition, the adversary may choose to obfuscate the real intent by performing misleading activities and operations.

The causal interpretation of networks is essential to understand how events and entities trigger each other, thereby indicating their causalities. Causal models help determine how the sequence of events or entities trigger each other. There can be numerous latent variables within a system that are not observable. Although it may be tolerable to not model some latent variables in answering probabilistic queries, it is highly desirable for causality analysis to identify latent variables when correlations between them represent causal relationships. In general, correlations between any set of variables may form a set of both causal and non-causal relationships. A causal model can be represented as a directed acyclic graph over random variables, where the value of each random variable is computed as a stochastic function of the values of its parents [33]. In [4], the triggering relations in causality reasoning about network events are addressed by comparing rule- and learning-based methods on network data of stealthy malware activities.

Our overall goal is not only to detect vulnerabilities and exploit but also to mitigate the adverse impact of vulnerability exploitations. Indeed, it is highly desirable that the adverse impact of vulnerability exploitations does not lead to an unacceptable level in mission assurance. This may be achieved by using the approaches of both reactive mitigations and proactive mitigations. Therefore, in addition to considering the cyber events of attacker, vulnerability detection/protection, and intrusion detection, we also consider the cyber events of agility and risk assessment. So, we consider five cyber processes in the temporal causality analysis of cyber events, where an event denotes any observable occurrence of an activity or action in a system or network. An event may have physical attributes (e.g., network topology, frequency of event occurrences over a period), meta-data attributes (e.g., IP addresses, port addresses, timestamps, control or user data types, TCP, or UDP), event interaction attributes (e.g., vector time, where the sequence of past values of vector-time indicate the interaction of causal events of different processes; lag time of event responses), or cross-layer attributes of OSI models (e.g., application type, file type, protocol type). In Figures 3.7 through 3.9, directed edges between events of different processes indicate causality, whereas undirected edges indicate that events exhibit temporal order but are not necessarily causal. To keep track of interactions between five cyber processes, we use the vector-time concept in distributed system events. Vector time characterizes causality and temporal order such that the kth entry of a vector time that corresponds to process P_k is incremented by one each time an event occurs in process P_k. Whenever an event of P_k receives the vector time of another process' event, the vector time entries of P_k's event are aggregated with the vector time entries of the other process.

As an example, let us consider an SQL injection attack that takes advantage of the ability of influencing SQL queries formed and submitted to a backend database by an application such as a web application using inputs received from potentially untrusted sources [13]. Figure 3.7 shows that the attacker activities can be classified into at least seven categories, labeled as a_1 to a_7, corresponding to (a_1) performing

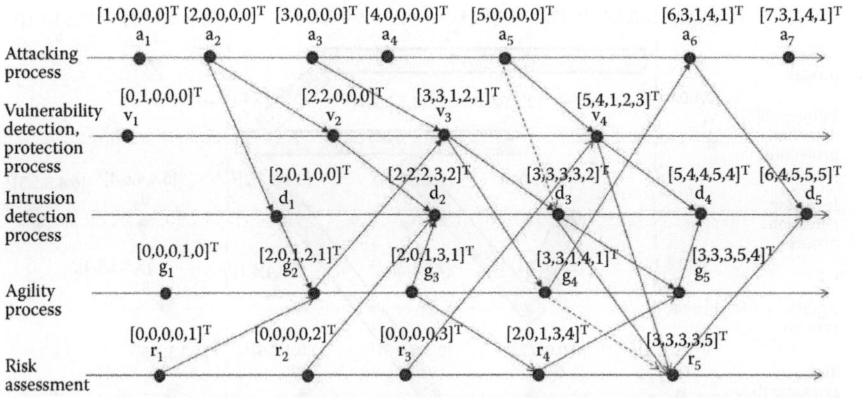

Figure 3.7 Causality edges of cyber events for an SQL use case. Attacking process events (a_1: reconnaissance; a_2: use SQL injection to exploit v_2 of webserver; a_3: use SQL injection to exploit v_3 of database server; a_4: deliver malware and tools to escalate privileges; a_5: install a backdoor on system by exploiting v_4; a_6: exfiltration of system credentials; a_7: theft of data); vulnerability process events (v_1, v_2: web server; v_3: database server; v_4: backdoor); intrusion detection process events (d_1, d_2, d_3, d_4, d_5); agility events (g_1, g_2, g_3, g_4, g_5); and risk assessment events (r_1, r_2, r_3, r_4, r_5).

reconnaissance, (a_2) exploiting vulnerabilities of (a_3) the webserver and (a_4) the database server, (a_5) delivering malware to escalate privileges, (a_6) installing a backdoor on system, and (a_7) stealing data. Some of these attacker events involved events of other cyber processes. For instance, network-based IDS and/or host-based IDS may detect some of these attacker events and generate alerts; some vulnerabilities may get exploited and then recovered; agility events may help avoid or mitigate impact of attacks, with the help of risk assessment events; and the tasks prioritization of vulnerability and intrusion detection processes can be strengthened with the guidance of risk assessment events. The causality between different processes in Figure 3.7 is illustrated by directed edges.

Once the causality edges and the vector-times of events are established as shown in Figure 3.7, time intervals with predefined durations can be designated so that all causal and temporal edges of each time interval can be studied in-depth. Figure 3.8 illustrates how all those directed edges that are involved with vulnerability v_4 can form causal pairs. However, some temporal edges can also be causal, and, therefore, the next step is to find out which temporal edges are causal (see Figure 3.9). Then, all causal edges are used to form the so-called vulnerability-centric pairing graph (VCP), as shown in Figure 3.9. The cyber data corresponding to the interactions of the VCP edges can represent the quality data of its time interval. These quality data are stored properly in the database so that they can be extracted easily and instantaneously by database queries formed by cyber analysts. Hence, big data of cyber events can be reduced to a smaller size of the aggregated quality data of temporal causal events.

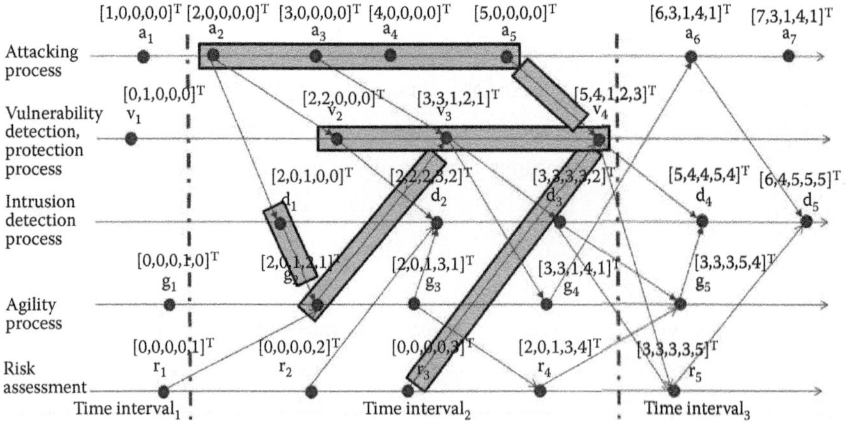

Figure 3.8 Causality edges of SQL cyber events within the middle time interval, where vulnerability v4 is found to be exploited.

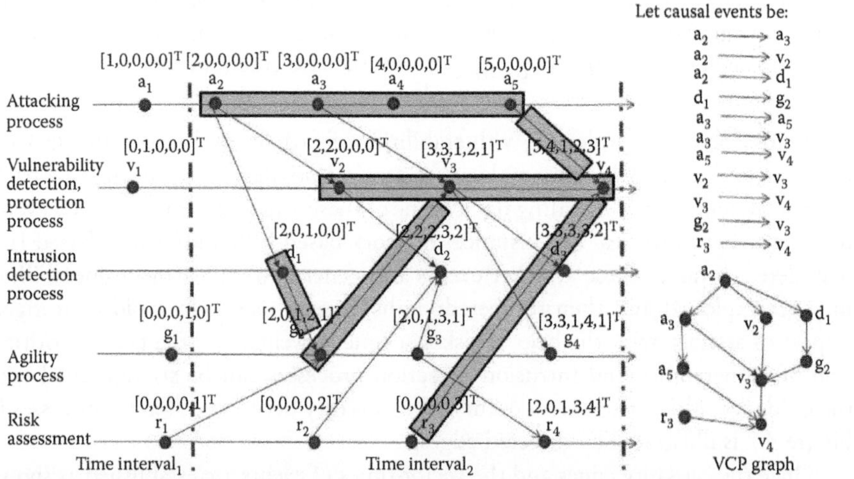

Figure 3.9 Causality edges of SQL cyber events with the VCP graph.

3.5 Summary and Future Directions

Computer systems and networks have become so essential to the functioning of modern society that they have become a primary target for adversaries, for ideological or nationalistic purposes as an element of modern day warfare, as well as for individual personal or financial gain. Trusted networks are penetrated and exploited to commit espionage and intelligence gathering, perpetrate a denial of service, corrupt data or disseminate misinformation, achieve kinetic or cyber-physical effects, and potentially hijack control of valuable assets. In each vulnerable sector of society, it is essential to prioritize mission essential functions by conducting dependency and risk analysis of network assets, engineering robust and resilient architectures, and identifying the optimal network locations to monitor and swiftly detect compromise of key computer assets.

Many industry and open source tools exist to collect, aggregate, summarize, and organize data collected from hosts and at strategic network locations. Antivirus software and vulnerability scanning tools can systematically search hosts for signatures of malicious code or security flaws in benign code. Intrusion detection and prevention systems can generate alerts that indicate unusual or suspicious activity on computers in the trusted network. The difficulty with these tools is that they generate far too many alerts and indicators, many of which do not truly have security implications. Although an SIEM can be used to assemble, organize, and query the data, and help analysts to cope with the large data volumes being generated, existing methods to prioritize the alerts and indicators suffer from various problems and could be improved.

We submit that detecting and comprehending actual threats that exist on the network requires a more dynamic approach. We suggest that correlations between various signatures on a host and indicators of potential exposure to an adversarial entity that may exist in the traffic passing to and from the host might be used to escalate the priority of a known vulnerability. The difficulty is in the sheer volume of signatures and traffic to be processed; it is not a tractable problem for a human being to perform a correlation analysis on each and every set of indicators. We propose certain methods for identifying events of interest, summarizing them, and storing them properly in a database so that cyber analysts can query them easily and instantaneously. Such methods could be combined with SIEM data architectures to provide a more seamless integration with existing methodologies.

The challenge of detecting, assessing, and mitigating vulnerabilities and intrusions necessitates collecting, correlating, and analyzing cyber vulnerability and intrusion data in real-time because cybersecurity situations evolve rapidly and get complicated with incomplete information and uncertainties. However, current cybersecurity tools and methods have limited capability extensibility and scalability to deal with such complicated situations and big data in real-time. In this chapter, we first presented the basics of vulnerability assessment, data sources and tools, and main components of big data analytics. We then provided a use case on identification and attribution of vulnerability exploitations. Temporal causality analysis of cyber events is described to determine the quality data needed for the analysis of vulnerabilities and exploitation by determining the temporal interactions and causality of various types of cyber events, including attacker activities, vulnerability detection and protection, and intrusion alerts. This analysis may also assist detecting zero-day vulnerabilities and exploitations whenever the known vulnerabilities and exploits do not provide sufficient reasoning for explaining the suspicious interactions and uncertainties among the observed interactions of attacker activity, vulnerability, and intrusion alerts. For future research, we suggest that this detection process of zero-day vulnerability and attack be enhanced further by incorporating outlier detection capability into cyber data analytics and causality analysis. To have a better management of cyber events, it would be desirable to add interventions [33] on the values of causality parameters so that the values are not just observed but are also manipulated. In order for cyber analysts to benefit from these scalable data analytics and causality analyses, they should have the capability of forming accurate queries and receiving fast responses by the analytics-driven processing environment of cybersecurity.

References

1. G.H. Baker. A Vulnerability Assessment Methodology for Critical Infrastructure Sites. DHS Symposium: R&D Partnerships in Homeland Security, 2005.
2. E. Cole. Detect, Contain and Control Cyberthreats. A SANS Whitepaper, SANS Institute, June 2015.
3. A. Vijayakumar and G.A. Muthuchelvi. Discovering Vulnerability to Build a Secured System Using Attack Injection. 2011 3rd International Conference on Electronics Computer Technology (ICECT), Vol. 6. IEEE, 2011.
4. H. Zhang, D. Yao, N. Ramakrishnan, and Z. Zhang. Causality reasoning about network events for detecting stealthy malware activities. *Computers and Security*, 58, 180–198, 2016.
5. A. Kim, M.H. Kang, J.Z. Luo, and A. Velazquez. A Framework for Event Prioritization in Cyber Network Defense. Technical Report, Naval Research Laboratory, July 15, 2014.
6. S.M. Sawyer, T.H. Yu, M.L. Hubbell, and B.D. O'Gwynn. LLCySA: Making Sense of Cyberspace. *Lincoln Laboratory Journal*, 20(2), 67–76, 2014.
7. H. Cam. Risk Assessment by Dynamic Representation of Vulnerability, Exploitation, and Impact. Proceedings of Cyber Sensing 2015, SPIE Defense, Security, and Sensing. April 20–24, 2015, Baltimore, MD.
8. FIRST: Improving Security Together. Common Vulnerability Scoring System (CVSS-SIG). Available from: http://www.first.org/cvss.
9. National Vulnerability Database. NVD Common Vulnerability Scoring System Support v2. Available from: http://nvd.nist.gov/cvss.cfm.
10. P. Mell, K. Scarfone, and S. Romanosky. CVSS—A Complete Guide to the Common Vulnerability Scoring System Version 2.0. June 2007.
11. K. Scarfone and P. Mell. An Analysis of CVSS Version 2 Vulnerability Scoring. Proceedings of IEEE 3rd International Symposium on Empirical Software Engineering and Measurement, 2009.
12. GAO: Government Accountability Office. Defense Department Cyber Efforts: DOD Faces Challenges in Its Cyber Activities, 62 (GAO-11-75), July 2011. Available from: http://itlaw.wikia.com/wiki/GAO.
13. AlienVault Unified Security Management. Available from: https://www.alienvault.com/products/.

14. AlienVault Unified Security Management. Available from: https://www.alienvault.com/doc-repo/USM-for-Government/all/Correlation-Reference-Guide.pdf.
15. AlienVault Unified Security Management. Available from: https://www.alienvault.com/open-threat-exchange.
16. AlienVault. Available from: https://www.alienvault.com/products/ossim.
17. HP Inc. HP to Acquire ArcSight. Available from: http://www8.hp.com/us/en/hp-news/press-release.html?id=600187#.V1zA5Kpf1R0.
18. Enterprise Security Management (ESM). Available from: http://www8.hp.com/us/en/software-solutions/arcsight-esm-enterprise-security-management/.
19. HP. Protect 2104. Available from: http://h71056.www7.hp.com/gfs-shared/downloads-220.pdf.
20. Available from: http://www.hp.com/hpinfo/newsroom/press_kits/2011/risk2011/HP_ArcSight_Express_Product_Brief.pdf.
21. Hewlett Packard Enterprise. Available from: http://www8.hp.com/h20195/V2/GetPDF.aspx/4AA4-3483ENW.pdf.
22. HP. Available from: http://www.hp.com/hpinfo/newsroom/press_kits/2015/RSA2015/ThreatCentralDataSheet.pdf.
23. Kahn Consulting Inc. Available from: http://www.kahnconsultinginc.com/images/pdfs/KCI_ArcSight_ESM_Evaluation.pdf.
24. HP. Available from: http://www8.hp.com/h20195/v2/GetPDF.aspx/4AA5-2823ENW.pdf.
25. US-CERT. Information Sharing Specifications for Cybersecurity. Available from: https://www.us-cert.gov/Information-Sharing-Specifications-Cybersecurity.
26. Github. Available from: https://stixproject.github.io/supporters/.
27. Splunk. Available from: http://www.splunk.com/view/SP-CAAAGBY.
28. Splunk. http://www.splunk.com/en_us/products/premium-solutions/splunk-enterprise-security.html.
29. Splunk. Available from: http://docs.splunk.com/Documentation/Splunk/latest/Search/Aboutthesearchlanguage.
30. Splunk. Available from: https://conf.splunk.com/session/2015/conf2015_ANekkanti_SPal_ATameem_Splunk_SplunkClassics_Harnessing63PerformanceAnd_a.pdf.
31. Splunk. Availbale from: https://www.splunk.com/en_us/.
32. R. Schwarz and F. Mattern, Detecting Causal Relationships in Distributed Computations: In Search of the Holy Grail. *Distributed Computing*, 7(3) 149–174, 1994.
33. D. Koller and N. Friedman. *Probabilistic Graphical Models*. MIT Press, 2009.

Chapter 4

Root Cause Analysis for Cybersecurity

Engin Kirda and Amin Kharraz

Contents

The cybersecurity landscape is evolving constantly. High-profile breaches in large enterprise networks [1–5] have demonstrated serious challenges for organizations and entities. These attacks are increasingly getting more complex, and usually tend to stay low profile while targeting critical data including intellectual property and financial assets. For this reason, they often go undetected for several months, and leave the enterprise networks unprotected during this period. Recent threat reports published by major security companies have also acknowledged the fact that the cyber-crime scene is becoming increasingly more organized, and more consolidated [6,7].

4.1 Introduction

On the other end of the spectrum, victims of such attacks are pressured to disclose who is behind the attack once the attack is detected [8]. Consequently, security analysts are often asked to attribute attacks to a specific threat actor in the early stages of the investigation, a point where they should start to gather evidence of the compromise. Clearly, this approach does not result in a systematic approach to identifying the underlying root causes of the attacks, and rigorously investigating root causes of the attack phenomena.

Over the past few years, big data analytics for security, data mining, and machine learning techniques have been proposed [9–16] to tackle this shortcoming by providing insights about an attack based on large-scale datasets. These techniques are often designed to automatically identify suspicious actions, extract knowledge from raw network data, and provide insightful results from a large number of logs generated every day. These research efforts cover a wide range of topics in security data mining from improving alert classification or intrusion detection capabilities [10,11,13,15] to automatically reporting infected machines within an enterprise network [9,16,17].

The main focus of this chapter is to elaborate on techniques to perform attack attribution which can assist security analysts to analyze security incidents more effectively, identify security breaches, and determine root causes of attack phenomena. More specifically, these techniques can potentially help cybersecurity analysts to gain deeper insights about an attack such as characterizing the malicious behavior inside the enterprise or getting insights into their global behavior. That is, the aim is to try to answer questions such as: how long do attacks stay active, what is their average size, their spatial distribution, how do they evolve over time with respect to their origins, or the type of malicious activities they perform?

The rest of this chapter is structured as follows. Section 4.2 explains the fundamentals of root cause analysis and the definition. Section 4.3 introduces a generic model to perform casual analysis of security threats. In Section 4.4, two case studies are provided, and finally, the chapter is concluded in Section 4.5.

4.2 Root Cause Analysis and Attack Attribution

In the field of threat intelligence, root cause analysis is a collection of procedures for identifying the causes of an attack, and effectively attributing new attack events. This potentially allows a security analyst to get a better understanding of the observed attacks, and also to characterize emerging threats from a global viewpoint. For example, from the defense perspective, it is useful to know who is really behind an observed attack, i.e., how many organizations are responsible for them? Where do they originate from? What are the emerging strategies used in cyber-crime?

This chapter primarily focuses on large-scale attacks which could be launched by criminal organizations or profit-oriented underground campaigns rather than tracing back a single attack to an ordinary hacker that penetrated an organization. The chapter also provides insights on effective methods that have been practiced recently in real-world scenarios which can help security analysts to determine the root causes of global attack phenomena (which usually involves a large number of sources), and to easily derive their modus operandi. These phenomena can be observed through different means such as honeypots, intrusion detection systems (IDSs), sandboxes, or malware collecting systems.

Unsurprisingly, such attacks are often largely distributed on the Internet, and their lifetime can vary from only a few days to several months depending on the nature of the attacks. This makes the attribution of distinct events having the same root phenomenon a challenging task, since several attack characteristics may evolve over time.

The generic approach described in this chapter allows security analysts to identify and characterize large-scale security events on the Internet based on network traces collected with easily deployable sensors. In most cases, it is assumed that security events can be observed with well-placed distributed sensors that collect logs. Examples of typical attack events that are considered in this chapter can range from malware families through code injection attacks to rogue software campaigns, which aim at deploying numerous malicious websites in order to host and sell rogue software.

4.3 The Causal Analysis of Security Threats

This section elaborates on general challenges to perform root cause analysis for large-scale security events, and then explains in more detail the tools and techniques to systematically perform a comprehensive analysis on security incidents.

4.3.1 Challenges in Detecting Security Incidents

There are several challenges that need to be addressed to accurately identify security incidents in enterprise networks and characterize their root causes. For example, the volume of events logged by various systems inside the enterprise networks usually results in a major challenge in log analysis and detection of security incidents. For example, performing efficient analysis and also timely detection of critical threats requires reliable data-reduction algorithms to maintain security-relevant information in the logs [16]. This step is often challenging because we need to retain the communication characteristics of internal hosts and external services. Furthermore, most current attacks tend to stay low profile, and easily blend in with millions of legitimate events. Given enormous volumes of logs every day, discovering meaningful security incidents is quite challenging considering the gaps between the raw logs collected by the monitoring systems and the insightful information that security analysts require to identify suspicious behaviors. Like other data mining applications, the features to extract meaningful information from the data should be carefully selected to achieve low false positive cases given the large datasets. Finally, a major challenge in detecting security threats is that limited ground truth is available for enterprise infections since the only way they are identified is when they are detected and blocked (by anti-virus, intrusion detection tools, or blacklists), making the evaluation of the proposed techniques quite challenging.

4.3.2 Root Cause Analysis for Security Data Mining

Over the past few years, a considerable research effort has been devoted to applying data mining techniques to security-related problems. However, a significant part of this effort has been exclusively focused on improving the efficiency of intrusion detection systems rather than on providing new fundamental insights into the nature of attacks, or their underlying root causes [18,19]. A comprehensive survey of data mining techniques applied to intrusion detection can be found in [20,21]. These techniques are designed to improve alert classification or intrusion detection capabilities, or construct more accurate detection models by automatically generating new rules (e.g., using an inductive rule generation mechanism).

The objective here is not only to identify attack events occurring at a larger scale, but also to understand their root causes, and get insights into the modus operandi of attackers. This allows security analysts to systematically discover patterns from a given dataset with limited knowledge of the security event under scrutiny. To achieve this goal, the underlying analytical methods must be sufficiently generic so that they can be applied to virtually any type of dataset comprising security events (e.g., attack events observed by honeypots, network attack events, IDS alerts, malware samples, spam messages, etc.).

In order to discover new insights about the nature of attacks and their underlying root causes, we explain a generic model to address this issue in a systematic way. In this model, the datasets contain malicious activities from different sources (high and low-interaction honeypots, malware samples, honeyclients, etc.). The model employs unsupervised data mining techniques to discover *a priori* unknown attack patterns, and gain insights into their global behavior. It also leverages multi-criteria decision analysis (MCDA) [22] to attributing attacks based on the output of the clustering process.

In fact, this framework consists of the following three main components:

1. **Feature selection for security events:** To perform the security analysis and extract meaningful patterns from a given dataset, the security analyst should introduce a set of relevant features to be applied on the dataset. Each security event in the dataset is characterized by a set of selected features (i.e., feature vectors), denoted by $F = \{F_k\}$ where $k = 1, \ldots, n$.
2. **Graph-based clustering:** To measure pairwise similarity, an undirected edge-weighted graph can be created with respect to every feature F_k. As an additional step, a graph analysis can be performed on a single feature basis to identify strongly connected components within each graph. This graph analysis allows the security analyst to extract the structure of the dataset and the relationship among different groups of security events with regard to a specific feature.
3. **Multi-criteria aggregation:** This step leverages different weighted graphs using an aggregation function that models the expected behavior of the security event under scrutiny.

In the following, we briefly explain each component in more detail.

4.3.2.1 Feature Selection for Security Events

Similar to other data mining applications, one of the first steps to perform an analysis on large datasets is to select features that may reveal interesting patterns. More specifically, the feature selection is the process of identifying the most effective subset of features to employ in the clustering process, and construct well-separated clusters.

More formally, we have the dataset D composed of t objects, which are usually defined as security events. We define a feature set F made of n different features F_k, $k = 1, \ldots, n$, that can be extracted for each event e_i from D where $i = 1, \ldots, t$. Let us denote $x_i^{(k)}$ as the feature vector extracted for the event e_i using the feature set F_k. In fact, $x_i^{(k)} \in R^d$ is a d-dimensional vector of real values, i.e.:

$$X_i^{(k)} = \left\{x_{i,1}^{(k)}, \ldots, x_{i,d}^{(k)}\right\}$$

Here, d is the dimension of the feature vector of the feature F_k. We can then group all feature vectors defined for the given feature F_k as $X^{(k)} = \left\{X^{(k)}, \ldots, X_t^{(k)}\right\}$.

To summarize, a security analyst needs to define three parameters: t is the number of security events, n is the number of attack features, and d is the dimensionality of the feature vector. The security analyst could employ any possible feature in order to discover insightful patterns from a given dataset, and that may be useful for the root cause analysis. Depending on the type of dataset and the attack being studied, the analyst may include features such as network-related features such as IP addresses considering different subnets, DNS queries or WHOIS information of the contacting domain names, malware payload analysis (e.g., MD5, PE header, and behavioral features through dynamic analysis), timing information of security incidents, or other application-specific features (e.g., embedded URIs and from-domains used in spam messages).

4.3.2.2 Graph-Based Clustering

A clustering process refers to the task of unsupervised classification by which unlabeled patterns are grouped into clusters based on a similarity measure. A valid cluster results in discovering interesting patterns from the given dataset without prior knowledge on the phenomena being studied. For attack attribution purposes, the extracted patterns from the constructed clusters allow security analysts to analyze the underlying causes that may have created the security events. These clusters also allow constructing a data abstraction level that provides a compact representation of each cluster containing all attack patterns being grouped in that particular cluster.

Unsurprisingly, clustering real-world datasets can be a difficult task since the clustering process is mostly a data-driven process, and different clustering methods will quite probably yield different results using the same dataset. Thus, the proposed framework should not be limited to a given clustering algorithm. The only requirement that a security analyst should consider is to use a graph-based representation (i.e., edge-weighted graphs) in which all pairwise distances are calculated ahead of time for every attack feature.

The analyst could use any classical clustering algorithm, such as K-means, hierarchical clustering (single or complete-linkage) [23], or connected components to perform the analysis. One approach is to leverage a graph-theoretic model [24] that allows extracting dominant sets from a graph by simply formulating the problem as a continuous optimization problem. Once the edge-weighted graphs for different attack features become available, they can be combined using MCDA aggregation functions that model the behavior of the attack under the analysis.

For each attack feature F_k, an edge-weighted graph G_k is generated in which the vertices (or nodes) are mapped to the feature vectors $X_i^{(k)}$, and the edges reflect the similarity between data objects regarding the considered feature. The undirected edge-weighted graph for a given feature F_k can be represented by:

$$G_k = (V_k, E_k, \omega_k)$$

where V_k is the vertex set, E_k is the edge set, and ω_k is a positive weight function.

The technique proposed by Pavan and Pelillo [25] iteratively finds dominant sets in an edge-weighted graph, and then removes them from the graph until all vertices have been clustered, or once a given stopping criterion is met, which could give eventually an incomplete partition as output. We refer the interested reader to [26] for a more detailed discussion and an objective comparison of various clustering algorithms against dominant sets.

4.3.2.2.1 Distance Measures

Most clustering techniques use distance metrics to group objects into clusters. In fact, distance measures are used to calculate the dissimilarity between two patterns based on the given feature space. As mentioned earlier, the security analyst could employ any technique to perform the clustering task. However, in order to generate compact clusters, it is crucial to check whether the specified measure suits the intrinsic data structure. For example, one of the commonly used distance measures is the Euclidean distance [27]. However, the authors in [28] demonstrated that Euclidean metrics only work well when the dataset contains compact or isolated clusters. Furthermore, they can be completely inefficient with high-dimensional data due to the exponential increase in the volume of the dataset. In fact, several previous works have shown that in a high-dimensional space, the concept of proximity, distance, or nearest neighbor may not even be qualitatively meaningful when relying on commonly used metrics such as L_k norms—especially in data mining applications [29].

There are other similarity measures that can be employed to cluster attack patterns. For example, another common similarity measure is the sample correlation between observations treated as sequences of values. The sample correlation reflects the strength of the linear dependence between two real-valued vectors. For example, a correlation value of 1 implies a perfect linear relationship between the two vectors. The interpretation of a correlation value depends on the context. However, a value between 0.5 and 1 is usually considered an indication of a strong dependence between observations.

To assess the quality and consistency of the clustering results, several cluster validity indices have been proposed. In [30], the authors review validity indices that are particularly appropriate for evaluating graph clustered structures. These techniques are based on different definitions of inter- and intra-cluster connectivity. To assess the quality of the experimental results presented in this model, we will mainly focus on the graph compactness, which is a quite effective validity index. We refer the interested reader to [26,30] for more information on the other cluster validity indices.

4.3.2.3 MCDA-Based Attack Attribution

As mentioned earlier, a security analyst can benefit from graph-based clustering to extract informative patterns from a set of security events. If the graph-based

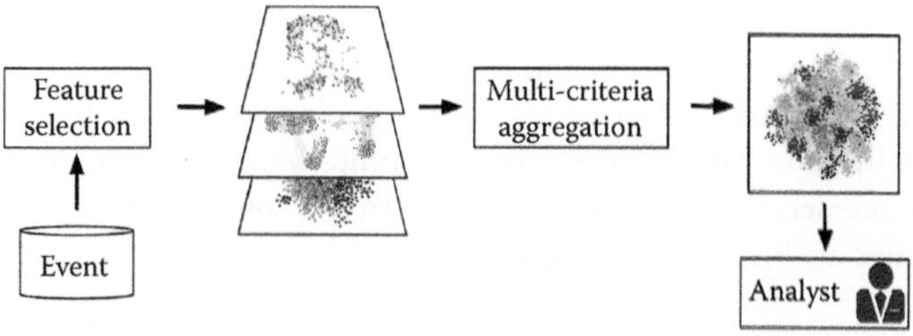

Figure 4.1 A generic attack attribution method which aggregates multiple weighted graphs into a combined graph using an MCDA approach.

clustering is repeated for different attack features, a set of clusters for each attack feature can be extracted which provides interesting viewpoints on the underlying phenomena.

An attack attribution problem can be represented as an application of MCDA in which the criteria of concern are given by the distance values during the graph-based clustering for each attack feature. That is, the distance values between two security events are used to decide whether they are likely due to the same root phenomenon. A representative MCDA attack is depicted in Figure 4.1.

In an MCDA problem, a global score is calculated for each alternative (decision) by using a well-defined aggregation method that models the preferences of the decision-maker or a set of constraints. In fact, the aggregation process is a form of averaging function, like a simple weighted means (e.g., simple additive weighting, weighted product method, analytical hierarchy process [31]), or the ordered weighted average (OWA) [32,33], and Choquet or Sugeno integrals [33]. The OWA [32] as aggregation function provides more flexibility on how to model more complex relationships among criteria. Moreover, one should not assume that events observed by different sensors are always independent.

The power of such an aggregation function lies in the fact that different combinations of criteria may apply to each pair of events. Furthermore, the decision-maker does not need to specify in advance which criteria (or features) must be satisfied to link two events to the same phenomenon.

4.4 Case Studies

In this section, we provide two case studies proposed with regard to the generic model presented in Section 4.3. The case studies demonstrate how applying data mining techniques allows the identification of an attack event, and assists security analysts to perform root cause analysis.

4.4.1 Attack Attribution via Multi-Criteria Decision Making

This case study shows a set of techniques to perform a behavioral analysis of botnets. The case study is based on a research paper [17] that employs a combination of a knowledge discovery technique and a fuzzy inference system. The authors show that by applying this method on attack traces, it is possible to identify large-scale attack phenomena with a high degree of confidence.

Attack events. The dataset used in this research is network attack traces collected from honeypots across 20 different countries from 18 different class A-subnets. The assumption here is that any network connection established with a remote IP can be safely considered as malicious since honeypots are deployed for the sole purpose of being compromised. Consequently, as a first step, each remote IP observed on honeypots is attributed to an attack cluster according to its network characteristics, such as the number of IP addresses targeted on the sensor, the number of packets and bytes sent to each IP, the attack duration, the average inter-arrival time between packets, the port sequence being targeted, and the packet payload. Therefore, all IP sources belonging to a given attack cluster with similar network traces on a given sensor can be considered as having the same attack profile. Consequently, an attack event in this context refers to a subset of IP sources having the same attack profile on a given sensor, and whose suspicious activity has been observed within a specific time window.

4.4.1.1 Defining Attack Characteristics

To provide meaningful patterns and extract knowledge from the attack events, a set of attack characteristics should be defined. In this context, attack characteristics are defined as follows:

The attack origin. One of the first questions that arises is that, based on the given dataset, what is the origin of the observed attacks? The geographical location of attack activities can be used to identify attack activities that have specific distribution in terms of originating countries. For example, the IP network blocks can provide an interesting insight about the attack. In fact, IP subnets can give a good indication of compromised machines involved in an attack event. Consequently, for each attack event, a feature vector is created to represent the distribution of originating countries, or of IP addresses grouped by Class A-subnet.

Targets of the attack. During an attack event, an attacker attempts to check all the active services on the sensors, and find vulnerable services to exploit. To identify the potential targets of an attack, each source of the attack is associated with a complete sequence of ports that it has targeted on a sensor for the duration of the attack session. To look whether there is a relationship between the attack events and the types of services on deployed sensors, the attack events that occurred within the same time window should be grouped together, and then each group of attack events should be used to create the feature vector representing how many sensors have been targeted.

Attack capabilities. Another interesting characteristic is to find out what a source of an attack is capable of doing on the target during the course of the attack. For example, examining the specific commands that a bot issues during an attack session can provide important insights on the capabilities that a bot may possess. The logs can be used to look for similarities between the sequences of actions that sources of attack events perform during an attack session.

Common characteristics. It is also reasonable to expect if two distinct attack events have a high percentage of IP addresses in common, then the probability that those two events are somehow related to the same global phenomenon increases.

4.4.1.2 Extracting Cliques of Attackers

As described in Section 4.3, for the clustering task, after selecting features, a similarity measure between pairs of patterns is defined in order to effectively group similar patterns. The similarity measure is a simple unsupervised graph to formulate the problem. In fact, the vertices of the graph are the patterns of all attack events. The edges express the similarity relationships between those vertices by calculating the distance metrics based on the square root of the Jensen–Shannon divergence [33]. The clustering is performed by extracting maximal cliques from the graph that is defined as an induced sub-graph in which the vertices are fully connected and it is not contained within any other clique. As mentioned in Section 4.3, to perform this unsupervised clustering, the dominant sets approach [25] was used which proved to be an effective method for finding maximal-weighted cliques. We refer the interested reader to [34,35] for a more detailed description of this clique-based clustering technique applied to this case study.

4.4.1.3 Multi-Criteria Decision Making

One of the objectives of this work is to reconstruct sequences of attack events that can be attributed to the same root phenomenon. This allows one to classify incoming attack events into either known attacks or a new attack. The intuition here is that two consecutive attack events should have the same root causes if and only if they share at least two different attack characteristics out of the complete set of criteria (see Section 4.4.2). The reason is that current types of attacks are highly dynamic, and the distribution of the attack events changes rapidly (i.e., a botmaster employs new bots and old bots [infected machines] become clean over time). Therefore, two consecutive attack events from the same botnet must not necessarily have all their attributes in common.

In order to decide whether two attack events are related, attack events should have a certain degree of relatedness. In this case study, the decision-making process that determines if attack events have the same root causes is based on a fuzzy inference system (FIS). More specifically, the knowledge obtained from the extraction of cliques is used to build the fuzzy rules that describe the behavior of each phenomenon. To detect a new attack, the characteristics of the new attack events are provided as input to the fuzzy inference systems which model the identified phenomena.

The multi-criteria inference method was applied to the set of attack traces obtained with the Leurre.com honeynet for over 640 days. The dataset was collected by 36 platforms located in 20 different countries and belonging to 18 different class A-subnets [17]. During this period, 32 global phenomena were identified and 348 attack events were attributed to a large-scale phenomenon. The method was also capable of characterizing the behaviors of the identified phenomena. For example, the largest botnet that attacked the deployed honeypots had 69,884 sources with 57 attack events. During this period, on average, the size of botnets was about 8,500 based on the observed sources, a mean number of 658 sources per event. Figures 4.2 and 4.3 exhibit the geographical distribution of cliques of attacks with regard to top attacking countries and the port sequence targeted by attackers.

The interested reader can refer to the original research work [17] for more information on the global behavior of detected phenomena.

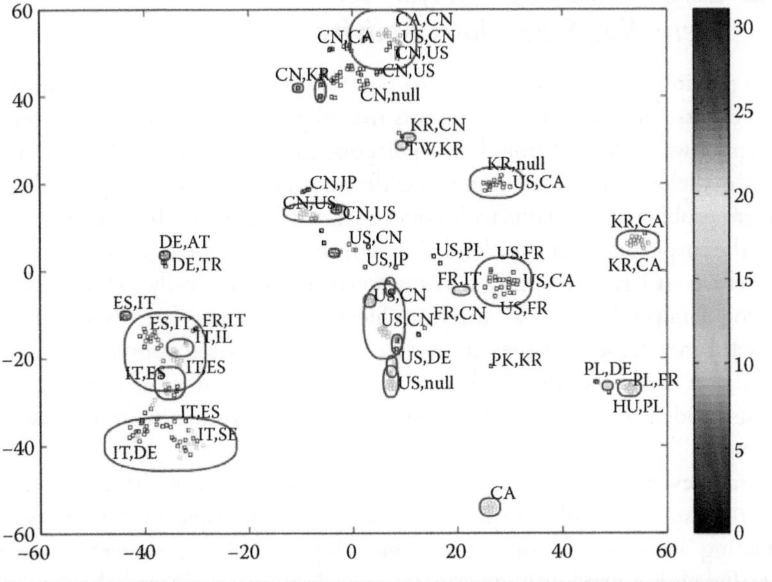

Figure 4.2 The distribution and size of cliques of attackers with the two top attacking countries.

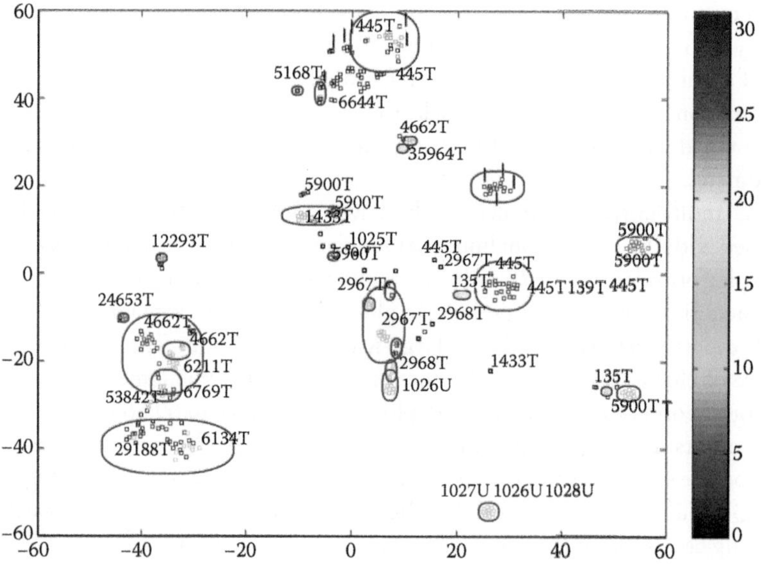

Figure 4.3 The geographical cliques of attackers with regard to the port sequences targeted by the attackers.

4.4.2 Large-Scale Log Analysis for Detecting Suspicious Activity

In the previous case study, the ultimate goal was to reconstruct the sequences of attack events and find the attack events that may have the same root causes. Since the dataset was collected from honeypots, one can safely assume that the collected data is malicious, and is the result of different attack events. This part addresses a different problem. It explains techniques that can be used to discover attack events when the suspicious traffic is blended in with millions of benign events.

Beehive [16] is a system that is proposed to automatically extract knowledge from log data produced by security products in large enterprises. Such approaches are useful in a sense that they improve on signature-based approaches by mainly focusing on characterizing the behavior of suspicious traffic. This allows security analysts to identify suspicious host behaviors and determine the root causes of the incidents.

Attack event. Beehive aims to facilitate the detection of threats by reporting network hosts that exhibit suspicious behaviors. These suspicious behaviors include contacting an attack website, communicating with C&C servers, or exchanging traffic with a previously unseen external destination. These behaviors may be the results of malware activities in the compromised host, direct control of hosts by an external attacker, or benign users being tricked into performing dangerous behavior.

4.4.2.1 Defining Attack Characteristics

In order to discover an attack event, Beehive employs a wide range of logs generated by network devices including web proxies, DHCP servers, VPN servers, authentication servers, and antivirus software logs. In order to characterize outbound traffic from the enterprise, for each dedicated host, a feature vector with 15 features is generated. In the following, we provide more details on how Beehive characterizes the outbound traffic.

Suspicious origins. Exchanging traffic with uncommon external origins may be indicative of suspicious behaviors. One may be interested in identifying hosts that communicate with new, external destinations that have never been contacted before. For example, the number of new external destinations contacted by each host per day is recorded as a history of external destinations by internal hosts over time. In addition to new, uncommon destinations, the system also collects unpopular external raw IP addresses. The assumption is that connections to unpopular IPs can indicate suspicious activity, as legitimate services can usually be reached by their domain names.

Suspicious hosts. Hosts in organizations are often very homogeneous in their software configurations. Installing new software on a host is, in fact, indicative of suspicious behavior.

Beehive infers the software configurations of a host from the user-agent string included in http request headers. A UserAgent (UA) string includes the name of the application making the request, its version, capabilities, and the operating environment. Beehive maintains the number of new UA strings from the host, and builds a history of UA strings per host over a month-long period.

Policy enforcement. If the origin of a request is unknown, and has not yet been categorized, the user must explicitly agree to respect the company's policy before being allowed to proceed. The domains (and connections) that require this acknowledgment are called challenged, and those to which the user has agreed are called consented. For each host, the number of domains (and connections) contacted by the host that are blocked, challenged, or consented is counted.

Suspicious traffic. Abrupt changes in the host's traffic volume can be the result of malware infection, or the presence of automated processes. Beehive is designed to extract these activities by defining a connection spike as a one-minute window and monitoring the host's traffic. An appropriate threshold for high traffic volume is determined over a sufficiently long period of time by counting the number of connections for each host.

Figure 4.4 shows the cumulative distribution across all one-minute windows for all dedicated hosts. Approximately 90% of the hosts generated less than 101 connections, and contacted fewer than 17 distinct domains, per minute.

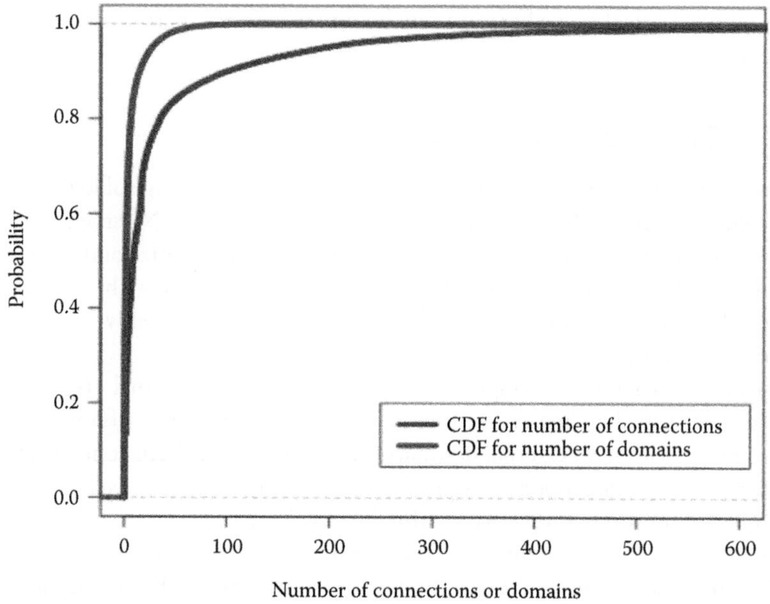

Figure 4.4 CDF for number of web connections and number of domains contacted by a host per one-minute interval.

4.4.2.2 Discovering Outliers in the Network

Beehive allows security analysts to observe groups of hosts that exhibit similar behaviors as well as misbehaving hosts with unique behavioral patterns. Based on the attack characteristics explained in Section 4.4.2.1, each host is represented as a multidimensional feature vector. In order to remove potential dependencies between features and reduce the dimensionality of the vectors, principal component analysis (PCA) [36] is applied on the dataset. The data reduction is performed by projecting the original vectors onto a set of principal components. Each principal component is chosen to capture as much of the variance in the data as possible [16]. By selecting the top m principal components, the projection of the original vectors decreases to the dimensionality m.

The clustering algorithms to the projected vectors are an adaptation of the K-means clustering algorithm, but do not require the number of clusters to be specified in advance [37]. Beehive discovers incidents for the top outlying hosts, and reports them to the security analyst. The algorithm forms clusters by iteratively identifying the nodes that are furthest away from other clusters.

After discovering the outliers, incidents are reported to security analysts to perform further investigations. In order to facilitate the manual investigation, an incident report includes contextual information about the cluster in which the host belongs to, other hosts in the cluster, and the value of the feature vectors.

Table 4.1 "Suspicious" Incidents Categorized by the Security Operation Center

SOC Label	*# of Suspicious Incidents*	
Adware or spyware	35	43.21%
Further investigation	26	32.09%
Other malware	9	11.11%
Policy violation – gaming	1	1.23%
Policy violation – IM	1	1.23%
Policy violation – streaming	2	2.47%
Other – uncategorized sites	7	8.64%

Beehive showed effectiveness in detecting contacted domains created by domain-generation algorithms (DGAs). The destination-based features (i.e., suspicious origins) was effective in clustering hosts that generated malicious traffic, as most of the DGA hosts belong to clusters with high numbers of new destinations.

Beehive also showed effectiveness by discovering 81 incidents where the corresponding hosts communicated with low-reputation websites, downloaded zipped files or executables, used malformed UA strings in http requests, or repeatedly contacted the same URL. Table 4.1 represents the suspicious incidents categorized by the Security Operation Center (SOC) of the company.

4.5 Conclusion

In this book chapter, a set of techniques was introduced to address the complex problem related to attack attribution and root cause analysis. The chapter also explains two case studies based on recent research and shows their effectiveness in discovery knowledge from the attack events. In the first case study, the chapter explained how apparently unrelated attack events could be attributed to the same global attack root. The chapter also provided details on techniques to automatically extract knowledge in a large enterprise from millions of event logs collected every day from several network devices.

References

1. Krebs, Brian, FBI: North Korea to Blame for Sony Hack. http://krebsonsecurity.com/2014/12/fbi-north-korea-to-blame-for-sony-hack/, 2014.

2. Krebs, Brian, Home Depot breach. http://krebsonsecurity.com/tag/home-depot-breach/, 2015.
3. CROWE, Portia. JPMorgan fell victim to the largest theft of customer data from a financial institution in US history, http://www.businessinsider.com/jpmorgan-hacked-bank-breach-2015-11, 2015.
4. Krebs, Brian, Anthem breach. http://krebsonsecurity.com/tag/anthem-breach/, 2015.
5. Krebs, Brian, Target data Breach, http://krebsonsecurity.com/tag/target-data-breach/, 2014.
6. McAfee Labs, 2016 Threat Prediction, http://www.mcafee.com/us/resources/reports/rp-threats-predictions-2016.pdf, 2016.
7. FireEye Inc., The 2016 Security Landscape, https://www2.fireeye.com/rs/848-DID-242/images/2016-Security-Landscape-RPT.pdf?mkt_tok=3RkMMJWWfF9wsRolvqzId%2B%2FhmjTEU5z17OkqXKexgokz2EFye%2BLIHETpodcMT8ZqPLHYDBceEJhqyQJxPr3NKNgN3tx5RhPmCg%3D%3D, 2016.
8. Basu, Eric, Target CEO Fired—Can You Be Fired If Your Company Is Hacked?, http://www.forbes.com/sites/ericbasu/2014/06/15/target-ceo-fired-can-you-be-fired-if-your-company-is-hacked/#311a62727bc1, 2014.
9. Antonakakis, Manos, Roberto Perdisci, Yacin Nadji, Nikolaos Vasiloglou, Saeed Abu-Nimeh, Wenke Lee, and David Dagon. From throw-away traffic to bots: Detecting the rise of DGA-based malware. In *Presented as part of the 21st USENIX Security Symposium (USENIX Security 12)*, pp. 491–506, 2012.
10. Gu, Guofei, Roberto Perdisci, Junjie Zhang, and Wenke Lee. BotMiner: Clustering analysis of network traffic for protocol-and structure-independent botnet detection. In *USENIX Security Symposium*, 5(2) (2008):139–154.
11. Holz, Thorsten, Christian Gorecki, Konrad Rieck, and Felix C. Freiling. Measuring and detecting fast-flux service networks. In *NDSS*. 2008.
12. Antonakakis, Manos, Roberto Perdisci, David Dagon, Wenke Lee, and Nick Feamster. Building a dynamic reputation system for DNS. In *USENIX security symposium*, pp. 273–290, 2010.
13. Antonakakis, Manos, Roberto Perdisci, Wenke Lee, Nikolaos Vasiloglou II, and David Dagon. Detecting malware domains at the upper DNS hierarchy. In *USENIX Security Symposium*, p. 16, 2011.
14. Bilge, Leyla, Davide Balzarotti, William Robertson, Engin Kirda, and Christopher Kruegel. Disclosure: Detecting botnet command and control servers through large-scale netflow analysis. In *Proceedings of the 28th Annual Computer Security Applications Conference*, pp. 129–138. ACM, 2012.
15. Bilge, Leyla, Engin Kirda, Christopher Kruegel, and Marco Balduzzi. "EXPOSURE: Finding malicious domains using passive DNS analysis." In *NDSS*, 2011.
16. Yen, Ting-Fang, Alina Oprea, Kaan Onarlioglu, Todd Leetham, William Robertson, Ari Juels, and Engin Kirda. Beehive: Large-scale log analysis for detecting suspicious activity in enterprise networks. In *Proceedings of the 29th Annual Computer Security Applications Conference*, pp. 199–208. ACM, 2013.
17. Thonnard, Olivier, Wim Mees, and Marc Dacier. Addressing the attack attribution problem using knowledge discovery and multi-criteria fuzzy decision-making. In *Proceedings of the ACM SIGKDD Workshop on Cyber Security and Intelligence Informatics*, pp. 11–21. ACM, 2009.
18. Kaufman, Leonard, and Peter J. Rousseeuw. Finding Groups in Data: An Introduction to Cluster Analysis. Vol. 344. John Wiley & Sons, 2009.

19. Julisch, Klaus, and Marc Dacier. Mining intrusion detection alarms for actionable knowledge. In Proceedings of the Eighth ACM SIGKDD International Conference on Knowledge Discovery and Data Mining, pp. 366–375. ACM, 2002.
20. Barbará, Daniel, and Sushi Jajodia (Eds.). *Applications of Data Mining in Computer Security,* volume 6 of *Advances in Information Security*. Springer, 2002.
21. Brugger, S. Terry. Data mining methods for network intrusion detection. University of California at Davis (2004).
22. Thonnard, Olivier, Wim Mees, and Marc Dacier. On a multicriteria clustering approach for attack attribution. *ACM SIGKDD Explorations Newsletter* 12(1) (2010): 11–20.
23. Ferreira, Laura, and David B. Hitchcock. A comparison of hierarchical methods for clustering functional data. *Communications in Statistics-Simulation and Computation* 38(9) (2009): 1925–1949.
24. Raghavan, Vijay V., and C. T. Yu. A comparison of the stability characteristics of some graph theoretic clustering methods. *Pattern Analysis and Machine Intelligence, IEEE Transactions on* 4 (1981): 393–402.
25. Pavan, Massimiliano, and Marcello Pelillo. A new graph-theoretic approach to clustering and segmentation. In *Computer Vision and Pattern Recognition, 2003. Proceedings. 2003 IEEE Computer Society Conference on*, vol. 1, pp. I-145. IEEE, 2003.
26. Thonnard, Olivier. A multi-criteria clustering approach to support attack attribution in cyberspace. PhD diss., PhD thesis, École Doctorale d'Informatique, Télécommunications et Électronique de Paris, 2010.
27. Draisma, Jan, Emil Horobet, Giorgio Ottaviani, Bernd Sturmfels, and Rekha R. Thomas. The Euclidean distance degree of an algebraic variety. *arXiv preprint arXiv:1309.0049* (2013).
28. Mao, Jianchang, and Anil K. Jain. A self-organizing network for hyperellipsoidal clustering (HEC). *Neural Networks, IEEE Transactions on* 7(1) (1996): 16–29.
29. Aggarwal, Charu C., Alexander Hinneburg, and Daniel A. Keim. *On the Surprising Behavior of Distance Metrics in High Dimensional Space.* Berlin: Springer, 2001.
30. Boutin, Francois, and Mountaz Hascoet. Cluster validity indices for graph partitioning. In *Information Visualisation, 2004. IV 2004. Proceedings. Eighth International Conference on*, pp. 376–381. IEEE, 2004.
31. Yoon, K. Paul, and Ching-Lai Hwang. *Multiple Attribute Decision Making: An Introduction*. Vol. 104. Sage Publications, 1995.
32. Yager, Ronald R. On ordered weighted averaging aggregation operators in multicriteria decisionmaking. *Systems, Man and Cybernetics, IEEE Transactions on* 18(1) (1988): 183–190.
33. Beliakov, Gleb, Ana Pradera, and Tomasa Calvo. *Aggregation Functions: A Guide for Practitioners*. Vol. 221. Heidelberg: Springer, 2007.
34. Fuglede, Bent, and Flemming Topsoe. Jensen-Shannon divergence and Hilbert space embedding. In *IEEE International Symposium on Information Theory*, pp. 31–31, 2004.
35. Thonnard, Olivier, and Marc Dacier. A framework for attack patterns' discovery in honeynet data. *Digital Investigation* 5 (2008): S128–S139.
36. Thonnard, Olivier, and Marc Dacier. Actionable knowledge discovery for threats intelligence support using a multi-dimensional data mining methodology. In *Data Mining Workshops, 2008. ICDMW'08. IEEE International Conference on*, pp. 154–163. IEEE, 2008.
37. Jolliffe, Ian. *Principal Component Analysis*. John Wiley & Sons, Ltd, 2002.

Chapter 5

Data Visualization for Cybersecurity

Lane Harrison

Contents

Data visualization is an indispensable means for analysis and communication, particularly in cyber security. Promising techniques and systems for cyber data visualization have emerged in the past decade, with applications ranging from threat and vulnerability analysis to forensics and network traffic monitoring. We revisit several of these milestones in this chapter.

Beyond recounting the past, however, we uncover and illustrate the emerging themes in new and ongoing cyber data visualization research. We explore the need for principled approaches toward combining the strengths of the human perceptual system with analytical techniques like anomaly detection, for example, as well as the increasingly urgent challenge of combating suboptimal visualization designs—designs that waste both analyst time and organization resources.

5.1 Introduction

Unfortunately, cyber security needs data visualization.

Cyber security needs visualization because—in practice—security requires substantial human involvement. Even small organizations require constant time and attention from trained Security Information Workers (SIWs) to ensure acceptable levels of security. SIWs spend much of their time in security operations: scanning devices on their network for vulnerabilities, for example, or analyzing incoming network traffic for malicious activity. Their limited time and attention is fragmented between collecting and analyzing data, and using it to form and prioritize changes in their organization's network and systems. While hardly noticeable at first glance, visual representations of data—bar charts, pie charts, line charts, and the like—are ubiquitous in these operations.

The need for data visualization in cyber security is unfortunate because many organizations would happily relegate their security operations to intelligent systems, if it were possible.

Intelligent systems operate much faster than human operators, and are less prone to error than we are. The transition to intelligent systems is tempting for many organizations, especially given recent advances in artificial intelligence and machine-learning. Machine learning can now process massive streams of diverse types of data from both inside and outside an organization, for example, providing models that capture malicious behavior. Artificial intelligence, similarly, can analyze network infrastructure to suggest changes that help avoid misconfiguration. These advances represent new ways of thinking in security.

While promising, these advances have not been adopted in operational contexts, nor will they replace the security analyst. Experts in machine learning argue that, even when intelligent systems reach the point of making operational decisions, human judgment will still be necessary for managing the systems themselves.

This gap aligns with the goal of data visualization: to aid human analysis and judgment with data. Visualization combines the inherent strengths of our visual system with the powerful graphical and computational abilities of the computer. A properly designed visualization allows our eyes to quickly discern patterns in data, which feeds our understanding of the underlying features and phenomena in our data. Visual inspection leads us to new insights about our data, helping us form hypotheses about where to focus next. Interaction allows us to further pursue these hypotheses either by showing other parts of the data, or by showing the same data from a different perspective. These features make data visualization an invaluable tool for exploration, analysis, and communication.

Effective data visualization is difficult, however. Most of us are familiar with basic graphs and charts. Given the prevalence of tools like Microsoft Excel, it would be difficult to find a colleague who has never spent time creating bar charts and pie charts. If you were to ask the same colleague to explain whether their bar chart is superior to a pie chart, however, no answer they give would be complete. The relative effectiveness of even the most basic charts is still a topic of debate. (Most research suggests that pie charts are the inferior choice, though some disagree, and recent work has begun investigating just how people read them.) Charts common in more technical contexts are no exception: histograms, box-plots, and scatterplots are frequently the topic of ongoing studies.

Given its ongoing study, one might wonder exactly when data visualization is useful in cyber security. Examples are readily available. When analyzing system-level logs, for instance, two of the most commonly used tools are command-line utilities and Excel. Command-line utilities are used to access, manipulate, and filter the logs, while Excel is used for inspection, analysis, and visualization. SIWs use these visualizations not only to aid in their analysis, but also to communicate their results to other security teams and stakeholders.

Examples of techniques developed through data visualization research are also plentiful. For instance, the data visualization capabilities of tools like Excel rapidly become difficult when the number of columns is large. If an analyst needed to look for relationships across 20 columns, for instance, using Excel they would need to manually create multiple charts comparing pairs of columns. Data visualization research offers several scalable alternatives. One is the parallel-coordinates plot (see Figure 5.1), which shows multiple dimensions side-by-side, and affords several interaction techniques to allow users to arrange columns to look for hidden correlations and outliers.

Cyber security is much more than log analysis, however. SIWs handle everything from threat and vulnerability management to forensics, traffic analysis, and more. As we cover these topics in the remainder of the chapter, bear in mind that our focus is not on covering the entire space, but rather on a sample of applicable data visualization techniques for each area.

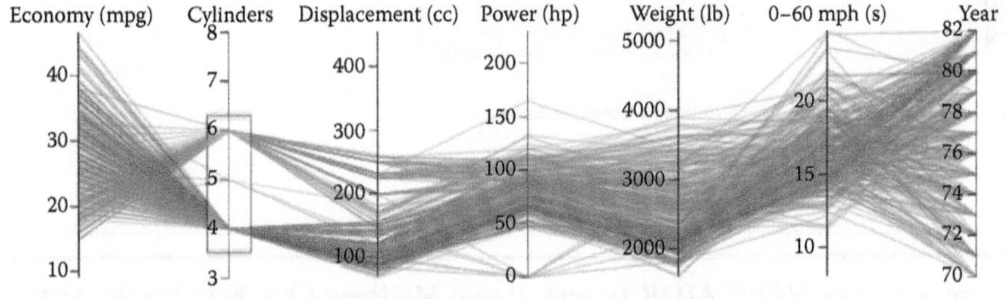

Figure 5.1 A parallel-coordinates plot [1]. Each axis represents a dimension (column) of the data. Each line represents a row (a particular car, in this case).

5.2 Threat Identification, Analysis, and Mitigation

Threat analysis involves identifying and categorizing actions (both purposeful and accidental) that could interrupt day-to-day operations. Threat analysis uses many data sources, for instance, the risk of host or section of the network on its known vulnerabilities, as well as data on the possible paths an attacker might take through a network or into a system. SIWs spend a significant amount of time on threat analysis in their organizations because it is the primary means of prioritizing ongoing maintenance and response procedures in the event of a breach (Figure 5.2).

ATTACK GRAPHS Diagrams can help illustrate the possible ways an attacker can traverse through a network toward a high value target. Commonly called attack graphs, these diagrams enable SIWs to computationally quantify threat analysis. These graphs can be computationally constructed from several pieces of information available in organizations, such as the network structure, the systems running on the network, and their associated vulnerabilities. Attack graphs allow SIWs to identify necessary changes in their networks and systems, and to test whether their changes were actually successful in stopping potential attacks.

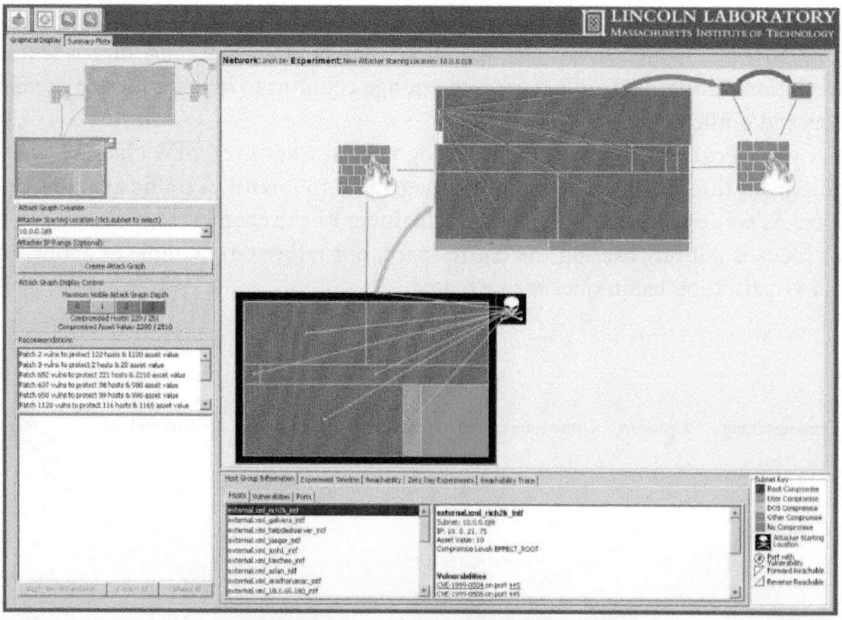

Figure 5.2 The NAVIGATOR system. (From Matthew Chu, Kyle Ingols, Richard Lippmann, Seth Webster, and Stephen Boyer. In *Proceedings of the Seventh International Symposium on Visualization for Cyber Security*, pp. 22–33. ACM, 2010.) Attack graph reachability information is combined with vulnerability information through node-link diagrams with treemap diagrams as the nodes.

From a data analysis perspective, the challenge with attack graphs is that they quickly become large and multifaceted. There are usually multiple possible paths (edges) between systems (nodes) in a network. Each of these edges and nodes may have several attributes, leading to a large multidimensional graph. Visual representations of large graphs often lead to a "hairball," where the large number of node and edge-crossings makes it difficult to see the underlying structure of the graph.

Challenges in graph visualization are a perennial topic in data visualization research. In security visualization, several recent approaches have focused on showcasing how careful encoding and interaction design can improve cyber analysis with attack graphs.

Generally, attack graphs are represented as node-link diagrams and use different colors or shapes for the nodes and links to represent risk, vulnerability-type, and other available variables [2–5]. Since node-link diagrams are often one of the best visual representations for following links [6], analysts are able to explore how attackers might gain access to critical machines through existing vulnerabilities. Node-link diagrams have several well-documented limitations, however [6], so researchers have proposed novel visual metaphors for attack graphs, including pixel-based matrix views and treemaps [7,8] (see Figure 5.3).

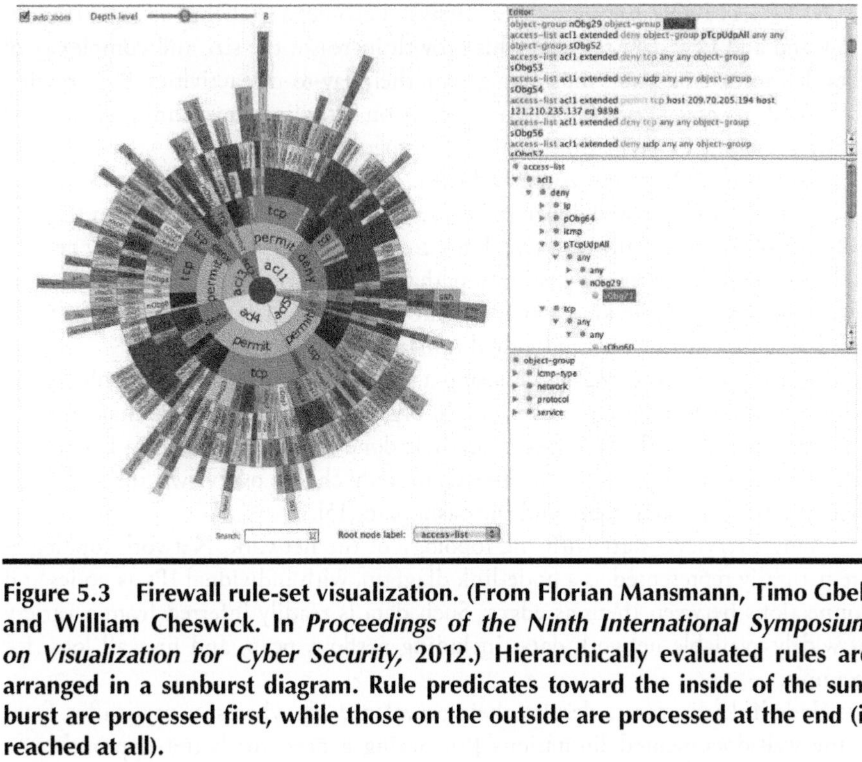

Figure 5.3 Firewall rule-set visualization. (From Florian Mansmann, Timo Gbel, and William Cheswick. In *Proceedings of the Ninth International Symposium on Visualization for Cyber Security,* 2012.) Hierarchically evaluated rules are arranged in a sunburst diagram. Rule predicates toward the inside of the sunburst are processed first, while those on the outside are processed at the end (if reached at all).

Given the complexity of visualizing graphs, each attack graph technique has relative strengths and limitations. SIWs may benefit from having several of these techniques at their disposal.

CONFIGURATION There are several research efforts that attempt to make the configuration of security assets, particularly firewalls and routers, easier for SIWs.

Firewall configuration remains an open and difficult problem for security analysts. Rules can conflict in a number of ways, and firewall configuration remains computationally intractable. Therefore, effective firewall configuration in large networks may benefit through a hybrid approach that combines configuration algorithms with human-centered visualization techniques. Recent developments in this area have visualized different types of rule conflicts [9], and focused on accurately representing the dimensions of firewall configuration [10].

It is also important for analysts to understand router configuration. This problem differs from firewalls in that it requires the analysis of large traffic data, reachability data, routing data, and more. Basic visualizations such as scatterplots and stacked graphs can help SIWs identify patterns in DNS traffic [11]. Given the diverse data types, coordinated multiple view visualizations have been shown useful in representing these data sources together, allowing analysts to find important connections in the data [12,13].

NAVIGATION Orienting threat analysis becomes a challenge as organizations grow and add new data sources. This growth increases the size and complexity of data that security analysts must navigate in their day-to-day activities. Recognizing this trend, several researchers have focused on visualization techniques that aid security analysts in navigating complex heterogeneous data.

The mantra "Overview, zoom and filter, details on demand" is one of the most widely known and followed design guidelines in interactive data visualization [14]. An overview of data is usually intuitive. For a company focused on sales, it may be sales and related metrics over the past year, perhaps shown weekly or a month at a time. Overviews like this provide a starting point for an analyst at the company to zoom and filter into daily or even individual transactions of interest.

In cyber security, however, choosing a good overview is more difficult. Given the large and varied sources of data in an organization, an overview that serves as a starting point for all the types of analysis done in a security setting is not possible. This complexity has led to three commonly chosen overviews: the node-link diagram, the geospatial map, and the dashboard [15].

Many overviews start with the topology of the network. Network topologies are naturally represented as a node-link diagram, with individual IPs as nodes and connections between them as edges. Such data is readily inferred from a variety of widely available network data, including netflow, pcap, and firewall logs, for example.

Node-link diagrams, despite their prevalence in cyber security, suffer from many well-documented limitations [6]. Seeing a need for better approaches to overviews in security settings, Fowler and colleagues created IMap—a map-based overview of a large network [16].

The IMap algorithm begins with a node-link representation of a network, and leverages this structure to build a geographic map, like the familiar maps we use for directions. The resulting maps resemble continents with country boundaries, indicating different portions of the network. This transformation eliminates several problematic features of node-link diagrams, like hairballs of edge-crossings and difficult-to-decipher positions of nodes.

Beyond mitigating the tradeoffs of representations commonly used for overviews, map-inspired representations bring several immediate benefits to analysts. For one, they capitalize on these results and other research demonstrating that two-dimensional spatializations of data aid navigation [17]. Another way to think of IMap is as an even higher-level overview than the node-link diagrams typically used. This is true by definition, as the authors demonstrate that individual nodes and links can be shown on demand from inside the IMap. Further benefits have yet to be investigated. However, decades of research in cartography have pointed to spatial maps as a useful tool for helping analysts find "common ground," and orienting themselves when facing new data and scenarios [18].

Now having discussed overviews, consider a situation in which an analyst has used an overview to identify activity of interest in their network. Navigation is still a challenge in this situation because the analyst must identify the context in which the activity occurred to determine what actions are appropriate to take. In this case, context might include information like what subnet the activity was on, which user was logged in, and what machines are in the "vicinity" of the activity (in a connectivity sense, not necessarily meaning that the machines are physically close).

Analysts must reason about the context of suspicious activity when deciding how to respond. Few tools explicitly support this type of reasoning, however. An analyst might use tools to trace the route of one machine to another to discover other IPs of interest, yet this information must also be combined with context about the IPs along the route themselves.

Recognizing this need, Gray et al. have contributed the notion of contextual network navigation [19]. In their work, the primary activity of interest is placed at the center of a network (i.e., egocentric), while other machines of interest are placed around it. This context can extend well beyond an organizational network and into the Internet. Context outside of a network can be useful in helping analysts reason about the origin of attacks, for instance, providing information that can be used to strengthen the borders of the network.

5.3 Vulnerability Management

In order to assess the security posture of the servers and workstations in their network, security analysts and systems administrators use vulnerability assessment tools to scan their network and deploy code for potential exploits. In an organization with many services and systems, the number of open vulnerabilities is typically large and constantly changing.

It is unreasonable to expect all vulnerabilities to be patched—employees introduce new software to their machines weekly, and even new versions of trusted software can introduce vulnerabilities. SIWs must prioritize where they spend their time. Relying on lists of vulnerabilities and SIW's mental models of a network to determine what should be prioritized can lead to troubling results, however. Industry reports show that unpatched systems are to blame for some of the largest and most harmful breaches in recent years [20].

NETWORK VULNERABILITIES Nessus and similar tools can produce an overwhelming amount of data for large networks. Network vulnerability scanners probe machines to determine which network ports are open, what services are running on the ports, and, most importantly, what versions of those services are running. Identifying the services and the versions enables these tools to match them with known vulnerabilities.

Scan analysis tools usually present the data in tables, sometimes with color coding to attempt to provide an overview of each vulnerability's severity. But scan data can be very large. With little support for comparing individual or logical groupings of machines, it can be difficult for SIWs to build a mental picture of what the overall vulnerability status is in the network. Further, it can be difficult to determine how the vulnerability status of a network has changed between scans at different points in time.

NV uses treemaps and linked histograms to allow security analysts and systems administrators to discover, analyze, and manage vulnerabilities on their networks [21] (see Figure 5.4). In addition to visualizing single Nessus scans, NV supports the analysis of sequential scans by showing which vulnerabilities have been fixed, remain open, or are newly discovered.

SOFTWARE VULNERABILITIES Vulnerabilities are not limited to commercial software. Organizations may run a number of scripts and services in their network for business operations. In fact, one of the main concerns of SIWs is discovering the "known unknowns" of the threats that exist in their organization's infrastructure [20].

Organizations must detect and manage vulnerabilities not only in the software they deploy, but also in the software they make. Similar to network vulnerability scanning, there are many tools for detecting and logging vulnerabilities in a given source code.

Recognizing this need, Goodall et al. developed a visual analysis tool to help understand and correct vulnerabilities in code bases [22]. Their system includes multiple views of not only the vulnerabilities detected by logging tools, but also the code itself. Exploiting the simplicity of the problem allows a unique self-contained system in which analysts can prioritize and fix vulnerabilities in a single tool.

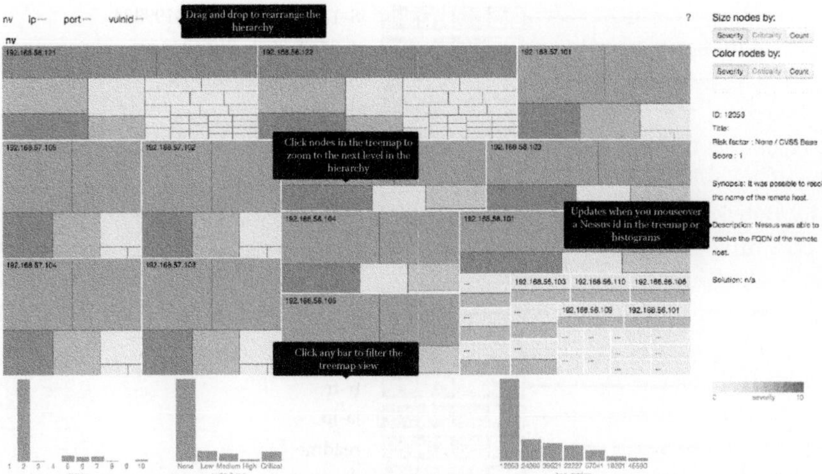

Figure 5.4 NV system. (From Lane Harrison, Riley Spahn, Mike Iannacone, Evan Downing, and John R Goodall. In *Proceedings of the Ninth International Symposium on Visualization for Cyber Security,* 2012.) A vulnerability scan of multiple machines at once is shown in a treemap diagram. Users can rearrange the hierarchy to focus on ports, IPs, or individual vulnerabilities.

Vulnerability management and remediation make up a large portion of how SIWs spend their time. There are few data-oriented tools and workflows specifically targeted at vulnerability management, however—this is an opportunity for future work.

5.4 Forensics

Visualization can benefit forensic analysis after a network or system is determined to be compromised. Forensic analysis requires in-depth data from one or several machines and devices. While these data sources can often be visualized with traffic and activity monitoring tools, the views in these tools are often of limited use in forensics, where the SIW needs to build a story of how an attack occurred. A distinguishing feature of forensics tools is the lower level of detail they present to analysts. Research focusing on forensic analysis has dealt with network data, individual device data, or behavioral data (e.g., email) in a post-intrusion setting (Figure 5.5).

Forensics tools focus on smaller subsets of the network, favoring features that show more detail and allow analysts to pivot between machines or subnetworks. For example, instead of relying solely on text-based command-line utilities like

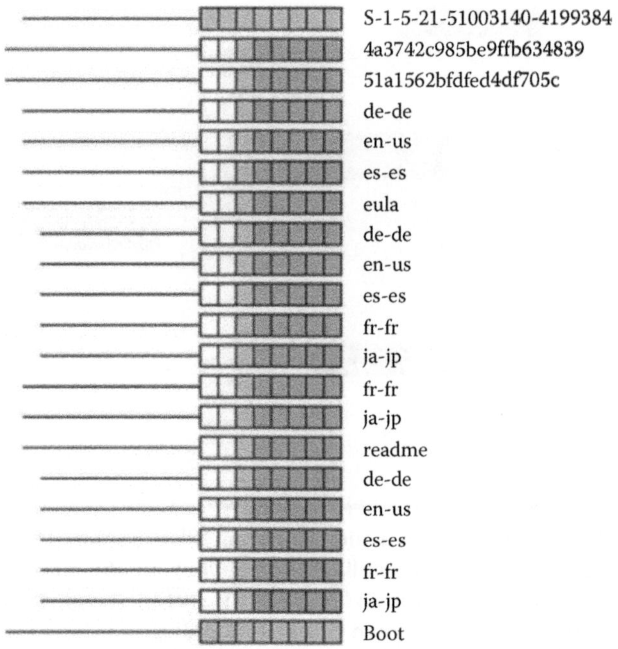

Figure 5.5 Change-Link system. (From Timothy R Leschke and Alan T Sherman. In *Proceedings of the Ninth International Symposium on Visualization for Cyber Security,* 2012.) Malicious processes and patches often change directory structures temporarily, deleting evidence of their work as they finish. Change-Link shows how directories have been changed over time.

grep, detailed search results can be visualized to assist analysts in exploring and filtering historical network traffic and events [23]. Several approaches have combined visualization with machine-learning to create and refine classification models for historic data, which can then be used to aid future forensics efforts [24,25].

Visualization has also supported device-level forensics, particularly in digital string search, a core component of forensic analysis. In particular, traditional search algorithms have been used in conjunction with visual techniques to provide an overview of the search results and to display file and string interactively [26]. Another approach is to visualize changes to directory trees, as many attacks can be identified by how they modify files on a system [27].

Other applications have explored how visualization can benefit the behavioral forensics, such as attacks that involve email and chat. Email flow and group analysis results have been visualized to provide insight into both a user's typical usage pattern history [28] and to uncover malicious spam campaigns [29].

5.5 Traffic

Many data visualization tools in cyber security are designed to facilitate network monitoring and intrusion detection, or situation awareness. Situation awareness refers to knowing what is happening in a specific, rapidly changing environment.

Situation awareness can be broken down into three stages: perception, comprehension, and projection [30]. Perception involves monitoring the status of a network and systems within a network, while comprehension involves synthesizing the status of the individual elements in the first stage to recognize patterns that should be investigated further. In contrast, projection involves extrapolating the current state of the network toward the immediate future. In security visualization, most efforts and tools target perception and comprehension.

There are several stages of network analysis and defense [31]. These include monitoring and initial detection, as well as the network forensics and reporting and decision making activities that follow. Other studies have examined how analysts make decisions and how visualization might benefit that process [32], as well as how high-level security goals relate to low-level data [33].

Another focus area in situation awareness research is to examine analysts' existing toolkits to identify the strengths and limitations of current tools and workflows. These studies lay the groundwork for new visualization techniques and systems. For instance, although command-line search tools such as grep remain a staple in the analysts' toolkit, few visualization systems incorporate even basic search functionality [34], potentially damaging their adoption. Similarly, analysts often need to relate external security information to activity on their network (e.g., from websites, mailing lists, and other online sources). Recent data visualization systems have begun to process external information and visualize how it relates to internal network operations [35].

Visualization designs have taken many forms in support of situation awareness. Given the time-focused nature of network security data, some visualization techniques emphasize time and support interactions that allow SIWs to move forward and backward through the temporal dimensions of their data. One such approach is event plots, which visually encodes events by category using visual marks to represent events [36]. Challenges for event plots include defining what an event is (e.g., packets are low-level events, whereas emails are high-level events) and defining how to represent an event (e.g., color, shape). While clutter can become an issue, event plots becoming more widely used because they can provide both an overview and a detailed view of a large number of machines.

5.6 Emerging Themes

Data visualization has been applied to many areas of security analysis. Security analysis is changing, however. Two emerging themes are a push to move analysis toward intelligent systems, and a realization that data analysis benefits not only the individual SIW, but their team, their organization, and their community.

HUMAN-IN-THE-LOOP MACHINE LEARNING Machine learning has had considerable success in some areas of cyber security, but limited success in others. Spam filters are a machine learning success story. With numerous examples of spam emails, machine learning is used to accurately vet incoming mail for spam-like features (most of the time, at least). This reduces the number of phishing emails that make it to end-users, considerably improving the security of the organization. Yet as we have seen, SIWs focus on much more than email.

Machine learning has been repeatedly applied toward helping SIWs identify anomalous traffic and connections in their networks. These efforts have not seen widespread adoption, however, for several reasons: Attacks are rare, meaning the number of false positives a model produces will be much larger than the actual number of attacks [37]. (In spam the situation is different, given the large number of malicious emails.) This false alarm problem is multiplied when machine-learning models are built using different data sources or sub-networks. Smaller models like this are often necessary for building a model of what normal activity looks like.

High-frequency data such as traffic and connections in a network can lead to an overwhelming number of false positives that SIWs must investigate. In these cases, the analysts' ability to defend the network is significantly reduced [32,33].

A deeper problem is the understandability of the models produced by machine learning. While some learning algorithms produce human-readable output, a sequence of questions about features in the data, for example, other algorithms produce models that are difficult for humans to internalize. This is a general problem in machine learning, but because security events must be vetted by SIWs, the gap between humans and models in machine learning remains a longstanding challenge [37–39].

Given the potential impact, researchers have been actively working to close this gap. One approach is to add constraints to the learned models that align with SIW's ability to understand them [40]. Another emerging approach is to conduct assessments of the tools SIWs would need to better manage multiple models [41]. These approaches hold promise to meld the operational needs of SIWs with the structure, capabilities, and limitations of machine learning.

EXPLORATION VERSUS EXPOSITION Security has become more data-driven in recent years. Data manipulation tools have become more usable, analysis techniques have become more scalable, and visualization techniques have become more aligned with the strengths and limitations of our perceptual and cognitive abilities. But data analysis and exploration is only part of the story.

Beyond exploration, the communication and exposition of data have become central topics in security. Part of this is driven by data-laden industry reports. The Verizon Data-Breach Investigations Report [20], for example, collects breach reports from multiple organizations and identifies emerging trends and gaps in the past year. Reports such as these are invaluable as organizations plan and pull-together resources for future years.

Given the expansion beyond exploratory data visualization to expository data visualization, new challenges have arrived. Best practices such as only using the absolute best perceived visual stimuli in data visualization (such as position or length) make sense in exploratory contexts where it is assumed that you have the full attention of the viewer. In exposition, however, accuracy in visual stimuli may need to be sacrificed for stimuli that are engaging.

Unfortunately, many practitioners, companies, and academics remain unaware of best practices in data visualization. This leads to a number of flashy (yet ineffective) analysis tools and attractive (yet misleading) industry reports. More study is necessary to navigate this space. As research moves from focusing on techniques to focusing on the SIW [42,43], security visualization will become an even more integral part of day-to-day security operations and communication.

References

1. Parallel coordinates. https://syntagmatic.github.io/parallel-coordinates/. Accessed: 2016-06-01.
2. John Homer, Ashok Varikuti, Xinming Ou, and Miles A McQueen. Improving attack graph visualization through data reduction and attack grouping. In *Visualization for Computer Security*, pp. 68–79. Springer, 2008.
3. Steven Noel and Sushil Jajodia. Managing attack graph complexity through visual hierarchical aggregation. In *Proceedings of the 2004 ACM Workshop on Visualization and Data Mining for Computer Security*, pp. 109–118. ACM, 2004.
4. Scott OHare, Steven Noel, and Kenneth Prole. A graph-theoretic visualization approach to network risk analysis. In *Visualization for Computer Security*, pp. 60–67. Springer, 2008.
5. Williams L., Lippmann R., Ingols K. (2008) GARNET: A graphical attack graph and reachability network evaluation tool. In: Goodall J.R., Conti G., Ma K.-L. (eds). *Visualization for Computer Security. Lecture Notes in Computer Science*, vol. 5210. Springer, Berlin, Heidelberg.
6. Mohammad Ghoniem, Jean-Daniel Fekete, and Philippe Castagliola. A comparison of the readability of graphs using node-link and matrix-based representations. In *Information Visualization*, 2004. INFOVIS 2004. IEEE Symposium on, 2004.
7. Matthew Chu, Kyle Ingols, Richard Lippmann, Seth Webster, and Stephen Boyer. Visualizing attack graphs, reachability, and trust relationships with navigator. In *Proceedings of the Seventh International Symposium on Visualization for Cyber Security*, pp. 22–33. ACM, 2010.
8. Steven Noel, Michael Jacobs, Pramod Kalapa, and Sushil Jajodia. Multiple coordinated views for network attack graphs. In *Visualization for Computer Security*, 2005. (VizSEC 05). IEEE Workshop on, pages 99–106. IEEE, 2005.
9. Shaun P Morrissey and Georges Grinstein. Visualizing firewall configurations using created voids. In *Visualization for Cyber Security*, 2009. VizSec 2009. 6th International Workshop on, 2009.

10. Florian Mansmann, Timo Gbel, and William Cheswick. Visual analysis of complex firewall configurations. In *Proceedings of the Ninth International Symposium on Visualization for Cyber Security*, 2012.
11. Pin Ren, John Kristoff, and Bruce Gooch. Visualizing dns traffic. In *Proceedings of the 3rd International Workshop on Visualization for Computer Security*, 2006.
12. James Shearer, Kwan-Liu Ma, and Toby Kohlenberg. Bgpeep: An ip-space centered view for internet routing data. In *Visualization for Computer Security*, 2008.
13. Soon Tee Teoh, Supranamaya Ranjan, Antonio Nucci, and Chen-Nee Chuah. Bgp eye: A new visualization tool for real-time detection and analysis of bgp anomalies. In *Proceedings of the 3rd International Workshop on Visualization for Computer Security*, 2006.
14. Ben Shneiderman. The eyes have it: A task by data type taxonomy for information visualizations. In *Visual Languages*, 1996. Proceedings, IEEE Symposium on, 1996.
15. Jay Jacobs and Bob Rudis. Data-Driven Security: Analysis, Visualization and Dashboards. John Wiley & Sons, 2014.
16. J Joseph Fowler, Thienne Johnson, Paolo Simonetto, Michael Schneider, Carlos Acedo, Stephen Kobourov, and Loukas Lazos. Imap: Visualizing network activity over internet maps. In *Proceedings of the Eleventh Workshop on Visualization for Cyber Security*, 2014.
17. Melanie Tory, David W Sprague, Fuqu Wu, Wing Yan So, and Tamara Munzner. Spatialization design: Comparing points and landscapes. *Visualization and Computer Graphics, IEEE Transactions on*, 2007.
18. Alan M MacEachren. *How Maps Work: Representation, Visualization, and Design*. Guilford Press, 1995.
19. Cameron C Gray, Panagiotis D Ritsos, and Jonathan C Roberts. Contextual network navigation to provide situational awareness for network administrators. In *Visualization for Cyber Security (VizSec), 2015 IEEE Symposium on*, 2015.
20. Verizon RISK Team et al. Verizon data breach investigations report, 2016.
21. Lane Harrison, Riley Spahn, Mike Iannacone, Evan Downing, and John R Goodall. Nv: Nessus vulnerability visualization for the web. In *Proceedings of the Ninth International Symposium on Visualization for Cyber Security*, 2012.
22. John R Goodall, Hassan Radwan, and Lenny Halseth. Visual analysis of code security. In *Proceedings of the Seventh International Symposium on Visualization for Cyber Security*, 2010.
23. Kiran Lakkaraju, Ratna Bearavolu, Adam Slagell, William Yurcik, and Stephen North. Closing-the-loop in nvisionip: Integrating discovery and search in security visualizations. In *Visualization for Computer Security*, 2005. (VizSEC 05). IEEE Workshop on, 2005.
24. Chris Muelder, Kwan-Liu Ma, and Tony Bartoletti. A visualization methodology for characterization of network scans. In *Visualization for Computer Security*, 2005. (VizSEC 05). IEEE Workshop on, 2005.
25. Charles Wright, Fabian Monrose, and Gerald M Masson. Hmm profiles for network traffic classification. In *Proceedings of the 2004 ACM Workshop on Visualization and Data Mining for Computer Security*, 2004.
26. TJ Jankun-Kelly, David Wilson, Andrew S Stamps, Josh Franck, Jeffery Carver, J Edward Swan et al. A visual analytic framework for exploring relationships in textual contents of digital forensics evidence. In *Visualization for Cyber Security*, 2009. VizSec 2009. 6th International Workshop on, 2009.

27. Timothy R Leschke and Alan T Sherman. Change-link: A digital forensic tool for visualizing changes to directory trees. In *Proceedings of the Ninth International Symposium on Visualization for Cyber Security*, 2012.
28. Wei-Jen Li, Shlomo Hershkop, and Salvatore J Stolfo. Email archive analysis through graphical visualization. In *Proceedings of the 2004 ACM Workshop on Visualization and Data Mining for Computer Security*, 2004.
29. Orestis Tsigkas, Olivier Thonnard, and Dimitrios Tzovaras. Visual spam campaigns analysis using abstract graphs representation. In *Proceedings of the Ninth International Symposium on Visualization for Cyber Security*, 2012.
30. Mica R Endsley. Toward a theory of situation awareness in dynamic systems. *Human Factors: The Journal of the Human Factors and Ergonomics Society*, 1995.
31. Anita D'Amico and Michael Kocka. Information assurance visualizations for specific stages of situational awareness and intended uses: Lessons learned. In *Visualization for Computer Security*, 2005 (VizSEC 05). IEEE Workshop on, 2005.
32. Jamie Rasmussen, Kate Ehrlich, Steven Ross, Susanna Kirk, Daniel Gruen, and John Patterson. Nimble cybersecurity incident management through visualization and defensible recommendations. In *Proceedings of the Seventh International Symposium on Visualization for Cyber Security*, 2010.
33. Chris Horn and Anita D'Amico. Visual analysis of goal-directed network defense decisions. In *Proceedings of the 8th International Symposium on Visualization for Cyber Security*, 2011.
34. Sergey Bratus, Axel Hansen, Fabio Pellacini, and Anna Shubina. Backhoe, a packet trace and log browser. In *Visualization for Computer Security*, 2008.
35. William A Pike, Chad Scherrer, and Sean Zabriskie. Putting security in context: Visual correlation of network activity with real-world information. In *VizSEC 2007*. 2008.
36. Doantam Phan, John Gerth, Marcia Lee, Andreas Paepcke, and Terry Winograd. Visual analysis of network flow data with timelines and event plots. In *VizSEC 2007*. 2008.
37. Stefan Axelsson. The base-rate fallacy and the difficulty of intrusion detection. *ACM Transactions on Information and System Security (TISSEC)*, 2000.
38. Pooya Jaferian, David Botta, Fahimeh Raja, Kirstie Hawkey, and Kon-stantin Beznosov. Guidelines for designing IT security management tools. In *Proceedings of the 2nd ACM Symposium on Computer Human Interaction for Management of Information Technology*, 2008.
39. Robin Sommer and Vern Paxson. Outside the closed world: On using machine learning for network intrusion detection. In *Security and Privacy (SP), 2010 IEEE Symposium on*, 2010.
40. Michael Gleicher. Explainers: Expert explorations with crafted projections. *Visualization and Computer Graphics, IEEE Transactions on*, 2013.
41. Simon Walton, Eamonn Maguire, and Min Chen. A visual analytics loop for supporting model development. In *Visualization for Cyber Security (VizSec), 2015 IEEE Symposium on*, 2015.
42. Sean McKenna, Diane Staheli, and Miriah Meyer. Unlocking user-centered design methods for building cyber security visualizations. In *Visualization for Cyber Security (VizSec), 2015 IEEE Symposium on*, 2015.
43. Diane Staheli, Tamara Yu, R Jordan Crouser, Suresh Damodaran, Kevin Nam, David O'Gwynn, Sean McKenna, and Lane Harrison. Visualization evaluation for cyber security: Trends and future directions. In *Proceedings of the Eleventh Workshop on Visualization for Cyber Security*, 2014.

Chapter 6

Cybersecurity Training

Bob Pokorny

Contents

Cybersecurity defense must be practiced by everyone in your organization. Not only do cyber-warriors and IT members need to fend off cyber attackers, but the most casual computer user, from the Contracts Office personnel to company officers, needs to follow good procedures and maintain the organization's cybersecurity boundary. While the IT and cybersecurity staff certainly know more about identifying, responding to, and warding off cybersecurity attacks than other computer users in your organization, everyone in the company will need to know and follow procedures, such as setting strong passwords and applying caution when opening email attachments or downloading files.

To address these needs, this chapter focuses on cybersecurity training. The chapter first discusses specific characteristics of training cybersecurity. In particular, smart humans competing against smart humans, the power and complexity of networks and computers, and human-made nature of computers and networks are discussed. Second, general principles of training and learning are discussed in detail. Topics of interest include desired result of training, use of media in training, context in which to present general learning principles, learning with understanding, reflections and interactions, immersive environments of simulations and games, building on what learners know, metacognition, teamwork, feedback, motivation, transfer, and misconceptions. Third, some of the practical factors that influence the design of a course are discussed. These practical factors include managing sponsor's expectations, understanding available resources, subject matter experts, and cognitive task analysis, identifying what trainees need to learn, underlying representation that supports computerized assessment and instruction, pilot-testing the instruction, putting it all together, and the role of Big Data in cybersecurity training.

6.1 Specific Characteristics of Training Cybersecurity

Cybersecurity is special in that cybersecurity approaches and tools change much faster than other domains change. Relative to some domains that change infrequently (e.g., budgeting rules) or evolve as more is learned (e.g., medical practices), cybersecurity changes rapidly due to a few factors.

First, smart humans compete with other smart humans in cybersecurity. Cyber-attackers try to infiltrate and access data from some other organization's networks while cyber-defenders do their best to squelch attacks. The tools that both attackers and defenders can use are evolving to leverage any potential weakness, and to plug those weaknesses and limit damage once a network has been infiltrated. Cybersecurity changes are fueled by competition and human ingenuity.

Second, the power and complexity of computer networks and communication protocols are increasing. As networks and communication protocols change, methods by which they can be attacked and defended change.

Third, computers and networks are human-made and arbitrary. This differs from other domains, such as chemistry or biology, in which building blocks can be discovered but not changed. One consequence of the rapid evolution of cybersecurity approaches and techniques is that cybersecurity experts must spend more time learning new threats and defensive approaches.

6.2 General Principles of Training and Learning

6.2.1 Desired Result of Training: Better Performance

Before discussing training, consider the bigger goals for the organization. The organization wants its staff to support the mission. Frequently this involves training to follow effective procedures, but not always. Alternatives to training include setting up automated procedures, or providing incentives for excellent performance [1]. A decision maker in charge of human performance must decide which approach to use to yield good performance [2]. Within your organization, different user types may need different kinds of solutions.

For the everyday user of computers, many solutions to good cybersecurity performance can be entrusted to engineered procedures rather than training. Some examples are requiring users to create strong passwords and forcing users to change them regularly. More stringent cybersecurity requirements would restrict users from opening selected types of attachments or installing programs on their computers. These kinds of solutions to potentially dangerous actions that users might make do not involve training. While training may offer the best solution to a performance problem, training should be considered within the wider set of performance improvement tools.

Decision makers who determine how to keep the organization's computer network safe and productive will have to specify which approach to use for each user type. One possible answer is to provide in-depth cybersecurity training for the IT staff and cybersecurity experts, while creating processes with which other users must abide, such as requiring frequent password changes, which force them to follow good procedures, even if they would not choose them.

6.2.2 Use of Media in Training

Training can be provided by an instructor, by a computer, or by a blended solution of an instructor and a computer. An instructor can make run-of the-mill curriculum lead to excellent learning and inspired students; or a not-so-good instructor can take excellent curriculum and use it poorly to yield ineffective training. Generally, good instructors can adapt content to learners' needs and backgrounds, and provide inspiration and relevance to training.

Computers provide two capabilities that human instructors cannot. First, computers can provide realistic, simulated environments in which trainees can be immersed in situations they might find themselves in their future. Many learning principles take advantage of immersive environments, as interacting with simulations can improve learning. Fortunately, for learning cybersecurity, many cybersecurity simulations exist that can be used for training. Second, computerized training is much more consistent than instructor-led training. Thus, data about training effectiveness can be referenced back to specific training successes or weaknesses much more easily with computer-led training than with instructors.

6.2.3 Context in which to Present General Learning Principles

To describe general principles of training and creating an environment for efficient learning, we will use a computerized presentation of content as our example. By using a prescribed training environment, the explanations and examples of effective learning can be tied directly to programmed interventions and instructional approaches rather than presenting ambiguous and less repeatable human interventions. The rest of this chapter assumes computer-based instruction. Even if you will be creating material for or leading instructor-led training, you will get more out of reading this chapter if you consider how to have instructors apply the principles described specifically with computer-led presentations.

6.2.4 Learning with Understanding

Current instructional theory states that people perform better if they learn not simply facts and rules, but also learn so they understand the connections between facts, concepts, models, and conditions. This is referred to as Learning with Understanding [3]. People who understand a domain not only recall facts, procedures, and concepts, but also organize their knowledge so they can apply it to perform accurately and efficiently, produce new solutions if needed, and transfer their knowledge to new situations.

In cybersecurity, understanding a particular network enabled personnel to more accurately detect when a sequence of cyber events was due to a cyber-attack [4]. This supports the generally accepted notion that experience in a domain improves performance in that domain.

6.2.5 Reflection and Interactions

One approach that supports learning with understanding is having students reflect on the content they are learning. When learning from a computerized simulation, learners can be led to reflect on the domain and what they have observed in the simulation by tasks such as (1) answering questions, which requires them to construct relationships between entities shown in the simulation or (2) creating a reasoned solution to a difficult problem presented within the simulation. As learners reflect on the content with the task of creating a new representation of the domain presented via the simulation, they construct their understanding of the simulated environment [5].

While reflection has been a specific technique used to yield learning with understanding, another viewpoint is that any rich interaction with content helps learners gain understanding [6]. Potential rich interactions involve solving problems, creating new designs, listening to others as they solve problems, creating examples in which concepts they are learning are evident, connecting concepts that they had not previously understood as connected, or developing logical arguments. Applying knowledge from a domain in novel ways can help learners organize their knowledge and apply it in new situations. In cybersecurity, Abawajy [7] analyzed users' preferences, including advantages of reflection within classroom courses.

6.2.6 Immersive Environments of Simulations and Games

Learners can reflect on and interact with a domain's principles through simulations and games. Simulations and games have many benefits as instructional environments:

1. Simulations and games provide contexts that are similar to the environment in which learners apply their knowledge. So learners (a) practice applying content that is helpful for their jobs, and (b) understand that what they are learning will be helpful to their job productivity, which most learners find motivating.
2. Simulations and games enable learners to condition their knowledge so they apply it when it is appropriate [8]. It is common to teach theory but not the conditions to which it applies. Simulations and games give learners opportunities to develop this skill. There are many theories of cognition that express the view that learning is easier if it is done in context. This view is often described as "situated cognition." It gained popularity when it was observed that learners can both (a) learn theoretical content in a classroom that they cannot apply to the real world, and (b) learn content in the real world that they cannot apply in classroom exercises, even if similar procedures are invoked [9].
3. Simulations or games can be built to adapt the environment to learners' current level of understanding. This is unlike the real world, in which many cases may be too easy or too complicated for most workers. A simulation can modify a problem that is too easy for learning by either adding complexity to the situation in real-time (if the training simulation has that capability), or to select a more complex problem for the next learning challenge. A simulation can adapt to presenting problems that are too difficult by reducing the

complexity in real time (if the training simulation has that capability), or to provide more assistance to the learner.

4. Simulations and games can expose learners to the concepts that the student needs to know within a natural progression of slightly increasing complex simulations [10]. The first task in a simulation or game could be the simplest curricular item in the course. As the learner gains competency, the simulation or game will present increasingly complex challenges. New concepts can be introduced within the sequence of increasingly complex environments.

There have also been many simulations that have been proposed for training cybersecurity personnel including those reported by Fite [11] and Thompson and Irvine [12].

6.2.7 Building on What Learners Know

For knowledge to be effectively applied, it must be integrated with learners' existing knowledge. As noted above, studies demonstrate that learners do not always generalize what they learn in school to the real world, or apply methods they have developed in the real world to school tests [13]. When a new concept is presented, the training system should try to connect the new concepts that are to be taught with experiences that learners have already experienced in life. Otherwise, the concepts that learners acquire in the simulation may not be integrated with the learners' existing knowledge, and the learner may not use the new knowledge.

When learners have to learn some concept for which they already have a misconception, evidence suggests that the misconception should be directly brought up, and learners should be told why they may possess the misconception [14]. New concepts should be presented so learners integrate the new concept with their previous misconception.

6.2.8 Metacognition

One effective instructional approach asks learners to monitor their own learning. Learners should assess what they know and what they should learn. The skill of understanding one's own cognition is called metacognition. Learners who are thinking about their strengths and weaknesses will be able to target their weaknesses as instructional targets. While recognizing a learner's own strengths and weaknesses is an advanced skill for learners [15], it is necessary for learners when they have to learn outside the context of a course.

6.2.9 Teamwork

Another instructional target that can be addressed in a simulation is the ability to communicate well with others. Communication is vital to success in complex situations such as warfighters conducting military operations, first responders dealing with emergencies, and medical staff attending to patients. Similar to those environments, the cybersecurity team members must communicate well in order for the value provided by each member to contribute to the performance of the team. Developing team communication skills is nearly its own course; but practicing the skills in context can be done well in a simulation [16]. The simulation must present conditions in which communication is important, and provide a channel in which teammates should communicate. The communication can be monitored and tracked for assessment and instruction, though natural language processing challenges must be overcome.

6.2.10 Feedback

Instructional feedback and assessment are very challenging topics that have their own rich scientific literature and specialists. The goal of feedback should be to improve performance. Hence, feedback is reliant on assessment to identify performance weaknesses. Some interesting research and practical questions regarding feedback are associated with (1) using student performance to make assertions about the knowledge or skill that a learner does or does not possess; and (2) designing feedback that supports student learning and leads to long-term gains in performance.

As most of our focus is on immersive environments, we will address assessment for simulations and games. Even if we were only developing assessment for objectives tests, assessment and feedback are complex [17]. But assessing performance in complex environments is more difficult than determining if objective test items are correct; and feedback in simulations and games is trickier than giving feedback to multiple choice or true/false questions. The feedback might simply explain to the trainee how to perform better. But to improve performance more, the feedback should take into account the principles of learning that were discussed earlier. Feedback should engage the learner in a process in which learner actions can be reviewed, and the trainee can interact with content to support improved understanding and decisions.

Assessment that leads to feedback should address practical and theoretically motivated issues:

1. The assessment of performance within simulations and games should be conducted for a practical consequence. Two primary purposes of assessment are to trigger an instructional intervention or to classify a person's specific level of competence. Assessing performance that does not lead to a practical instructional consequence is wasteful.
2. The assessment could trigger many different types of instructional intervention. In particular, three types of instruction could focus on instructional intervention. The instruction may seek to improve (1) the learner's

metacognitive approach to learning, (2) the learner's mental model of a complex situation, or (3) a specific, fine-grained weakness in a learner's understanding of a situation. To follow the principles of basing learning on reflection and interactions, the intervention that is triggered should involve more than a simple explanation. Rather, the intervention could include an interactive task that induces the learner to reflect on the applications of concepts within the domain.

The triggering of an interaction is somewhat different from the approach used in traditional Intelligent Tutoring Systems (ITS). Typically, ITS attempted to create a detailed analysis of learner knowledge in order to provide just the right content that the learner did not possess or apply that would support improved performance. Current theories of learning for understanding take the perspective that learners need to construct their understanding and build cognitive organizations through rich interaction with content [18]. Following this view of learning, the instructional intervention should provide an interaction in which learners are exposed to content that they reflect on and integrate into their mental organization of a topic. This should lead to improved understanding, and thus, performance. Common types of interaction include scaffolding messages that direct the learner to a desired action via a series of hints that become progressively more revealing.

Feedback is also frequently given to learners in classroom or computerized instruction when the learners are at the end of a lecture, chapter, or computer-presented problem. At the end of a lecture or chapter, learners should integrate the information that they have just been exposed to. At the end of a problem, learners are no longer striving to solve a problem, and can pay attention and reflect on the actions that they took to try to solve the problem, and organize whatever they learned in the problem with their existing knowledge. This is frequently related to following principles of instruction that aim to not overwhelm students with excessive cognitive load [19]. As applied to presenting abstract concepts when solving problems, good practice normally follows the pattern of focusing on the current problem that the learner is struggling with, through to the point of the student solving the problem. After the student solves the problem, the problem can be reviewed, and general principles can be raised without interfering or distracting the learner from solving the problem.

6.2.11 Motivation

Motivation is a very complex topic. In training and education, many researchers have investigated what helps students' motivation [20]. Immersive environments are often seen as supporting motivation, as students can see direct connections between their training and what they need to do in the real world. Games are expressly designed to be engaging; as students play to win, they also learn.

Still, there are some issues that should be addressed to improve motivation in simulations and games. One concern is to make the challenges given to learners to be neither too difficult nor too easy. If a problem is too difficult, learners might give up. If a problem is too easy, learners will not learn anything. Making problems so they are neither too easy nor too hard can be addressed most obviously by selecting an appropriately difficult problem [21]. Even if a problem is selected that is too difficult or too easy, remedies can be provided. For problems that are too difficult, students can receive more assistance from the instructional system (which can be presented as a coach in a simulation or a co-conspirator character in a game). For problems that are too easy and the learner reached a solution too quickly, an adaptable scenario could make the challenge greater.

One question about students' approach to learning is whether their primary concern is to become smart or look like they are smart [22]. Whether a student is interested in becoming smart or in "looking smart" is related to whether the student is intrinsically interested in the topic. With simulations and games, even if students are primarily interested in looking smart, they have to perform and apply knowledge, increasing the likelihood that they will learn.

One method to increase motivation for the game is to have learners interact with other students who also participate in the same learning environment. Students may be motivated by interest in the topic, and they may be encouraged to learn well due to the social interaction forces. Of course, it is also possible that disinterested, cynical students may spoil the motivating social effects.

6.2.12 Transfer

Having students apply what they have learned, beyond the specific examples used in training, is a common educational goal. As with motivation, immersive environments provide some advantages to transfer, relative to more common educational techniques. Approaches used in immersive environments that promote transfer include specifying problems that include a number of different situations and promoting learning with understanding [23]. Simulations can provide student encounters with different classes of problems, in which learners apply general principles in different contexts. The reflective period after a problem can provide an interaction in which learners are exposed to abstract principles that can be applied across many contexts.

One of the abstract principles that can be explicit for learners is the specification of a mental model. "Mental models" have been explored in depth for decades and a rich literature abounds for them. The basic idea is for learners to have a pictorial representation of a complex system. The pictorial representation enables the learner to quickly grasp the connections between components of the system. Experts possess mental models of systems in their domain, and learners are constructing their own mental model. Often the mental model presents some general principle that can be widely applied across problems and can be used when learners perform different tasks. A few examples of such principles can be seen with common electrical theories that apply across many domains, cooking methods that apply across foods, and requirements for editing computer files that are common across nearly all editing programs. Within cybersecurity, a mental model might address how opening an attachment with malware infects a host's computer. Explicitly making learners aware of the mental model supports transfer.

6.2.13 Misconceptions

One situation that presents a transfer problem for learners is when they hold incorrect knowledge. The effects of pre-existing knowledge are often seen in studies of physics students who possess the theoretical knowledge of physics that they learned in class, but also continue to hold "folk physics" knowledge that is not correct, yet part of the common culture. These are examples of not transferring new knowledge to situations it should transfer to. To overcome this pre-existing knowledge, the discrepancies between existing, incorrect knowledge and new knowledge should be explicitly addressed in the learning environment [24]. Misconceptions are common in cybersecurity, given the fast rate at which threats and defensive tactics change.

6.3 Practical Design

When designing a course, in addition to applying principles from current learning theory to training and instruction, there are many practical factors that will influence the design of your course. This section raises some of these factors so you can incorporate them into your overall plans.

6.3.1 Sponsor's Expectations

The most obvious practical factor is the expectation of the sponsor. Sponsors will have many expectations about a course they wish to create. Some expectations they can make explicit and others they cannot. You should discuss with sponsors the overall budget that can be spent, deadlines, and the expected technology to be used, such as using human-led or computerized instruction. Often their implicit expectations will include training methods with which they are familiar. This tendency to use familiar methods may be overcome by some leader's call to revamp and improve the instruction, or to reduce the costs of the training. The use of technology unfamiliar to the sponsor, such as simulations and games, may require persuasive discussion with sponsors.

The sponsor and the designer need to discuss and agree on many features of the instruction beyond technology:

1. The importance of evaluating the training effectiveness must be clarified. Some sponsors may assume that if learners work through the instruction, they will learn the material. Other sponsors may have more interest or need to have the instructional benefits accurately assessed. Sometimes the developers of new instruction may wish to compare it to the effectiveness of older instruction. Assessing current instructional effectiveness is sometimes politically difficult.
2. How to use the data after the course is completed should be clarified. The sponsor may wish to store student data for later analysis, or may not. It is important for the sponsors and the designers to have a shared vision of the end use and disposition of the data.

One sponsor input that must be followed is the budget. Difficult decisions will be required, and some instructional features will not be affordable. The costs of some factors are decreasing (such as virtual reality), while other costs are increasing (as expectations for production values increase, the appearance of simulations and games rise). You should consider both the costs to develop the training and the costs to maintain it. The course should be designed to create the maximal instructional power given the budget available for the instruction.

6.3.2 Available Resources

Another practical factor is to collect and use existing available resources. Example resources that you might be able to use are existing curriculum, graphics, or videos. Using existing materials translates into less content you must create.

A critical resource is access to subject matter experts (SMEs) who will help develop and refine instructional material. If these experts are plentiful and inexpensive, you can use them in your plan with less carefully planned processes. Another important resource for creating instruction is access to students in order to pilot test the effectiveness of the instruction. With cybersecurity instruction, access to SMEs and students is critical, given the fast rate of change in the domain. Access to these resources may be assisted by course sponsors.

6.3.3 Subject Matter Experts and Cognitive Task Analysis

Of great practical importance are methods used to acquire expertise from SMEs. There are many methods by which experts' expertise can be drawn out and made explicit for training [25]. These methods are often referred to as "cognitive task analysis" (CTA), or simply "task analysis." The most valuable insight from all these methods is that asking experts to explain their thought processes in performing complex tasks is much more difficult than commonly assumed [26]. Experts have access to some of their ability and knowledge, but not to all of it. The content that they cannot express but use anyway is called tacit knowledge. In addition to studies that show tacit knowledge, some experts are poor at communicating what they know, even if they are aware they are using specific kinds of knowledge [27]. It is important to apply CTA methods that efficiently elicit their knowledge.

CTA methods make tacit knowledge of SME explicit. Many CTA methods involve some form of situated cognition. Experts are placed in a situation similar to the one in which they must apply their knowledge. They may be asked to (1) make decisions and explain those decisions in context, (2) critique decisions that others made, or (3) indicate critical factors in their decisions. The knowledge of SMEs made explicit in these situated cognition contexts needs to be unified into a representation that can be applied across many contexts.

6.3.4 Identify What Trainees Need To Learn

While CTA clarifies expert performers' knowledge and skill which helps identify the content trainees need to learn, the SME's knowledge and skill that he or she applies to solve the most difficult problems defines the most complicated aspect of what trainees need. We also need to know the knowledge and skill learners possess at the beginning of a course. This incoming knowledge of trainees is important as it is inefficient to create instruction for what learners already know or to create instruction that relies on knowledge trainees have not yet learned. Training content should include material that learners can learn but do not now know.

6.3.5 The Underlying Representation That Supports Computerized Assessment and Instruction

Computerized training systems that assess learner knowledge and adapt instruction to student needs are called Intelligent Tutoring Systems (ITSs). In this field researchers have developed many formats of assessment and instruction. Places to read about them include a set of books sponsored by the Army Research Laboratory [28], and an excellent summary by Dr. Beverly Woolf [29]. The general framework for an ITS specifies a model of the domain to be learned, a model of the student's knowledge, a pedagogical module that plans and manages instructional intervention, and an interface that manages user input and the presentation of a complex environment from a learning system.

As you design computer-based training, you should use the concepts and methods developed for ITS that can apply to your situation. Many ITSs have been developed for research purposes; if you are developing an effective and affordable training method, you would apply resources to those modules that are most important for good performance.

Many research ITSs have a pedagogical module that applies different instructional strategies based on student need. While a pedagogical component is reasonable within a research framework, it would not be used in a practical application.

For any specific training, the design of an instructional environment will use the pedagogical approaches deemed most efficient for a target set of learners and content. The pedagogical module will be chosen during design and implemented as part of the interface between the system and the learner. The interface will be designed to be cost-effective and beneficial for learners.

The domain model and the student model will be built to support the learner's training interactions. The representation of the student model frequently takes on one of three forms. One form is to overlay the representation of the learner's assessed knowledge and skill on a model of the domain. The domain model will represent the knowledge of an expert. The overlay model of a learner identifies which nodes or portions of the expert model each learner is believed to possesses (this knowledge can be represented probabilistically). The overlay model compares the student model to an experts' model, and indicates which parts of the experts' model that a learner does not have [30].

A second representation of a student model lists mistakes that students commonly make. A learner will be marked as making a mistake or not. This approach is frequently called a bug library. Historically, the concept of a bug library comes from software development: a bug is an incorrect specification of steps used to complete the desired task. For student models, a bug refers to some deficit in knowledge or skill which, if remediated, would lead to improved performance. The bug library model does not bother to specify the content of the expert model when specifying a student's weakness; rather, student performance is identified as exhibiting one of a known set of mistakes [31].

A third diagnostics approach is to identify which constraints of good performance a student violates [32]. While this resembles a bug library, its relationship with the violation of good performance is often seen as different from a bug. A bug library has traditionally been associated with local remediation that refers to misapplication of local rules. A constraint violation can also lead to local repairs, though it may also lead to an intervention that addresses larger misconceptions.

Whether an assessment uses an overlay model, bug library, or constraint violation, they all are intended to trigger a beneficial instructional intervention. And while they have different names and different processes are often used to construct them, their differences in application are more in degree than in category. An overlay model is often used when diagnoses refer to underlying knowledge and skill that enable complex performance. The intervention with an overlay model tries to help the student learn the underlying knowledge that is required for the complex performance. A bug model is used when a specific rule that should lead to good performance is not followed. The intervention targets an incorrectly applied rule. Bug models are often used when all the rules for good performance can be specified. The classical example of a bug model is with rules for simple mathematical computations. The constraint violation model is typically related to specific performance mistakes, and associated constraints that the trainee seems to be applying. Constraint-based models can be used when there are multiple good paths to a solution.

One computer representation that links diagnosed student weaknesses to instructional interventions is a process explorer [33]. A process explorer specifies how a process is executed. For example, the process explorer has a description of a Cross Site Scripting attack. The assessment system identifies what the student should know to perform well, and can present a remedial explanation from the process explorer.

6.3.6 Pilot Test the Instruction

Ideally, instructional interventions for the trainee to learn content should be tested before the computer programming of the interactions is implemented. While the computer programming of the simulation or game environment can be constructed in order to support the student interactions, it will likely require little adjustment based on interactions with the trainee. But testing the interactions [34] is important because if the designed training interactions are ineffective, modifying them is easier and less expensive before the programming is completed. The pilot test should investigate:

- The instructional effectiveness of interactions designed to help trainees learn.
- The ability of the assessment system to inform instructional interventions.
- The capability of the computer representation to support the planned computerized instruction and assessment system.
- The costs to develop instructional and assessment systems that should be collected and used to estimate costs for the designed intervention.

The pilot test should be conducted in an early and small iteration of the entire development. This allows some experimentation of the instructional interactions and assessment capabilities. After the pilot test helps determine effective processes, the creation of instructional content, the assessment system, and the underlying computer representation can be constructed in a streamlined fashion.

6.4 Putting it All Together

This chapter has presented many elements that the developer of a training system needs to develop, organize, and integrate. To help the developer coalesce this knowledge, the following section leads the reader through applying these concepts to an example learning context. In addition to following through the decisions that this section leads you through, you should consider applying the questions to a situation with which you are familiar.

1. Clarifying sponsor expectations and budget
   Clarify the expectations of your sponsor, and the budget that is assigned to the project. Earlier, we raised questions that should be answered by discussions

between the sponsor and the leader of the instructional development team. A vision that illustrates what the instruction is expected to look like can be presented to the sponsor, the development team, and various stakeholders, including users. This will clarify questions such as the media used and the role of SMEs and instructors.

Members of the instructional development team, such as the artist, the software lead, and the instructional design team, should estimate costs for the content and programming needed to develop the instruction. This must fall within the budget that the sponsor wishes to spend. The sponsor will be informed regarding progress toward goals that had been defined in earlier phases of development.

When reviewing cyber-training, some examples indicate that the cybersecurity training world applies a traditional model of training that does not take full use of the capabilities of current instructional theory [35]. A report from the National Institute of Standards and Technology (NIST) on cybersecurity training [36] involves situated cognition to only a limited degree. The report discussed many different roles for which training should be created. It is worth considering an alternative view that would focus on training common mental models that would cut across many cybersecurity roles. The report also assumed that the instruction would be instructor-led, and did not always include the use of simulations, which could increase training effectiveness.

2. Take stock of resources

Collect the resources that are at the disposal of the instructional design team. This has been described previously, including such concrete assets as a curriculum and graphics. The instructional team leader should also consider the relative strengths and weaknesses of the development team. An example is identifying the strengths of the programming staff and the computer systems in which they have expertise.

In cybersecurity training, potentially valuable assets that training might use are cybersecurity testbeds that have been built to test cybersecurity tools. Some of these are used in training [37]. They are a valuable set of assets that could be widely exploited in cybersecurity training.

3. Design the learner interaction

In this phase, the learning team creates a mock-up of the instructional interactions by which the learner gains knowledge and skill. The instructional team needs to consider many factors:

1. What does the learner need to learn? This helps clarify the skills that the instructional interaction imparts to the learner. This will require access to knowledge of the task. Usually, this is obtained via an SME and assessment of trainees' incoming skill. It is possible that the sponsor provides the SME to the instructional team.

2. What media will be used in this instruction? If the course is entirely instructor led, there is less design work, and more decisions are left to the instructor. The entire course may be given by a computer, or the computer might simply provide a practice environment in which the instructor provides assessment of learner performance and leads a discussion in which learners are exposed to instructional objectives and interesting and appropriate cybersecurity situations.
3. If the course involves a simulation or game, common interactions by the learner within the game should be made clear, as well as how evaluation initiates an instructional intervention, and what the sequence of interactions between the learner and the instructional system looks like.
4. Sketch the environment in which the learner interactions occur. This might be a simulation or a game, and may include more traditional didactic instruction.

As cybersecurity is a quickly evolving environment, it would be beneficial to construct the interactions with trainees, so they can be easily revised. The cybersecurity environment should also be easy to revise as new tools for use by cyber-defenders become available and as new threats are observed.

4. Conduct a pilot study of the instruction interaction

The instructional interactions should be tested for user acceptance and user effectiveness before the computer interactions are implemented in code. The interactions should be tested by pilot participants that are similar to the eventual learners. This allows observation of the instructional interactions to see if they have the intended effect. Testing the interaction at this stage allows for the opportunity to revise the instruction. In general, any feedback that can be obtained from typical learners is valuable to understand how the instruction can be made more effective.

5. Develop more instructional and assessment content, and represent it in a computer.

After settling on the environment and instructional intervention (hopefully after a pilot test), the computer format for the assessment and instruction content must be finalized. This is followed by content creation. There are quite a few formats which have been used to represent and apply computerized instruction. Many examples are given in [29].

For cybersecurity, the domain is evolving quickly, and new attack and defense approaches are being tried. The computer representation should be designed with this nature of the domain in mind; the computer representation should be simple in order to support flexibility.

To conduct cybersecurity CTA, it would be valuable to embed the SMEs within a testbed for observing cybersecurity tools and techniques. If possible, for the study of cyber-defense, one expert could be the cyber-defender; another expert could be the cyber-attacker. The cyber-defender would not know what line of attack will be followed, and the attacker will not know the defender's tool or approach. The task analyst would conduct a structured talk-aloud protocol with the two cyber SMEs. One description of such a talk aloud protocol is described in [38].

6. Test the completed instruction to observe and revise instructional weaknesses.

   After creating the instruction, test it with a few participants to identify weaknesses in the content that need to be revised before wide deployment. This is ideally done before conducting a full test of instructional effectiveness. The instruction should be revised based on the results from this test.

7. Test the completed instruction for full instructional effectiveness.

   After the content has been reviewed with a few participants, test the entire course for instructional effectiveness. The test should use a sufficient number of participants to reasonably assess instructional effectiveness. Ideally, this would be conducted within an experiment designed to report the effectiveness of this instruction.

   Ideally, the test of instructional effectiveness would be designed so that much of it could be used repeatedly; it would be ideal if the assessment of the instruction could be repeated regularly.

8. Once the instruction is deployed, monitor it for continued effectiveness.

   Once the system is deployed, monitor its effectiveness. Internal measures of learner progress through the instruction should provide information whether the training is proving to be effective. Try to get measures from the field of the practical skill of trainees who have worked through the instruction. Use these indicators to design revisions and improvements to the instruction.

6.5 Using Big Data to Inform Cybersecurity Training

In describing how big data should be applied to cybersecurity training, we will begin by looking at how data is used now, and then consider how big data can improve cybersecurity training.

Data is used to establish the capabilities of workers as they complete their tasks. In cybersecurity, analysts' performance in maintaining security and investigating attacks can be measured with two kinds of measures: first is data that reveals the overall success of cybersecurity operations; second is more detailed data that reveals processes used by cybersecurity personnel. If performance is constantly being monitored and an instructional intervention (or a new tool) is provided to cyber-analysts, the resultant change in performance can be linked to the changes from newly acquired training or tools.

Monitoring performance of cyber-analysts as they conduct their work can lead to a cycle of improved effectiveness. Data is collected, which initially establishes a baseline. An intervention is introduced while all else stays the same. Continual monitoring of performance reveals how performance is changed by the intervention. This performance can inspire another intervention—ideally, the change selected would yield the biggest performance improvement for the lowest cost. The next change would, given the current situation, again yield the biggest change from the current situation for the lowest cost.

Besides the overall outcome performance change as a result of new training or tools, another use in using data is to examine details of processes used by workers who received new training. For example, if a training improvement leads defensive cyber analysts to inspect the computers in a network that have a newly discovered vulnerability first, outcome measures would assess if the training led to improved cyber-defense (if the monitors wanted to be sure that the change was due to the new training intervention and not a change in the kind of attacks the network receives, comparison to a network supported by cyber-defenders who did not receive the new training could be used as an experimental control group). Process data could be investigated in more detail to see if trainees followed the guidance they received from the training by tracking details of how they responded to attacks.

Big data is perfect for examining both outcome and process effects of training. Big data can be applied to the two big questions addressed above: monitoring of current performance, and process changes in how workers execute their tasks differently following training.

In a report for the U.S. Army, Ososky et al. [39] foresee two uses for big data and training. The first is to collect overall effectiveness measures of each worker. As data of workers' performance will be collected as they do their jobs, big data could be used to reveal their overall effectiveness.

Collecting and analyzing big data to assess overall effectiveness and worker experiences informs targets for instruction. In a cybersecurity context, the data that assesses overall competencies might reveal that trained cyber-defenders are excellent at one task (e.g., recovery after malware has been detected) but perform worse than expected or desired at a second task (e.g., identifying the origin of an intrusion). Big data could reveal which training, life experience, or other characteristics of workers differentiates highly successful performers from less successful performers. Additionally, each worker would know how well he or she performs relative to other workers. Training decision makers would use big data to adjust training content, experiences, and emphasis. Big data informs improvement in the large-scale design of courses.

The second use of big data is to collect very detailed data of the processes that trainees used while interacting with a training system. The training systems would, using big data capabilities, collect very detailed accounts of training system efficiency. If big data reveals that training on a topic is inefficient, then a solution would seek to improve the effectiveness of training on that topic. A second result might be that workers are learning about intrusion detection efficiently, but they just need more training time to become as proficient as needed.

Big data that examines the relationships across trainee behaviors, instructional system interactions, and assessment that shows trainee improvement will reveal if trainees are actually improving at some skills or knowledge as expected by the instruction plan. Collecting big data of trainee interactions can answer questions of training efficiency.

When using big data to inform training effectiveness and efficiency, there are a few classic problems with data to which big data is susceptible. Big data may not collect the data that illuminates the factors that lead to correct conclusions. A cautionary tale about the use of big data came from a study of the worst places to live in America [40]. In this article, a *Washington Post* reporter, Christopher Ingraham, had used a variety of variables to identify good and poor places to live. Example factors included were economic conditions, educational attainment, crime, climate, and cultural diversity. Based on these factors, Red Lake Falls, Minnesota was ranked the worst place to live in America. The townspeople of Red Lake Falls invited Ingraham to visit their city. He took them up on their offer, and visited Red Lake Falls. He enjoyed it so much, he moved there, as described in the referenced article. The data collected about the town did not include factors that were actually important to Ingraham, such as the friendliness of the people in the town or the quality of life that his two young boys enjoyed as they explored the town.

As applied to training and cybersecurity, data must include those factors that enable analysts to make correct judgments about network cybersecurity. For example, big data may capture the number of network intrusions, but not the methods that led to successful intrusions. To guide training improvement, the data must be sufficiently rich to capture the details that are critical to successful or unsuccessful intrusion detection. Big data will collect data that can be collected; but it should not miss the pertinent data. Experts that understand cybersecurity processes and analysis of big data will be required to use the data collected to make beneficial interpretations of data for training.

Additionally, big data can contribute in two more ways to training cybersecurity analysts, though these contributions go beyond training. First, big data can monitor the types of cybersecurity tactics used by opponents. This can inform what analysts should be trained in, as well as what kinds of tools and tactics should be used by cybersecurity analysts. Second, big data is used to visualize a computer network, including its currently understood vulnerability and current state. Big data visualization should be used in training and by cybersecurity analysts as they perform their real-world tasks.

6.6 Conclusions

This chapter, if successful, should lead the reader to see that training goes far beyond the presentation of information, or interacting with a simulation. Effective training requires interactions that engage trainees with concepts that they apply to their tasks and lead them to deeply understand not only actions they take, but why other tasks that they could take will be less successful than the preferred task.

Simulations and games can be a great environment for learning, and they should be used with applications of good learning principles for maximum effect.

Developing training is a technical enterprise in defining the right content and presenting it effectively and efficiently to trainees. Developing training is also a social and business enterprise that involves managing relationships with sponsors, users, and existing training professionals, all of who have idiosyncratic perspectives based on their personal learning and training history. Creating the best training for the available funds requires attention to both technical and social factors.

Big data in cybersecurity will undoubtedly have large consequences in the near term future of training cybersecurity. Big data will influence the visualization which cybersecurity analysts use and are trained with. Use of big data in training cybersecurity analysts also has a responsibility to the future use of big data in training. Cybersecurity is an ideal domain in which to collect big data. The environment in which cybersecurity plays out is an electronic network with tremendous amounts of available data; big data abounds in computer networks. Big data is not as easily available in interactions that are not electronic. For example, healthcare, childhood education, and business interactions involve many face to face communications that are not tracked electronically. Training in cybersecurity should use carefully and analytically applied big data in order to illustrate the benefits of big data for learning and performance improvement. The benefits of big data for training can be illustrated in cybersecurity training, which can then serve as a model for other domains.

References

1. Shute, V. (2008). Focus on Formative Feedback. *Review of Educational Research*, 153–189.
2. Zaguri, Y., & Gal, E. (2016). An Optimization of Human Performance Technology Intervention Selection Model: A 360-Degree Approach to Support Performance. *Performance Improvement*, 55(6), 25–31.
3. Bransford, J., Brown, A., & Cocking, R. (2000). *How People Learn: Brain, Mind, Experience, and School.* Washington, D.C.: National Academy Press.
4. Ben-Asher, N., & Gonzalez, C. (2015). Effects of Cyber Security Knowledge on Attack Detection. *Computers in Human Behavior*, 51–61.
5. Lajoie, S., Guerrera, D., Muncie, S., & Lavigne, N. (2001). Constructing Knowledge in the Context of BioWorld. *Instructional Science*, 29(2), 155–186.
6. Chi, M. (2009). Active-Constructive-Interactive: A Conceptual Framework for Differentiating Learning Activities. *Topics in Cognitive Science*, 1(1), 1–33.
7. Abawajy, J. (2014). User Preference of Cyber Security Awareness Delivery Methods. *Behavior and Information Technology*, 236–247.
8. Wilson, B., Jonassen, D., & Cole, P. (1993). Cognitive approaches to instructional design. In G. Piskurich, Ed., *The ASTD Handbook of Instructional Technology.* New York: McGraw-Hill, pp. 1–21.

9. Lave, J., & Wenger, E. (1991). *Situated Learning Legitimate Peripheral Participation.* Cambridge: Cambridge University Press.
10. Jonaguchi, T., & Hirashima, T. (2005). Graph of Microworlds: A Framework for Assisting Progressive Knowledge Acquisition in Simulation-based Learning Environments. *Artificial Intelligence in Education.* Amsterdam, the Netherlands.
11. Fite, B. (2014, February 11). SANS Institute InfoSec Reading Room. Retrieved from https://www.sans.org/reading-room/whitepapers/bestprac/simulating-cyber-operations-cyber-security-training-framework-34510.
12. Thompson, M., & Irvine, C. (2015, September). CyberCIEGE: A Video Game for Constructive Cyber Security Education. *Call Signs*, pp. 4–8.
13. Minstrell, J. (1989). Teaching Science for Understanding. In L. Resnick, & L. Klopfer, Eds., *Toward the Thinking Curriculum: Current Cognitive Research.* Alexandria, VA: Association of Supervision and Curriculum Develoment, pp. 129–149.
14. Leonard, M., Kalnowski, S., & Andrews, T. (2014). Misconceptions Yesterday Today and Tomorrow. *CBE—Life Sciences Education*, 13, 179–186.
15. Prins, F., Veenman, M., & Eishout, J. (2006). The Impact of Intellectual Ability and Metacognition on Learning New Support for the Threshold of Problematicity Theory. *Learning and Instruction*, 16, 374–387.
16. Rosen, M. S. (2008). Promoting Teamwork: An Event-based Approach to Simulation-based Teamwork Training for Emergency Medicine Residents. *Academic Emergency Medicine*, 15, 1190–1198.
17. Mason, R. (2005). The Assessment of Workplace Learning. In *Handbook of Corporate University Development.* Gower, pp. 181–192.
18. Sack, W., Soloway, E., & Weingrad, P. (1993). Re: Writing Cartesian Student Models. *Journal of Artificial Intelligence in Education*, 3(4).
19. van Merrienboer, J., & Ayres, P. (2005). Research on Cognitive Load Theory and its Design Implications for e-Learning. *Educational Technology Research and Development*, 5–13.
20. Keller, J. (2009). *Motivational Design for Learning and Performance.* New York: Springer.
21. Baker, R., D'Mello, S., Rodrigo, M., & Graesser, A. (2010). Better to be Frustrated than Bored: The Incidence, Persistence, and Impact of Learners' Cognitive-Affective States During Interactions with Three Different Computer-Based Learning Environments. *International Journal of Human-Computer Studies*, 68(4), 223–241.
22. Tirri, K., & Kujala, T. (2016). Students' Mindsets for Learning and Their Neural Underpinnings. *Psychology*, 1231.
23. National Research Council. (2004). *How People Learn: Brain, Mind, Experience, and School.* Washington, DC: National Academy Press.
24. Lucariello, J., & Naff, D. (2016). How Do I Get My Students Over Their Alternative Conceptions (Misconceptions) for Learning? (American Psychological Association) Retrieved October 3, 2016, from American Psychological Association: http://www.apa.org/education/k12/misconceptions.aspx.
25. Crandell, B., & Hoffman, R. (2013). Cognitive Task Analysis. In J. Lee, & A. Lirlik, Eds., *Oxford Handbook of Cognitive Engineering.* Oxford: Oxford University Press, pp. 229–239.
26. Hoffman, R. (2008). Human Factors Contributions to Knowledge Elicitation. *Human Factors*, 481–488.

27. Koedinger, K., Corbett, A., & Perfetti, C. (2012). The Knowledge-Learning-Instruction (KLI Framework: Toward Bridging the Science-Practice Chasm to Enhance Robust Student Learning). *Cognitive Science*, 757–798.
28. Army Research Laboratory. (2016). Documents. Retrieved from ARL GIFT: https://gifttutoring.org/projects/gift/documents.
29. Woolf, B. (2010). *Building Intelligent Interactive Tutors: Student-centered Strategies for Revolutionizing e-Learning.* Morgan Kaufmann.
30. Brusilovsky, P., & Millan, E. (2007). User Models for Adaptive Hypermedia and Adaptive Edcuational Systems. In *The Adaptive Web*. Berlin: Springer-Verlag, pp. 3–53.
31. Ohlsson, S. (2016). Constraint-Based Modeling: From Cognitive Theory to Computer Tutoring—and Back Again. *International Journal of Artificial Intelligent in Education,* 457–473.
32. Mitrovic, A., & Ohlsson, S. (2016). Implementing CBM: SQL-Tutor after Fifteen Years. *International Journal of Artificial Intelligence in Education*, 150–159.
33. Lesgold, A., & Nahemow, M. (2001). Tools to Assist Learning by Doing: Achieving and Assessing Efficient Technology for Learning. In D. Klahr, & S. Carver, Eds., *Cognition and Instruction: Twenty-five Years of Progress.* Mahwah, NJ: Erlbaum, pp. 307–346.
34. Snyder, C. (2003). *Paper Prototyping: The Fast and Easy Way to Design and Refine User Interfaces.* San Francisco: Morgan Kaufmann.
35. Dodge, R., Toregas, C., & Hoffman, L. (2012). Cybersecurity Workforce Development Directions. *Sixth International Symposium on Human Aspects of Information Security and Assurance.* Crete, Greece.
36. Toth, P., & Klein, P. (2014). *A Role-Based Model for Federal Information Technology/Cyber-Security Training.* Gaithersburg, MD: National Institute for Science and Technology.
37. Furfarao, A., Piccolo, A., & Sacca, D. (2016). SmallWorld: A Test and Training System for Cyber-Security. *European Scientific Journal,* 1857–1881.
38. Hall, E., Gott, S., & Pokorny, B. (1995). *A Procedure Guide to Cognitive Task Analysis: The PARI Methodology.* San Antonio, TX: Air Force Armstrong Laboratory.
39. Ososky, S., Sottilare, R., Brawner, K., Long, R., & Graesser, A. (2015). *Authoring Tools and Methods for Adaptive Training and Education in Support of the U.S. Army Learning Model.* Aberdeen Proving Ground: Army Research Laboratory.
40. Washington Post. (2016, August 23). What Life Is Really Like in "America's Worst Place to Live." Retrieved from *Washington Post*: https://www.washingtonpost.com/news/wonk/wp/2016/08/23/what-life-is-really-like-in-americas-worst-place-to-live/.

Chapter 7

Machine Unlearning: Repairing Learning Models in Adversarial Environments

Yinzhi Cao

Contents

Today's systems produce a rapidly exploding amount of data, and the data further derives more data, forming a complex data propagation network that we call the data's lineage. There are many reasons that users want systems to forget certain data including its lineage. From a privacy perspective, users who become concerned with new privacy risks of a system often want the system to forget their data and lineage. From a security perspective, if an attacker pollutes an anomaly detector by injecting manually crafted data into the training data set, the detector must forget the injected data to regain security. From a usability perspective, a user can remove noise and incorrect entries so that a recommendation engine gives useful recommendations. Therefore, we envision forgetting systems, capable of forgetting certain data and their lineages, completely and quickly.

In this chapter, we introduce machine unlearning, or simply unlearning, capable of forgetting certain data and their lineages in learning models completely and quickly. We present a general, efficient unlearning approach by transforming learning algorithms used by a system into a summation form. To forget a training data sample, our approach simply updates a small number of summations—asymptotically faster than retraining from scratch. Such an approach is general because the summation form is from the statistical query learning in which many machine learning algorithms can be implemented. Such an approach also applies to all stages of machine learning, including feature selection and modeling.

7.1 Introduction

7.1.1 The Need for Systems to Forget

Today's systems produce a rapidly exploding amount of data, ranging from personal photos and office documents to logs of user clicks on a website or mobile device [1].

From this data, the systems perform a myriad of computations to derive even more data. For instance, backup systems copy data from one place (e.g., a mobile device) to another (e.g., the cloud). Photo storage systems re-encode a photo into different formats and sizes [2,3]. Analytics systems aggregate raw data such as click logs into insightful statistics. Machine learning systems extract models and properties (e.g., the similarities of movies) from training data (e.g., historical movie ratings) using advanced algorithms. This derived data can recursively derive more data, such as a recommendation system predicting a user's rating of a movie based on movie similarities. In short, a piece of raw data in today's systems often goes through a series of computations, "creeping" into many places and appearing in many forms. The data, computations, and derived data together form a complex data propagation network that we call the data's lineage.

For a variety of reasons, users want a system to forget certain sensitive data and its complete lineage. Consider privacy first. After Facebook changed its privacy policy, many users deleted their accounts and the associated data [4]. The iCloud photo hacking incident [5] led to online articles teaching users how to completely delete iOS photos including the backups [6]. New privacy research revealed that machine learning models for personalized warfarin dosing leak patients' genetic markers [7], and a small set of statistics on genetics and diseases suffices to identify individuals [8]. Users unhappy with these newfound risks naturally want their data and its influence on the models and statistics to be completely forgotten. System operators or service providers have strong incentives to honor users' requests to forget data, both to keep users happy and to comply with the law [9]. For instance, Google had removed 171,183 links [10] by October 2014 under the "right to be forgotten" ruling of the highest court in the European Union.

Security is another reason that users want data to be forgotten. Consider anomaly detection systems. The security of these systems hinges on the model of normal behaviors extracted from the training data. By polluting* the training data, attackers pollute the model, thus compromising security. For instance, Perdisci et al. [11] show that PolyGraph [12], a worm detection engine, fails to generate useful worm signatures if the training data is injected with well-crafted fake network flows. Once the polluted data is identified, the system must completely forget the data and its lineage to regain security.

Usability is a third reason. Consider the recommendation or prediction system Google Now [13]. It infers a user's preferences from his or her search history, browsing history, and other analytics. It then pushes recommendations, such as news about a show, to the user. Noise or incorrect entries in analytics can seriously degrade the quality of the recommendation. One of our lab members experienced this problem first-hand. He loaned his laptop to a friend who searched for a TV show ("Jeopardy!") on Google [14]. He then kept getting news about this show on his phone, even after he deleted the search record from his search history.

* In this chapter, we use the term pollute [11] instead of poison [15,16].

We believe that systems must be designed under the core principle of completely and quickly forgetting sensitive data and its lineage for restoring privacy, security, and usability. Such forgetting systems must carefully track data lineage even across statistical processing or machine learning, and make this lineage visible to users. They let users specify the data to forget with different levels of granularity. For instance, a privacy-conscious user who accidentally searches for a sensitive keyword without concealing his or her identity can request that the search engine forget that particular search record. These systems then remove the data and revert its effects so that all future operations run as if the data had never existed. They collaborate to forget data if the lineage spans across system boundaries (e.g., in the context of web mashup services). This collaborative forgetting potentially scales to the entire Web. Users trust forgetting systems to comply with requests to forget because the aforementioned service providers have strong incentives to comply, but other trust models are also possible. The usefulness of forgetting systems can be evaluated with two metrics: how completely they can forget data (completeness) and how quickly they can do so (timeliness). The higher these metrics, the better the systems at restoring privacy, security, and usability.

Forgetting systems can be easily adopted because they benefit both users and service providers. With the flexibility to request that systems forget data, users have more control over their data, so they are more willing to share data with the systems. More data also benefits the service providers because they have more profit opportunity services and fewer legal risks. In addition, we envision forgetting systems playing a crucial role in emerging data markets [17–19] where users trade data for money, services, or other data because the mechanism of forgetting enables a user to cleanly cancel a data transaction or rent out the use rights of his or her data without giving up the ownership.

Forgetting systems are complementary to much existing work [12,20,21]. Systems such as Google Search [22] can forget a user's raw data upon request, but they ignore the lineage. Secure deletion [23–25] prevents deleted data from being recovered from the storage media, but it largely ignores the lineage, too. Information flow control [26,27] can be leveraged by forgetting systems to track data lineage. However, it typically tracks only direct data duplication, not statistical processing or machine learning, to avoid taint explosion. Differential privacy [20,21] preserves the privacy of each individual item in a data set equally and invariably by restricting accesses only to the whole data set's statistics fuzzed with noise. This restriction is at odds with today's systems such as Facebook and Google Search which, authorized by billions of users, routinely access personal data for accurate results. Unsurprisingly, it is impossible to strike a balance between utility and privacy in state-of-the-art implementations [7]. In contrast, forgetting systems aim to restore privacy on select data. Although private data may still propagate, the lineage of this data within the forgetting systems is carefully tracked and removed completely and in a timely manner upon request. In addition, this fine-grained data removal caters to an individual user's privacy consciousness and the data item's sensitivity.

Forgetting systems conform to the trust and usage models of today's systems, representing a more practical privacy versus utility tradeoff. Researchers also proposed mechanisms to make systems more robust against training data pollution [12,28]. However, despite these mechanisms (and the others discussed thus far such as differential privacy), users may still request systems to forget data due to, for example, policy changes and new attacks against the mechanisms [7,11]. These requests can be served only by forgetting systems.

7.1.2 Machine Unlearning

While there are numerous challenges in making systems forget, this chapter focuses on one of the most difficult challenges: making machine learning systems forget. These systems extract features and models from training data to answer questions about new data. They are widely used in many areas of science [12,29–35]. To forget a piece of training data completely, these systems need to revert the effects of the data on the extracted features and models. We call this process *machine unlearning*, or *unlearning* for short. A naive approach to unlearning is to retrain the features and models from scratch after removing the data to forget. However, when the set of training data is large, this approach is quite slow, increasing the timing window during which the system is vulnerable.

We present a general approach to efficient unlearning, without retraining from scratch, for a variety of machine learning algorithms widely used in real-world systems. To prepare for unlearning, we transform learning algorithms in a system to a form consisting of a small number of summations [36]. Each summation is the sum of some efficiently computable transformation of the training data samples. The learning algorithms depend only on the summations, not individual data. These summations are saved together with the trained model. (The rest of the system may still ask for individual data and there is no injected noise as there is in differential privacy.) Then, in the unlearning process, we subtract the data to forget from each summation, and then update the model. As Figure 7.1 illustrates, forgetting a data item now requires recomputing only a small number of terms, asymptotically faster than retraining from scratch by a factor equal to the size of the training data set. It is general because the summation form is from statistical query (SQ) learning [37]. Many machine learning algorithms, such as naive Bayes classifiers, support vector machines, and k-means clustering, can be implemented as SQ learning. Our approach also applies to all stages of machine learning, including feature selection and modeling.

While prior work proposed incremental machine learning for several specific learning algorithms [38–40], the key difference is that unlearning is a general efficient unlearning approach applicable to any algorithm that can be converted to the summation form, including some that currently have no incremental versions, such as normalized cosine similarity and one-class SVM. In addition, the unlearning approach handles all stages of learning, including feature selection and modeling approach on real systems.

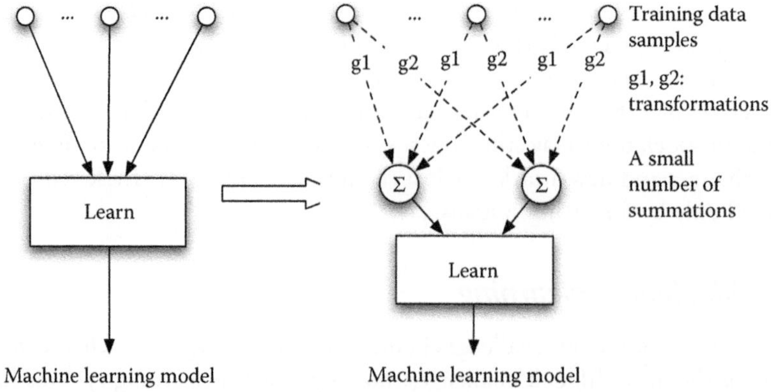

Figure 7.1 *Unlearning idea.* **Instead of making a model directly depend on each training data sample (left), we convert the learning algorithm into a summation form (right). Specifically, each summation is the sum of transformed data samples, where the transformation functions g_i are efficiently computable. There are only a small number of summations, and the learning algorithm depends only on summations. To forget a data sample, we simply update the summations and then compute the updated model. This approach is asymptotically much faster than retraining from scratch.**

7.1.3 Chapter Organization

The rest of the chapter is organized as follows. In Section 7.2, we present some background on machine learning systems and the extended motivation of unlearning. In Section 7.3, we present the goals and work flow of unlearning. In Section 7.4, we present the core approach of unlearning, i.e., transforming a system into the summation form, and its formal backbone. In Section 7.5, we report one case study on LensKit. In Section 7.6, we discuss related work.

7.2 Background and Adversarial Model

This section presents some background on machine learning (Section 7.2.1) and the extended motivation of unlearning (Section 7.2.2).

7.2.1 Machine Learning Background

Figure 7.2 shows a general machine learning system with three processing stages.

Feature selection. During this stage, the system selects, from all features of the training data, a set of features most crucial for classifying data. The selected feature set is typically small to make later stages more accurate and efficient.

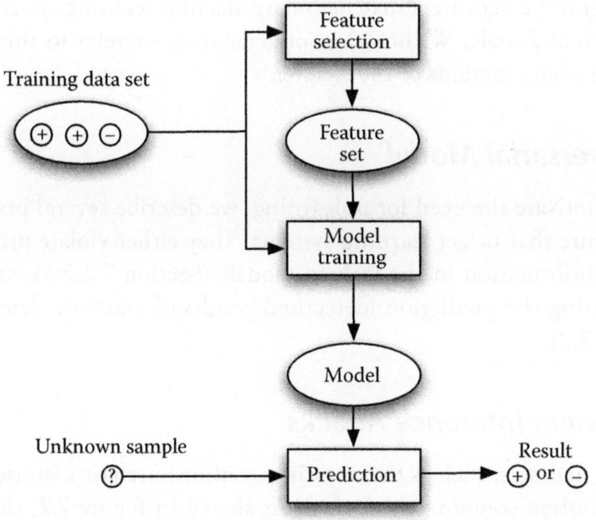

Figure 7.2 ***A general machine learning system.*** **Given a set of training data including both malicious (+) and benign (–) samples, the system first selects a set of features most crucial for classifying data. It then uses the training data to construct a model. To process an unknown sample, the system examines the features in the sample and uses the model to predict the sample as malicious or benign. The lineage of the training data thus flows to the feature set, the model, and the prediction results. An attacker can feed different samples to the model and observe the results to steal private information from every step along the lineage, including the training data set (system inference attack). The attacker can pollute the training data and subsequently every step along the lineage to alter prediction results (training data pollution attack).**

Feature selection can be (1) manual where system builders carefully craft the feature set or (2) automatic where the system runs some learning algorithms such as clustering and chi-squared test to compute how crucial the features are and select the most crucial ones.

Model training. The system extracts the values of the selected features from each training data sample into a feature vector. It feeds the feature vectors and the malicious or benign labels of all training data samples into some machine learning algorithm to construct a succinct model.

Prediction. When the system receives an unknown data sample, it extracts the sample's feature vector and uses the model to predict whether the sample is malicious or benign.

Note that a learning system may or may not contain all three stages, work with labeled training data, or classify data as malicious or benign. We present the system in Figure 7.2 because it matches many machine learning systems for security purposes such as Zozzle. Without loss of generality, we refer to this system as an example in the later sections of the chapter.

7.2.2 Adversarial Model

To further motivate the need for unlearning, we describe several practical attacks in the literature that target learning systems. They either violate privacy by inferring private information in the trained models (Section 7.2.2.1), or reduce security by polluting the prediction (detection) results of anomaly detection systems (Section 7.2.2.2).

7.2.2.1 System Inference Attacks

The training data sets, such as movie ratings, online purchase histories, and browsing histories, often contain private data. As shown in Figure 7.2, the private data lineage flows through the machine learning algorithms into the feature set, the model, and the prediction results. By exploiting this lineage, an attacker gains an opportunity to infer private data by feeding samples into the system and observing the prediction results. Such an attack is called a system inference attack [41].*

Consider a recommendation system that uses item-item collaborative filtering which learns item-item similarities from users' purchase histories and recommends to a user the items most similar to the ones he or she previously purchased. Calandrino et al. [41] show that once an attacker learns (1) the item-item similarities, (2) the list of recommended items for a user before he or she purchased an item, and (3) the list after, the attacker can accurately infer what the user purchased by essentially inverting the computation done by the recommendation algorithm. For example, on LibraryThing [42], a book cataloging service and recommendation engine, this attack successfully inferred six book purchases per user with 90% accuracy for over one million users!

Similarly, consider a personalized warfarin dosing system that guides medical treatments based on a patient's genotype and background. Fredrikson et al. [7] show that with the model and some demographic information about a patient, an attacker can infer the genetic markers of the patient with accuracy as high as 75%.

7.2.2.2 Training Data Pollution Attacks

Another way to exploit the lineage in Figure 7.2 is using training data pollution attacks. An attacker injects carefully polluted data samples into a learning system, misleading the algorithms to compute an incorrect feature set and model. Subsequently, when processing unknown samples, the system may flag a big

* In this chapter, we use system inference instead of model inversion [7].

number of benign samples as malicious and generate too many false positives, or it may flag a big number of malicious samples as benign so the true malicious samples evade detection.

Unlike system inference in which an attacker exploits an easy-to-access public interface of a learning system, data pollution requires an attacker to tackle two relatively difficult issues. First, the attacker must trick the learning system into including the polluted samples in the training data set. There are a number of reported ways to do so [11,16,43]. For instance, the attacker may sign up as a crowdsourcing worker and intentionally mislabel benign emails as spam [16]. He or she may also attack the honeypots or other baiting traps intended for collecting malicious samples, such as sending polluted emails to a spamtrap [44], or compromising a machine in a honeynet and sending packets with polluted protocol header fields [11].

Second, the attacker must carefully pollute enough data to mislead the machine learning algorithms. In the crowdsourcing case, the administrator of the crowdsourcing sites directly pollutes the labels of some training data [16]. Approximately 3% mislabeled training data turned out to be enough to significantly decrease detection efficacy. In the honeypot cases [11,44], the attacker cannot change the labels of the polluted data samples because the honeypot automatically labels them as malicious. However, the attacker controls what features appear in the samples, so he or she can inject benign features into these samples, misleading the system into relying on these features for detecting malicious samples. For instance, Nelson et al. injected words that also occur in benign emails into the emails sent to a spamtrap, causing a spam detector to classify 60% of the benign emails as spam. Perdisci et al. injected many packets with the same randomly generated strings into a honeynet, so that true malicious packets without these strings evade detection.

7.3 Overview

This section presents the goals (Section 7.3.1) and work flow (Section 7.3.2) of machine learning.

7.3.1 Unlearning Goals

Recall that forgetting systems have two goals: (1) completeness, or how completely they can forget data, and (2) timeliness, or how quickly they can forget. We discuss what these goals mean in the context of unlearning.

7.3.1.1 Completeness

Intuitively, completeness requires that once a data sample is removed, all its effects on the feature set and the model are also cleanly reversed. It essentially captures how consistent an unlearned system is with the system that has been retrained from scratch. If, for every possible sample, the unlearned system gives the same prediction result as the retrained system, then an attacker, operator, or user has no way of discovering that the unlearned data and its lineage existed in the system by feeding input samples to the unlearned system or even observing its features, model, and training data. Such unlearning is complete. To empirically measure completeness, we quantify the percentage of input samples that receive the same prediction results from both the unlearned and the retrained system using a representative test data set. The higher the percentage, the more complete the unlearning. Note that completeness does not depend on the correctness of prediction results: an incorrect but consistent prediction by both systems does not decrease completeness.

Our notion of completeness is subject to such factors as how representative the test data set is and whether the learning algorithm is randomized. In particular, given the same training data set, the same randomized learning algorithm may compute different models which subsequently predict differently. Thus, we consider unlearning complete as long as the unlearned system is consistent with one of the retrained systems.

7.3.1.2 Timeliness

Timeliness in unlearning captures how much faster unlearning is than retraining at updating the features and the model in the system. The more timely the unlearning, the faster the system is at restoring privacy, security, and usability. Analytically, unlearning updates only a small number of summations and then runs a learning algorithm on these summations, whereas retraining runs the learning algorithm on the entire training data set, so unlearning is asymptotically faster by a factor of the training data size. To empirically measure timeliness, we quantify the speedup of unlearning over retraining. Unlearning does not replace retraining. Unlearning works better when the data to forget is small compared to the training set. This case is quite common. For instance, a single user's private data is typically small compared to the whole training data of all users. Similarly, an attacker needs only a small amount of data to pollute a learning system. When the data to forget becomes large, retraining may work better.

7.3.2 Unlearning Work Flow

Given a training data sample to forget, unlearning updates the system in two steps, following the learning process shown in Figure 7.2. First, it updates the set of selected features. The inputs at this step are the sample to forget, the old feature set, and the summations previously computed for deriving the old feature set. The outputs are the updated feature set and summations. For example, Zozzle [30], a JavaScript malware detection engine, selects features using the chi-squared test, which scores a feature based on four counts (the simplest form of summations):

how many malicious or benign samples contain or do not contain this feature. To support unlearning, we can augment Zozzle to store the score and these counts for each feature. To unlearn a sample, we can update these counts to exclude this sample, rescore the features, and select the top scored features as the updated feature set. This process does not depend on the training data set, and is much faster than retraining which has to inspect each sample for each feature. The updated feature set in our experiments is very similar to the old one with a couple of features removed and added.

Second, unlearning updates the model. The inputs at this step are the sample to forget, the old feature set, the updated feature set, the old model, and the summations previously computed for deriving the old model. The outputs are the updated model and summations. If a feature is removed from the feature set, we simply splice out the feature's data from the model. If a feature is added, we compute its data in the model. In addition, we update summations that depend on the sample to forget, and update the model accordingly. For Zozzle which classifies data as malicious or benign using naive Bayes, the summations are probabilities (e.g., the probability that a training data sample is malicious given that it contains a certain feature) computed using the counts recorded in the first step. Updating the probabilities and the model is thus straightforward, and much faster than retraining.

7.4 Unlearning Approach

As previously depicted in Figure 7.1, the unlearning approach introduces a layer of a small number of summations between the learning algorithm and the training data to break down the dependencies. Now, the learning algorithm depends only on the summations, each of which is the sum of some efficiently computable transformations of the training data samples. Chu et al. [36] show that many popular machine learning algorithms, such as naive Bayes, can be represented in this form. To remove a data sample, we simply remove the transformations of this data sample from the summations that depend on this sample, which has $O(1)$ complexity, and compute the updated model. This approach is asymptotically faster than retraining from scratch.

More formally, the summation form follows statistical query (SQ) learning [37]. SQ learning forbids a learning algorithm from querying individual training data samples. Instead, it permits the algorithm to query only statistics about the training data through an oracle. Specifically, the algorithm sends a function $g(x,l_x)$ to the oracle where x is a training data sample, l_x is the corresponding label, and g is an efficiently computable function. Then, the oracle answers an estimated expectation of $g(x,l_x)$ over all training data. The algorithm repeatedly queries the oracle, potentially with different g-functions, until it terminates.

Depending on whether all SQs that an algorithm issues are determined upfront, SQ learning can be nonadaptive (all SQs are determined upfront before the algorithm starts) or adaptive (later SQs may depend on earlier SQ results). These two different types of SQ learning require different ways to unlearn, described in the following two subsections.

7.4.1 Nonadaptive SQ Learning

A nonadaptive SQ learning algorithm must determine all SQs upfront. It follows that the number of these SQs is constant, denoted m, and the transformation g-functions are fixed, denoted $g_1, g_2, \ldots, g_m$. We represent the algorithm in the following form:

$$Learn\left(\sum_{x_i \in X} g_1(x_i, l_{x_i}), \sum_{x_i \in X} g_2(x_i, l_{x_i}), \ldots, \sum_{x_i \in X} g_m(x_i, l_{x_i})\right)$$

where x_i is a training data sample and l_{x_i} is its label. This form encompasses many popular machine learning algorithms, including linear regression, chi-squared test, and naive Bayes.

With this form, unlearning is as follows. Let G_k be $\sum g_k(x_i, l_{x_i})$. All G_ks are saved together with the learned model. To unlearn a data sample x_p, we compute G_k' as $G_k - g_k(x_p, l_{x_p})$. The updated model is thus

$$Learn\left(G_1 - g_1(x_p, l_{x_p}), G_2 - g_2(x_p, l_{x_p}), \ldots, G_m - g_m(x_p, l_{x_p})\right)$$

Unlearning on a nonadaptive SQ learning algorithm is complete because this updated model is identical to

$$Learn\left(\sum_{i \neq p} g_1(x_i, l_{x_i}), \sum_{i \neq p} g_2(x_i, l_{x_i}), \ldots, \sum_{i \neq p} g_m(x_i, l_{x_i})\right)$$

the model computed by retraining on the training data excluding x_p. For timeliness, it is also much faster than retraining because (1) computing G_k' is easy: simply subtract $g_k(x_p, l_{x_p})$ from G_k and (2) there are only a constant number of summations G_k.

We now illustrate how to convert a nonadaptive SQ learning algorithm into this summation form using naive Bayes as an example. Given a sample with features

F_1, F_2, ..., and F_k, naive Bayes classifies the sample with label L if $P(L|F_1,..., F_k)$, the conditional probability of observing label L on a training data sample with all these features, is bigger than this conditional probability for any other label. This conditional probability is computed using Equation 7.1.

$$P\left(L|F_1,\dots,F_k\right)=\frac{P(L)\prod_{i=0}^{k}P\left(F_i|L\right)}{\prod_{i=0}^{k}P(F_i)} \tag{7.1}$$

We now convert each probability term P in this equation into summations. Consider $P(F_i|L)$ as an example. It is computed by taking (1) the number of training data samples with feature F_i and label L, denoted $N_{F_i,L}$, and dividing by (2) the number of training data samples with label L, denoted N_l. Each counter is essentially a very simple summation of a function that returns 1 when a sample should be counted and 0 otherwise. For instance, N_l is the sum of an indicator function $g_l(x,lx)$ that returns 1 when l_x is L and 0 otherwise. Similarly, all other probability terms are computed by dividing the corresponding two counters. $P(L)$ is the division of N_l over the total number of samples, denoted N. $P(F_i)$ is the division of the number of training data samples with the feature F_i, denoted N_{F_i}, over N.

To unlearn a sample, we simply update these counters and recompute the probabilities. For instance, suppose the training sample to unlearn has label L and one feature F_j. After unlearning, $P(F_j|L)$ becomes $\frac{N_{F_jL}-1}{N_L-1}$, and all other $P(F_i|L)$s become $\frac{N_{F_iL}}{N_L-1}$. $P(L)$ becomes $\frac{N_L-1}{N}$. $P(F_j)$ becomes $\frac{N_{F_j}-1}{N-1}$, and all other $P(F_i)$s become $\frac{N_{F_i}}{N-1}$.

7.4.2 Adaptive SQ Learning

An adaptive SQ learning algorithm issues its SQs iteratively on the fly, and later SQs may depend on results of earlier ones. (Nonadaptive SQ learning is a special form of adaptive SQ learning.) Operationally, adaptive SQ learning starts by selecting an initial state s_0, randomly or heuristically. At state s_j, it determines the transformation functions in the SQs based on the current state, sends the SQs to the oracle, receives the results, and learns the next state s_{j+1}. It then repeats until the algorithm converges. During each iteration, the current state suffices for determining the transformation functions because it can capture the entire history starting from s_0. We represent these functions in each state S_j as $g_{s_j,1}, g_{s_j,2}, \ldots, g_{s_j,m}$. Now, the algorithm is in the following form:

(1) S_0: initial state;

(2) $s_{j+1} = Learn\left(\sum_{x_i \in X} g_{s_j,1}(x_i, l_{x_i}), \sum_{x_i \in X} g_{s_j,2}(x_i, l_{x_i}), \ldots, \sum_{x_i \in X} g_{s_j,m}(x_i, l_{x_i})\right)$;

(3) Repeat (2) until the algorithm converges.

The number of iterations required for the algorithm to converge depends on the algorithm, the initial state selected, and the training data. Typically the algorithm is designed to robustly converge under many scenarios. This adaptive form of SQ learning encompasses many popular machine learning algorithms, including gradient descent, SVM, and k-means.

Unlearning this adaptive form is more changing than nonadaptive because, even if we restart from the same initial state, if the training data sample to forget changes one iteration, all subsequent iterations may deviate and require computing from scratch. Fortunately, the insight is that, after removing a sample, the previously converged state often becomes only slightly out of convergence. Thus, unlearning can simply "resume" the iterative learning algorithm from this state on the updated training data set, and it should take much fewer iterations to converge than restarting from the original or a newly generated initial state.

Operationally, the adaptive unlearning approach works as follows. Given the converged state S computed on the original training data set, it removes the contributions of the sample to forget from the summations that *Learn* uses to compute S, similar to unlearning the nonadaptive form. Let the resultant state be S'. Then, it checks whether S' meets the algorithm's convergence condition. If not, it sets S' as the initial state and runs the iterative learning algorithm until it converges.

We now discuss the completeness of the adaptive unlearning approach in three scenarios. First, for algorithms such as SVM that converge at only one state, the approach is complete because the converged state computed from unlearning is the same as that retrained from scratch. Second, for algorithms such as k-means that converge at multiple possible states, the approach is complete if the state S' is a possible initial state selected by the algorithm (e.g., the algorithm selects initial state randomly). A proof sketch is as follows. Since S' is a possible initial state, there is one possible retraining process that starts from S' and reaches a new converged state. At every iteration of this retraining process, the new state computed by *Learn* is identical to the state computed in the corresponding iteration in unlearning. Thus, they must compute the same exact converged state, satisfying the completeness goal (Section 7.3.1.1). Third, the approach may be incomplete if (a) S' cannot be a possible initial state (e.g., the algorithm selects the initial state using a heuristic that happens to rule out S') or (b) the algorithm does not converge or converges at a state different than all possible states retraining converges to. We expect these scenarios to be rare because adaptive algorithms need to be robust anyway for convergence during normal operations.

The adaptive unlearning approach is also timely. The speedup over retraining is twofold. First, unlearning is faster at computing the summations if there are old results of the summations to use. For example, it updates the state S by removing contributions of the removed sample. Second, unlearning starts from an almost-converged state, so it needs fewer iterations to converge than retraining. In practice, we expect that the majority of the speedup comes from the reduced number of iterations. The implication is that, in principle, the adaptive unlearning approach should speed up any robust iterative machine learning algorithm, even if the algorithm does not follow SQ learning. In practice, however, very few practical learning algorithms cannot be converted to the adaptive SQ learning form. Specifically, many machine learning problems can be cast as optimization problems, potentially solvable using gradient descent, an adaptive SQ learning algorithm.

Now, we illustrate how to convert an adaptive SQ learning algorithm into the summation form using k-means clustering as an example. K-means clustering starts from an initial set of randomly selected cluster centers, $c_i,\ldots, c_k$, assigns each data point to a cluster whose center has the shortest Euclidean distance to the point, and then updates each c_i based on the mean value of all the data points in its cluster. It repeats this assignment until the centers no longer change.

To support unlearning, we convert the calculation of each c_i into summations. Because k-means clustering is unsupervised, labels are not involved in the following discussion. Let us define $g_{c_i,j}(x)$ as a function that outputs x when the distance between x and c_i is minimum, and otherwise 0; and define $g'_j(x)$ as a function that outputs 1 when the distance between x and c_i is minimum, and otherwise 0. Now, the new c_i in the $j + 1$ iteration equals $\dfrac{\sum_{x\in X} g_{c_i,j}(x)}{\sum_{x\in X} g'_{c_i,j}(x)}$.

To unlearn a sample x_p, we update $\sum_{x\in X} g_{c_i,j}(x)$ and $\sum_{x\in X} g'_{c_i,j}(x)$ by subtracting $g_{c_i,j}(x_p)$ and $g'_{c_i,j}(x_p)$ from the summations. Then, we continue the iteration process until the algorithm converges.

7.5 Unlearning in LensKit

In this section, we use LensKit [33] as an example to describe the unlearning approach. We start by describing LensKit's recommendation algorithm. Recall that by default it recommends items to users using item-item collaborative filtering [31,33] that computes the similarity of every two items based on user ratings of the items because, intuitively, similar items should receive similar ratings from the same user. Operationally, LensKit starts by constructing a user-item matrix based on historical user ratings of items, where row i stores all ratings given by user i, and column j all ratings received by item j. Then, LensKit normalizes all ratings in the matrix to reduce biases across users and

$$
\begin{aligned}
sim(k,l) &= \frac{\sum_{i=1}^{n} a_{ik}a_{il}}{\sqrt{\sum_{i=1}^{n} a_{ik}^2 \sum_{i=1}^{n} a_{il}^2}} = \frac{\sum_{i=1}^{n}(r_{ik}-\mu_i-\eta_k+g)(r_{il}-\mu_i-\eta_l+g)}{\sqrt{\sum_{i=1}^{n}(r_{ik}-\mu_i-\eta_k+g)^2\sum_{i=1}^{n}(r_{il}-\mu_i-\eta_l+g)^2}} \\
&= \left\{\sum_{i=1}^{n}(r_{ik}-\mu_i)(r_{il}-\mu_i)-\eta_k\sum_{i=1}^{n}(r_{il}-\mu_i)-\eta_l\sum_{i=1}^{n}(r_{ik}-\mu_i)\right. \\
&\quad \left. -g(\eta_k+\eta_l)N+\eta_k\eta_l N+g^2N+g\sum_{i=1}^{n}(r_{ik}+r_{il}-2\mu_i)\right\} \\
&\quad \div\sqrt{\sum_{i=1}^{n}(r_{ik}-\mu_i)^2-2(\eta_k-g)\sum_{i=1}^{n}(r_{ik}-\mu_i)+(\eta_k-g)^2N} \\
&\quad \div\sqrt{\sum_{i=1}^{n}(r_{il}-\mu_i)^2-2(\eta_l-g)\sum_{i=1}^{n}(r_{il}-\mu_i)+(\eta_l-g)^2N} \\
&= \frac{S_{kl}-\eta_k S_l-\eta_l S_k+g(S_k+S_l)-g(\eta_k+\eta_l)N+\eta_k\eta_l N+g^2N}{\sqrt{S_{kk}-2(\eta_k-g)S_k+(\eta_k-g)^2N}\sqrt{S_{ll}-2(\eta_l-g)S_l+(\eta_l-g)^2N}} \\
&= Learn(S_{kl},S_k,S_l,S_{kk},S_{ll},g,\eta_k,\eta_l)
\end{aligned}
\tag{7.4}
$$

items. For instance, one user's average rating may be higher than another user's, but both should contribute equally to the final item-item similarity. Equation 7.2 shows the normalized rating a_{ij} for r_{ij}, user i's original rating of item j, where μ_i is the average of all ratings given by user i, η_j the average of all ratings received by item j, and g is the global average rating.

$$
a_{ij} = \begin{cases} r_{ij}-\mu_i-\eta_j+g & when \quad rij \neq null \\ 0 & when \quad rij = null \end{cases} \tag{7.2}
$$

Based on the normalized user-item rating matrix, LensKit computes an item-item similarity matrix within which the cell at row k and column l represents the similarity between items k and l. Specifically, as shown in Equation 7.3, it computes the cosine similarity between columns k and l in the user-item rating matrix, where $\|\vec{x}\|_2$ represents the Euclidean norm of $\vec{x}$, and $\vec{a}_{*,k}$ is a vector, $(a_{1k}, a_{1k},..., a_{nk})$, representing all the ratings received by item k.

$$sim(k,l) = \frac{\vec{a}_{*,k} \cdot \vec{a}_{*,l}}{\|\vec{a}_{*,k}\|_2 \|\vec{a}_{*,l}\|_2} \tag{7.3}$$

Now, to recommend items to a user, LensKit computes the most similar items to the items previously rated by the user.

The workload that we use is a public, real-world data set from movie recommendation website MovieLens [45]. It has three subsets: (1) 100,000 ratings from 1,000 users on 1,700 movies, (2) 1 million ratings from 6,000 users on 4,000 movies, and (3) 10 million ratings from 72,000 users on 10,000 movies. The LensKit's default settings are used in all experiments.

7.5.1 The Attack–System Inference

Since there exists a prior system inference attack against recommendation systems [41], we reproduced this attack against LensKit and verified the effectiveness of the attack. As described by Calandrino et al. [41], the attacker knows the item-item similarity matrix and some items that the user bought from the past. To infer a newly bought item of the user, the attacker computes a delta matrix between the current item-item similarity matrix and the one without the item. Then, based on the delta matrix, the attacker could infer an initial list of items that might lead to the delta matrix, i.e., potential items that the user might have newly bought. Comparing the list of inferred items and the user's purchasing history, the attacker could infer the newly bought item. Following the attack steps, we first record the item-item similarity matrix of LensKit and one user's rating history. Then, we add one item to the user's rating history, compute the delta matrix and then successfully infer the added rating from the delta matrix and the user's rating history.

7.5.2 Analytical Results

To support unlearning in LensKit, we converted its recommendation algorithm into the summation form. Equation 7.4 shows this process. We start by substituting $\vec{a}_{*,k}$ and $\vec{a}_{*,l}$ in Equation 7.3 with their corresponding values in Equation 7.2 where n is the number of users and m is the number of items, and expanding the multiplications. We then simplify the equation by substituting some terms using the five summations listed in Equation 7.5. The result shows that the summation approach applies to item-item recommendation using cosine similarity.

$$
\begin{aligned}
S_{kl} &= \sum_{i=1}^{n} (r_{ik} - \mu_i)(r_{il} - \mu_i) \\
S_k &= \sum_{i=1}^{n} (r_{ik} - \mu_i) \quad S_l = \sum_{i=1}^{n} (r_{il} - \mu_i) \\
S_{kk} &= \sum_{i=1}^{n} (r_{ik} - \mu_i)^2 \quad S_{ll} = \sum_{i=1}^{n} (r_{il} - \mu_i)^2
\end{aligned}
\tag{7.5}
$$

We now discuss analytically the completeness and timeliness of unlearning in LensKit. To forget a rating in LensKit, we must update its item-item similarity matrix. To update the similarity between items k and l, we simply update all the summations in Equation 7.4, and then recompute $sim(k,l)$ using the summations. This unlearning process is 100% complete because it computes the same value of $sim(k,l)$ as recomputing from scratch following Equation 7.3. The asymptotic time to unlearn $sim(k,l)$ is only $O(1)$ because there is only a constant number of summations, each of which can be updated in constant time. Considering all m^2 pairs of items, the time complexity of unlearning is $O(m^2)$. In contrast, the time complexity of retraining from scratch is $O(nm^2)$ because recomputing $sim(k,l)$ following Equation 7.3 requires the dot-product of two vectors of size n. Thus, unlearning has a speedup factor of $O(n)$ over retraining. This speedup is quite huge because a recommendation system typically has many more users than items (e.g., Netflix's users vs. movies).

Now that we have shown mathematically how to convert LensKit's item-item similarity equation into the summation form and its analytical completeness and timeliness, we proceed to show algorithmically how to modify LensKit to support unlearning. While doing so is not difficult once Equation 7.4 is given, we report the algorithms we added to provide a complete picture of how to support unlearning in LensKit.

We added two algorithms to LensKit. Algorithm 1 runs during the learning stage of LensKit, which occurs when the system bootstraps or when the system operator decides to retrain from scratch. This algorithm computes the necessary summations for later unlearning. To compute the average rating of each user i (μ_i, line 13), it tracks the number of ratings given by the user ($Count_{\mu_i}$, line 6) and the sum of these ratings (Sum_{μ_i}, line 5). It similarly computes the average rating of each item k (η_k, line 17) by tracking the number of all ratings received by item k ($Count_{\eta_k}$, line 8) and the sum of these ratings (Sum_{η_k}, line 7). It computes the average of all ratings (g, line 15) by tracking the total number of ratings ($Count_g$, line 10) and the sum of them (Sum_g, line 9). In addition, it computes additional summations S_k and *Skl* (*line*

19 and 23) required by Equation 7.4. Once all summations are ready, it computes the similarity of each pair of items following Equation 7.4. It then stores the summations μi and $count_{\mu_i}$ for each user, η_j and $count_{\eta_i}$ for each item, g and $count_g$, S_k for each item, and S_{kl} for each pair of items for later unlearning.

Algorithm 1 Learning Stage Preparation in LensKit

Input:

All the users: 1 to n

All the items: 1 to m

Process:

1: Initializing all the variables to zero
2: **for** $i = 1$ to n **do**
3: **for** $j = 1$ to m **do**
4: **if** $r_{ij} \neq null$ **then**
5: $Sum_{\mu i}\ Sum_{\mu i} + r_{ij}$
6: $Count_{\mu i}$++
7: $Sum_{\eta j} \leftarrow Sum_{\eta j} + r_{ij}$
8: $Count_{\eta j}$++
9: $Sum_g \leftarrow Sum_g + r_{ij}$
10: $Count_g$++
11: **end if**
12: **end for**
13: $\mu_i \leftarrow Sum_{\mu i}/Count_{\mu i}$
14: **end for**
15: $g \leftarrow Sum_g/Count_g$
16: **for** $k = 1$ to m **do**
17: $\eta_k \leftarrow Sum_{\eta k}/Count_{\eta k}$
18: **for** $i = 1$ to n **do**
19: $S_k \leftarrow S_k + (r_{ik} - \mu_i)$
20: **end for**
21: **for** $l = 1$ to m **do**
22: **for** $i = 1$ to n **do**
23: $S_{kl} \leftarrow S_{kl} + (r_{ik} - \mu_i) * (r_{il} - \mu_i)$
24: **end for**
25: Calculate $sim(k; l)$
26: **end for**
27: **end for**

Algorithm 2 is the core algorithm for unlearning in LensKit. To forget a rating, it updates all relevant summations and relevant cells in the item-item similarity matrix. Suppose that user u asks the system to forget a rating she gave about item t.

Algorithm 2 first updates user *u*'s average rating μ_i, item *t*'s average rating η_j, and the global average rating *g* by multiplying the previous value of the average rating with the corresponding total number, subtracting the rating to forget r_{ut}, and dividing by the new total number (lines 1–3). It then updates item *t*'s summations S_t and S_{tt} by subtracting the value contributed by r_{ut} which simplifies to the assignments shown on lines 4–5. It then updates S_j and S_{jj} (lines 6–11) for each of the other items *j* that received a rating from user *m*. Because the ratings given by the other users and their averages do not change, Algorithm 2 subtracts the old value contributed by user *u* and adds the updated value. Algorithm 2 updates S_{jk} similarly (lines 12–20). Finally, it recomputes *sim(j,k)* based on updated summations following Equation 7.4 (line 21).

Algorithm 2 Unlearning Stage in LensKit

Input:

u : the user who wants to delete a rating for an item ▷ *User u*
t : the item, of which the user wants to delete the rating ▷ *Item t*
r_{ut} : the original rating that the user gives ▷ *Rating* r_{ut}

Process:

1: $old\mu_u \leftarrow \mu_u$
2: $\mu_u \leftarrow (\mu_u * Count_{\mu u} - r_{ut})/(Count_{\mu u} - 1)$
3: $\eta_t\ (\eta_t * Count_{\eta t} - r_{ut})/(Count_{\eta t} - 1)$
4: $g \leftarrow (g * Count_g - r_{ut})/(Count_g - 1)$
5: $S_t \leftarrow S_t - (r_{ut} - old\mu_u)$
6: $S_t \leftarrow S_{tt} - (r_{ut} - old\mu_u) * (r_{ut} - old\mu_u)$
7: **for** $j = 1$ to m **do**
8:     **if** $r_{uj} \neq null\ \&\&\ j \neq t$ **then**
9:         $S_j \leftarrow S_j + old\mu_u - \mu_u$
10:         $S_{jj} \leftarrow S_{jj} - (r_{uj} - old\mu_u) * (r_{uj} - old\mu_u) + (r_{uj} - \mu_u) * (r_{uj} - \mu_u)$
11:     **end if**
12: **end for**
13: **for** $k = 1$ to m **do**
14:     **for** $l = 1$ to m **do**
15:         **if** $r_{uk} \neq null\ \&\&\ r_{ul} \neq null\ \&\&\ k \neq l$ **then**
16:             **if** $j = t || l = t$ **then**
17:                 $S_{kl} \leftarrow S_{kl} - (r_{uk} - old\mu_u) * (r_{ul} - old\mu_u)$
18:             **else**
19:                 $S_{kl} \leftarrow S_{kl} - (r_{uk} - old\mu_u) * (r_{ul} - old\mu_u) + (r_{uk} - \mu_u) * (r_{ul} - \mu_u)$
20:             **end if**
21:         **end if**
22:         Update *sim*(*k*; *l*)
23:     **end for**
24: **end for**

Note that while these algorithms require additional $n + m^2 + 2m$ space to store the summations, the original item-item recommendation algorithm already uses $O(nm)$ space for the user-item rating matrix and $O(m^2)$ space for the item-item similarity matrix. Thus, the asymptotic space complexity remains unchanged.

7.5.3 Empirical Results

To modify LensKit to support unlearning, we have inserted 302 lines of code into nine files spanning over three LensKit packages: lenskit-core, lenskit-knn, and lenskit-data-structures.

Empirically, we evaluated completeness using two sets of experiments. First, for each data subset, we randomly chose a rating to forget, ran both unlearning and retraining, and compared the recommendation results for each user and the item-item similarity matrices computed. We repeated this experiment 10 times and verified that in all experiments, the recommendation results were always identical. In addition, the maximum differences between the corresponding similarities were less than 1.0×10^{-6}. These tiny differences were caused by imprecision in floating point arithmetic.

Second, we verified that unlearning successfully prevented the aforementioned system inference attack [41] from gaining any information about the forgotten rating. After unlearning, LensKit gave exactly the same recommendations as if the forgotten rating had never existed in the system. When we launched the attack, the delta matrices (Section IV in [41]) used in the attack contained all zeros, so the attacker cannot infer anything from these matrices.

We evaluated timeliness by measuring the time it took to unlearn or retrain. We used all three data subsets and repeated each experiment three times. Table 7.1 shows the results. The first row shows the time of retraining, and the second row the time of unlearning, and the last row the speedup of unlearning over retraining. Unlearning consistently outperforms retraining. The speedup factor is less than the $O(n)$ analytical results because there are many empty ratings in the data set, i.e., a

Table 7.1 Speedup of Unlearning Over Retraining for LensKit

	100K Ratings from 1,000 Users and 1,700 Items	*1M Ratings from 6,000 Users and 4,000 Items*	*10M Ratings from 72,000 Users and 10,000 Items*
Retraining	4.2 s	30 s	4 min 56 s
Unlearning	931 ms	6.1 s	45 s
Speedup	4.51	4.91	6.57

Note: The time of retraining increases by the factor of the number of total ratings, and the overhead of unlearning increases by the factor of the number of total users.

user does not give ratings for every movie. Therefore, the retraining speed is closer to $O(Nm)$, and the speedup factor is closer to $O(N/m)$, where N is the number of ratings and m is the number of users. For a larger data set, the speedup may be even larger. For example, IMDb contains 2,950,317 titles (including TV shows, movies, etc.) and 54 million registered users [46,47], which may produce billions or even trillions of ratings. In that case, the unlearning may take several hours to complete, while the retraining may take several days.

7.6 Related Work

In Section 7.1, we briefly discussed related work. In this section, we discuss related work in detail. We start with some attacks targeting machine learning (Section 7.6.1), then the defenses (Section 7.6.2), and finally incremental machine learning (Section 7.6.3).

7.6.1 Adversarial Machine Learning

Broadly speaking, adversarial machine learning [15,48] studies the behavior of machine learning in adversarial environments. Based on a prior taxonomy [15], the attacks targeting machine learning are classified into two major categories: (1) *causative attacks* in which an attacker has "write" access to the learning system—he or she pollutes the training data and subsequently influences the trained models and prediction results; and (2) *exploratory attacks* in which an attacker has "read-only" access—he or she sends data samples to the learning system hoping to steal private data inside the system or evade detection. In the rest of this subsection, we discuss these two categories of attacks in greater detail.

7.6.1.1 Causative Attacks

These attacks are the same as data pollution attacks (Section 7.2.2.2). Perdisci et al. [11] developed an attack against PolyGraph [12], an automatic worm signature generator that classifies network flows as either benign or malicious using a naive Bayes classifier. In this setup, the attacker compromises a machine in a honeynet and sends packets with polluted protocol header fields. These injected packets make PolyGraph fail to generate useful worm signatures. Nelson et al. [43] developed an attack against a commercial spam filter called SpamBayes [49], which also uses naive Bayes. They showed that, by polluting only 1% of the training data with well-crafted emails, an attacker successfully causes SpamBayes to flag a benign email as spam 90% of the time. While these two attacks target Bayesian classifiers, other classifiers can also be attacked in the same manner, as illustrated by Biggio et al.'s attack on SVM [50]. Instead of focusing on individual classifiers, Fumera et al. [51] proposed a framework for evaluating classifier resilience against causative attacks at the design stage. They applied their framework on several real-world applications and showed that the classifiers in these applications are all vulnerable.

Our practical pollution attacks targeting Zozzle [30], OSNSF [32], and PJScan [52] fall into this causative attack category. All such attacks, including prior ones and ours, serve as a good motivation for unlearning.

7.6.1.2 Exploratory Attacks

There are two sub-categories of exploratory attacks. The first sub-category of exploratory attacks is system inference or model inversion attacks, as discussed in Section 7.2.2.1. Calandrino et al. [41] showed that, given some auxiliary information of a particular user, an attacker can infer the transaction history of the user. Fredrikson et al. [7] showed that an attacker can infer the genetic markers of a patient given his or her demographic information. These attacks serve as another motivation for unlearning.

In the second sub-category, an attacker camouflages malicious samples as benign samples, and influences the prediction results of a learning system. In particular, for those systems that detect samples with malicious intentions, an attacker usually crafts malicious samples to mimic benign samples as much as possible, e.g., by injecting benign features into malicious samples [16,53–55]. As suggested by Srndic et al. [55], in order to make learning systems robust to those attacks, one needs to use features inherent to the malicious samples. These attacks are out of the scope of this chapter because they do not pollute training data nor leak private information of the training data.

7.6.2 Defense of Data Pollution and Privacy Leakage

In this subsection, we discuss current defense mechanisms for data pollution and privacy leakage. Although claimed to be robust, many of these defenses are subsequently defeated by new attacks [7,11]. Therefore, unlearning serves as an excellent complimentary method for these defenses.

7.6.2.1 Defense of Data Pollution

Many defenses of data pollution attacks apply filtering on the training data to remove polluted samples. Brodley et al. [28] filtered mislabeled training data by requiring absolute or majority consensus among the techniques used for labeling data. Cretu et al. [56] introduced a sanitization phase in the machine learning process to filter polluted data. Newsome et al. [12] clustered the training data set to help filter possible polluted samples. However, they are defeated by new attacks [11]. None of these techniques can guarantee that all polluted data is filtered. Another line of defense is to increase the resilience of the algorithms. Dekel et al. [57] developed two techniques to make learning algorithms resilient against attacks. One technique formulates the problem of resilient learning as a linear program, and the other uses the Perceptron algorithm with an online-to-batch conversion technique. Both techniques try to minimize the damage that an attacker could cause, but the attacker may still influence the prediction results of the learning system. Lastly, Bruckner et al. [58] model the learner and the data-pollution attacker as a game and prove that the game has a unique Nash equilibrium.

7.6.2.2 Defense of Privacy Leaks

In general, differential privacy [20,21] preserves the privacy of each individual item in a data set equally and invariably. McSherry et al. [59] built a differentially private recommendation system and showed that in the Netflix Prize data set the system can preserve privacy without significantly degrading the system's accuracy. Recently, Zhang et al. [21] proposed a mechanism to produce private linear regression models, and Vinterbo [20] proposed privacy-preserving projected histograms to produce differentially private synthetic data sets. However, differential privacy requires that accesses to data fit a shrinking privacy budget, and are only to the fuzzed statistics of the data set. These restrictions make it extremely challenging to build usable systems [7]. In addition, in today's systems, each user's privacy consciousness and each data item's sensitivity varies wildly. In contrast, forgetting systems aim to restore privacy on select data, representing a more practical privacy versus utility tradeoff.

7.6.3 Incremental Machine Learning

Incremental machine learning studies how to adjust the trained model incrementally to add new training data or remove obsolete data, so it is closely related to our work. Romero et al. [39] found the exact maximal margin hyperplane for linear SVMs so that a new component can be easily added or removed from the inner product. Cauwenberghs et al. [38] proposed using adiabatic increments to update an SVM from l training samples to $l + 1$. Utgoff et al. [60] proposed an incremental algorithm to induce decision trees equivalent to the trees formed by Quinlan's ID3 algorithm. Domingos et al. [61] proposed a high performance construction algorithm of decision trees to deal with high-speed data streams. Recently, Tsai et al. [40] proposed using warm starts to practically build incremental SVMs with linear kernels.

Compared to prior incremental machine learning work, our unlearning approach differs fundamentally because we propose a general efficient unlearning approach applicable to any algorithm that can be converted to the summation form, including some that currently have no incremental versions. For instance, we successfully applied unlearning to normalized cosine similarity which recommendation systems commonly use to compute item-item similarity. This algorithm had no incremental versions prior to our work. In addition, we applied our learning approach to real-world systems, and demonstrated that it is important that unlearning handles all stages of learning, including feature selection and modeling.

Chu et al. [36] used the summation form to speed up machine learning algorithms with map-reduce. Their summation form is based on SQ learning, and provided inspiration for our work. We believe we are the first to establish the connection between unlearning and the summation form. Furthermore, we demonstrated how to convert non-standard machine learning algorithms, e.g., the normalized cosine similarity algorithm, to the summation form. In contrast, prior work converted nine standard machine learning algorithms using only simple transformations.

Further Reading

Y. Cao and J. Yang. Towards making systems forget with machine unlearning. In Proceedings of the 2015 IEEE Symposium on Security and Privacy, 2015.

M. Barreno, B. Nelson, A. D. Joseph, and J. D. Tygar. The security of machine learning. *Mach. Learn.*, 81(2):121–148, Nov. 2010.

D. Beaver, S. Kumar, H. C. Li, J. Sobel, and P. Vajgel. Finding a needle in haystack: Facebook's photo storage. In Proceedings of the 9th USENIX Conference on Operating Systems Design and Implementation, OSDI, 2010.

B. Biggio, B. Nelson, and P. Laskov. Poisoning attacks against support vector machines. In Proceedings of International Conference on Machine Learning, ICML, 2012.

M. Brückner, C. Kanzow, and T. Scheffer. Static prediction games for adversarial learning problems. *J. Mach. Learn. Res.*, 13(1):2617–2654, Sept. 2012.

J. A. Calandrino, A. Kilzer, A. Narayanan, E. W. Felten, and V. Shmatikov. You might also like: Privacy risks of collaborative filtering. In Proceedings of 20th IEEE Symposium on Security and Privacy, May 2011.

Y. Cao, X. Pan, Y. Chen, and J. Zhuge. JShield: Towards real-time and vulnerability-based detection of polluted drive-by download attacks. In Proceedings of the 30th Annual Computer Security Applications Conference, ACSAC, 2014.

G. Cauwenberghs and T. Poggio. Incremental and decremental support vector machine learning. In Advances in Neural Information Processing Systems (NIPS*2000), volume 13, 2001.

C. T. Chu, S. K. Kim, Y. A. Lin, Y. Yu, G. R. Bradski, A. Y. Ng, and K. Olukotun. Map-reduce for machine learning on multicore. In B. Schlkopf, J. C. Platt, and T. Hoffman, Eds., *NIPS*, pp. 281–288. MIT Press, 2006.

G. F. Cretu, A. Stavrou, M. E. Locasto, S. J. Stolfo, and A. D. Keromytis. Casting out demons: Sanitizing training data for anomaly sensors. In Proceedings of the 2008 IEEE Symposium on Security and Privacy, SP, 2008.

M. Fredrikson, E. Lantz, S. Jha, S. Lin, D. Page, and T. Ristenpart. Privacy in pharmacogenetics: An end-to-end case study of personalized warfarin dosing. In Proceedings of USENIX Security, August 2014.

G. Fumera and B. Biggio. Security evaluation of pattern classifiers under attack. IEEE Transactions on Knowledge and Data Engineering, 99(1), 2013.

L. Huang, A. D. Joseph, B. Nelson, B. I. Rubinstein, and J. D. Tygar. Adversarial machine learning. In Proceedings of the 4th ACM Workshop on Security and Artificial Intelligence, AISec, 2011.

M. Kearns. Efficient noise-tolerant learning from statistical queries. *J. ACM*, 45(6):983–1006, Nov. 1998.

M. Kearns and M. Li. Learning in the presence of malicious errors. In Proceedings of the Twentieth Annual ACM Symposium on Theory of Computing, STOC, 1988.

R. Perdisci, D. Dagon, W. Lee, P. Fogla, and M. I. Sharif. Misleading worm signature generators using deliberate noise injection. In Proceedings of the 2006 IEEE Symposium on Security and Privacy, 2006.

E. Romero, I. Barrio, and L. Belanche. Incremental and decremental learning for linear support vector machines. In Proceedings of the 17th International Conference on Artificial Neural Networks, ICANN, 2007.

C.-H. Tsai, C.-Y. Lin, and C.-J. Lin. Incremental and decremental training for linear classification. In Proceedings of the 20th ACM SIGKDD International Conference on Knowledge Discovery and Data Mining, KDD, 2014.

G. Wang, T. Wang, H. Zheng, and B. Y. Zhao. Man vs. machine: Practical adversarial detection of malicious crowdsourcing workers. In Proceedings of USENIX Security, August 2014.

References

1. New IDC worldwide big data technology and services forecast shows market expected to grow to $32.4 billion in 2017. http://www.idc.com/ getdoc.jsp?containerId =prUS24542113.
2. Doug Beaver, Sanjeev Kumar, Harry C. Li, Jason Sobel, and Peter Vajgel. Finding a needle in a haystack: Facebook's photo storage. In *Proceedings of the 9th USENIX Conference on Operating Systems Design and Implementation*, OSDI, 2010.
3. Subramanian Muralidhar, Wyatt Lloyd, Sabyasachi Roy, Cory Hill, Ernest Lin, Weiwen Liu, Satadru Pan, Shiva Shankar, Viswanath Sivaku-mar, Linpeng Tang, and Sanjeev Kumar. F4: Facebook's warm blob storage system. In *Proceedings of the 11th USENIX Conference on Operating Systems Design and Implementation*, OSDI, 2014.
4. John Sutter. Some quitting facebook as privacy concerns escalate. http: //www.cnn .com/2010/TECH/05/13/facebook.delete.privacy/.
5. iCloud security questioned over celebrity photo leak 2014: Apple officially launches result of investigation over hacking. http: //www.franchiseherald.com/articles/6466 /20140909/celebrity-photo-leak-2014.htm.
6. Victoria Woollaston. How to delete your photos from iCloud: Simple step by step guide to stop your images getting into the wrong hands. http://www.dailymail.co.uk /sciencetech/article-2740607/How-delete-YOUR-photos-iCloud-stop-getting-wrong -hands.html.
7. Matthew Fredrikson, Eric Lantz, Somesh Jha, Simon Lin, David Page, and Thomas Ristenpart. Privacy in pharmacogenetics: An end-to-end case study of personalized warfarin dosing. In *Proceedings of USENIX Security*, August 2014.

8. Rui Wang, Yong Fuga Li, XiaoFeng Wang, Haixu Tang, and Xiaoyong Zhou. Learning your identity and disease from research papers: Information leaks in genome wide association study. In *Proceedings of the 16th ACM Conference on Computer and Communications Security*, CCS, pp. 534–544, New York, 2009. ACM.
9. The Editorial Board of the *New York Times*. Ordering google to forget. http://www.nytimes.com/2014/05/14/opinion/ordering-google-to-forget.html?_r=0.
10. Arjun Kharpal. Google axes 170,000 'right to be forgotten' links. http: //www.cnbc.com/id/102082044.
11. Roberto Perdisci, David Dagon, Wenke Lee, Prahlad Fogla, and Monirul I. Sharif. Misleading worm signature generators using deliberate noise injection. In *Proceedings of the 2006 IEEE Symposium on Security and Privacy*, 2006.
12. James Newsome, Brad Karp, and Dawn Song. Polygraph: Automatically generating signatures for polymorphic worms. In *Proceedings of the 2005 IEEE Symposium on Security and Privacy*, 2005.
13. Google now. http://www.google.com/landing/now/.
14. Private Communication with Yang Tang in Columbia University.
15. Ling Huang, Anthony D. Joseph, Blaine Nelson, Benjamin I. P. Rubinstein, and J. D. Tygar. Adversarial machine learning. In *Proceedings of the 4th ACM Workshop on Security and Artificial Intelligence*, AISec, 2011.
16. Gang Wang, Tianyi Wang, Haitao Zheng, and Ben Y. Zhao. Man vs. machine: Practical adversarial detection of malicious crowdsourcing workers. In *Proceedings of USENIX Security*, August 2014.
17. BlueKai—Big Data for Marketing—Oracle Marketing Cloud. http: //www.bluekai.com/.
18. Gil Elbaz. Data markets: The emerging data economy. http: //techcrunch.com/2012/09/30/data-markets-the-emerging-data-economy/.
19. Christopher Riederer, Vijay Erramilli, Augustin Chaintreau, Balachander Krishnamurthy, and Pablo Rodriguez. For sale: Your data: By: You. In *Proceedings of the 10th ACM Workshop on Hot Topics in Networks*, HotNets-X, 2011.
20. Staal A. Vinterbo. Differentially private projected histograms: Construction and use for prediction. In Peter A. Flach, Tijl De Bie, and Nello Cristianini, Eds., *ECML/PKDD (2)*, volume 7524 of *Lecture Notes in Computer Science*, pp. 19–34. Springer, 2012.
21. Jun Zhang, Zhenjie Zhang, Xiaokui Xiao, Yin Yang, and Marianne Winslett. Functional mechanism: Regression analysis under differential privacy. *Proceedings of VLDB Endow.*, 5(11):1364–1375, July 2012.
22. Delete search history. https://support.google.com/websearch/ answer/465?source=gsearch.
23. Jim Chow, Ben Pfaff, Tal Garfinkel, and Mendel Rosenblum. Shredding your garbage: Reducing data lifetime through secure deallocation. In *Proceedings of the 14th Conference on USENIX Security Symposium*, 2005.
24. Joel Reardon, Srdjan Capkun, and David Basin. Data node encrypted file system: Efficient secure deletion for flash memory. In *Proceedings of the 21st USENIX Conference on Security Symposium*, Security, 2012.
25. Yang Tang, Patrick P. C. Lee, John C. S. Lui, and Radia Perlman. Secure overlay cloud storage with access control and assured deletion. *IEEE Trans. Dependable Secur. Comput.*, 9(6):903–916, November 2012.

26. William Enck, Peter Gilbert, Byung-Gon Chun, Landon P. Cox, Jaeyeon Jung, Patrick McDaniel, and Anmol N. Sheth. Taintdroid: An information-flow tracking system for realtime privacy monitoring on smartphones. In *Proceedings of the 9th USENIX Conference on Operating Systems Design and Implementation*, OSDI, 2010.
27. Riley Spahn, Jonathan Bell, Michael Z. Lee, Sravan Bhamidipati, Roxana Geambasu, and Gail Kaiser. Pebbles: Fine-grained data management abstractions for modern operating systems. In *Proceedings of the 11th USENIX Conference on Operating Systems Design and Implementation*, OSDI, 2014.
28. Carla E. Brodley and Mark A. Friedl. Identifying mislabeled training data. *Journal of Artificial Intelligence Research*, 11:131–167, 1999.
29. Michael Brennan, Sadia Afroz, and Rachel Greenstadt. Adversarial sty-lometry: Circumventing authorship recognition to preserve privacy and anonymity. *ACM Trans. Inf. Syst. Secur.*, 15(3):12:1–12:22, November 2012.
30. Charlie Curtsinger, Benjamin Livshits, Benjamin Zorn, and Christian Seifert. Zozzle: Fast and precise in-browser javascript malware detection. In *Proceedings of the 20th USENIX Conference on Security*, 2011.
31. Mukund Deshpande and George Karypis. Item-based top-n recommendation algorithms. *ACM Trans. Inf. Syst.*, 22(1):143–177, January 2004.
32. Hongyu Gao, Yan Chen, Kathy Lee, Diana Palsetia, and Alok N. Choud-hary. Towards online spam filtering in social networks. In *Proceedings of Network and Distributed Systems Security Symposium*, NDSS, 2012.
33. Badrul Sarwar, George Karypis, Joseph Konstan, and John Riedl. Item-based collaborative filtering recommendation algorithms. In *Proceedings of the 10th International Conference on World Wide Web*, WWW, 2001.
34. D. Sculley, Matthew Eric Otey, Michael Pohl, Bridget Spitznagel, John Hainsworth, and Yunkai Zhou. Detecting adversarial advertisements in the wild. In *Proceedings of the 17th ACM SIGKDD International Conference on Knowledge Discovery and Data Mining*, KDD, 2011.
35. Margaret A. Shipp, Ken N. Ross, Pablo Tamayo, Andrew P. Weng, Jeffery L. Kutok, Ricardo C. T. Aguiar, Michelle Gaasenbeek, et al. Diffuse large B-cell lymphoma outcome prediction by gene-expression profiling and supervised machine learning. *Nature Medicine*, 8(1):68–74, January 2002.
36. Cheng T. Chu, Sang K. Kim, Yi A. Lin, Yuanyuan Yu, Gary R. Bradski, Andrew Y. Ng, and Kunle Olukotun. Map-reduce for machine learning on multicore. In Bernhard Schlkopf, John C. Platt, and Thomas Hoffman, Eds., *NIPS*, pp. 281–288. MIT Press, 2006.
37. Michael Kearns. Efficient noise-tolerant learning from statistical queries. *J. ACM*, 45(6):983–1006, November 1998.
38. G. Cauwenberghs and T. Poggio. Incremental and decremental support vector machine learning. In *Advances in Neural Information Processing Systems* (NIPS*2000), volume 13, 2001.
39. Enrique Romero, Ignacio Barrio, and Lluis Belanche. Incremental and decremental learning for linear support vector machines. In *Proceedings of the 17th International Conference on Artificial Neural Networks*, ICANN, 2007.
40. Cheng-Hao Tsai, Chieh-Yen Lin, and Chih-Jen Lin. Incremental and decremental training for linear classification. In *Proceedings of the 20th ACM SIGKDD International Conference on Knowledge Discovery and Data Mining*, KDD, 2014.

41. Joseph A. Calandrino, Ann Kilzer, Arvind Narayanan, Edward W. Felten, and Vitaly Shmatikov. You might also like: Privacy risks of collaborative filtering. In *Proceedings of 20th IEEE Symposium on Security and Privacy*, May 2011.
42. LibraryThing. https://www.librarything.com/.
43. Blaine Nelson, Marco Barreno, Fuching Jack Chi, Anthony D. Joseph, Benjamin I. P. Rubinstein, Udam Saini, Charles Sutton, J. D. Tygar, and Kai Xia. Exploiting machine learning to subvert your spam filter. In *Proceedings of the 1st Usenix Workshop on Large-Scale Exploits and Emergent Threats*, LEET, 2008.
44. Project honey pot. https://www.projecthoneypot.org/.
45. Movielens. http://movielens.org/login.
46. IMDb database status. http://www.imdb.com/stats.
47. Wikipedia: Internet Movie Database. http://en.wikipedia.org/wiki/ Internet_Movie _Database.
48. Marco Barreno, Blaine Nelson, Anthony D. Joseph, and J. D. Tygar. The security of machine learning. *Mach. Learn.*, 81(2):121–148, November 2010.
49. SpamBayes. http://spambayes.sourceforge.net/.
50. Battista Biggio, Blaine Nelson, and Pavel Laskov. Poisoning attacks against support vector machines. In *Proceedings of International Conference on Machine Learning*, ICML, 2012.
51. Giorgio Fumera and Battista Biggio. Security evaluation of pattern classifiers under attack. *IEEE Transactions on Knowledge and Data Engineering*, 99(1), 2013.
53. Yinzhi Cao, Xiang Pan, Yan Chen, and Jianwei Zhuge. JShield: Towards real-time and vulnerability-based detection of polluted drive-by download attacks. In *Proceedings of the 30th Annual Computer Security Applications Conference*, ACSAC, 2014.
52. Pavel Laskov and Nedim Srndic. Static detection of malicious javascript-bearing pdf documents. In *Proceedings of the 27th Annual Computer Security Applications Conference*, ACSAC, 2011.
54. Michael Kearns and Ming Li. Learning in the presence of malicious errors. In *Proceedings of the Twentieth Annual ACM Symposium on Theory of Computing*, STOC, 1988.
55. Nedim Srndic and Pavel Laskov. Practical evasion of a learning-based classifier: A case study. In *Proceedings of the 2014 IEEE Symposium on Security and Privacy*, 2014.
56. G. F. Cretu, A. Stavrou, M. E. Locasto, S. J. Stolfo, and A. D. Keromytis. Casting out demons: Sanitizing training data for anomaly sensors. In *Proceedings of the 2008 IEEE Symposium on Security and Privacy*, SP, 2008.
57. Ofer Dekel, Ohad Shamir, and Lin Xiao. Learning to classify with missing and corrupted features. *Mach. Learn.*, 81(2):149–178, November 2010.
58. Michael Brückner, Christian Kanzow, and Tobias Scheffer. Static prediction games for adversarial learning problems. *J. Mach. Learn. Res.*, 13(1):2617–2654, September 2012.
59. Frank McSherry and Ilya Mironov. Differentially private recommender systems: Building privacy into the netflix prize contenders. In *Proceedings of the 15th ACM SIGKDD International Conference on Knowledge Discovery and Data Mining*, KDD, 2009.
60. Paul E. Utgoff. Incremental induction of decision trees. *Mach. Learn.*, 4(2):161–186, November 1989.
61. Pedro Domingos and Geoff Hulten. Mining high-speed data streams. In Proceedings of the Sixth ACM SIGKDD International Conference on Knowledge Discovery and Data Mining, KDD, 2000.

II

BIG DATA IN EMERGING CYBERSECURITY DOMAINS

Chapter 8

Big Data Analytics for Mobile App Security

Doina Caragea and Xinming Ou

Contents

This chapter describes mobile app security analysis, one of the new emerging cybersecurity issues with rapidly increasing requirements introduced by the predominant use of mobile devices in people's daily lives, and discusses how big data techniques such as machine learning (ML) can be leveraged for security analysis of mobile applications. In particular, the discussion focuses on malware detection for Android apps. ML is a promising approach in triaging app security analysis, in which it can leverage the big datasets in the app markets to learn a classifier, incorporating multiple features to separate apps that are more likely to be malicious from the benign ones. Recently, there have been several efforts focused on applying ML to app security analysis. However, there are still some significant challenges in making the solution practical, most of which are due to the unique operational constraints and the "big data" nature of the problem. This chapter systematically studies the impacts of these challenges as a set of questions and provides insights to the answers based on systematic experimentation results obtained from authors' past research. Meanwhile, this chapter also demonstrates the impact of some challenges on some existing machine learning-based approaches. The large (market-scale) dataset (benign and malicious apps) used in the above experiments represents the real-world Android app security analysis scale. This chapter is particularly written to encourage the practice of employing a better evaluation strategy and better designs of future machine learning-based approaches for Android malware detection.

8.1 Introduction to Mobile App Security Analysis

Mobile platforms such as Android are becoming the predominant computing utilities for end users. These platforms usually adopt an open-market model where developers submit applications to an "app store" for users to purchase and download to devices. The app store operators want to ensure that apps entering the market are trustworthy and free of malware. However, this is a non-trivial task due to the inherent undecidable nature of determining code behavior statically and the limitation of testing. Thus, app store operators adopt a variety of approaches to reduce the likelihood of "bad apps" entering the market and harming end users. This includes vetting of an app when it is first uploaded to the app store, and continuous vetting of apps that become popular. In addition, they constantly monitor issues reported by users, researchers, and companies to identify and remove malicious apps not flagged by the vetting process.

While app stores such as Google Play and Apple App Store have existed for years, current vetting technologies are still lagging behind the threats. This is evident from periodic reports of malware from these markets. The situation is worse in third-party markets. Even though the average malware rate for official markets like Google Play is low, with thousands of new apps uploaded to Google Play, new malicious apps are entering the official Google Play market without being detected on a daily basis. While we did not find any official explanation from Google on why it has not done a better job at stopping malware, the scale of the app vetting process is clearly a factor. Early studies done by researchers showed that Google's app vetting service Bouncer only scans an app for 30 seconds each time to detect security problems [1].

While the extent of damage caused by those malicious apps is not clear, the possibility of them getting into app stores poses a non-trivial risk. Such risks need to be minimized by (1) curtailing the number of apps with security problems getting into the market and (2) quickly removing apps with security problems at the first sign. Both require effective analysis methods so that one can make quick and accurate decisions on which app has what security problems. This has to scale up to the large volumes of apps uploaded to app stores on a daily basis.

It is definitely not easy to achieve this. Common practice in industry, e.g., Google Bouncer and Amazon ATS, has adopted a variety of approaches including static and dynamic analysis. The research community has also designed advanced analysis methods and tools. But there needs to be an effective approach to address the *scale problem* in the vetting process. We observe that (1) although the number of apps in a market is huge, the number of malicious apps is not. If a "triage" process can effectively direct attention to the "right apps" for further examination, it could dramatically reduce the amount of compute and manual efforts; (2) the large number of apps in the markets actually provides an edge for defenders: it will allow us to identify patterns and trends that would be hard to find with smaller amounts of data [2]. The key to success is to identify, in an efficient and precise way, which apps are more likely to have security problems, so that the precious resources (human or computer) can be directed to those apps first. This triage problem has been examined in prior work [3] with promising results. The effect of big data in helping identify malware is further illustrated in the recent MassVet work [4], which aimed at quickly identifying malware created by repackaging existing legitimate apps with malicious payload. MassVet adopts a simple yet effective approach where an app is compared with a large number of existing apps in the market to identify "visually similar apps" with different components and "visually non-similar apps" with common components. The "DiffComm" analysis yields anomalous different or common components between apps which become the basics for identifying repackaged malware. This analysis can be done efficiently at a market scale. While these analysis techniques were invented to identify malware that are built in specific ways like repackaging existing popular apps, the threat landscape is certain to move toward more sophisticated malware creation processes that require more efforts from the malware writers, e.g., they may have to create their own apps that become popular instead of getting free rides on existing popular apps, or they may invent techniques to obfuscate the repackaging relations to break the assumptions of the specific detection techniques such as MassVet, and so on. This is inevitable given the rising stakes mobile devices bring to both individuals and organizations—mobile devices are now used for critical functions such as payments and are becoming an integral part of organizations' enterprise IT systems. All this indicates that app vetting will be a highly complex and evolving process and it is not likely that a completely automated process without human intervention can do an adequate job. This is highlighted in Google's recent announcement to change its vetting process which now involves human review before an app can be published, instead of the completely automated process in the past. This puts more urgent need for better triaging capabilities since human labor is scarce given the amount of work needed, and expensive. An effective triaging can increase productivity by helping analysts to focus their effort on apps that are more likely to be malicious, and spending less time on those that are more likely to be benign. In the end, more general methods for triaging the vetting of apps on a large scale will be needed to address the evolving threats.

8.2 Applying Machine Learning (ML) in Triaging App Security Analysis

Machine learning is a promising approach in triaging app security analysis, in that it can leverage the big data in the app markets to learn a classifier, incorporating multiple app features to separate apps that are more likely to be malicious from the benign ones. Such separations are often times subtle and cannot be easily expressed by logical rules; machine learning is good at identifying hidden relationships in big data. A typical machine learning-based approach for Android malware app detection employs a classifier (e.g., an off-the-shelf machine learning classifier, such as k-NN) which is trained on a training set consisting of known benign apps and known malware apps. To evaluate the classification performance, the number of correctly and incorrectly classified apps is measured on a test set whose labels are unknown to the classifier at the time of evaluation.

Recently, there have been several efforts focused on applying machine learning to app security analysis [5–8]. However, there are still some significant challenges in effectively using a machine learning approach to triage mobile app security analysis, most of which are due to the unique operational constraints and the "big data" nature of the problem.

- *Noise and uncertainty on labels.* It is hard to obtain ground truths to train a machine-learned classifier for mobile app security. The degree of "truths" on the labels assigned to samples varies depending on the quality of information sources based on which the labels are assigned. The learning algorithm must account for this.
- *Imbalance on data.* The overwhelming majority of data samples for mobile apps are benign applications. The amount of malicious apps is minuscule

compared to the millions of good apps on the markets. This both presents a challenge in learning and puts a high requirement on the classifier's performance. For example, with a 0.1% malware prevalence, a 1% false positive rate would mean 10 times false alarms than true alarms on the market, clearly unacceptable in operations.

- *Feature limitation.* Features that can be extracted from an app in a computationally cheap way are weak indicators of security problems and many of them can be easily evaded by malware writers. To improve triage quality, a higher quality set of features is needed and more computation needs to be involved to derive features with more reliable attack semantics that cannot be easily evaded. This comes at odds with the scale challenge of the problem. In addition, the highly dynamic nature of adversarial behaviors means that predictive features *will change* over time. An effective triage must account for that and identify the optimal window for training.
- Although the results of the machine learning-inspired approaches look promising, many critical research questions still remain unanswered. There exists substantial room for clarification and improvement.

The above "big data" challenges result in additional concrete challenges when applying machine learning to Android malware detection, as described below:

Ensuring proper evaluation: These challenges arise in selecting the evaluation metrics as well as in collecting and preparing the data (e.g., correctly labeling the apps in training/test set). We see that in most of the current ML-approaches, (1) the evaluation strategy does not follow a common standard; and (2) the ground truth on which these approaches are evaluated lack reliability.

Algorithm design: These challenges arise in the design space of the machine learning approaches. One such challenge is to construct an informative feature set for the classifier. For example, in some works (e.g., [5]) the feature set contains hundreds of thousands of items, and many items (such as the names of the app components) are arbitrary strings at the app developer's choice. This raises a question on whether all items in this large feature set are really helping the classifier or if a subset can be sufficient (or even better).

The previously proposed ML-approaches focused more on a specific setting defined by factors such as specific evaluation metrics, ground truth quality, composition of the training/test data, the feature set, and others. The reported performance results are then measured in that particular setting. However, since the setting varies widely across different approaches, it is difficult (if not impossible) to fairly compare the results. For many of the recently proposed solutions, we are not aware of the impact of the above factors on the classifier performance.

8.3 The State-of-the-Art ML Approaches for Android Malware Detection

Drebin [5] works with a massive feature set (more than 500K features) containing different types of manifest features (permissions, etc.) and "code" features (URLs, APIs, etc.). Yet, Drebin authors demonstrated that the malware detection system is scalable, and it can even run on a phone in the order of seconds. Drebin's performance results are also very impressive.

DroidSIFT [8] is unique in designing features in terms of distance among API dependency graphs. It builds the API dependency graphs G for each app, and then constructs the feature vector of the app. The features represent the similarity of the graphs G with a reference database of graphs of known benign apps and malware apps. Finally, the feature vectors are used in anomaly or signature detection.

MAST [3] is a triage architecture whose goal is to spend more resources on apps that have a higher probability of being malicious, thereby reducing the average computation overhead for app vetting. This system utilizes a statistical method called multiple correspondence analysis (MCA). It uses permissions, intents, and the presence of native code to determine the probabilities of being malicious.

MUDFLOW [6] argues that the pattern of sensitive information flows in malware is statistically different from those in benign apps, which can be utilized for malware detection. From an app, it extracts the flow paths through static analysis, and these paths are then mapped to a feature vector that is used in a classifier.

8.4 Challenges in Applying ML for Android Malware Detection

Figure 8.1 illustrates the overall pipeline for using machine learning for mobile app security analysis. The large number of app samples goes through a labeling and feature extraction process. Then part of the data is used in constructing a machine-learned classifier, and the rest is used in evaluation. There are multiple challenges in each stage of the process.

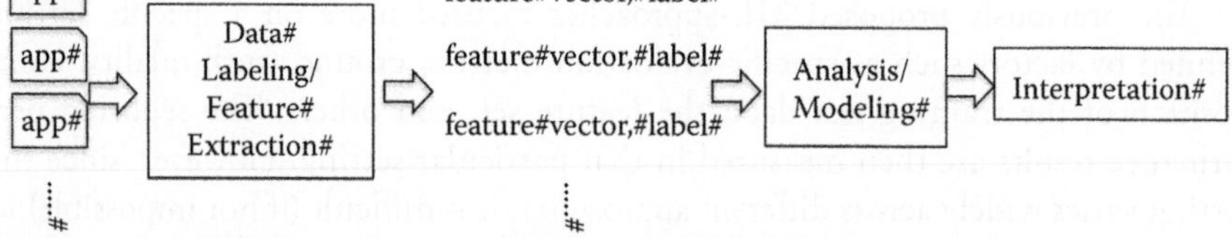

Figure 8.1 Big data analysis pipeline for mobile apps.

8.4.1 Challenges in Ensuring Proper Evaluation

To ensure that the ML-approach is evaluated properly is not straightforward. The related challenges fall under two subcategories as follows.

1. **Challenges in deciding the evaluation metrics.** The evaluation metrics for an ML-approach are not yet standardized and different ML-approaches rely on different metrics. For instance, DroidSIFT [8] and MUDFLOW [6] report the performance results in terms of true positive rate (TPR) and false-positive rate (FPR). Other existing works, such as MAST [3] and Drebin [5] present the receiver operating characteristic (ROC) plot, which is a generalized representation of TPR and FPR while the separating threshold is varied. Further, the ML-community has reported [9] that if the dataset is highly imbalanced, the PRC (precision-recall curve) is a better metric for measuring classifier performance than the traditional ROC curve. Given that the Android malware domain is highly imbalanced, i.e., the ratio of malware to benign apps in the real-world is highly skewed (1:100 or up), the above facts raise substantial doubt on whether current works are using the best metric.
2. **Challenges due to characteristics of the input data.** These challenges are related to data preparation, e.g., labeling the apps, composing the training/testing set, and so on. We see that these challenges are applicable to all the current ML-approaches. For instance, the age of input data may pose one challenge. Dated apps versus recent apps could lead to very different evaluation results in some cases. Deciding the data composition is another challenge, e.g., selecting the ratio between positive class (malware apps) size and negative class (benign apps) size in the test data, which may lead to different performance results of the classifier. To ensure realistic evaluation, we should conform to the real-life ratio of malware and good apps in the app store, but unfortunately this is not practiced in many existing works. Furthermore, the ground truth is noisy in reality while manually labeling a million plus apps is not feasible. So, we have to depend on security companies' reports on those apps (if available), which effectively lead to imperfect ground truth. We see that the ground truth on which the current ML-approaches depend is not fully reliable, which has a negative impact in two ways: (i) if training data has noise (mislabeled apps), the classifier mislearns things, which will negatively influence the classification performance. (ii) If test data has noise, we evaluate on the wrong ground truth, and then the reported performance results can be misleading. In addition, the presence of adware apps (which show unwanted advertisements to the user) in the dataset leads to further challenges. As adware has similarities to both benign and malware apps, it is often challenging to label an adware, e.g., including adware in the malware set or in the benign set, or dropping adware from the dataset altogether. The existing works differ on this choice, which further complicates attempting to compare their performance.

8.4.2 Challenges in the Algorithm Design

These challenges are related to the design of the ML approach itself. One challenge is to construct an informative (i.e., discriminative across the classes) feature set for the classifier. Some of the existing approaches are overwhelmed by this challenge. As an example, the Drebin approach [5] uses a very large feature set. One may want to know whether the classifier really needs this large feature set or only a subset of these items could be sufficient. We note that the size of Drebin's feature set is correlated with the size of its dataset—it has nearly 500K features while applied on the authors' dataset [5], but when we emulated Drebin feature's extraction on our larger dataset we achieved more than 1 million features. Do we really need these many features? How to identify and select strong, discriminative features is a challenge.

8.4.3 Challenges in Data Collection

We have discussed above the challenges due to characteristics of the dataset. Collecting a large dataset of apps poses a formidable challenge. Attempting to collect modern apps is an even more challenging task. Although Google Play provides the whole set of "free" apps (over 1.4 million), there is no "download API" available. So, we need to rely on app store crawlers like PlayDrone [10] that periodically scan the Google Play app store and collect entire snapshots of the store. The most recent apps, however, are not always available in the PlayDrone archive. Moreover, collecting a large set of adware and malware apps is also challenging—we have to rely on several sources. VirusShare and anti-virus companies provide large datasets of potentially malicious apps. These sets, however, are often noisy and impure, sometimes containing benign apps, Win32 binaries, and even blank apps. We believe that the large amount of data, even if somewhat noisy, provides further credibility to the results. To reduce the computation complexity of the machine learning approach is a further challenge. It is not straightforward how to design a scalable machine learning approach. When considering the millions of apps in the Play store, and the thousands of new apps added every day, scalability is of paramount importance. As an example of the degree of this challenge, we take note of MUDFLOW [6] authors' comment that sometimes their system took more than 24 hours to analyze one single Android app.

8.4.4 Insights Based on Our Own Study

Our research team has recently conducted an investigation of challenges that are faced in applying ML for Android security analysis [11]. We found that previously proposed machine learning approaches vary widely in terms of factors such as specific evaluation metrics, ground truth quality, composition of the training/test data, the feature set, and others, making it difficult (if not impossible) to fairly compare the results. Some findings relevant to this chapter are listed below.

- *Is ROC the best metric to evaluate ML-based malware detection approaches?* The evaluation metrics for an ML-approach are not yet standardized and different ML-approaches rely on different metrics, such as true positive rate (TPR) and false-positive rate (FPR), receiver operating characteristic (ROC) plot, and the PRC (precision-recall curve). Given that the Android malware domain is highly imbalanced, i.e., the ratio of malware to benign apps in the real-world is highly skewed (1:100 or up), it is likely that PRC is a better metric for measuring classifier performance than the traditional ROC curve. Our investigation shows that indeed, the area under the PRC is a better metric for comparing results of different approaches in machine learning-based Android malware detection [11].
- *Does having dated malware in training/test set mislead performance?* The Genome Malware Project [12] has been used for many years as a main source of malware for many machine learning-based works. However, the Genome set, with malware from 2010–2012, has become a dated source of malware. We hypothesized that using dated malware sources together with more modern benign sources can lead to misleading results, and our study supports this hypothesis [11].
- *Does classifier performance degrade as we approach real-world ratio of malware and benign apps?* The occurrence of malware in the app stores is relatively low. This imbalance in the amount of malware and benign apps can contribute an interesting factor in classifier performance. Specifically, our results [11] show that the area under the PRC substantially degrades as the ratio increases (although the commonly used TPR and FPR do not change much), suggesting that results based on datasets that do not conform to the real data distribution could be misleading.
- *Does quality of ground truth affect the performance?* Peer works generally do some form of ground truth preparation for a machine learning classifier. Some works [5] require that a minimum of 20% of VirusTotal reports indicate the app is malicious. Other works [8] hold stringent standards and require that the reports return a matching malware family to be used in their dataset. In our own research [11], we investigated the effect of the quality of the ground truth data on the performance of the classifier, and found that the higher quality malware leads to substantially better results.

8.5 Recommendations

Below we present a number of recommendations for applying big data analysis to mobile apps. Some of them are specifically about the application of machine learning, while others involve complementary methods that could benefit the problem domain.

8.5.1 Data Preparation and Labeling

The community should explore and experiment with different ways to obtain ground truth information. In general, based on returned antivirus scanning results, we can separate Android samples into three categories:

1. *Ideal malware.* Apps in this category have highly credible labels and a high rate of shared labels among different antivirus companies, e.g., more than 25 different scanners are showing the sample as malicious and 20 of them give a shared keyword "DroidKungFu" in their scanning results. Thus, we can safely choose the shared label "DroidKungFu" as their family information.
2. *Candidate malware.* Apps in this category have either an unclear or a low rate of shared labels. For instance, only 10 out of 50 scanners identify the sample as malicious, even though 20 different scanners recognize it as malicious but only 5 scanners return a shared label. In either case, we cannot make a confident decision about the exact malware family, and only know that the sample is malicious.
3. *Unknown type.* Apps in this category do not have enough meaningful scanning results. The app could be benign but we are not really sure due to possible false negative in the antivirus products.

We expect the *ideal malware* datasets to be relatively small compared to the other two types of datasets, but cleaner. The *candidate malware* dataset is expected to be noisier, in the sense that we cannot label samples with high confidence. The *unknown type* dataset is the noisiest. By using such datasets, one can thoroughly study how a classifier's performance varies with the amount of noise.

Furthermore, given the uncertainty on the data label, it is interesting to study different approaches to labeling. For example, one can use the majority voting strategy to assign *hard* 0/1 labels to the samples. Alternatively, one can assign confidence scores to labels, based on the number of antivirus scanners that agree on that label, the trustworthiness of each scanner, and also the *freshness* of the application. By using information about "freshness," one can avoid a situation where all or most scanners identify an app as legit, and as a result the app will be labeled as benign with high confidence, when in fact it is a new type of malware. On the other hand, if a very small number of scanners identify an application as malware, while that application has been on the market for a long time, then there is a good chance that the application is legitimate. The confidence scores (which take values in between 0 and 1) associated with the two possible class labels of an app can be seen as *soft* labels (or probabilistic labels), and they essentially represent a probability distribution over labels for each instance. Intuitively, the soft labels can help capture (to some extent) the uncertainty on labels.

8.5.2 Learning from Large Data

To deal with large datasets, we recommend representing the classification problems at hand into a small hierarchy, where the problem at the root is the easiest, and has the largest amount of data, while the most specific problems—assigning malware to specific groups or categories—are the hardest, and have smaller amounts of data. More basic features can be used to address the more general problem (one advantage being that it will be less expensive to generate those features for a large number of apps), while semantics-richer features can be used for the more specific problems (such features will be more expensive to extract, but they will be generated for a smaller number of apps).

8.5.3 Imbalanced Data

Generally, the number of good Android apps is significantly larger than the number of malicious ones, leading to the challenge of learning from highly imbalanced data. We recommend the use of different standard strategies (such as under-sampling, over-sampling, cost-based learning, ensemble-based learning, etc.) to address the class imbalance problem.

8.5.4 Expensive Features

We envision systems that can help a human analyst in the vetting process. As part of this process, each new app will be classified using a hierarchy of classifiers. Furthermore, the classification process has to be fast. However, some classifiers (the most specific ones) may require expensive features whose construction can slow down the process, while a particular test app may be relatively easy to classify. To address this challenge and avoid generating expensive features unnecessarily, we suggest learning multiple classifiers for the same classification problem—from simpler classifiers that are based on more basic features to more complex classifiers that require more sophisticated features. Building a set of classifiers for each problem can be computationally expensive, but this task is done offline and, therefore, time is not the biggest concern (assuming the resources to perform the computation are available). At runtime, for a given app, we will first extract the most basic features, and use the classifier learned using those features to classify the app. If the app is classified with high confidence as benign or as malicious, nothing else needs to be done on the machine part. Otherwise, we will incrementally extract the next set of features required by the next classifier available for the problem at hand.

8.5.5 Leveraging Static Analysis in Feature Selection

An Android app is composed of one or more components and components interact (mostly) through mediated channels in the form of *intent*. While this nature of Android apps makes static analysis challenging, it also creates an opportunity for presenting an app's behavior in a compact format that can help to extract rich features for machine learning.

As an example, consider a recent malware app called HijackRAT that we studied (illustrated in Figure 8.2). One of the malware's components—MyActivity—has the following behaviors: (1) By calling an Android system API, it attempts to hide the app's icon from the phone home screen and prevents the app from being stopped by garbage collection, and (2) it constructs an intent and sends it to DevicePolicyManager (a system service) to ask for administrative privilege. These two behaviors are suspicious and we can detect them by examining the code of this single component. We can detect behavior (1) by looking for the relevant API call in the code. We can detect behavior (2) by performing data flow analysis to resolve the target for the ICC call of the intent.

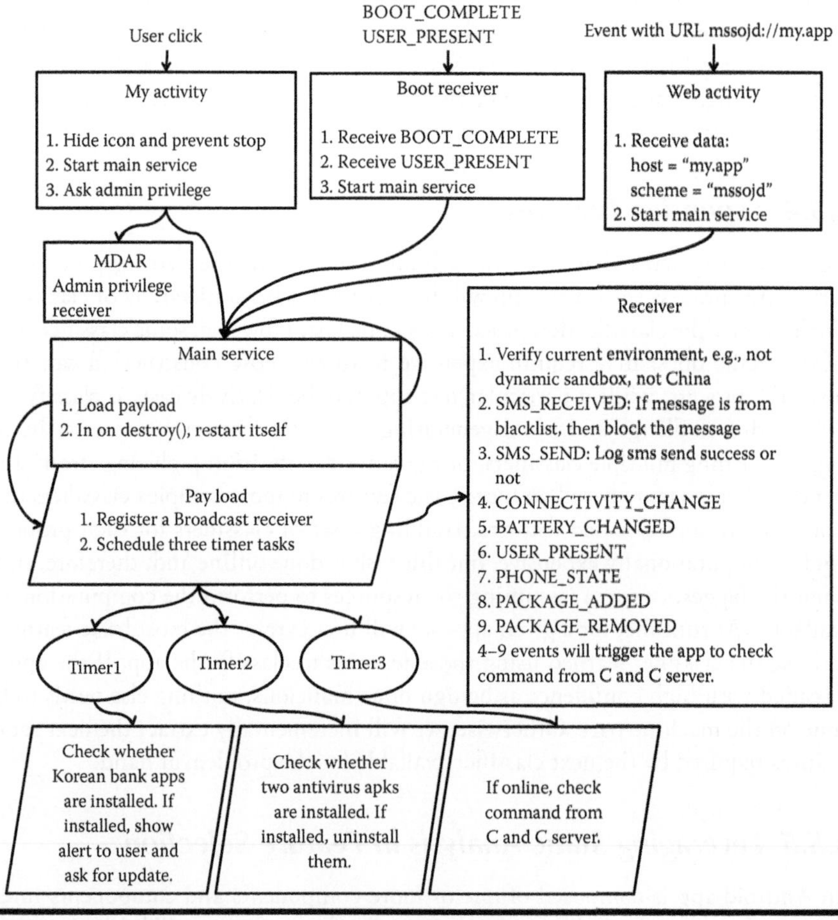

Figure 8.2 The ICC graph of malware HijackRAT.

On the other hand, this app also has inter-component behavior. After the component asks for admin privilege, it will save the user's decision (acceptance/rejection) to the SharedPreference (internal storage of an app). This will be retrieved by another component before it tries to perform actions that require admin privilege. If the user has not granted the privilege, the app will try to acquire it again. SharedPreference is a channel that the above two components use to communicate, which can be captured using static analysis.

MainService is the major component of the malware app. It dynamically loads a payload that is packaged in a separate file in the app's apk file. Upon running, the payload will register a broadcast receiver—a type of Android component that works like a mailbox receiving intents that can be filtered by it. Based on the type of the intent received, Receiver will perform various malicious functions, e.g., blocking messages from legitimate bank numbers so users are not aware of the nefarious transactions the app is trying to perform on the user's behalf. MainService will also initialize three times to perform other malicious functionalities.

A static analyzer like Amandroid [13] can detect the above behaviors and output them in the form of inter-component interaction graph (shorthand ICC graph) like the one shown in Figure 8.2. The unique advantage of this type of graph is that they provide a richer set of features that reveal an app's semantics in addition to other features such as API calls, source-to-sink flows, etc. Extracting a richer set of semantic features from an app is critical to the effectiveness of applying ML in triaging malware analysis, since malware writers can adapt and try to evade detection by changing the way the code is written. If features are based on code properties that can easily be changed, such as the choice of strings to name URLs or components, they will not be robust to evasion even if the classifier has very good performance results on the current malware data set. Features that are based on an app's behaviors are harder to evade since this would require the malware writer to change how the app achieves its objectives, which may only have a limited set of choices.

8.5.6 Understanding the Results

In addition to learning classifiers that can help in the malware triage process, one also needs to understand the results of the classifiers, especially to identify features that are predictive of problematic behaviors within an application. Information about predictive features can be used to inform how to better detect the problem using perhaps a slightly different static analysis plugin, and can help analysts in confirming/ruling out the results. A variety of methods can be used to perform feature ranking: wrapper methods, filter-based methods, and embedded methods [14]. Similar to learning classifiers from large Android app datasets, gaining insight into the results of the classifiers by performing feature ranking poses several challenges. Most importantly, the amount of labeled data available could be small for some classification tasks, while exhibiting high class imbalance. To address such challenges, methods for performing feature ranking from imbalanced data will be beneficial, including semi-supervised/unsupervised methods. First, to address the imbalance challenge, one can use under-sampling, over-sampling, and ensemble-type methods to perform feature ranking [15]. As an example of the ensemble-type methods, one approach for learning from highly imbalanced data with an imbalanced ratio of 1:n works as follows. Construct n balanced subsets, where all subsets contain the same positive data (the minority class) and different subsets of non-overlapping negative data. Perform filter-based feature ranking on each subset and use the average scores to perform an overall ranking for the dataset. A similar approach, where the subsets could have overlapping negative data, was successfully used [16] on the problem of predicting software defects. Furthermore, semi-supervised-like approaches (e.g., transductive SVM) together with sampling approaches can be used to perform feature ranking using a recursive feature elimination-type algorithm [17].

8.6 Summary

In this chapter we discussed a number of challenges in applying big data analytic techniques, in particular machine learning, to mobile app security analysis. Many of the challenges are due to the scale of the mobile app market, e.g., Google Play. We present results from our own research that shows that consistent application of evaluation metrics in ML classifier performance is paramount to producing comparable results. The high imbalance in the positive and negative data samples in mobile data sets present unique challenges in both ML algorithm design and evaluation. We provide a few recommendations to approaches that can potentially address these challenges, and hope that they are useful for the research community to further research in this area.

References

1. Nicholas J. Percoco and Sean Schulte. Adventures in Bouncerland. *Black Hat USA*, 2012.
2. Alexandros Labrinidis and H. V. Jagadish. Challenges and opportunities with big data. *Proc. VLDB Endow.*, 5(12):2032–2033, August 2012.
3. Saurabh Chakradeo, Bradley Reaves, Patrick Traynor, and William Enck. MAST: Triage for market-scale mobile malware analysis. In *Proceedings of the Sixth ACM Conference on Security and Privacy in Wireless and Mobile Networks*, WiSec, pp. 13–24, 2013.
4. Chen Kai, Wang Peng, Lee Yeonjoon, Wang XiaoFeng, Zhang Nan, Huang Heqing, Zou Wei, and Liu Peng. Finding unknown malice in 10 seconds: Mass vetting for new threats at the Google-Play scale. In *Proceedings of the USENIX Security Symposium*, 2015.

5. Daniel Arp, Michael Spreitzenbarth, Malte Hubner, Hugo Gascon, and Konrad Rieck. Drebin: Effective and explainable detection of Android malware in your pocket. In *Proceedings of the NDSS*, 2014.
6. Vitalii Avdiienko, Konstantin Kuznetsov, Alessandra Gorla, Andreas Zeller, Steven Arzt, Siegfried Rasthofer, and Eric Bodden. Mining apps for abnormal usage of sensitive data. In *Proceedings of the ICSE*, 2015.
7. Hao Peng, Chris Gates, Bhaskar Sarma, Ninghui Li, Yuan Qi, Rahul Potharaju, Cristina Nita-Rotaru, and Ian Molloy. Using probabilistic generative models for ranking risks of Android apps. In *Proceedings of the 2012 ACM Conference on Computer and Communications Security* (CCS'12), October 2012.
8. Mu Zhang, Yue Duan, Heng Yin, and Zhiruo Zhao. Semantics-aware Android malware classification using weighted contextual API dependency graphs. In *Proceedings of the 2014 ACM Conference on Computer and Communications Security* (CCS), pp. 1105–1116, 2014.
9. J. Davis and M. Goadrich. The relationship between Precision-Recall and ROC curves. In *Proc. of the ICML*, 2006.
10. N. Viennot et al. A measurement study of Google Play. In *Proc. of the SIGMETRICS*, 2014.
11. S. Roy, J. DeLoach, Y. Li, N. Herndon, D. Caragea, X. Ou, V. P. Ranganath, H. Li, and N. Guevara. Experimental study with real-world data for android app security analysis using machine learning. In *Proceedings of the 2015 Annual Computer Security Applications Conference* (ACSAC 2015), Los Angeles, CA, 2015.
12. Yajin Zhou and Xuxian Jiang. Dissecting Android malware: Characterization and evolution. In *Proceedings of the IEEE SP*, 2012.
13. Fengguo Wei, Sankardas Roy, Xinming Ou, and Robby. Amandroid: A precise and general inter-component data flow analysis framework for security vetting of android apps. In *Proceedings of the 2014 ACM Conference on Computer and Communications Security* (CCS'14), pp. 1329–1341, 2014.
14. I. Guyon and A. Elisseeff. An introduction to variable and feature selection. *J. Mach. Learn. Res.*, 3:1157–1182, March 2003.
15. N. Chawla. Data mining for imbalanced datasets: An overview. In Oded Maimon and Lior Rokach, Eds., *Data Mining and Knowledge Discovery Handbook*, pp. 853–867. Springer US, 2005.
16. T.M. Khoshgoftaar, K. Gao, and J. Van Hulse. A novel feature selection technique for highly imbalanced data. In *Proceedings of the 2010 IEEE International Conference on Information Reuse and Integration* (IRI), pp. 80–85, Aug. 2010.
17. J. Weston and I. Guyon. Support vector machine—Recursive feature elimination (svmrfe), January 10, 2012. US Patent 8,095,483.

Chapter 9

Security, Privacy, and Trust in Cloud Computing

Yuhong Liu, Ruiwen Li, Songjie Cai, and Yan (Lindsay) Sun

Contents

Cloud computing is revolutionizing the cyberspace by enabling convenient, on-demand network access to a large shared pool of configurable computing resources (e.g., networks, servers, storage, applications, and services) that can be rapidly provisioned and released. While cloud computing is gaining popularity, diverse security, privacy, and trust issues are emerging, which hinders the rapid adoption of this new computing paradigm.

To address the cybersecurity needs for this new computing paradigm, this chapter introduces important concepts, models, key technologies, and unique characteristics of cloud computing, which helps readers better understand the fundamental reasons for current security, privacy, and trust issues in cloud computing. Furthermore, critical security, privacy and trust challenges, and the corresponding state-of-the-art solutions are categorized and discussed in detail, and followed by future research directions.

9.1 Introduction to Cloud

Cloud computing is defined as a service model that enables convenient, on-demand network access to a large shared pool of configurable computing resources (e.g., networks, servers, storage, applications, and services) that can be rapidly provisioned and released with minimal management effort or service provider interaction [1].

This innovative information system architecture, which is fundamentally changing the way how computing, storage, and networking resources are allocated and managed, brings numerous advantages to users, including but not limited to reduced capital costs, easy access to information, improved flexibility, automatic service integration, and quick deployment [2]. Many businesses and organizations are attracted by the cloud's nearly unlimited data storage capacity and processing power. In addition, the highly scalable and flexible resource consumption services provided by the cloud make it ideal for businesses that require a cost-effective solution for computationally intensive operations.

Cloud computing has been adopted by a wide range of applications and forms the backbone for many of them. For example, many social media sites rely on the cloud to enable the global access of their users from anywhere, any device, and at any time, to conduct efficient big data analytics on their user behaviors and activities, to host their heavy multimedia content (e.g., videos and photographs), which is the most popular content generated and shared by individual users every day. Another example is that in the Internet of Things applications, anything, no matter if it is a washer and dryer, a car, or a piece of medical equipment, can communicate with each other through the cloud, where significant amounts of messages can be efficiently processed, stored, and analyzed in real time.

In this section, we will introduce the cloud's deployment models, service models, and distinct characteristics, as well as key technologies that enable these characteristics. In addition, we also provide brief discussions on the potential security, privacy, and trust challenges introduced by these components, which serve as the basis for later sections.

9.1.1 Deployment Models

Cloud users have different options to deploy the cloud based on their budget and security requirements. This section will introduce some popular cloud deployment models, as shown in Figure 9.1, their characteristics as well as the security analysis.

1. **Public Cloud:** Public cloud is the most popular form of the cloud computing deployment model. It is made available for the general public users through interfaces on web browsers in a pay-as-you-go manner [1–3]. Cloud service provider (CSP) has full ownership of the public cloud's policy, value, and charging model [4]. Some examples of public cloud services include Amazon EC2, S3, Google AppEngine, and Force.com. Compared to other deployment models, the public cloud minimizes cloud users' cost by achieving economies of scale. However, it also leads to more security issues due to the public access to shared IT resources [5].

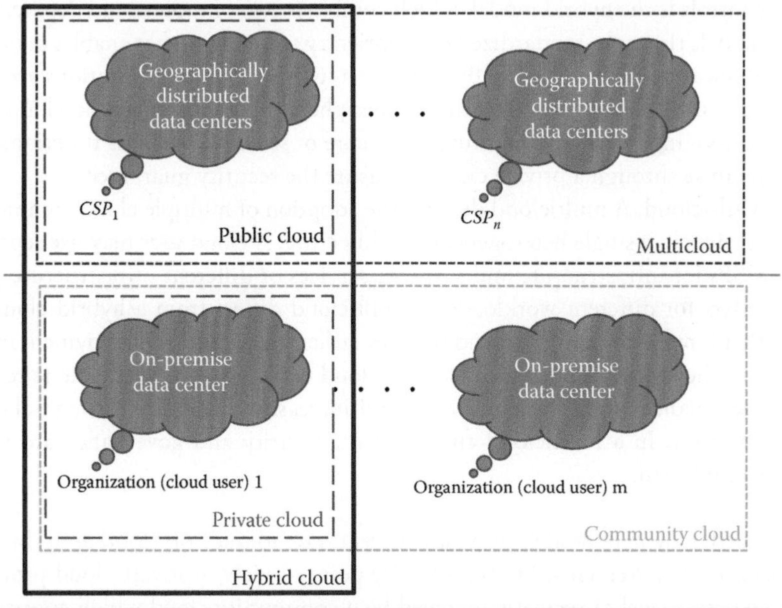

Figure 9.1 Cloud deployment models.

2. **Private Cloud:** To enjoy the cost reduction from resource sharing while avoiding security issues caused by public access, some businesses or organizations choose to deploy a private cloud, which only provides services for internal usage and is not available to the general public [3]. It may be managed and operated by the organization itself or a third party. One example of a private cloud is academic use for research and teaching purposes [4,5]. The advantages of a private cloud include maximization of in-house resources utilization, higher security guarantee compared to public clouds, and full access control over the activities that reside behind the firewalls [1]. Nevertheless, compared to other deployment models, it still generates high costs due to the on-premises hardware maintenance/upgrade and IT management.
3. **Community Cloud:** To further reduce the cost from operating a private cloud while still keeping the security control to some extent, multiple organizations can collaborate with one another and form a community cloud. A community cloud is similar to a private cloud in that it provides services to a specific community of users, who trust one another and share the same interests [1,6]. It could be hosted by a third party or within one of the organizations in the community [5]. Specifically, the community members cooperate on security controls over the cloud and meanwhile also share the operational costs. As a consequence, a community cloud may provide a balance between users' budget and security requirements.
4. **Hybrid Cloud:** Another model to balance cloud users' budget and security controls is the hybrid model, which combines two or more cloud deployment models through standardized or proprietary technology that enables data and application portability [1]. By utilizing a hybrid cloud, organizations are able to outsource their non-significant, peripheral activities to public clouds for cost-savings while maintaining those core or sensitive business functions on-premise through a private cloud to ensure the security guarantee.
5. **Multicloud:** A multicloud denotes the adoption of multiple cloud computing services in a single heterogeneous architecture. A cloud user may use separate CSPs for infrastructure and software services or different infrastructure providers for different workloads. A multicloud differs from a hybrid cloud in that it refers to multiple cloud services rather than multiple deployment models. The motivations of using a multicloud deployment model include reducing reliance on any single vendor and increasing flexibility through choice. However, in a multicloud environment, security and governance are more complicated.

These deployment models provide different ways to trade off cloud users' budget and security requirements. From a security point of view, a private cloud provides the maximum level of security, followed by a community cloud which consists of only collaborative organizations. In a hybrid cloud, users may lose part of their security controls by outsourcing their non-significant data/tasks to a public cloud.

The security over a public cloud goes beyond the control of cloud users. They have to heavily rely on CSPs to provide a security guarantee. The least secured model is a multicloud which has the most complicated security governance scenarios by involving multiple CSPs. From a cost perspective, however, these models are ranked in the reverse order. Multicloud provides the cheapest solution by involving multiple CSPs to avoid single vendor lock-in, followed by public cloud, which is operated by a single CSP. Both of these two models reduce cloud users' costs by achieving economics of scale through resource sharing among disparate users. Cloud users' costs in a hybrid cloud, community cloud, and private cloud are usually much higher than that in the two previous models because of the on-premise deployment and maintenance of IT resources.

9.1.2 Service Models

A cloud provides various services to satisfy different levels of user requirements, including software as a service (SaaS), platform as a service (PaaS), and infrastructure as a service (IaaS), as shown in Figure 9.2.

1. **Software as a Service (SaaS)**: Software as a service (SaaS), sometimes referred to as on-demand software, is a software delivery model that provides software services to cloud users remotely as an Internet-based service. In particular, CSPs deploy software applications on their servers. Cloud users can order application software and services via the Internet according to their demands, and they are usually charged based on their usage or through a subscription fee. The key features of the SaaS model include: (a) central management on software upgrades and patches and (b) web access from users. Some examples of the SaaS model are Google Apps, Salesforce, Workday, Dropbox, and Cisco WebEx.

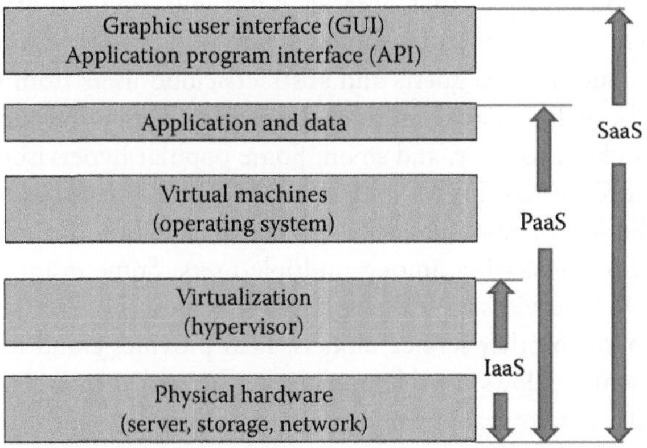

Figure 9.2 Cloud service models.

The broad web access from heterogeneous user devices introduces high access control risks and requires more robust authentication and access control schemes.

2. **Platform as a Service (PaaS):** Platform as a service (PaaS) provides cloud users with an application development environment, which typically includes operating system, programming-language execution environment, databases, and web servers. Cloud users can design their own graphical user interface (GUI) and determine what application program interface (API) (provided by the CSP) to call. Cloud users' applications will be running on top of the cloud and the data generated by these applications will be stored in the cloud.

   In the PaaS model, users can save their costs by focusing more on their software development while not maintaining the underlying hardware and software environment. Furthermore, the underlying computing and storage resources scale automatically to meet the application requirement and users will be charged according to their actual usage. The key features for the PaaS model include (1) services for quick, easy, and cost-effective application development, testing, and deployment, (2) allowance of multiple concurrent users of the same development application, and (3) support for development team collaboration [7]. Some examples of the PaaS model are Apprenda, Microsoft Azure, Google Compute Engine (GCE), and Salesforce Heroku.

   The PaaS receives increasing concerns from users who store their business data in the cloud about their data confidentiality, integrity, availability, and privacy breach. In addition, the lack of a secure software development process may lead to insecure code [8].

3. **Infrastructure as a Service (IaaS):** Infrastructure as a service (IaaS) provides cloud users with fundamental IT resources, such as servers, storage, network, and operating systems, as an on-demand service. In an IaaS model, cloud users will be assigned one or multiple virtual machines (VMs), over which they have full control, such as installing operating systems and application software, and running different tasks. A virtualization software on top of the cloud physical infrastructure, named hypervisor, hosts VMs owned by one or multiple cloud users as guests and abstracts cloud users from the infrastructure details, such as management of the physical servers, resource sharing and scaling, backup, security, and so on. Some popular hypervisors include Xen, VMware ESX/ESXi, KVM, and Hyper-V. The key features of IaaS include (a) distribution of resources as a service, (b) dynamic scaling of resources, and (c) resource sharing among multiple users. Some examples of IaaS are Amazon Web Services (AWS) and Cisco Metapod [7].

   Compared to other service models, IaaS provides cloud users with more controls, which allows capable users to further enhance their security levels. Meanwhile, it also grants cloud users more privilege and thus opens more opportunities for malicious users to exploit hypervisor vulnerabilities and to even penetrate the virtual isolation among different cloud users.

9.1.3 Distinct Characteristics

Cloud computing is revolutionizing cyberspace through its distinct characteristics such as broad-based network access, resource pooling, rapid elasticity, pay-as-you-go services, and federated environment. While these essential characteristics distinguish cloud computing from conventional Internet-based services and are attracting tremendous users, they also introduce new vulnerabilities and open a new frontier for cyber security and defense researches. The understanding of these essential characteristics can serve as a basis to analyze security, privacy, and trust challenges in the cloud environment.

1. **Broad-Based Network Access:** Broad-based network access indicates that cloud computing resources can be easily accessed by cloud users over the Internet [9]. Specifically, through a single user account logged on from diverse devices located anywhere in the world, a cloud user can access its data and applications running on a single logical location which is usually the integration of multiple physical or virtual devices.

   This characteristic attracts users by providing them a convenient way to access cloud services. However, it also provides a much larger attack surface by introducing a dynamic series of access points that have a variety of security postures [10]. The heterogeneity of various access points raises high access control risks such as account hijacking, browser vulnerabilities, and unauthorized users [11], which dramatically increase the possibility for illegitimate users to obtain unauthorized access to data and services.
2. **Resource Pooling:** Resource pooling indicates the joining of IT resources from a variety of locations around the world [9]. These resources, including both physical and virtual resources, are shared among multiple customers or tenants to significantly improve resource utilization efficiency and reduce operating costs [12].

   However, various security, privacy, and trust challenges are raised due to the imperfect isolation and the risk of having untrustworthy tenants reside in the same physical hardware. For instance, the malware injection attack involves an attacker uploading a malicious instance of an unsuspecting user into the cloud who can steal data from the victim [11]. Other attacks that exploit resource pooling include co-resident attacks and attacks against the hypervisor that manages multiple VMs.
3. **Rapid Elasticity:** The cloud provides dynamic resource expanding/contracting based on users' capacity needs, which is defined as rapid elasticity. This allows a user to upgrade or degrade the cloud services at run time in order to promote scalability. For instance, to increase the data processing speed of a system, the number of VMs can be increased automatically to meet the demand of the system.

Nevertheless, the constantly changing allocation of resources among disparate users dramatically increases the risk of resource compromises. If an attacker manages to hijack a resource and run malicious code, the compromised resource could be assigned to multiple users before its abnormal behavior is identified [11]. This service-injection attack could allow attackers to steal confidential information or data from its victim.

4. **Pay-As-You-Go Service:** Pay-As-You-Go service, derived from utility computing, considers cloud resources as one type of utility, so that cloud users are billed according to their actual usage of these resources. It allows a user to scale, customize, and provision computing resources, including software, storage, and development platforms.

   However, the metering information, which determines the cost of each cloud user, has become a potential vulnerability that can be manipulated by attackers [11]. This information is more detailed than in previous IT implementations due to the dynamic and resource sharing attributes of the cloud [10]. Moreover, a theft of service attack presents an even greater threat to the cloud, and it specifically targets the measured service feature. This type of attack is made possible by the scheduling vulnerabilities of the hypervisors. As a result, the attacker is able to consume cloud resources without the knowledge of the CSP and avoid the billing charges [11].

9.1.4 Key Technologies

Diverse technologies have been developed in cloud computing scenarios to provide high quality and cost-efficient solutions for cloud users. Among these technologies, multi-tenancy, virtualization, distributed data storage, and cloud federation are essential elements that enable the distinct characteristics of cloud computing.

1. **Multi-tenancy:** Multi-tenancy is defined as "the practice of placing multiple tenants on the same physical hardware to reduce costs of the user by leveraging economies of scale" [13]. It indicates sharing of computational resources, storage, services, and applications with other tenants, hosted by the same physical or logical platform at the provider's premises [14]. Specifically, the concept of multi-tenancy varies for different service models [13].
   a. In SaaS, multiple tenants have their applications share a single instance of object code.
   b. In PaaS, each tenant may have various layers of their hosted solution, such as business logic, data access logic and storage, or presentation logic, hosted across multiple physical servers.
   c. In IaaS, the hosted environment for each tenant is partitioned and controlled by a single instance of hypervisor and virtualization software.

2. **Virtualization:** Virtualization refers to the logical abstraction of computing resources from physical constraints. Such computing resources include operating systems, networks, memory, and storage. One representative example of virtualization technology is the virtual machine (VM), a piece of software emulating a physical machine to execute programs. Virtualization can be implemented at different layers, including hardware virtualization, software virtualization, network virtualization, and desktop virtualization. In practice, virtualization at multiple layers may be integrated to flexibly provide services based on users' requirements [15]. In a virtualized environment, computing resources can be dynamically created, expanded, shrunk, or moved according to users' demands, which greatly improves agility and flexibility, reduces costs, and enhances business values for cloud computing [9].
3. **Distributed Data Storage:** The cloud stores a user's data in a logical storage pool which may physically span multiple geographically distributed data centers. It dramatically decreases the cost of massive data storage since different available storage pieces can be effectively integrated and managed to store data. On the other hand, high data reliability is achieved by backing up data using redundant storage at different places around the globe [15].
4. **Cloud Federation:** Cloud federation is the practice of interconnecting the cloud computing resources from multiple cloud service providers [16]. The federation of cloud resources allows a cloud user to optimize its operations by distributing workloads around the globe and moving data between disparate clouds [17]. It provides more choices to cloud users, so that they can choose the best cloud service provider to meet a particular business or technological need.

Despite enabling substantial benefits, these technologies are still at their developing stage. Attacks exploiting the vulnerabilities of these imperfect technologies are gaining popularity and threatening the security of cloud infrastructure. We will discuss such attacks in detail in Section 9.3.

9.2 Security, Privacy, and Trust Challenges in Cloud Computing

Although cloud computing brings numerous attractive features, it does not come without costs. The computing society has to face emerging security, privacy, and trust challenges raised by cloud services.

9.2.1 Security Attacks against Multi-Tenancy

While the multi-tenancy architecture allows CSPs to maximize the organizational efficiency and significantly reduce a cloud user's computing expenses, it also results in a number of security challenges by hosting multiple tenants with heterogeneous security settings and diverse behaviors on the same physical or logical platform.

1. Uncoordinated security controls among disparate tenants: In the multi-tenant environment, the security policies made by different tenants may disagree or even conflict with one another. Such disagreements or conflicts could introduce threats to tenants' needs, interests, or concerns [18]. More important, different tenants' security controls are heterogeneous. The tenant with fewer security controls or misconfigurations is easier to compromise, which may later serve as a stepping stone to the more secured tenants located in the same host. This could reduce the overall security level for all the tenants to that of the least secured one [19].
2. **Attacks against general co-residents:** Adversaries taking advantage of the co-residency opportunities may launch diverse attacks against their co-residents [20]. This type of attack usually does not target specific tenants in the cloud. Instead, the attackers' goal is to exhaust shared resources in the system such as thread execution time, memory, storage requests, and network interfaces, so that other users sharing the same physical resources are not able to consume the cloud services [21]. In [22], a Shrew attack is proposed where the attackers are able to launch low-rate DoS attacks by identifying the bottlenecks of the cloud through a loss-based probe.
3. **Attacks against target co-residents:** There are also attacks focusing on a specific target tenant (i.e., victim). Attackers may manage to place their malicious tenants in the same physical device that hosts the target tenant and then launch attacks against it. There are usually three steps in this type of attack. Different attack strategies can be involved in each step.
   Step 1: Determine the location of the targeted tenant through network probing. In [23], different tools, such as nmap, hping, and wget, are employed to perform network probes. And the geographical zone of a target tenant can be located by its IP information. A malicious tenant can verify its co-residence by having an identical DOM_0 IP address and small packet round-trip times (RTT) with the target tenant [24].
   Step 2: Place a malicious tenant on the same host as the targeted tenant. A brute-force placement strategy is proposed in [23], with which the attacker runs numerous malicious tenants over a relatively long time period and achieves co-residency with 8.4% of the target tenants. By taking advantage of the CSP's placement locality, an instance flooding strategy, where the attacker launches as many tenants in parallel as possible, has successfully achieved co-residency with a specific target tenant [23].
   Step 3: Attack the target tenant. With the success of the first two steps, attackers are able to place malicious tenants at the same physical server as the target tenant.

Malicious tenants may be able to infer confidential information of the target tenant via covert side channel attacks. A side channel attack is any attack based on unauthorized access to information through physical implementation of a system, named side channels [25]. Generally speaking, the potential side channels can be any physical resources shared between multiple tenants, such as network access, CPU branch predictors and instruction cache [26–29], DRAM memory bus [30], CPU pipelines [31], scheduling of CPU cores and timeslices, disk access [32], and so on. Some typical side channel attacks include: (1) timing attack, one of the most common side channel attacks, in which the attacker attempts to gain information by measuring the time it takes for a unit to perform operations [33], (2) power consumption attacks where the attacker can identify system processes by analyzing the power consumed by a unit while performing different operations [33], and (3) differential fault analysis where the attacker studies the behavior of a system by injecting faults into it [33], (4) cache usage attacks where the attacker measures the utilization of CPU caches on its physical machine to monitor the activities on co-resident's activities [23], (5) load-based co-residence attack where the attacker measures the load variation of its co-resident to verify whether it is co-located with the target VM [23], and (6) co-resident traffic rates estimation [23].

Furthermore, malicious tenants may also penetrate the isolation among tenants by exploiting system vulnerabilities. For example, the attacker who obtains access to the underlying operating system memory could potentially capture the sensitive information from other tenants. A misconfigured hypervisor which hosts multiple tenants may serve as a conduit for information leakage [19].

Last but not least, malicious tenants may also degrade victim's performance by over-consuming computing resources, such as CPU, memory, storage space, I/O resources, and so on. A Swiper attack is proposed in [24], with which the attacker uses a carefully designed workload to incur significant delays on the victim's targeted application. In [34], the authors propose and implement an attack which modifies the workload of a target VM in a way that frees up resources for the attacker's VM. The reason for the success of such an attack is that an overload created by one tenant may negatively impact the performance of another tenant [35].

9.2.2 Security Attacks against Virtualization

Serving as an essential component of the cloud foundation, virtualization technology receives extensive security attacks from different aspects.

1. **Physical vulnerabilities:** Vulnerabilities in the physical infrastructure still threaten the virtual environment [19]. On the one hand, the virtualized implementation is also subject to risks and attacks against the physical resources. For example, the attacks penetrating the misconfigured physical firewalls are also able to compromise the virtual firewall with the same configuration

settings. On the other hand, the virtualized environment will be exposed to threats if the underlying physical infrastructure has been compromised.

2. **New access context:** Virtualization brings new challenges to user authentication, authorization, and accounting in terms of properly defining roles and policies [19]. Virtualization technology enables users to access their data and applications running on a single logical location which is usually the integration of multiple physical or virtual devices. The lack of security border and isolation introduces the possibility of information leakage [36]. Furthermore, such access can be done through a single user account logged on from diverse devices located anywhere in the world. This new access context raises many challenges, such as whether a user has the same privileges to access different physical or virtual devices; whether the accounts logged on from multiple distant geographic locations belong to the same user. Granular separation of user roles is required to address these challenges [19].
3. **Attacks against hypervisor:** The hypervisor that manages multiple VMs becomes the target of attacks [19]. Different from physical devices which are independent from one another, VMs in the cloud are usually residing in one physical device managed by the same hypervisor. The compromise of the hypervisor therefore will put multiple VMs at risk. For example, if an attacker gains access over the hypervisor, he or she is able to manipulate the network traffic, configuration files, and even the connection status of the VMs located on top of the hypervisor [37,38].

   Furthermore, the immaturity of the hypervisor technology, such as isolation, access control, security hardening, and so on, provides attackers with new potentials to exploit the system. Attackers gaining access to the host running multiple VMs are able to access the resources shared by the VMs, and even bring down these resources and turn off the hypervisor [38].
4. **Attacks against VMs:** Diverse attacks can be launched against virtual machines. For example, VMs can exist in either active or dormant states. Although the dormant VMs may still hold sensitive user data, they can easily be overlooked and not updated with the latest security settings, leading to potential information leakage [19].

   In addition, when a VM is launched, the information required to invoke the VM is created and saved on the host. In the multi-tenant scenario, this information for all the VMs located in the same server will be stored on a common storage system. The attackers gaining access to this storage space will be able to break into the VMs, which is called VM hijacking [39].

   Moreover, since a VM can be copied over network or through a USB, and the source configuration files are recreated when the VM is moved to a new location, the attackers may be able to modify the configuration file as well as the VM's activities during the VM migration [37]. Once a VM is infected and readmitted to its original host, the infection can potentially spread out to other VMs located on the same host. Such an attack is also known as virtual library check-out [40].

9.2.3 Data Security and Privacy in Cloud

Different from traditional IT infrastructure, where organizations have complete control over their data, cloud computing diminishes users' control over their data when they move it from local servers to cloud servers. Such loss of control has raised a great number of concerns on data protection and privacy, such as where the data is stored, how the data is backed up, who has the access to the data, whether the deleted data will be permanently removed from the cloud, and so on, making organizations hesitant to move to cloud.

1. **Data loss and data breach:** Data loss and data breaches are recognized as the top threats in the cloud computing environment in 2013 [41]. A recent survey shows that 63% of customers would be less likely to purchase a cloud service if the cloud vendor reported a material data breach involving the loss or theft of sensitive or confidential personal information [42]. Whether a CSP can securely maintain customers' data has become the major concern of cloud users. The frequent outages occurring on reputable CSPs [43], including Amazon, Dropbox, Microsoft, Google drive and so on, further exacerbate such concerns.

   To help customers recover in case of service failures, data proliferation is conducted in the cloud where customers' data is replicated in multiple data centers as backups [44]. However, the distributed storage for multiple data copies may increase the risks of data breaches and inconsistency. For example, due to the heterogeneity of security settings for the multiple storage devices, the overall security level of the data is only determined by the "weakest link in the chain." The attackers can obtain the data if any one of the storage devices is compromised. In addition, the multiple data copies need to be synchronized when customers make any data updates, including insertion, modification, and deletion. The failures of data synchronization will lead to data inconsistency. Last but not least, it is more challenging for a cloud user to track the appropriateness of a CSP's data operations. For example, it is extremely difficult to ascertain whether the CSP will completely delete all the data copies when such a request is made by the user [44].
2. **Cheap data and data analysis:** The rapid development of cloud computing has facilitated the generation of big data, leading to cheap data collections and analysis [45]. For example, many popular online social media sites, such as Facebook, Twitter, and LinkedIn, are utilizing cloud computing technology to store and to process their customers' data [46]. Cloud providers who store the data are gaining considerable business revenue by either retrieving

user information through data mining and analysis by themselves or selling the data to other businesses for secondary usage [44]. One example is that Google is using its cloud infrastructure to collect and analyze users' data for its advertising network [45].

Such data usage has raised extensive privacy concerns since the sensitive information of cloud users may be easily accessed and analyzed by unauthorized parties. The Electronic Privacy Information Center (EPIC) asked to shut down Gmail, Google Docs, Google Calendar, and the company's other Web apps until government-approved "safeguards are verifiably established" [47]. Netflix had to cancel its $1 million prize data challenge due to a legal suit that it violated customers' privacy during the data sharing process [48]. While technologies such as data anonymization are under investigation [44], users' data privacy has to be fundamentally protected by standards, regulations, and laws.

According to a research survey conducted by Ponemon Institute, the level of commitment a CSP has for protecting data privacy has an important impact on cloud users' purchase decisions [42]. Specifically, such commitment includes policies and practices about setting up strict processes to separate customer data, disclosing physical location of customers' data, and not mining user data for advertising.

3. **Data storage and transmission under multiple regional regulations:** Due to the distributed infrastructure of the cloud, cloud users' data may be stored on data centers geographically located in multiple legal jurisdictions, leading to cloud users' concerns about the legal reach of local regulations on data stored out of region [49]. For example, data privacy laws are not the same for every country. Furthermore, the local laws may be violated since the dynamic nature of the cloud makes it extremely difficult to designate a specific server or device to be used for the transborder data transmission [44]. As one solution, cloud service providers, such as Amazon, allow customers to control the geographic location of their cloud services [50].

9.2.4 Lack of Trust among Multiple Stakeholders in Cloud

Trust, originated from social science, is defined as a relationship between two parties. That is, how much confidence one party has about whether the other party will perform a certain action or possess a certain property. Lack of trust has been identified as one of the major obstacles that hinders the rapid adoption of cloud computing [51].

1. **Cloud users' trust on CSPs:** The adoption of cloud, especially public cloud, heavily relies on cloud users establishing trust on CSPs. Such a trust establishment process is challenging. It relies on the development of technology, people's changing of mindset, and transparency between cloud users and service providers.

Take task scheduling as an example. In the cloud, users' tasks are usually divided into smaller subtasks which are executed on multiple computing nodes in parallel. Computing nodes involved in a given task can be very diverse in their security settings. The less secured computing nodes, once compromised by attackers, may lead to the failure of the entire task. Thus, developing technologies to ensure the security of computing nodes plays a critical role in increasing the overall trustworthiness of large-scale cloud computation [52].

Take cloud data storage service as another example. Data, especially sensitive business data, is always the last thing that an organization would like to give up control over [53]. In traditional IT infrastructure, organizations build up their own data centers on-premise and place all of their data and applications locally on their own servers, over which they have complete control. In contrast, in cloud computing, organizations have to give up at least part of their control and outsource it to CSPs, which makes them hesitate to adopt this new computing paradigm. In many cases, even organizations using the cloud, for most of the time, only store their less sensitive data on the cloud. It takes time to persuade organizations to change their mindset and establish trust in CSPs [45].

In addition, providing transparent services could often facilitate trust establishment. It requires CSPs to be more open and disclose more details on their security readiness. But CSPs often consider some of the information as trade secret and thus are not willing to share.

2. **CSPs' trust in cloud users:** On the other hand, it is also important for CSPs to monitor and evaluate the trustworthiness of their users, since not all cloud users can be trusted. However, this problem has been neglected due to several reasons. First, cloud service providers' potential loss caused by malicious users is often underestimated. Second, cloud's open nature and the economies of scale feature drive CSPs to attract more cloud users, as long as they honestly pay for their resource consumption. Third, evaluating users' trustworthiness by tracking and analyzing their behaviors is not trivial and usually leads to extra resource consumption and management costs.

   Nevertheless, these statements are not true in reality. Untrustworthy cloud users managing to reside in the same physical device with normal users may be able to launch co-resident attacks and steal sensitive information [54]. Without CSP's appropriate monitoring and logging about users' behaviors, it is extremely difficult for normal cloud users to protect themselves from being attacked by malicious users. As a consequence, even malicious attacks targeting only cloud users may eventually hurt CSPs' reputation and undermine normal users' trust in the cloud. More important, compared to the Internet attackers, untrustworthy cloud users may cause more severe damage because they can directly access the software, platform, and even infrastructure of the cloud [51]. Smart attacks have already been developed to deceive CSPs' billing schemes for free riding, which causes CSPs' economic loss.

3. **Trust in other parties:** Beyond the explicit trust relationship between cloud users and service providers, there are other different stakeholders involved in the trustworthy cloud computing scenario, such as multiple collaborating CSPs or third parties, making the trust evaluation process even more complicated. For example, a multicloud model may be deployed where multiple CSPs work together to provide services for a cloud user's different workloads. In such cases, the cloud user's overall security guarantee has to rely on the collaborations from multiple CSPs. The delegation of security responsibilities among different CSPs becomes a challenging issue. In addition, some third parties, such as third party audit, authentication, encryption, and so on, are proposed to facilitate trust development between cloud users and CSPs through recommendations. These third parties, however, can only help when they are trusted by both cloud users and service providers, which brings in new types of trust issues.

9.3 Security, Privacy, and Trust Solutions in Cloud Computing

Various solutions have been proposed to handle the above-mentioned security, privacy, and trust challenges in cloud computing. In this section, we first discuss the adoption of some "conventional" security solutions, such as logging and monitoring, access control, and encryption, which serve as general equations to solve security issues in different cyber systems. Then we introduce emerging solutions specifically designed to work in a cloud computing scenario, such as virtual isolation and defense against co-resident attacks. At the end, we investigate different ways to establishing trust among different parties in the cloud scenario.

9.3.1 Logging and Monitoring

Logging and monitoring collect ample evidence of user behaviors as well as system status to assist anomaly detection.

User behavior monitoring. Selective monitoring of user activities is proposed in [55], where all users are assigned a security label based on prior activities, and additional surveillance is given to those with previous security violations. Any abnormalities will result in denied permission and immediate alerting. In [56], the authors propose to combine user monitoring tools with the intrusion detection system for immediate action against malicious users and alerting of proper system administrators. This proposed framework suggests a strong user authentication, monitoring of user activity and all media transfers, and resource checking. If security violations occur, a defense manager will immediately deny permissions. By taking user behaviors as input, machine learning techniques can be applied to identify malicious users (1) cloning a virtual machine, (2) copying everything from a virtual machine, and (3) taking snapshots of the virtual machine [57].

System status monitoring. In [58], it was proposed that anomaly detection should be based on the effects on the system caused by malicious events rather than on the behavior of individual users. Network activities are monitored from user perspective, database server perspective, and file server perspective. Hoda et al. [59] proposed to build a global model for the entire set of available domains to detect both blending anomalies and irregular user behavior. In their work, the term "domain" refers to separate categories of data (e.g., email domain or logon domain, etc.) that may exhibit different behavior and therefore requires suitable processing and analysis techniques.

Logging and monitoring are indirect defense solutions that do not directly prevent or stop malicious attacks. However, results generated by the logging and monitoring process provide critical evidence to facilitate other later mentioned defense solutions, such as access control, isolation, co-resident attack detection, trustworthiness evaluation, and so on.

9.3.2 Access Control

As previously mentioned, cloud computing has introduced new access context, which significantly increases the risks of fraudulent users obtaining unauthorized access to data and services [10,11].

Access control, consisting of authentication, authorization, and accountability, is the way of ensuring that the access is provided only to the authorized users and hence the data is stored in a secure manner [60].

Research has been conducted to develop advanced access control techniques in terms of properly defining roles and policies [36,40]. For example, a role-based multi-tenancy access control (RM-MTAC) model, which applies identity management to determine the user's identity and applicable roles, is designed to efficiently manage a user's access privilege to achieve application independence and data isolation [61]. In [62], the authors define and enforce access policies based on data attributes and allow the data owner to delegate most of the computation tasks involved in fine-grained data access control to untrusted cloud servers without disclosing the underlying data contents. Furthermore, physical measures are also proposed to ensure the access control to the hypervisor or VMs. An example is a hardware token possessed by the administrator in order to launch the hypervisor [63].

9.3.3 Encryption-Based Security Solutions

At the current stage, encryption is still one of the major solutions to address data confidentiality, integrity, and privacy issues in cloud computing [64,65]. Through encryption algorithms, sensitive information is encrypted and can only be accessed by users possessing the encryption keys.

There are many encryption schemes available. For example, El-Etriby et al. [66] compared eight modern encryption methods in the context of cloud computing. However, due to the involvement of multiple parties in the cloud environment, the adoption of encryption schemes has to face a critical question as to which party should encrypt the data and manage the encryption keys.

Cloud users can simply rely entirely on CSP for their encryption needs. For example, Amazon Simple Storage Service (S3) encrypts users' data by default. In this case, the problem is that cloud users lose control over ensuring the confidentiality of their data, since CSP has full access to the data. Even if the CSP does not intend to do any harm to the cloud users' data, there is still a risk associated with malicious insiders. Since cloud users' data are stored on distributed storage nodes in the cloud, one or multiple compromised nodes may breach the confidentiality, integrity, and privacy of the entire data set. To prevent this possibility, a ciphertext policy-attribute-based-encryption (CP-ABE) can be used to achieve a fine-grained data access control by enabling cloud users to define their own access policies over the data encrypted by CSP [67]. Specifically, cloud users can grant differential access rights to different parties according to their attributes. Such access rights will be used to generate private keys for each party. As a consequence, only a party with a set of attributes satisfying the access policy of the encrypted data can decrypt the ciphertext and obtain the data. It does not rely on CSPs for preventing unauthorized data access.

To avoid the full access of data from CSP, cloud users can choose their own encryption method, encrypt their data, and store it in the cloud. Many cloud users are using this approach today to protect their data. This approach, however, raises a challenging question as to how CSPs can provide data services to cloud users, such as search, insertion, and deletions, while not decrypting their data. Homomorphic encryption [68] is useful in this scenario because it allows CSPs to manage users' data by providing services, such as searches, correctness verification, and error localization [69], without having to decrypt it. Specifically, Craig Gentry [70], using lattice-based cryptography, describes the first plausible construction for a fully homomorphic encryption scheme. Gentry's scheme supports both additions and multiplications on ciphertexts, which provide the basis to perform arbitrary computation. Later in 2010, a second fully homomorphic encryption scheme was proposed [71], which replaces the ideal lattice-based scheme with a much simpler integer-based scheme while maintaining similar properties for homomorphic operations and efficiency. In 2013, IBM presented an open source software library, Helib [72], which has implemented fully homomorphic encryption with some optimization. Although promising, the homomorphic encryption has its own disadvantages such as expensive computational and bandwidth costs. Another weakness is exposed when attackers can detect certain patterns in the communications associated with operations using the homomorphic encryption [73].

Recently, efforts have been made to partially leverage homomorphic encryption algorithms for only efficient operations in cloud computing. For example, CryptDB has been proposed to prevent a curious database administrator (DBA) from learning private data (e.g., health records, financial statements, personal information). One of the key techniques involved is an SQL-aware encryption strategy, which executes SQL queries over encrypted data. Homomorphic encryption has been adopted for summation, where the encryption of two values' summation can be calculated by multiplying the encryption of these two values [74]. The SQL-aware encryption algorithms are also adopted by the SecureDBaaS architecture [75], which allows multiple, independent, and geographically distributed cloud users to execute concurrent operations on encrypted data in the cloud.

If cloud users choose to do the encryption by themselves, they have to be responsible for the heavy computation introduced by encryption algorithms. In addition, the quality of encryption algorithms arbitrarily chosen by individual cloud users could be questionable. More problems arise when cloud users lose their encryption keys, or in an even worse case, have encryption keys stolen by an attacker who compromises their workstations.

Another approach is to have a trusted third-party organization to be in charge of encryption and managing the encryption keys. Although this option solves some security problems such as the lost encryption keys or weak encryption algorithms, cloud users still face the possibilities of losing privacy and confidentiality since the third-party encryption service still has full access to their data. Newly emerging cloud encryption methods take a step further in terms of key management. They do not allow any one party to take full ownership of an encryption key. Instead, they divide the key into pieces, each of which is kept by a cloud user, a CSP, and a third-party data encryption service.

9.3.4 Virtual Isolation

To keep the benefits generated by resource sharing among different cloud users, while addressing security issues caused by it, much research focuses on enhancing virtual isolation, which aims to provide a certain level of isolation among tenants' data, computing, and application processes.

With perfect isolation, the execution of one user's service should not interfere with the performance of another user. In particular, it should achieve

- Segregation of VMs' storage, processing, memory, and access path networks in IaaS.
- Segregation of running services and API calls as well as operating system level process in PaaS.
- Segregation of transactions carried out on the same instance by different tenants and tenants' data or information in SaaS [9,15].

Current studies implement virtual isolation from different levels of the cloud. First, some isolation solutions are proposed to directly work on the hardware level, such as allocating memory bandwidth [76] and processor caches [77] in a better way. Second, isolation can also be facilitated by utilizing hypervisors or virtual machine monitor (VMM), a piece of computer software, firmware, or hardware that creates and runs virtual machines. For example, the original development of the Xen hypervisor aimed to realize isolation [78]. Third, some software level resource management mechanisms are proposed to perform isolation for cache [79], disk [80], memory bandwidth [81], and network [82]. Fourth, security models are established to ensure isolation. In [83], the concept of tenant-ID is introduced on the data-link layer to securely segment, isolate, and identify tenants and their assets in the cloud. The authors in [84] propose a security model and a set of principles to secure logical isolation between tenant resources in a cloud storage system.

9.3.5 Defense against Co-Resident Attacks

Various schemes have been proposed to defend against co-resident attacks. We classify them into two categories. Schemes in the first category aim at detecting malicious residents by analyzing their unique behavior patterns. Different from such solutions, schemes in the second category do not explicitly differentiate malicious residents from normal ones. Instead, they treat all residents as potential attackers and provide more general solutions, such as increasing the difficulties of achieving or verifying co-residence, obfuscating side channel information, or running VMs at isolated physical servers.

1. **Detecting co-resident attacks:** The straightforward way to defend against co-resident attacks is to identify the attack patterns. For example, the authors in [85] have proposed a cache-based side channel detection approach (i.e., CSDA), which identifies the attack patterns as high cache miss time at the physical host side as well as frequent changes in CPU/memory utilization at the VM side. Sundareswaran et al. [86] have proposed a detection framework, in which an "observer" VM identifies VMs launching excess system calls and interrupts as suspicious VMs, and then a "defender" further searches suspicious VMs' behavior for particular attack patterns.

   However, such detection schemes suffer from three limitations. First, the noisy resource consumption from either the physical server itself or other normal residents makes it very challenging to differentiate attack patterns from normal behaviors. Second, different types of co-resident attacks usually do not share the same attack patterns, requiring detection schemes to handle them separately. As a consequence, detection schemes are usually ad-hoc and application specific. Third, such detection schemes need to monitor, aggregate, and analyze the behavior of each individual process, which may cause high overhead and even drop the performance of the physical server.

2. **Preventing co-resident attacks:** Due to the challenges to detect co-resident attacks accurately and efficiently, many defense solutions are proposed to minimize the possibilities for co-resident attacks to succeed. We further discuss them according to their working mechanisms.

Security aware VM allocation policy. Attackers who aim to launch co-resident attacks against a certain target have to first place their malicious VMs on the same physical host where the target VM locates. Co-resident attacks cannot succeed if this first step fails. Therefore, researches are launched to design security aware VM allocation policies which significantly increase the difficulties for attackers to achieve co-residence.

Many VM allocation policies are studied to assign different initial positions to VMs. For instance, a randomization way to assign VMs has been proposed [87] to make VMs' deployment unpredictable to attackers. Han et al. have proposed a co-resident attack resistant VM allocation policy [88], which distributes VMs by optimizing security, workload balance, and power consumption needs of cloud servers.

Beyond the VM initial position allocation policy, there is also some research investigating VM migration policies to reduce the possibility of co-resident attacks. For example, Li and Zhang et al. have designed a Vickrey–Clarke–Groves (VCG) mechanism to migrate VMs periodically, so that malicious VMs cannot stay co-located with their target VM for a long time even if they can achieve co-residence [89].

Increasing the difficulty of verifying co-residence. As discussed in Section 9.2.1, malicious VMs can confirm their co-residence status by having an identical DOM_0 IP address with the target VM. A straightforward solution is to hide the DOM_0's IP address from cloud users. Nevertheless, when attackers use more complicated strategies to verify the co-residence, more advanced defense solutions are required.

Obfuscating side channel information. Another approach to prevent sensitive information from being transferred between co-resident VMs is to hide or obfuscate information exposed to side channels at different levels of the cloud infrastructure. First, eliminating side channels from the hardware level [90–92] usually provides more effective defense. However, due to the complex process of introducing new hardware into existing cloud infrastructure, the adoption of such schemes is very difficult. Second, extensive research has been carried out at the hypervisor level [93–95]. For example, XenPump, proposed as a module located in the hypervisor [96], monitors the hypercalls used by timing channels and adds latency to potential malicious operations, which increases the error rate in timing channels. Another example is a scheduling mechanism that mitigates shared-core side channel attacks by limiting the frequency of preemptions [97]. In addition, the authors in [94] propose to make the timer substantially coarser by removing resolution clocks on Xen-virtualized x86 machines, so that malicious VMs can hardly obtain accurate time measurement. The key drawback of these schemes is that they often require significant modifications of the hypervisors. Third, more recently, a system called Düppel has been proposed to mitigate cross-VM side channels at the VM OS level, which does not require any hypervisor modifications [98]. Specifically, time-shared cache cleansing is periodically performed by this system to defend individual resident VM from cache-based side channel attacks in public clouds. Fourth, some schemes are proposed at the application level [99,100]. For instance, the authors in [101] propose to hide the real power consumption information from user VMs by deploying a police VM to generate false information. Such schemes do not require substantial changes in the cloud infrastructure and are thus easy to be adopted. Nevertheless, they often suffer from the heavy overhead caused by obfuscating side channel information at the upper level of the cloud infrastructure.

Running VMs at isolated physical servers. Due to the challenges to completely mitigate co-resident attacks in a multi-tenant cloud, some security-aware cloud users require the cloud service provider to run their VMs at isolated physical servers. Although this solution effectively avoids attacks from co-residents, it sacrifices the economic benefit of the public cloud due to the usage of dedicated physical servers, which leads to its limited adoption by individual or small business users who are cost-sensitive.

In addition, even cloud users who adopt this solution are still facing a challenging issue as to how to verify the physical isolation of their VMs. In this scenario, Zhang et al. have proposed that normal cloud users can also use side channel analysis to verify their exclusive usage of a physical server [102].

9.3.6 Establishing Trust in Cloud Computing

Trust-based solutions, which guide entities to detect misbehavior, to take actions by avoiding risks, and to stimulate cooperation among distributed entities, play a unique and indispensable role in making the cloud secure and trustworthy. Current cloud computing trust studies mainly focus on (1) establishing cloud users' trust on CSPs, (2) ensuring the trustworthiness of cloud computing resources, such as hardware, software, applications, and so on, (3) evaluating the trustworthiness of cloud users, and (4) trust evaluation on other parties or entities.

1. **Establishing users' trust on CSPs:** As discussed above, establishing users' trust on CSPs is critical for the rapid adoption of cloud computing. Therefore, it has become the most active field for trustworthy cloud computing research. A typical trust evaluation relies on three steps.

Step 1: Determining the evaluation criteria. Whether a CSP is trustworthy or whether a CSP A is more trustworthy than a CSP B is a subjective question. The answers can be different depending on what the evaluation criteria are. Therefore, determining the trust evaluation criteria is a fundamental step for trust studies. In [103], the authors propose that users' trust on CSP is related with several factors including data location, allowance of investigation, data segregation, availability, long-term viability, regulatory compliance, backup and recovery, and privileged user access. The impact of these factors is evaluated through survey and statistical analysis. In [104], the authors propose a multi-faceted trust management (TM) system architecture that evaluates the trustworthy CSP by integrating assessment from multiple sources on different CSP attributes (e.g., security, performance, compliance). Moreover, many schemes use the service level agreement (i.e., SLA) between the CSP and cloud users as the evaluation criteria. The authors in [105] propose an SLA-based trust model to select the most suitable CSP for cloud users. An SLA-aware trust model is proposed in [106], which considers various SLA parameters between cloud users and CSPs in the trust computation and compliance process. In [107], a hybrid distributed trust model is proposed to prevent SLA violations by identifying violation-prone services at the service selection stage.

Step 2: Collecting evidence about CSPs' behavior. The evidence of CSPs' behavior can be collected through CSPs' self-assessment, third-party auditing, and cloud users' own experience.

Multiple programs are initiated to collect CSPs' security control information through CSPs' self-assessment. Specifically, the "Security, Trust & Assurance Registry (STAR)" program was initiated by the Cloud Security Alliance (CSA) as a free publicly accessible registry, which allows CSPs to publish the self-assessment of their security controls [108]. Beyond the STAR program, the CloudTrust Protocol (CTP), which was proposed by the CSC.com [109] and adopted by CSA [110], provides a request-response mechanism for users to obtain transparency information of a specific cloud such as configuration, vulnerability, audit log, service management, and so on. Such programs provide standards for CSPs to reveal their security control information to users, which facilitates the establishment of cloud users' trust on CSPs. However, CSPs may hide the potential flaws in their security and privacy controls, which makes the reliability of the self-assessment based evidence collection questionable.

Third-party auditors are also involved in the evidence collection process. The Cloud Trust Authority (CTA) [111] was announced by RSA as a third party to provide trust as a service (TaaS). Specifically, the CTA enables cloud users to view the security profiles of multiple cloud providers against a common benchmark. In this scenario, the trustworthiness of the third-party auditors is the key to determining the reliability of the evidence.

Evidence can also be collected by cloud users themselves. Such evidence includes both users' direct experiences and indirect observations (i.e., recommendations). A cloud user will believe his or her own experiences most. However, as a single user, the number of direct experiences may be very limited to make informative decisions. In many current studies, cloud users' feedback (i.e., ratings and reviews) are collected to serve as indirect observations. For example, in [112], the authors propose that a service broker can help users to choose a trustworthy CSP based on users' ratings. Since the ratings/reviews may be provided by untrustworthy or even malicious users, an effective protection scheme is on demand. The authors in [113] introduce the uncertainty of users' opinion into the trust computation for CSPs. In [114], the authors protect the entity reputation in a hybrid cloud by detecting and filtering out dishonest feedback where a personalized similarity measure is involved to compute the credibility of feedback through personalized experiences.

Step 3: Deriving trust aggregation algorithm. Diverse trust models have been proposed to evaluate the trustworthiness of CSP. For example, a dynamic trust evaluation approach based on multi-level Dirichlet distribution is proposed in [115]. The authors in [116] propose a formal trust management model that evaluates the trustworthiness of the SaaS in the cloud computing environment by integrating various trust properties, such as direct trust, recommended trust, reputation factor, and so on. A trust management model based on fuzzy set theory is proposed in [117] to help cloud users selecting trustworthy CSP. In [118], an extensible trust evaluation model named ETEC is proposed to compute the trust of CSP by integrating a time-variant comprehensive evaluation method for expressing direct trust and a space-variant evaluation method for calculating recommendation trust. A multi-tenancy trusted computing environment model (i.e., MTCEM) has been designed as a two-level hierarchy transitive trust chain model to assure a trusted cloud infrastructure to customers [119].

In addition, a number of studies also integrate trust mechanisms with existing technologies to address specific security and privacy challenges in cloud computing. In [120], the authors proposed a cloud trust model which integrates the user authentication, authorization management, and access control based on a family gene tree. In [121], a collaborative trust model of firewall-through is proposed to ensure the security of the cloud by combining the strength of the domain-based trust model and the feature of a firewall. In [122], a watermark-aware trusted running environment is proposed to ensure to protect the software running in the cloud. In [123], a trust model is integrated with encryption-based schemes to ensure the data confidentiality in cloud computing.

2. **Evaluating the trustworthiness of cloud users.** Some research is launched to evaluate cloud users' trustworthiness. In [51], the authors propose

practical ways to collect evidence about users' behavior, and propose an analytic hierarchy process (AHP) based trust model to calculate user trust. In [124], a policy-based user trust model is proposed, based on which the CSP is able to restrict untrustworthy users' access to cloud resources. Compared to CSPs' trust evaluation, evaluating cloud users' trustworthiness has been underestimated, and therefore limited work has been conducted thus far.

3. **Trust evaluation on other parties or entities.** In addition to CSP and cloud users, there are other third parties whose trustworthiness may also affect the overall security of the cloud environment. Trust models are also developed to evaluate such parties. For example, a trust framework, which integrates various trust mechanisms based on evidence, attribute certification, and validation, is proposed to evaluate the trustworthiness of various parties in the cloud, such as CSP, cloud brokers, and third-party auditors [125]. In [126], a DHT-based trust management framework on all data centers is proposed to reinforce the security and privacy in cloud applications. Sato et al. proposed to establish mutual trust between CSP and cloud users through a multiple layer trust model that ensures cloud users' "internal trust" through the trusted platform module (TPM) and establish CSP's "contracted trust" on users through the agreement that contains three documents as service policy/service practice statement (SP/SPS), ID policy/ID practice statement (IDP/IDPS), and the contract [127].
4. **Strengths and limitations.** The establishment of trust in the cloud promotes collaborations among different parties and further facilitates the broad adoption of the cloud computing technology. Furthermore, trust can also support different parties to make their decisions. For example, with accurate trust values, cloud users can choose the most reliable CSP; a CSP can determine whether to allow a specific user to access certain resources; and the most trustworthy third parties could be selected to bridge the trust gap between cloud users and CSPs.

   There are also some limitations of current trust based schemes. (1) While extensive studies have been conducted on evaluating CSP's trustworthiness, the evaluations on cloud users and third parties are still in their initial stages. (2) Trust evaluation criteria in different studies are not consistent. The lack of standardized evaluation criteria makes it extremely difficult to compare different trust evaluation results. (3) Entities' trustworthiness is mainly evaluated qualitatively. Quantitative trust computation algorithms are required to accurately evaluate and compare the reliability of entities. (4) Current schemes are mostly ad-hoc, which can only partially ensure the cloud security and privacy [128]. A unified framework that integrates comprehensive trust evaluations on diverse entities involved in the cloud environment is on demand. Advanced trust-based solutions are under investigation to address such limitations.

9.4 Future Directions

While cloud computing is rapidly gaining popularity, diverse security, privacy, and trust issues are emerging against this new computing paradigm. However, the development of defense solutions is lagging behind. Based on discussions in this chapter, we envision three future research directions to secure the cloud environment.

First, some conventional security solutions, such as logging and monitoring, access control, and encryption, may still play important roles in ensuring a secured cloud environment. However, the unique characteristics and technologies used in cloud computing raise new challenges against these solutions, requiring them to be further tailored to meet the special needs in this new computing paradigm. For example, access control schemes have to be able to handle broad-based network access, a new challenge that never occurred in previous systems. Encryption-based solutions have to face the critical challenge as encryption key management due to the separation between data owner and data handler.

Second, emerging security solutions for cloud computing, such as virtual isolation, defense against co-resident attacks are not mature yet. The most challenging issue is how to enable dynamic sharing and scaling of resources while eliminating interference on users' legitimate resource consumption caused by malicious usage. Moreover, as sophisticated attacks are developed rapidly, enhanced solutions are required.

Third, stimulating the security cooperation among diverse stakeholders, including CSP, cloud users, and many third parties, in the cloud scenario is very challenging. The involvement of diverse parties in the cloud makes the security, privacy, and trust issues complicated since security objectives for different parties can be very different, and sometimes these objectives may even conflict with one another. For example, a cloud user may require CSPs to be more transparent about their security controls, while a CSP may need to protect its entire cloud infrastructure by not revealing details about its security settings. Establishing trust relationships among diverse parties, which enables negotiation and tradeoffs, may serve as a promising solution.

Last but not least, the integration of multiple solutions provides a great potential to address security, privacy, and trust issues that cannot be addressed by a single, ad-hoc solution. For example, by integrating encryption and access control, cloud users are able to ensure the fulfillment of their access control policies on the cloud server [62,129,130]. By integrating trust models with encryption schemes, users can protect their data confidentiality by only allowing trustworthy CSPs to decrypt and process their sensitive data [123]. However, how to seamlessly integrate different security solutions remains an open challenge.

To ensure a secure and trustworthy cloud computing environment, research challenges as well as opportunities remain. The resolution of these security, privacy, and trust issues will serve as the key to enable the rapid adoption of cloud computing.

9.5 Conclusion

As an emerging and rapidly developing computing scenario, cloud computing has introduced a number of security, privacy, and trust challenges. This chapter first introduces background knowledge about cloud computing, such as deployment model, service model, unique characteristics, and key technologies, followed by brief discussions about the reasons that these technologies raise diverse security, privacy, and trust challenges. Furthermore, critical security, privacy, and trust challenges as well as the corresponding state-of-the-art solutions are investigated in detail, followed by a discussion on future research directions, which concludes this chapter.

References

1. Peter Mell and Timothy Grance, The NIST definition of cloud computing, 2011, available at: http://dx.doi.org/10.6028/NIST.SP.800-145.
2. Priya Viswanathan, Cloud computing, is it really all that beneficial?, available at http://mobiledevices.about.com/od/additionalresources/a/Cloud-Computing-Is-It-Really-All-That-Beneficial.htm.
3. Michael Armbrust, Armando Fox, Rean Griffith, Anthony D. Joseph, Randy Katz, Andy Konwinski, Gunho Lee et al., A view of cloud computing, *Communications of the ACM*, 53(4): 50–58, 2010.
4. Yaju Jadeja and Kavan Modi, Cloud computing-concepts, architecture and challenges, in *2012 International Conference on Computing, Electronics and Electrical Technologies (ICCEET)*. IEEE, 2012, pp. 877–880.
5. Tharam Dillon, Chen Wu, and Elizabeth Chang, Cloud computing: Issues and challenges, in *2010 24th IEEE International Conference on Advanced Information Networking and Applications (AINA)*. IEEE, 2010, pp. 27–33.
6. Hassan Takabi, James B.D. Joshi, and Gail-Joon Ahn, Security and privacy challenges in cloud computing environments, *IEEE Security & Privacy*, (6): 24–31, 2010.
7. Understanding the Cloud Computing Stack: SaaS, PaaS, IaaS, https://support.rackspace.com/whitepapers/understanding-the-cloud-computing-stack-saas-paas-iaas/.
8. Cloud—Top 5 Risks with PAAS, https://www.owasp.org/index.php/Cloud_-_Top_5_Risks_with_PAAS.
9. Bhaskar Prasad Rimal, Eunmi Choi, and Ian Lumb, A taxonomy and survey of cloud computing systems, in *NCM '09: Fifth International Joint Conference on INC, IMS and IDC*, Aug 2009, pp. 44–51.
10. Burton S. Kaliski, Jr. and Wayne Pauley, Toward risk assessment as a service in cloud environments, in *Proceedings of the 2nd USENIX Conference on Hot Topics in Cloud Computing*. 2010, HotCloud'10, pp. 13–13, USENIX Association.
11. Issa M. Khalil, Abdallah Khreishah, and Muhammad Azeem, Cloud computing security: A survey, *Computers*, 3(1): 1–35, 2014.
12. Abdeladim Alfath, Karim Baina, and Salah Baina, Cloud computing security: Fine-grained analysis and security approaches, in *Security Days (JNS3), 2013 National*, April 2013, pp. 1–6.

13. Wayne J. Brown, Vince Anderson, and Qing Tan, Multitenancy–Security risks and countermeasures, *2012 15th International Conference on Network-Based Information Systems*, 2012, pp. 7–13.
14. Akhil Behl and Kanika Behl, An analysis of cloud computing security issues, in *Information and Communication Technologies (WICT), 2012 World Congress on*. IEEE, 2012, pp. 109–114.
15. Shufen Zhang, Hongcan Yan, and Xuebin Chen, Research on key technologies of cloud computing, *Physics Procedia*, 33: 1791–1797, 2012.
16. Cloud Federation, available at http://searchtelecom.techtarget.com/definition/cloud-federation.
17. Definition of Cloud Federation, http://apprenda.com/library/glossary/definition-cloud-federation/.
18. Pengfei Sun, Qingni Shen, Liang Gu, Yangwei Li, Sihan Qing, and Zhong Chen, Multilateral security architecture for virtualization platform in multi-tenancy cloud environment, in *Conference Anthology, IEEE*. 2013, pp. 1–5.
19. Virtualization Special Interest Group PCI Security Standards Council, PCI DSS Virtualization Guidelines.
20. Katie Wood and Mark Anderson, Understanding the complexity surrounding multi-tenancy in cloud computing, in *2011 IEEE 8th International Conference on e-Business Engineering (ICEBE)*. IEEE, 2011, pp. 119–124.
21. Jaydip Sen, Security and privacy issues in cloud computing, arXiv preprint arXiv:1303.4814, 2013.
22. Zhenqian Feng, Bing Bai, Baokang Zhao, and Jinshu Su, Shrew attack in cloud data center networks, in *2011 Seventh International Conference on Mobile Ad-hoc and Sensor Networks (MSN)*. IEEE, 2011, pp. 441–445.
23. Thomas Ristenpart, Eran Tromer, Hovav Shacham, and Stefan Savage, Hey, you, get off of my cloud: Exploring information leakage in third-party compute clouds, in *Proceedings of the 16th ACM Conference on Computer and Communications Security*. ACM, 2009, pp. 199–212.
24. Ron Chi-Lung Chiang, Sundaresan Rajasekaran, Nan Zhang, and H. Howie Huang, Swiper: Exploiting virtual machine vulnerability in third-party clouds with competition for i/o resources, *IEEE Transactions on Parallel and Distributed Systems*, 26: 1732–1742, 2015.
25. Hussain Aljahdali, Paul Townend, and Jie Xu, Enhancing multi-tenancy security in the cloud iaas model over public deployment, in *Service Oriented System Engineering (SOSE), 2013 IEEE 7th International Symposium on*. IEEE, 2013, pp. 385–390.
26. Onur Aciiçmez, Çetin Kaya Koç, and Jean-Pierre Seifert, On the power of simple branch prediction analysis, in *Proceedings of the 2nd ACM Symposium on Information, Computer and Communications Security*. ACM, 2007, pp. 312–320.
27. Onur Acıiçmez, Çetin Kaya Koç, and Jean-Pierre Seifert, Predicting secret keys via branch prediction, in *Topics in Cryptology–CT-RSA 2007*, pp. 225–242. Springer, 2006.
28. Onur Aciiçmez, Yet another microarchitectural attack: Exploiting i-cache, in *Proceedings of the 2007 ACM Workshop on Computer Security Architecture*. ACM, 2007, pp. 11–18.

29. Dirk Grunwald and Soraya Ghiasi, Microarchitectural denial of service: Insuring microarchitectural fairness, in *Proceedings of the 35th Annual ACM/IEEE International Symposium on Microarchitecture.* IEEE Computer Society Press, 2002, pp. 409–418.
30. Thomas Moscibroda and Onur Mutlu, Memory performance attacks: Denial of memory service in multi-core systems, in *Proceedings of 16th USENIX Security Symposium on USENIX Security Symposium.* USENIX Association, 2007, p. 18.
31. Onur Aciicmez and J-P Seifert, Cheap hardware parallelism implies cheap security, in *Fault Diagnosis and Tolerance in Cryptography, 2007. FDTC 2007. Workshop on.* IEEE, 2007, pp. 80–91.
32. Paul A. Karger and John C. Wray, Storage channels in disk arm optimization, in *2012 IEEE Symposium on Security and Privacy.* IEEE Computer Society, 1991, pp. 52–52.
33. François-Xavier Standaert, Introduction to side-channel attacks, in *Secure Integrated Circuits and Systems*, pp. 27–42. Springer, 2010.
34. Venkatanathan Varadarajan, Thawan Kooburat, Benjamin Farley, Thomas Ristenpart, and Michael M. Swift, Resource-freeing attacks: Improve your cloud performance (at your neighbor's expense), in *Proceedings of the 2012 ACM Conference on Computer and Communications Security.* ACM, 2012, pp. 281–292.
35. Christof Momm and Wolfgang Theilmann, A combined workload planning approach for multi-tenant business applications, in *Computer Software and Applications Conference Workshops (COMPSACW), 2011 IEEE 35th Annual.* IEEE, 2011, pp. 255–260.
36. Xiangyang Luo, Lin Yang, Linru Ma, Shanming Chu, and Hao Dai, Virtualization security risks and solutions of cloud computing via divide-conquer strategy, in *2011 Third International Conference on Multimedia Information Networking and Security (MINES).* IEEE, 2011, pp. 637–641.
37. Doug Hyde, A survey on the security of virtual machines, www1.cse.wustl.edu/˜jain /cse571-09/ftp/vmsec/index.html, 2009.
38. Ken Owens, Securing Virtual Computer Infrastructure in the Cloud, SavvisCorp.
39. Amarnath Jasti, Payal Shah, Rajeev Nagaraj, and Ravi Pendse, Security in multitenancy cloud, in *2010 IEEE International Carnahan Conference on Security Technology (ICCST).* IEEE, 2010, pp. 35–41.
40. Minjie Zheng, Virtualization security in data centers and cloud, http://www.cse .wustl.edu/ jain/cse571-11/ftp/virtual/.
41. Top Threats Working Group et al., The notorious nine: Cloud computing top threats in 2013, Cloud Security Alliance, 2013.
42. Independently Conducted by Ponemon Institute LLC, Achieving Data Privacy in the Cloud, sponsored by Microsoft.
43. J. R. Raphael, The worst cloud outages of 2013, *InfoWorld*, http://www.infoworld.com /slideshow/107783/the-worst-cloud-outages-of-2013-so-far-221831.
44. Siani Pearson and Azzedine Benameur, Privacy, security and trust issues arising from cloud computing, in *2010 IEEE Second International Conference on Cloud Computing Technology and Science (CloudCom).* IEEE, 2010, pp. 693–702.
45. Richard Chow, Philippe Golle, Markus Jakobsson, Elaine Shi, Jessica Staddon, Ryusuke Masuoka, and Jesus Molina, Controlling data in the cloud: Outsourcing computation without outsourcing control, in *Proceedings of the 2009 ACM Workshop on Cloud Computing Security.* ACM, 2009, pp. 85–90.

46. Rich Maggiani, Cloud computing is changing how we communicate, in *Professional Communication Conference*, 2009. IPCC 2009. IEEE international. IEEE, 2009, pp. 1–4.
47. FTC questions cloud-computing security, http://news.cnet.com/8301-13578 3-1019 8577-38.html?part=rss&subj=news&tag=2547-1 3-0-20.
48. Ryan Singel, NetFlix cancels recommendation contest after privacy lawsuit, http://www.wired.com/2010/03/netflix-cancels-contest/.
49. Alan Murphy, Storing data in the cloud raises compliance challenges, http://www.forbes.com/sites/ciocentral/2012/01/19/storing-data-in-the-cloud-raises-compliance-challenges/.
50. Cliff Saran, Amazon gives users control over geographic location of cloud services, http://www.computerweekly.com/news/2240105257/Amazon-gives-users-control-over-geographic-location-of-cloud-services.
51. Li qin Tian, Chuang Lin, and Yang Ni, Evaluation of user behavior trust in cloud computing, in *2010 International Conference on Computer Application and System Modeling (ICCASM)*. IEEE, 2010, 7: V7–567.
52. Wei Wang, Guosun Zeng, Junqi Zhang, and Daizhong Tang, Dynamic trust evaluation and scheduling framework for cloud computing, *Security and Communication Networks*, 5(3): 311–318, 2012.
53. Don Sheppard, Is loss of control the biggest hurdle to cloud computing?, available at http://www.itworldcanada.com/blog/is-loss-of-control-the-biggest-hurdle-to-cloud-computing/95131.
54. Mohamed Almorsy, John Grundy, and Amani S. Ibrahim, Collaboration-based cloud computing security management framework, in *2011 IEEE International Conference on Cloud Computing (CLOUD)*. IEEE, 2011, pp. 364–371.
55. Jung-Ho Eom, Min-Woo Park, Seon-Ho Park, and Tai-Myoung Chung, A framework of defense system for prevention of insider's malicious behaviors, in *2011 13th International Conference on Advanced Communication Technology (ICACT)*, Feb. 2011, pp. 982–987.
56. C. Nithiyanandam, D. Tamilselvan, S. Balaji, and V. Sivaguru, Advanced framework of defense system for prevention of insider's malicious behaviors, in *2012 International Conference on Recent Trends in Information Technology (ICRTIT)*, April 2012, pp. 434–438.
57. Ma Tanzim Khorshed, A.B.M. Shawkat Ali, and Saleh Wasimi, Monitoring insiders activities in cloud computing using rule based learning, in *2011 IEEE 10th International Conference on Trust, Security and Privacy in Computing and Communications (TrustCom)*, Nov. 2011, pp. 757–764.
58. Majid Raissi-Dehkordi and David Carr, A multi-perspective approach to insider threat detection, in *Military Communications Conference, 2011—MILCOM 2011*, Nov. 2011, pp. 1164–1169.
59. Hoda Eldardiry, Evgeniy Bart, Juan Liu, John Hanley, Bob Price, and Oliver Brdiczka, Multi-domain information fusion for insider threat detection, in *Security and Privacy Workshops (SPW)*, 2013 IEEE, May 2013, pp. 45–51.
60. Allen Oomen Joseph, Jaspher W. Katrine, and Rohit Vijayan, Cloud security mechanisms for data protection: A survey, *International Journal of Multimedia and Ubiquitous Engineering*, 9(9): 81–90, September 2014.
61. Shin-Jer Yang, Pei-Ci Lai, and Jyhjong Lin, Design role-based multi-tenancy access control scheme for cloud services, in *Biometrics and Security Technologies (ISBAST), 2013 International Symposium on*. IEEE, 2013, pp. 273–279.

62. Shucheng Yu, Cong Wang, Kui Ren, and Wenjing Lou, Achieving secure, scalable, and fine-grained data access control in cloud computing, in *INFOCOM, 2010 Proceedings IEEE*. IEEE, 2010, pp. 1–9.
63. Karen Scarfone, *Guide to Security for Full Virtualization Technologies*, DIANE Publishing, 2011.
64. Nasuni, Top 5 security challenges of cloud storage, available at http://www.nasuni.com/news/press releases/26-top 5 security challenges of cloud storage.
65. Yong Peng, Wei Zhao, Feng Xie, Zhong hua Dai, Yang Gao, and Dong Qing Chen, Secure cloud storage based on cryptographic techniques, *The Journal of China Universities of Posts and Telecommunications*, 19: 182–189, 2012.
66. Sherif El-etriby, Eman M Mohamed, and Hatem S. Abdul-kader, Modern encryption techniques for cloud computing, *ICCIT 2012*, 12–14 March 2012, Al-Madinah Al-Munawwarah, Saudi Arabia, 2012.
67. B. Raja Sekhar, B. Sunil Kumar, L. Swathi Reddy, and V. Poorna Chandar, Cp-abe based encryption for secured cloud storage access, *International Journal of Scientific & Engineering Research*, 3(9): 1–5, 2012.
68. Aderemi A. Atayero and Oluwaseyi Feyisetan, Security issues in cloud computing: The potentials of homomorphic encryption, *Journal of Emerging Trends in Computing and Information Sciences*, 2(10): 546–552, 2011.
69. Cong Wang, Qian Wang, Kui Ren, and Wenjing Lou, Ensuring data storage security in cloud computing, in *17th International Workshop on Quality of Service (IWQoS)*, July 2009, pp. 1–9.
70. Craig Gentry, Fully homomorphic encryption using ideal lattices, in *STOC*, 9: 169–178, 2009.
71. Marten Van Dijk, Craig Gentry, Shai Halevi, and Vinod Vaikuntanathan, Fully homomorphic encryption over the integers, in *Advances in Cryptology–EUROCRYPT* 2010, pp. 24–43. Springer, 2010.
72. Shai Halevi and Victor Shoup, Helib—An implementation of homomorphic encryption, https://github.com/shaih/HElib, 2014.
73. Cong Wang, Ning Cao, Kui Ren, and Wenjing Lou, Enabling secure and efficient ranked keyword search over outsourced cloud data, *Parallel and Distributed Systems, IEEE Transactions on*, 23(8): 1467–1479, 2012.
74. Raluca Ada Popa, Catherine Redfield, Nickolai Zeldovich, and Hari Balakrishnan, Cryptdb: Protecting confidentiality with encrypted query processing, in *Proceedings of the Twenty-Third ACM Symposium on Operating Systems Principles*. ACM, 2011, pp. 85–100.
75. Luca Ferretti, Michele Colajanni, and Mirco Marchetti, Distributed, concurrent, and independent access to encrypted cloud databases, *Parallel and Distributed Systems, IEEE Transactions on*, 25(2): 437–446, 2014.
76. Nauman Rafique, Won-Taek Lim, and Mithuna Thottethodi, Effective management of dram bandwidth in multicore processors, in *16th International Conference on Parallel Architecture and Compilation Techniques (PACT 2007)*. IEEE, 2007, pp. 245–258.
77. Kyle J. Nesbit, James Laudon, and James E Smith, Virtual private caches, *ACM SIGARCH Computer Architecture News*, 35(2): 57–68, 2007.
78. Paul Barham, Boris Dragovic, Keir Fraser, Steven Hand, Tim Harris, Alex Ho, Rolf Neugebauer et al., Xen and the art of virtualization, *ACM SIGOPS Operating Systems Review*, 37(5): 164–177, 2003.

79. Himanshu Raj, Ripal Nathuji, Abhishek Singh, and Paul England, Resource management for isolation enhanced cloud services, in *Proceedings of the 2009 ACM Workshop on Cloud Computing Security*. ACM, 2009, pp. 77–84.
80. Ajay Gulati, Arif Merchant, and Peter J. Varman, mclock: Handling throughput variability for hypervisor io scheduling, in *Proceedings of the 9th USENIX Conference on Operating Systems Design and Implementation*. USENIX Association, 2010, pp. 1–7.
81. Ben Verghese, Anoop Gupta, and Mendel Rosenblum, Performance isolation: Sharing and isolation in shared-memory multiprocessors, in *ACM SIGPLAN Notices*. ACM, 33: 181–192, 1998.
82. Alan Shieh, Srikanth Kandula, Albert Greenberg, and Changhoon Kim, Seawall: Performance isolation for cloud datacenter networks, in *Proceedings of the 2nd USENIX Conference on Hot Topics in Cloud Computing*. USENIX Association, 2010, pp. 1–1.
83. Sebastian Jeuk, Shi Zhou, and Miguel Rio, Tenant-id: Tagging tenant assets in cloud environments, in *Cluster, Cloud and Grid Computing (CCGrid), 2013 13th IEEE/ACM International Symposium on*. IEEE, 2013, pp. 642–647.
84. Michael Factor, David Hadas, Aner Hamama, Nadav Har'El, Elliot K. Kolodner, Anil Kurmus, Alexandra Shulman-Peleg, and Alessandro Sorniotti, Secure logical isolation for multi-tenancy in cloud storage, in *Mass Storage Systems and Technologies (MSST), 2013 IEEE 29th Symposium on*. IEEE, 2013, pp. 1–5.
85. Si Yu, Xiaolin Gui, and Jiancai Lin, An approach with two-stage mode to detect cache-based side channel attacks, in *2013 International Conference on Information Networking (ICOIN)*. IEEE, 2013, pp. 186–191.
86. Smitha Sundareswaran and Anna C. Squcciarini, Detecting malicious co-resident virtual machines indulging in load-based attacks, in *Information and Communications Security*, pp. 113–124. Springer, 2013.
87. Yossi Azar, Seny Kamara, Ishai Menache, Mariana Raykova, and Bruce Shepard, Co-location-resistant clouds, in *Proceedings of the 6th edition of the ACM Workshop on Cloud Computing Security*. ACM, 2014, pp. 9–20.
88. Yi Han, Jeffrey Chan, Tansu Alpcan, and Christopher Leckie, Using virtual machine allocation policies to defend against co-resident attacks in cloud computing, in *IEEE Transactions on Dependable and Secure Computing*, vol. 14, no. 1, Jan/Feb 2017.
89. Min Li, Yulong Zhang, Kun Bai, Wanyu Zang, Meng Yu, and Xubin He, Improving cloud survivability through dependency based virtual machine placement, in *SECRYPT*, 2012, pp. 321–326.
90. Zhenghong Wang and Ruby B. Lee, New cache designs for thwarting software cache-based side channel attacks, in *ACM SIGARCH Computer Architecture News*. ACM, 35: 494–505, 2007.
91. Georgios Keramidas, Alexandros Antonopoulos, Dimitrios N. Serpanos, and Stefanos Kaxiras, Non deterministic caches: A simple and effective defense against side channel attacks, *Design Automation for Embedded Systems*, 12(3): 221–230, 2008.
92. Robert Martin, John Demme, and Simha Sethumadhavan, Timewarp: Rethinking timekeeping and performance monitoring mechanisms to mitigate side-channel attacks, *ACM SIGARCH Computer Architecture News*, 40(3): 18–129, 2012.
93. Dan Page, Partitioned cache architecture as a side-channel defence mechanism, *IACR Cryptology ePrint Archive*, 2005: 280, 2005.
94. Bhanu C. Vattikonda, Sambit Das, and Hovav Shacham, Eliminating fine grained timers in xen, in *Proceedings of the 3rd ACM Workshop on Cloud Computing Security Workshop*. ACM, 2011, pp. 41–46.

95. Peng Li, Debin Gao, and Michael K. Reiter, Mitigating access-driven timing channels in clouds using stopwatch, in *2013 43rd Annual IEEE/IFIP International Conference on Dependable Systems and Networks (DSN)*. IEEE, 2013, pp. 1–12.
96. Jingzheng Wu, Liping Ding, Yuqi Lin, Nasro Min-Allah, and Yongji Wang, Xenpump: A new method to mitigate timing channel in cloud computing, in *2012 IEEE 5th International Conference on Cloud Computing (CLOUD)*. IEEE, 2012, pp. 678–685.
97. Venkatanathan Varadarajan, Thomas Ristenpart, and Michael Swift, Scheduler-based defenses against cross-vm side-channels, in *23rd USENIX Security Symposium (USENIX Security 14)*, 2014, pp. 687–702.
98. Yinqian Zhang and Michael K. Reiter, Düppel: Retrofitting commodity operating systems to mitigate cache side channels in the cloud, in *Proceedings of the 2013 ACM SIGSAC Conference on Computer & Communications Security*. ACM, 2013, pp. 827–838.
99. Bart Coppens, Ingrid Verbauwhede, Koen De Bosschere, and Bjorn De Sutter, Practical mitigations for timing-based side-channel attacks on modern x86 processors, in *Security and Privacy, 2009 30th IEEE Symposium on*. IEEE, 2009, pp. 45–60.
100. Robert Könighofer, A fast and cache-timing resistant implementation of the aes, in *Topics in Cryptology–CT-RSA 2008*, pp. 187–202. Springer, 2008.
101. Sajjad Waheed, Nazrul Islam, Barnaly Paul Chaity, and Saddam Hossain Bhuiyan, Security of side channel power analysis attack in cloud computing, *Global Journal of Computer Science and Technology*, 14(4): 2015.
102. Yinqian Zhang, Ari Juels, Alina Oprea, and Michael K. Reiter, Homealone: Co-residency detection in the cloud via side-channel analysis, in *Security and Privacy (SP), 2011 IEEE Symposium on*. IEEE, 2011, pp. 313–328.
103. Ahmad Rashidi and Naser Movahhedinia, A model for user trust in cloud computing, *International Journal on Cloud Computing: Services and Architecture (IJCCSA)*, 2(2): April, 2012.
104. Sheikh Habib, Sebastian Ries, and Max Muhlhauser, Towards a trust management system for cloud computing, in *2011 IEEE 10th International Conference on Trust, Security and Privacy in Computing and Communications (TrustCom)*, Nov 2011, pp. 933–939.
105. Mohammed Alhamad, Tharam Dillon, and Elizabeth Chang, Sla-based trust model for cloud computing, in *2010 13th International Conference on Network-Based Information Systems (NBiS)*, Sept 2010, pp. 321–324.
106. Tomar Deepak, Sla—Aware trust model for cloud service deployment, *International Journal of Computer Applications* (0975-8887), 90(10): 10, 2014.
107. Irfan Ul Haq, Rehab Alnemr, Adrian Paschke, Erich Schikuta, Harold Boley, and Christoph Meinel, Distributed trust management for validating sla choreographies, in *Grids and Service-Oriented Architectures for Service Level Agreements*, pp. 45–55. Springer, 2010.
108. CSA STAR (security, trust and assurance registry) program, Cloud Security Alliance. https://cloudsecurityalliance.org/star/. Accessed on Oct. 16, 2012.
109. R Knode, Digital trust in the cloud. CSC.com, 2009.
110. CSC, Cloudtrust protocol (CTP). Cloud Security Alliance, https://cloudsecurityalliance.org/research/ctp/, 2011.
111. RSA, RSA establishes cloud trust authority to accelerate cloud adoption. RSA, http://www.rsa.com/press release.aspx?id=11320, 2011.
112. Chaitali Uikey and D.S. Bhilare, A broker based trust model for cloud computing environment, *International Journal of Emerging Technology and Advanced Engineering*, 3(11): 247–252.

113. P.S. Pawar, M. Rajarajan, S. Krishnan Nair, and A. Zisman, Trust model for optimized cloud services, in *Trust Management VI*, Theo Dimitrakos, Rajat Moona, Dhiren Patel, and D. Harrison McKnight, Eds., vol. 374 of IFIP Advances in Information and Communication Technology, pp. 97–112. Springer Berlin Heidelberg, 2012.
114. Jemal Abawajy, Establishing trust in hybrid cloud computing environments, in *2011 IEEE 10th International Conference on Trust, Security and Privacy in Computing and Communications (TrustCom)*, Nov 2011, pp. 118–125.
115. Zhongxue Yang, Xiaolin Qin, Yingjie Yang, and Wenrui Li, A new dynamic trust approach for cloud computing, in *1st International Workshop on Cloud Computing and Information Security*. Atlantis Press, 2013.
116. Somesh Kumar Prajapati, Suvamoy Changder, and Anirban Sarkar, Trust management model for cloud computing environment, arXiv preprint arXiv:1304.5313, 2013.
117. Xiaodong Sun, Guiran Chang, and Fengyun Li, A trust management model to enhance security of cloud computing environments, in *2011 Second International Conference on Networking and Distributed Computing (ICNDC)*, Sept 2011, pp. 244–248.
118. Qiang Guo, Dawei Sun, Guiran Chang, Lina Sun, and Xingwei Wang, Modeling and evaluation of trust in cloud computing environments, in *2011 3rd International Conference on Advanced Computer Control (ICACC)*, Jan 2011, pp. 112–116.
119. Xiao-Yong Li, Li-Tao Zhou, Yong Shi, and Yu Guo, A trusted computing environment model in cloud architecture, in *Machine Learning and Cybernetics (ICMLC), 2010 International Conference on*, July 2010, vol. 6, pp. 2843–2848.
120. TieFang Wang, BaoSheng Ye, YunWen Li, and LiShang Zhu, Study on enhancing performance of cloud trust model with family gene technology, in *2010 3rd IEEE International Conference on Computer Science and Information Technology (ICCSIT)*, July 2010, vol. 9, pp. 122–126.
121. Zhimin Yang, Lixiang Qiao, Chang Liu, Chi Yang, and Guangming Wan, A collaborative trust model of firewall-through based on cloud computing, in *2010 14th International Conference on Computer Supported Cooperative Work in Design (CSCWD)*, April 2010, pp. 329–334.
122. Junning Fu, Chaokun Wang, Zhiwei Yu, Jianmin Wang, and Jia-Guang Sun, A watermark-aware trusted running environment for software clouds, in *ChinaGrid Conference (ChinaGrid), 2010 Fifth Annual*, July 2010, pp. 144–151.
123. Yuhong Liu, Jungwoo Ryoo, and Syed Rizivi, Ensuring data confidentiality in cloud computing: An encryption and trust-based solution, in *The 23rd Wireless and Optical Communication Conference (WOCC 2014)*, NJIT, Newark, NJ, May 9–10 2014.
124. Bendale Yashashree and Shah Seema, User level trust evaluation in cloud computing, *International Journal of Computer Applications*, 69(24): 2013.
125. Jingwei Huang and David M. Nicol, Trust mechanisms for cloud computing, *Journal of Cloud Computing*, 2(1): 1–14, 2013.
126. Kai Hwang, S. Kulkareni, and Yue Hu, Cloud security with virtualized defense and reputation-based trust management, in *2009 Eighth IEEE International Conference on Dependable, Autonomic and Secure Computing, 2009. DASC '09*, Dec 2009, pp. 717–722.
127. H. Sato, A. Kanai, and S. Tanimoto, A cloud trust model in a security aware cloud, in *Applications and the Internet (SAINT), 2010 10th IEEE/IPSJ International Symposium on*, July 2010, pp. 121–124.

128. Sheikh Mahbub Habib, Sascha Hauke, Sebastian Ries, and Max Mühlhäuser, Trust as a facilitator in cloud computing: A survey, *Journal of Cloud Computing*, 11: 1–18, 2012.
129. Sabrina De Capitani Di Vimercati, Sara Foresti, Sushil Jajodia, Stefano Paraboschi, and Pierangela Samarati, Over-encryption: Management of access control evolution on outsourced data, in *Proceedings of the 33rd International Conference on Very Large Data Bases*. VLDB endowment, 2007, pp. 123–134.
130. Vipul Goyal, Abhishek Jain, Omkant Pandey, and Amit Sahai, Bounded ciphertext policy attribute based encryption, in *Automata, Languages and Programming*, pp. 579–591. Springer, 2008.

Chapter 10

Cybersecurity in Internet of Things (IoT)

Wenlin Han and Yang Xiao

Contents

This chapter introduces the Internet of Things (IoT) as one of the most rapid expanding cybersecurity domains and presents the big data challenges faced by IoT, as well as various security requirements and issues in IoT. IoT is a giant network containing various applications and systems. Every application or system has its own devices, data sources, protocols, data formats, and so on. Thus, the data in IoT is extremely heterogeneous and big, and this poses heterogeneous big data security and management problems. Cybersecurity in IoT has attracted various interests when many smart devices are found vulnerable to hacking and reported on headline news recently. This chapter describes current solutions and also outlines how big data analytics can address security issues in IoT when facing big data.

10.1 Introduction

Internet of Things (IoT) is the network where physical objects are connected [1]. These physical objects may include every object in our daily lives, such as TV, refrigerator, car, wallet, and so on. In IoT, these objects are either electronic or have electronic devices, such as sensors or radio frequency identification (RFID) tags attached to them [2]. IoT has a huge market potential. Cisco estimated that IoT could create an economic value up to $19 trillion in the next decade [3].

However, people began to be concerned about the security of IoT when more and more devices in IoT were found vulnerable to hacking and it was reported on headline news recently. As McAfee reported, a Fisher-Price smart toy bear could be used by hackers to steal information from children [4]. Hackers can remotely kill a Jeep Cherokee, and the video was posted on YouTube and referred to by many online media [5]. IoT has a close relationship to our daily lives. Thus, the security of IoT has a bigger impact on humans than any other systems or networks [1].

Nowadays, many medical devices are becoming smart, and this raises the possibility for hackers to attack a human [6].

Cybersecurity in IoT faces many challenges. IoT is highly heterogeneous. The devices in IoT are heterogeneous. The data in IoT are heterogeneous. The protocols in IoT are heterogeneous. Thus, security issues in IoT are complicated. Security solutions in IoT have to address heterogeneous data management problems to efficiently manage keys and identities, to build trust between entities, to protect privacy, to prevent frauds, and so on.

These challenges have been studied in other fields, and we have some traditional security solutions, such as intrusion detection systems (IDS) [7–9], firewall [10], and so on. However, data volume in IoT is tremendously big. As Cisco reported, the data generated by IoT was over 100 zettabytes by 2013, and will reach 400 zettabytes by 2018, where a zettabyte is a trillion GB [11]. Cybersecurity in IoT is facing the big data challenge. The traditional security solutions cannot well address the challenges that big data brings to cybersecurity.

Big data analytic (BDA) methods for cybersecurity adopt big data analytic technologies (such as Hadoop) to solve big data cybersecurity problems. BDA can address some challenges that the traditional security solutions cannot address. BDA can analyze a single big data set, as well as a significant amount of small data sets. BDA can correlate heterogeneous data sources in IoT and manage big security data. Using BDA, security solutions in IoT can achieve dynamic feature selection and cross-boundary intelligence.

10.2 IoT and Big Data

Internet of Things (IoT) is formally defined in Recommendation ITU-T Y.2060 as "A global infrastructure for the information society, enabling advanced services by interconnecting (physical and virtual) things based on existing and evolving interoperable information and communication technologies" [12]. Simply speaking, IoT is a giant network of a huge amount of connected smart devices. As shown in Figure 10.1 [13], it is the conceptual framework of IoT.

IoT relates to our daily lives closely. The applications of IoT cover almost all the aspects of people's lives. The technology of IoT is used to build smart homes where all the home appliances, such as TV, refrigerator, microwave oven, and so on, are smart. When you set an alarm at 7 AM in the morning on your cell phone, your cell phone may notify the coffee maker to make a morning coffee for you automatically. Moreover, when you get up, your coffee is ready. When the cartridge is running low, the printer could place an order online automatically. The technology of IoT is used to build smart power grids, which is Smart Grid [14–17]. Smart Grid provides many advanced features including real-time energy usage monitoring, real-time pricing, self-healing, and so on. Using the technology of IoT, cars are

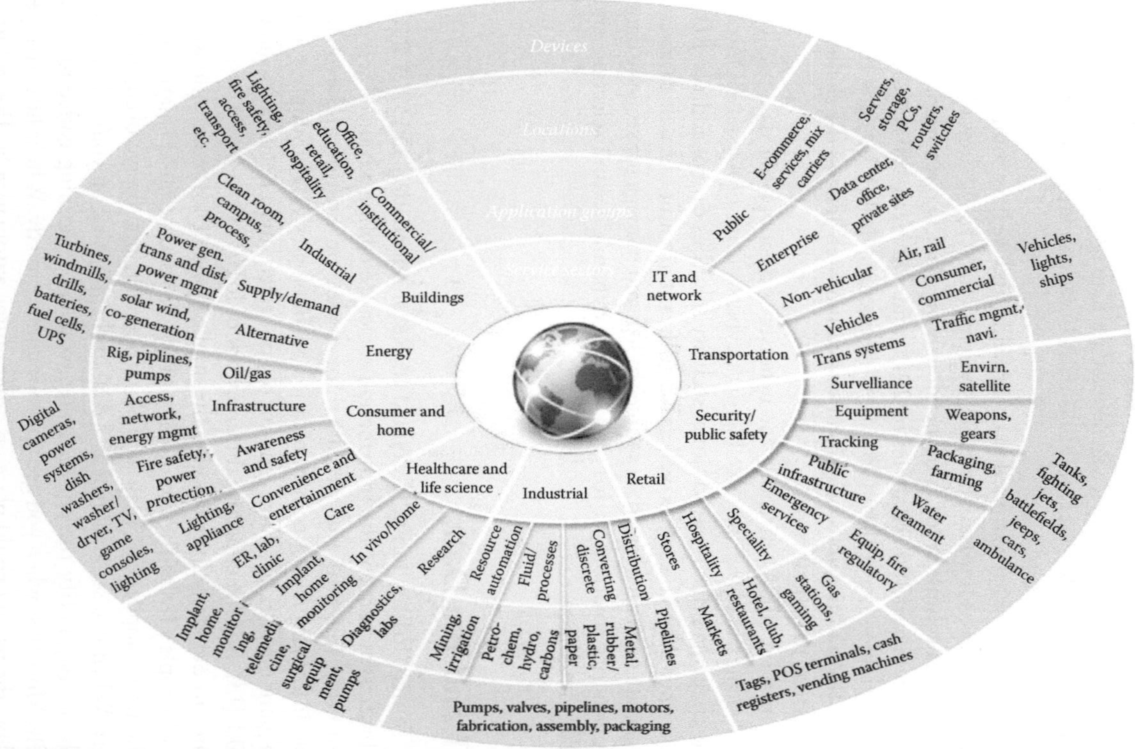

Figure 10.1 IoT conceptual framework. (Based on Jessgroopman. Visualizing the Internet of Things: A Round-up of Maps, Frameworks, and Infographics of IoT. https://jessgroopman.wordpress.com/2014/08/25/visualizing-the-internet-of-things-a-round-up-of-maps-frameworks-and-infographics-of-iot/, accessed June 1, 2016.)

becoming smart [18]. When you are late for a meeting, your car may automatically send a message to the meeting organizer based on your schedule. The technology of IoT has been applied to many other fields, such as industry, agriculture, retail, and so on, which are shown in Table 10.1 [19].

IoT has a huge emerging market. By 2011, the number of devices with RFID tags was 12 million [8]. These devices were used to monitor objects, collect data, or track movement. As estimated, this number will continue to increase and reach 209 billion by 2021 [20]. Gartner says the incremental revenue generated by IoT will exceed $300 billion by 2020 [21]. Cisco estimated that IoT could create an economic value up to $19 trillion in the next decade [3].

However, when more and more smart devices join IoT, the data in IoT becomes tremendously big. As Cisco reported, the data generated by IoT was over 100 zettabytes by 2013, and will reach 400 zettabytes by 2018, where a zettabyte is a trillion GB [11]. Take a Boeing 787 aircraft as an example; it generates 40 TB data on an hourly basis [11]. As shown in Figure 10.2 [22], smart devices collect data from factories, power grids, homes, and so on, and send to cloud servers.

It is well known that big data has four "Vs", which are volume, velocity, variety, and veracity. Volume refers to the scale of data. Velocity refers to the pace of data flow. Variety means the various sources and types of data. Veracity means the quality of data. In some fields, the big data problem may have only one "V". For example, the big data in video streaming only has "velocity". However, the big data in IoT has all four "V" properties. The volume of big data in IoT is extremely big. The pace of big data flow in IoT is very fast in some applications, such as patient survelliance. The sources and types of data are especially diverse and heterogeneous. Moreover, because of the variety of data, the quality of data in IoT also varies.

10.3 Security Requirement and Issues

IoT is a giant complicated network of many subnetworks involving a huge amount of devices, different protocols, different data structures, different message formats, and different system requirements. Thus, the security requirements and issues in IoT are complicated. The security threat map of IoT is shown in Figure 10.3 [23].

We will study various security requirements and issues in the context of IoT and present major security requirements and issues in this section.

10.3.1 Heterogeneous Big Data Security and Management

IoT is a giant network containing various applications and systems. Every application or system has its own devices, data sources, protocols, data formats, and so on. Thus, the data in IoT is extremely heterogeneous and big, and this poses a heterogeneous big data security and management problem.

Table 10.1 Applications and Devices in IoT

Application	*Function*	*Description*	*Device*
Smart cities	Structural health	Monitoring vibration of bridges, buildings, etc.	Sensor
	Waste management	Monitoring trash condition	Sensor
Transportation	Smart parking	Monitoring parking space	Sensor
	Traffic congestion	Monitoring traffic conditions	Sensor
	Smart drive	Assisting your schedule, route, etc. based on the calendar	Smart car
Home automation	Remote control appliances	Turning on/off home appliances remotely	Smart TV, smart refrigerator, smart microwave oven, etc.
	Energy and water use	Monitoring energy usage of home appliances	Smart meter
eHealth	Emergency notification	Assisting elderly or disabled people	Smart caregiver wearable heart monitors
	Patient surveillance	Assisting patient care	Pain relief wearables Smart chair
	Physical exercise assistance	Assisting physical exercise	Smart scale
Education	Child education assistance	Assisting child education	Smart toy

(Continued)

Table 10.1 (Continued) Applications and Devices in IoT

Application	*Function*	*Description*	*Device*
Smart environment	Forest fire detection	Monitoring forests to report fire	Sensor
	Air pollution	Monitoring air condition	Sensor
	Earthquake early detection	Monitoring earthquake zone	Sensor
Smart water	Chemical leakage detection in rivers	Monitoring rivers for chemical leakage	Sensor
	Water leakages	Monitoring pipes for water leakages	Sensor
	River floods	Monitoring rivers for floods	Sensor
Smart metering	Smart grid	Monitoring energy usage	Smart meter
	Tank level	Monitoring oil, gas level in tanks	Sensor
Retail	Supply chain control	Monitoring storage conditions	Sensor, RFID
	Smart product management	Controlling rotation of products	Sensor, RFID
Industrial control	Temperature monitoring	Controlling temperature during manufacturing	Sensor
Smart agriculture	Wine quality enhancing	Controlling the amount of sugar in grapes	Sensor
	Greenhouses	Controlling conditions in greenhouses	Sensor
	Animal tracking	Tracking locations of animals	RFID

Source: Top 50 Internet of Things Applications. http://www.libelium.com/top_50_iot_sensor_applications_ranking/ (accessed May 8, 2016).

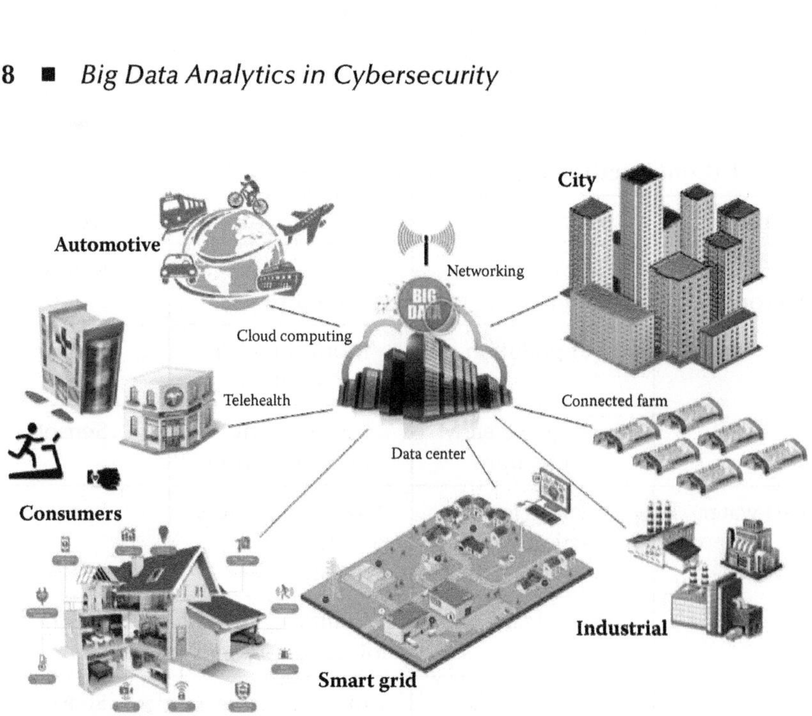

Figure 10.2 IoT and big data. (Based on Internet of Things World, Europe. https://opentechdiary.wordpress.com/tag/internet-of-things/, accessed May 19, 2016.)

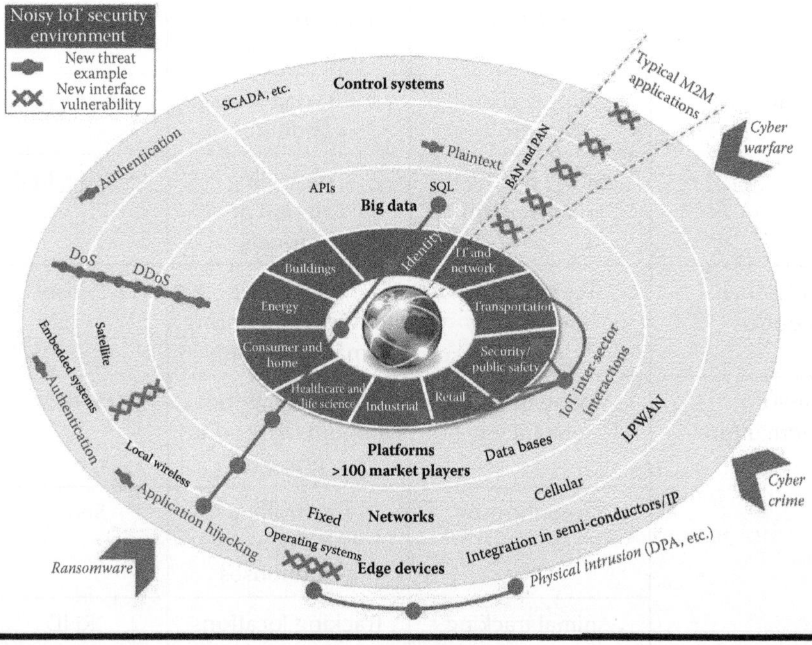

Figure 10.3 IoT security threat map. (Based on Beecham Research. IoT Security Threat Map. http://www.beechamresearch.com/download.aspx?id=43, accessed May 19, 2016.)

The input data in IoT is heterogeneous big data from both traditional cyberspace and the physical world. The traditional cyberspace data includes network traffic data, OS log data, workstation log data, cloud-based host log data, anti-virus log data, firewall log data, web proxy log data, and so on. Physical world data includes home appliance data, smart meter data, power substation data, smart car data, smart watch data, and so on. The output includes both archival data and real-time alerts.

10.3.2 Lightweight Cryptography

Many applications in IoT are human-centric, such as early education, home automation, and eHealth. The security of these applications is crucial and urgent, and data encryption is an essential requirement. However, the smart devices in these applications are usually resource-constrained, which have limited energy, storage, and processing capabilities, such as smart toys, body area sensors, and smart meters. These applications and devices require lightweight cryptography to encrypt and authenticate. But the security strength should not be "light" [24,25].

10.3.3 Universal Security Infrastructure

As shown in Table 10.1, IoT has many applications and systems. Every application or system has its own security infrastructure. In Smart Grid, supervisory control and data acquisition (SCADA) [5] is used to monitor the power generation, transmission, distribution, and redistribution process. Smart meters adopt symmetric key encryption and authentication, e.g., DES and AES. In RFID, various security systems have been proposed, such as Deckard [26]. Various encryption methods have been proposed for RFID devices, such as Hummingbird [27]. These security infrastructures have totally different encryption, authentication, and threat handling processes. The security events, logs, and alerts they generate are totally different [28].

Existing security solutions, such as various IDS, firewalls, anti-virus software, honeypots, and so on, usually work individually and seldom cooperate. They might perform similar redundant operations on the same threats in the systems. Or they might generate repeated or even conflicted security events and alerts. A universal security infrastructure for IoT is needed to integrate security infrastructures of various applications in IoT and correlate security information from different sources.

10.3.4 Trust Management

Trust management is to build and manage trust between each two entities in IoT. IoT is highly heterogeneous. The devices in IoT are heterogeneous. The frameworks of applications in IoT are heterogeneous. The security infrastructures in IoT are heterogeneous. Data source, data type, and format are also heterogeneous in IoT. Therefore, trust management is crucial in IoT to support information correlation, data fusion, and context-aware intelligence, as well as information security and privacy. The paper [29] summarizes objectives of trust management in IoT, which include trust relationship and decision, data perception trust, data fusion and mining trust, data transmission and communication trust, quality of IoT services, privacy preservation, human–computer trust interaction, and so on.

10.3.5 Key Management

Key management is the process to generate, distribute, and store encryption and authentication keys securely in security solutions. Public key infrastructure (PKI) is used for the most sophisticated authentication and key management system. PKI is widely used in Internet-based security solutions, and its security has been widely studied and proved. The development of PKI is to overcome some shortcomings of symmetric key, such as key distribution, storage, and revocation. However, symmetric key is easier to generate and more lightweight than public key.

Many devices in IoT are resource-constrained, which have limited processing and storage capabilities. These devices include various sensors, wearables, smart meters, RFID tagged objects, and so on. The traditional PKI does not apply to these devices because it is impossible to manage a tremendous amount of certificates. Developing lightweight cryptography is one trend toward solving this problem. Current lightweight cryptography, such as Hummingbird and AES-EAX [30], is symmetric key encryption, which is more expensive to manage.

Some recent studies propose using PKI with a lightweight certificate or no certificate. The paper [31] proposes a key management scheme based on a micro-certificate for IoT. The certificate only takes a few bytes. The paper [30] proposes using certificateless PKI for Smart Grid.

10.3.6 Privacy Preservation

Privacy preservation has attracted various interests in different application areas of IoT, including connected cars [32], connected smart meters [15], wireless sensor networks (WSN) [33,34], and so on. Privacy preservation in IoT is to carry out a series of technologies, mechanisms, legislation, and so on, to protect the privacy of smart device owners in IoT. However, the complexity of IoT involves many challenges in privacy preservation, and the main challenges include [35,36] the following.

10.3.6.1 Identity Privacy

Identity privacy is hiding the identities of smart devices and thus protecting the privacy of device owners. Traditionally, identities include real IDs, names, addresses, or pseudonyms of real IDs. But in IoT, emerging technologies, such as face recognition, speech recognition, surveillance camera, fingerprint identification, and so on, make it possible to use face, voice, fingerprints, and so on as identities. These bio-featured identities are more difficult to hide and the existing privacy-preserving techniques may not be applicable.

10.3.6.2 Location Privacy

Location privacy is hiding the locations and movements of smart devices and thus protecting the privacy of device owners. If the locations or movements of smart devices are exposed to adversaries, the information could be used for crimes, such as hijacking and stalking. However, localization and tracking are the main functionalities of many IoT applications. Moreover, the diversity of location resources in IoT could provide adversaries with multiple data sources.

10.3.6.3 Profiling Privacy

In many IoT applications, a business generates customer profiles based on user behavior analysis and uses these profiles to make marketing strategy. However, profiling may lead to privacy violation, such as unsolicited advertisements, price discrimination, and so on.

10.3.6.4 Linkage Privacy

Previously separated systems may have their own privacy preserving mechanisms and policies. However, the combination of data from different sources may potentially cause new privacy violation issues when these separated systems collaborate under the context of IoT.

10.3.6.5 Interaction Privacy

In many IoT applications, interaction between smart devices and device owners is one of the main functionalities. Interaction includes touching, shaking, or speaking to smart devices. However, these interactions could be observed by nearby people and thus causes privacy violation issues.

10.3.7 Transparency

The term transparency often co-occurs with privacy. Privacy preservation refers to how to protect user's privacy. Transparency closely relates to privacy, but it refers to letting the users know how their data are collected and used. In the traditional Internet-based systems, it is easier to integrate transparency into the privacy preservation design since the devices have enough displaying and processing ability to interact with end users. In IoT, devices are highly heterogeneous and resource-constrained. It is very difficult for devices to consider transparency when most of their capabilities are used to guarantee functionality.

10.3.8 Fraud Protection

Fraud is to use falsified objects or statements to deceive victims and gain illegal benefit. IoT creates new opportunities for fraud to spread over billions of smart devices. Smart devices are usually resource-constrained devices that have limited programming memory for security mechanisms to use [30]. Thus, they are more likely to be infected by malware and be utilized by fraudsters. Typical frauds in IoT include ad fraud [37], ATM fraud [38], non-technical loss (NTL) fraud [39], and so on.

10.3.8.1 Ad Fraud

Ad fraud is where fraudsters use botnet to stimulate human traffic to steal from advertisers' budgets. A typical case is an advertiser who wants to increase traffic to the site he or she owns. A traffic broker site promises to bring highly qualified customers. But in fact, the owner of the broker site is a fraudster who spreads malware to infect many smart devices and forms a botnet to increase traffic to the advertiser's site.

10.3.8.2 ATM Fraud

ATM fraud is where fraudsters force access to web-configurable ATMs to gain illegal benefit by changing system parameters or setting up fraudulent transactions. A typical case is that fraudsters use the web-based control to let banks ignore the balance on compromised accounts.

10.3.8.3 NTL Fraud

NTL fraud is a typical fraud in Smart Grid where fraudsters compromise smart meters and send fraudulent billing information to the utility to lower electricity bills. NTL fraud has a long history in the power grid. However, with the rise of smart meters, fraudsters have many more ways to commit NTL fraud.

10.3.9 Identity Management

Identity is a unique value to identify an object in a domain. In IoT, emerging technologies bring the possibilities of using face, voice, fingerprint, and so on, as identities, and this brings a new challenge of how to manage these identities. Meanwhile, the traditional identities, such as IP address, may not be used as identity in IoT, and this adds another new challenge. The main challenges of identity management in IoT include the following.

10.3.9.1 Identity and Address

Some of the devices in IoT are IP-based, such as smart meters, and they can use an address as identity. Some of the devices in IoT use RFID in applications such as animal trackers; they are not built on IP addresses and thus cannot use addresses as identities.

10.3.9.2 Identity and Ownership

The owners, users, or operators of smart devices could change over time. The relationship between identity and ownership in IoT affects other processes such as authentication. The ownership between devices is also a problem. For example, a fingerprint sensor embedded in a smart phone is a single device. Should it only be controlled by this phone?

10.3.9.3 Identity and Domain

In IoT, devices could be connected with each other using different protocols. For example, in Smart Grid, a smart meter is connected with several smart home appliances using ZigBee to form a Home Area Network [40]. At the same time, the meter and home appliances should join metering networks using ANSI C12 series of protocols [41]. It is a problem to manage the identity of the same device in different domains. Alternatively, should we use a universal identity for each device?

10.3.9.4 Identity and Lifecycle

Different from traditional user identity management where an identity usually has a long lifecycle, identity lifecycle in IoT varies from minutes to a lifetime.

10.4 Big Data Analytics for Cybersecurity in IoT

The traditional security solutions for IoT include IDS, firewall, anti-virus software, and monitoring systems. However, these solutions have difficulty in storing, processing, and integrating big data. Facing big data challenges, big data analytics (BDA) is a good choice to address cybersecurity issues in IoT. Hadoop technologies, such as MapReduce, HDFS, Hive, Pig, and so on, are often used by BDA solutions to process big data. MapReduce is a programming model that processes large datasets with a parallel and distributed algorithm [42]. HDFS is the distributed file system. Hive is the data warehouse and Pig is the database querying language similar to SQL. Hadoop has the ability to divide a large security analysis task or a large traffic dataset into many small subtasks or sub-datasets. When these subtasks or sub-datasets are processed in a parallel and distributed manner, the security analysis process will be accelerated thousands of times.

Besides big data processing, these traditional security solutions cannot simply store the data. NoSQL databases, such as MongoDB, HBase, Cassandra, CouchDB, and so on, are often used to store many security events, alerts, and logs.

In this section, we will introduce the shortcomings of the traditional IoT security solutions and the benefits of employing BDA solutions.

10.4.1 Single Big Dataset Security Analysis

IDS is one of the most used ways to combat cyberattack [7–9]. The traditional IDSs are either based on misuse detection or anomaly detection [43]. They analyze traffic and events of a host or a network and generate security alerts. However, a single dataset in IoT could be very big, such as space exploration. In 2018, Square Kilometre Array (SKA), the largest radio telescope, will be built. SKA will generate 700 terabytes of data per second [44]. As reported in the paper [44], a traffic flow with the speed of 1 Gbps is enough to cause big data issues for the traditional IDS. The big dataset contains "heavy" attributes such as image, video stream, and high dimensional scientific data, which makes it very difficult for the traditional IDS to perform deep analysis.

In the paper [45], the authors propose a Hadoop-based traffic monitoring system to detect DDoS attack. The playback files used in the experiments vary from 1 TB to 5 TB. They can achieve a throughput from 6 Gbps to 14 Gbps. In the paper [46], a BDA solution is proposed for IDS. The author proposes using HDFS to process big data if they are needed immediately and using a cloud computing storage system (CCSS) to store big data locally for later analysis. The authors in [47] introduce how Hadoop technologies can address big data problems in the traditional IDS and issues when applying BDA to intrusion detection.

10.4.2 Big Amount of Datasets Security Analysis

Compared to a single big dataset, some systems or applications in IoT generate small datasets. For example, road traffic data, weather data, and pollution data in a Smart City are small datasets with specific attributes [48]. A wind turbine adjusts itself by sensing and generating small datasets with the attributes of temperature, wind speed, wind direction, and vibration. However, a Smart City has a lot of wind turbines and other smart devices; the volume of these small datasets becomes tremendously big.

The traditional security solutions in IoT can process these small datasets, but it takes a long time. Instead of processing these small datasets one by one, BDA solutions can parallelize the process. As reported in the paper [49], it takes 20 minutes to one hour to query security data of one month using their traditional security solution. When they switch to BDA solutions, it takes only one minute to get the same results. In the paper [50], the authors propose a distributed BDA solution based on Hadoop and Snort. Their experiments employ eight slaves and a master node. The processing speed of using nine nodes increases more than four times compared to using only one node.

10.4.3 Big Heterogeneous Security Data

IoT data are heterogeneous, which have various data sources, data formats, and data types. When heterogeneous data meet big data, it becomes the problem of heterogeneous big data. The traditional security solutions in IoT cannot deal with heterogeneous data, or they lack scalability which is required by IoT systems. The paper [51] introduces different types of big heterogeneous security data as follows.

10.4.3.1 Heterogeneous Input Data

10.4.3.1.1 Big Heterogeneous Cyberspace Data

Big heterogeneous cyberspace data refer to the traditional traffic data collected by the network layer monitoring systems or associated with various hosts. The paper [52] introduces an example of outsourcing network traffic monitoring and IDS to cloud providers. The example used in the paper is a university network with a throughput up to 1 Gbps.

Besides network traffic data, another type of cyberspace data is the host event log. The types of hosts in IoT are various including workstations, servers, cloud-based hosts, appliances, and so on. The types of log files in IoT also vary from OS log, anti-virus software log, server log, proxy log, to firewall log, and so on. Beehive [53] is a BDA security solution based on large-scale log analysis. Beehive was implemented at EMC Corporation for two weeks, and it can well address the big heterogeneous data problem of EMC which has 1.4 bn log messages generated every day.

10.4.3.1.2 Big Heterogeneous Industrial Data

An important application of IoT is industrial process control, such as Smart Grid, Smart Water, Smart Factory, and so on. Big heterogeneous industrial data refer to the data generated by different devices during the industrial control process which has various types and formats. A typical security solution in the traditional industrial process control is SCADA. However, SCADA also faces big data challenges. The paper [54] studies the feasibility of applying BDA to SCADA. The experimental results show that the proposed BDA solution can meet the requirement of processing big heterogeneous data in SCADA.

10.4.3.2 Heterogeneous Output Data

10.4.3.2.1 Big Archival Security Data

Big archival security data refer to the output data that is archived for later analysis or digital forensic. Archival security data in IoT creates a big challenge with storing big heterogeneous data, especially when the data generated in each second might have to be stored. In the paper [55], a BDA model is proposed to improve the ability of long-term digital forensics. The study shows that 5 TB storage space is required for a traffic flow with the speed of 10 Gbps per hour. The paper also points out that the traditional security solutions, such as IDS and firewall, often do not obtain enough forensic information.

10.4.3.2.2 Big Alert Data

Another type of output data is big alert data. Security systems generate security alerts when they detect threats. An individual IDS could generate many security alerts. Various heterogeneous data sources in IoT generate heterogeneous security alerts and the volume of the alerts is big.

10.4.4 Information Correlation and Data Fusion

One benefit of applying BDA to cybersecurity in IoT is that BDA solutions can correlate security information from various data sources. The traditional security solutions in IoT, such as IDS, firewall, anti-virus software, and so on, have their specialties in addressing various threats. However, they often work separately. Or they work together to protect a system but they are not well-integrated. Information correlation and data fusion are to integrate and correlate security information, such as security events, security alerts, and so on, to improve detection accuracy and decrease the false alarm rate.

The basic idea behind information correlation and data fusion is to use a BDA method to build a correlation layer, and to analyze various security information generated by heterogeneous security systems. Shown in Figure 10.4 is a framework of information correlation and data fusion [56]. A number of observers are deployed in the network to monitor and collect data. A few slave nodes act as local analyzers that execute a given detection algorithm. Each analyzer relates to several observers. A master node acts as the global analyzer, which finalizes the correlation process.

Another type of information correlation is security alert correlation. Alert correlation is a technique used to stop continuously generating similar alerts. The paper [57] proposes a framework to improve the security situation awareness based

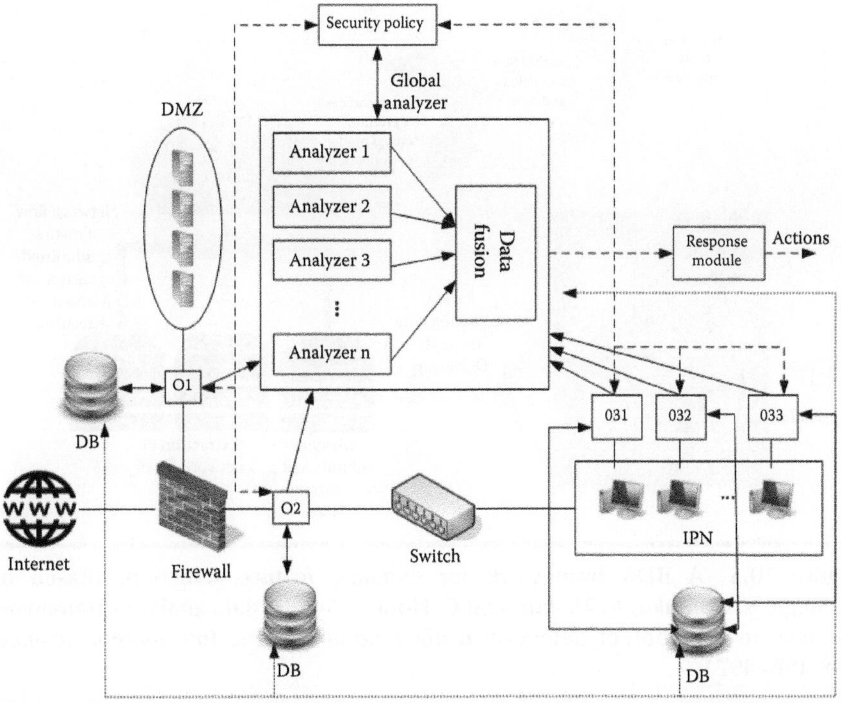

Figure 10.4 Information correlation and data fusion. (Based on Fessi B, Benabdallah S, Hamdi M, Rekhis S, and Boudriga N. 2010. Data collection for information security system. In *Engineering Systems Management and Its Applications (ICESMA), 2010 Second International Conference on.* IEEE, Sharjah, United Arab Emirates; 2010:1–8.)

on knowledge discovery. The basic idea is to collect security alerts from sensors and correlate them using correlation rules based on the network security situation.

10.4.5 Dynamic Security Feature Selection

Feature selection is a crucial technique used by security solutions to identify various threats, attacks, abnormal behaviors, and potential anomaly. Traditionally, security solutions study static datasets that contain abnormal traffic, extract features from the abnormal traffic using machine learning or other techniques, and classify attacks by matching these features with incoming traffic. A more accurate feature selection will significantly improve classification accuracy and reduce false alarm rate. The feature selection process takes storage and computational efforts especially when the data is big. Thus, most of the existing security solutions employ offline feature selection to achieve better accuracy.

However, cybersecurity in IoT is dynamically changing and diverse. More and more attacks are zero-day exploits. Features selected today might not be applicable

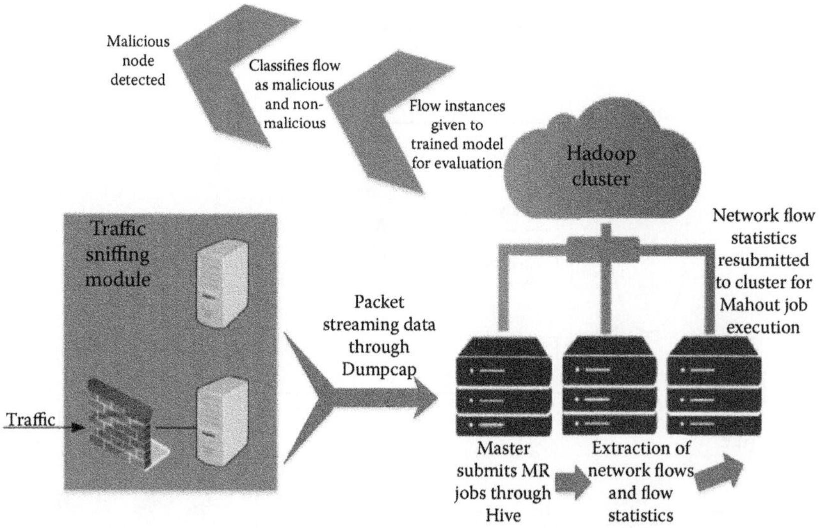

Figure 10.5 A BDA framework for dynamic feature selection. (Based on K. Singh, S. Guntuku, A. Thakur, and C. Hota. 2014. Big data analytics framework for peer-to-peer botnet detection using random forests. *Information Sciences* 278:488–497.)

tomorrow. Dynamic feature selection is to select features from incoming traffic in a real-time manner. Dynamic feature selection can greatly improve the efficiency and accuracy of threat detection. Dynamic feature selection requires the abilities of big data storage, fast big data processing, and fast big data classification, which are the abilities that BDA solutions can provide.

In the paper [58], a BDA framework is proposed to detect botnet attacks in real time. The framework is built on Hadoop, Hive, and Mahout. Hive is used for network traffic sniffing which enables dynamic feature selection. Mahout is used to build a random forest based decision tree model. The framework is shown in Figure 10.5.

10.4.6 Cross-Boundary Intelligence

The traditional security solutions in IoT, such as IDS, firewall, anti-virus software, and so on, address threats within their domains, but they work separately and seldom cooperate. BDA can help security solutions to achieve cross-boundary intelligence which contributes to making a better decision and protecting safety in various domains. For example, a BDA-enabled security solution in Smart Grid can detect threats and defend attackers. At the same time, it can send out alerts when there is a leaking or short loop. It can even remind customers of energy efficiency and savings.

The paper [59] proposes a BDA-enabled security solution supporting cross-boundary intelligence. As shown in Figure 10.6, the security solution integrates security events from multiple sources including network, host, application, database and directory. Multiple technologies, such as vulnerability management, anti-malware, firewall, IDS, and so on, cooperate to protect security. Intelligent actions and decisions are made based on multiple intelligence sources, such as threat intelligence, vulnerability intelligence, crowd intelligence, and so on. The paper [60] introduces how cross-boundary intelligence helps to build intelligent railway control systems in Russia. The intelligent railway control systems employ BDA tools to build multi-level intelligence and a better decision-making scheme based on a rough set.

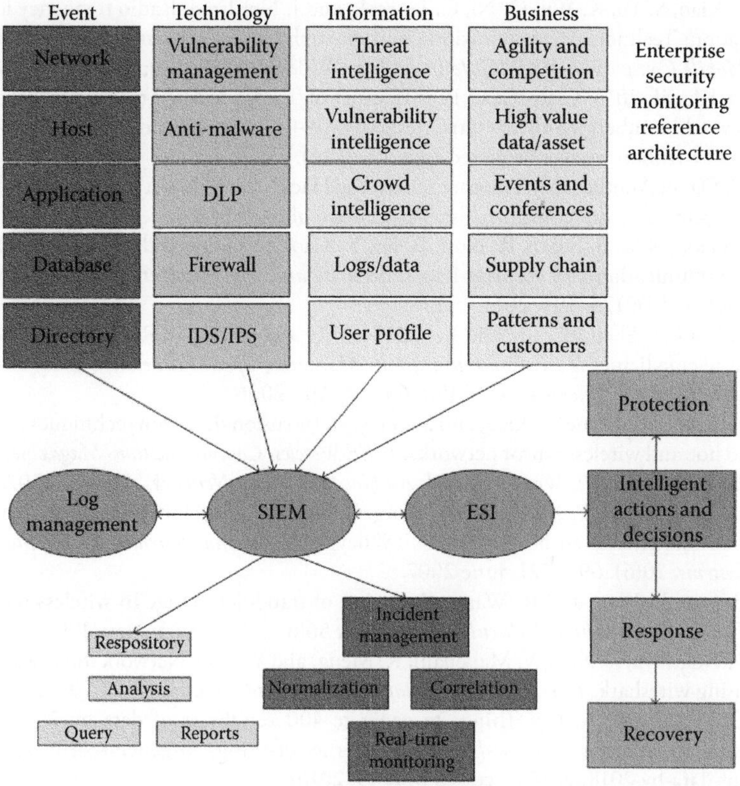

Figure 10.6 BDA-enabled cross-boundary intelligence. (Based on Li Y, Liu Y, and Zhang H. 2012. Cross-boundary enterprise security monitoring. In *Computational Problem-Solving (ICCP), 2012 International Conference on.* IEEE, Leshan, China, pp. 127–136.)

10.5 Conclusion

In this chapter, we introduced IoT and the big data challenges in IoT. We presented various security requirements and issues in IoT, including key management, identity management, lightweight cryptography, privacy preservation, and transparency. We introduced how BDA can address security issues in IoT when facing big data.

References

1. J. Liu, Y. Xiao, and C. L. P. Chen. Internet of Things' authentication and access control, *International Journal of Security and Networks (IJSN)*, 7(4): 228–241, 2012. doi:10.1504/IJSN.2012.053461.
2. Y. Xiao, S. Yu, K. Wu, Q. Ni, C. Janecek, and J. Nordstad. Radio frequency identification: Technologies, applications, and research issues, *Wireless Communications and Mobile Computing (WCMC) Journal*, John Wiley & Sons, 7(4): 457–472, May 2007.
3. O. Kharif. 2014. Cisco CEO Pegs Internet of Things as $19 Trillion Market. http://www.bloomberg.com/news/articles/2014-01-08/cisco-ceo-pegs-internet-of-things-as-19-trillion-market (accessed May 19, 2016).
4. G. Davis. Another Day, Another Smart Toy Hack: This Time, It's Fisher-Price. https://blogs.mcafee.com/consumer/fisher-price-toy-vulnerability/ (accessed May 19, 2016).
5. J. Gao, J. Liu, B. Rajan, R. Nori, B. Fu, Y. Xiao, W. Liang, and C. L. P. Chen. Scada communication and security issues. *Security and Communication Networks Security Comm*, 7(1): 175–194, 2014.
6. Y. Xiao, X. Shen, B. Sun, and L. Cai. Security and privacy in RFID and applications in telemedicine, *IEEE Communications Magazine, Special issue on Quality Assurance and Devices in Telemedicine*, 44(4): 64–72, Apr. 2006.
7. B. Sun, L. Osborne, Y. Xiao, and S. Guizani. Intrusion detection techniques in mobile ad hoc and wireless sensor networks, *IEEE Wireless Communications Magazine, Special Issue on Security in Wireless Mobile Ad Hoc and Sensor Networks*, 56–63, 2007.
8. B. Sun, K. Wu, Y. Xiao, and R. Wang. Integration of mobility and intrusion detection for wireless ad hoc networks, (Wiley) *International Journal of Communication Systems*, 20(6): 695–721, June 2007.
9. B. Sun, Y. Xiao, and R. Wang. Detection of fraudulent usage in wireless networks, *IEEE Transactions on Vehicular Technology*, 56(6): 3912–3923, Nov. 2007.
10. V. Ndatinya, Z. Xiao, V. Manepalli, K. Meng, and Y. Xiao. Network forensics analysis using wireshark, *International Journal of Security and Networks*, 10(2): 91–106, 2015.
11. D. Worth. Internet of Things to generate 400 zettabytes of data by 2018. http://www.v3.co.uk/v3-uk/news/2379626/internet-of-things-to-generate-400-zettabytes-of-data-by-2018, 2014 (accessed May 19, 2016).
12. Y.2060. Overview of the Internet of Things. https://www.itu.int/rec/T-REC-Y.2060-201206-I (accessed May 19, 2016).
13. JessGroopman. Visualizing the Internet of Things: A round-up of maps, frameworks, and infographics of IoT. https://jessgroopman.wordpress.com/2014/08/25/visualizing-the-internet-of-things-a-round-up-of-maps-frameworks-and-infographics-of-iot/ (accessed June 1, 2016).

14. J. Gao, Y. Xiao, J. Liu, W. Liang, and C. L. P. Chen. A survey of communication /networking in smart grids, (Elsevier) *Future Generation Computer Systems*, 28(2): 391–404, Feb. 2012. doi:10.1016/j.future.2011.04.014.
15. J. Liu, Y. Xiao, S. Li, W. Liang, and C. L. P. Chen. Cyber security and privacy issues in smart grids, *IEEE Communications Surveys & Tutorials*, 14(4): 981–997, 2012. doi:10.1109/SURV.2011.122111.00145.
16. W. Han and Y. Xiao. NFD: A practical scheme to detect non-technical loss fraud in smart grid. In *Proceedings of the 2014 International Conference on Communications (ICC'14)*, pp. 605–609, June 2014.
17. W. Han and Y. Xiao. FNFD: A fast scheme to detect and verify non-technical loss fraud in smart grid. *International Workshop on Traffic Measurements for Cybersecurity (WTMC'16)*, accepted, doi:http://dx.doi.org/10.1145/2903185.2903188, 2016.
18. W. Han and Y. Xiao. IP2DM for V2G networks in smart grid. In *Proceedings of the 2015 International Conference on Communications (ICC'15)*, pp. 782–787, June 2015.
19. Top 50 Internet of Things Applications. http://www.libelium.com/top_50_iot_sensor_applications_ranking/ (accessed May 8, 2016).
20. T. Dull. Big data and the Internet of Things: Two sides of the same coin? http://www.sas.com/en_us/insights/articles/big-data/big-data-and-iot-two-sides-of-the-same-coin.html (accessed May 19, 2016).
21. Gartner Says the Internet of Things Installed Base Will Grow to 26 Billion Units By 2020. http://www.gartner.com/newsroom/id/2636073 (accessed May 19, 2016).
22. Internet of Things World, Europe. https://opentechdiary.wordpress.com/tag/internet-of-things/ (accessed May 19, 2016).
23. Beecham Research. IoT Security Threat Map. http://www.beechamresearch.com/download.aspx?id=43 (accessed May 19, 2016).
24. A. Olteanu, Y. Xiao, F. Hu, B. Sun, and H. Deng. A lightweight block cipher based on a multiple recursive generator for wireless sensor networks and RFID, *Wireless Communications and Mobile Computing (WCMC) Journal*, John Wiley & Sons, 11(2): 254–266, Feb. 2011, doi:10.1002/wcm.988.
25. B. Sun, C. Li, K. Wu, and Y. Xiao. A lightweight secure protocol for wireless sensor networks, *Computer Communications Journal, special issue on Wireless Sensor Networks: Performance, Reliability, Security and Beyond*, 29(13–14): 2556–2568, Aug. 2006.
26. L. Mirowski and J. Hartnett. Deckard. A system to detect change of RFID tag ownership. *IJCSNS International Journal of Computer Science and Network Security*, 7(7); 2007.
27. B. J. Mohd, T. Hayajneh, and A. V. Vasilakos. A survey on lightweight block ciphers for low-resource devices: Comparative study and open issues. *Journal of Network and Computer Applications*, 58:73–93, 2015.
28. L. Zeng, Y. Xiao, and H. Chen. Auditing overhead, auditing adaptation, and benchmark evaluation in Linux, (Wiley Journal of) *Security and Communication Networks*, 8(18): 3523–3534, Dec. 2015, doi:10.1002/sec.1277.
29. Z. Yan, P. Zhang, and A. V. Vasilakos. A survey on trust management for Internet of Things. *Journal of Network and Computer Applications* 42:120–134, 2014.
30. W. Han and Y. Xiao. Non-technical loss fraud in advanced metering infrastructure in smart grid. *The 2nd International Conference on Cloud Computing and Security (ICCCS 2016)*, Nanjing, China, July 29–31, 2016.

31. L. Du, F. Feng, and J. Guo. Key management scheme based on micro-certificate for Internet of Things. *International Conference on Education Technology and Information System (ICETIS 2013)*, pp. 701–711, 2013.
32. W. Han and Y. Xiao. CO_2: A fault-tolerant relay node deployment strategy for throwbox-based DTNs. *The 11th International Conference on Wireless Algorithms, Systems, and Applications (WASA 2016)*, August 8–10, 2016, Bozeman, MT.
33. Y. Xiao, H. Chen, K. Wu, B. Sun, Y. Zhang, X. Sun, and C. Liu. Coverage and detection of a randomized scheduling algorithm in wireless sensor networks, *IEEE Transactions on Computers*, 59(4): 507–521, Apr. 2010. doi:10.1109/TC.2009.170.
34. Y. Xiao, V. Rayi, B. Sun, X. Du, F. Hu, and M. Galloway. A survey of key management schemes in wireless sensor networks, *Computer Communications Journal*, 30(11–12): 2314–2341, Sept. 2007.
35. J. Ziegeldorf, O. Morchon, and K. Wehrle. Privacy in the Internet of Things: Threats and challenges. *Security and Communication Networks*, 7(12), 2014.
36. W. Han and Y. Xiao. Privacy preservation for V2G networks in smart grid: A Survey. Submitted.
37. Here Are 4 Common Methods That Ad Fraudsters Use to Make Their Ill-Gotten Money. http://www.adweek.com/news/technology/here-are-4-common-methods-ad-fraudsters-use-make-their-ill-gotten-money-169285 (accessed May 19, 2016).
38. B. Baesens, W. Verbeke, and V. Vlasselaer. *Fraud Analytics Using Descriptive, Predictive, and Social Network Techniques*. Wiley, 2015.
39. W. Han and Y. Xiao. CNFD: A novel scheme to detect colluded non-technical loss fraud in smart grid. *The 11th International Conference on Wireless Algorithms, Systems, and Applications (WASA 2016)*, Bozeman, MT, August 8–10, 2016.
40. J. Liu, Y. Xiao, and J. Gao. Achieving accountability in smart grids, *IEEE Systems Journal*, 8(2): 493–508, June 2014. doi:10.1109/JSYST.2013.2260697.
41. W. Han and Y. Xiao. Combating TNTL: Non-technical loss fraud targeting time-based pricing in smart grid. *The 2nd International Conference on Cloud Computing and Security (ICCCS 2016)*, Nanjing, China, July 29–31, 2016.
42. Z. Xiao and Y. Xiao. Achieving accountable MapReduce in cloud computing, (Elsevier) *Future Generation Computer Systems*, 30(1): 1–13, Jan. 2014. doi:10.1016/j.future.2013.07.001.
43. W. Han, W. Xiong, Y. Xiao, M. Ellabidy, A. V. Vasilakos, and N. Xiong. A class of non-statistical traffic anomaly detection in complex network systems. In *Proceedings of the 32nd International Conference on Distributed Computing Systems Workshops (ICDCSW'12)*, pp. 640–646, June 2012.
44. M. Nassar, B. Bouna, and Q. Malluhi. Secure outsourcing of network flow data analysis. *2013 IEEE International Congress on Big Data*, pp. 431–432, 2013.
45. Y. Lee. Toward scalable internet traffic measurement and analysis with hadoop. *ACM SIGCOMM Comput Commun Rev.* 43(1): 5–13, 2013. 10.1145/2427036.2427038.
46. S. Suthaharan. Big data classification: Problems and challenges in network intrusion prediction with machine learning. In *Big Data Analytics Workshop, in Conjunction with ACM Sigmetrics*. ACM, Pittsburgh, PA, 2013.
47. H. Jeong, W. Hyun, J. Lim, and I. You. Anomaly teletraffic intrusion detection systems on hadoop-based platforms: A survey of some problems and solutions. In *15th International Conference on Network-Based Information Systems (NBiS)*, IEEE, Melbourne, Australia, pp. 766–770, 2012. 10.1109/NBiS.2012.139

48. Dataset Collection. http://iot.ee.surrey.ac.uk:8080/datasets.html (accessed May 19, 2016).
49. E. Chickowski. 2012. A case study in security big data analysis. http://www.darkreading.com/analytics/security-monitoring(accessed May 19, 2016).
50. J. Cheon and T-Y. Choe. Distributed processing of snort alert log using hadoop. *International Journal of Engineering & Technology* 5(3): 2685–2690, 2013.
51. R. Zuech, T. M Khoshgoftaar, and R. Wald. Intrusion detection and big heterogeneous data: A survey. *Journal of Big Data*, 2015.
52. M. Nassar, B. al Bouna, and Q. Malluhi. Secure outsourcing of network flow data analysis. In *IEEE International Congress on Big Data (BigData Congress)*, IEEE, Santa Clara, CA, pp. 431–432, 2013. 10.1109/BigData.Congress.2013.71.
53. T.-F. Yen, A. Oprea, K. Onarlioglu, T. Leetham, W. Robertson, A. Juels, and E. Kirda. Beehive: Large-scale log analysis for detecting suspicious activity in enterprise networks. In *Proceedings of the 29th Annual Computer Security Applications Conference.* ACM, New Orleans, LA, pp. 199–208, 2013. 10.1145/2523649.2523670.
54. X-B. Xu, Z-Q. Yang, J-P. Xiu, and C. Liu. A big data acquisition engine based on rule engine. *J China Universities Posts Telecommunications 2013*, 20: 45–49, 2013. 10.1016/S1005-8885(13)60250-2.
55. R. Hunt and J. Slay 2010. The design of real-time adaptive forensically sound secure critical infrastructure. In *The 4th International Conference on Network and System Security (NSS).* IEEE, Melbourne, Australia, pp. 328–333, 2010. 10.1109/NSS.2010.38.
56. B. Fessi, S. Benabdallah, M. Hamdi, S. Rekhis, and N. Boudriga. Data collection for information security system. In *Second International Conference on Engineering Systems Management and Its Applications (ICESMA)*, IEEE, Sharjah, United Arab Emirates, pp. 1–8, 2010.
57. F. Lan, W. Chunlei, and M. Guoqing. A framework for network security situation awareness based on knowledge discovery. In *2nd International Conference on Computer Engineering and Technology (ICCET)*, IEEE, Chengdu, China, pp. 1–226, 2010.
58. K. Singh, S. Guntuku, A. Thakur, and C. Hota. Big data analytics framework for peer-to-peer botnet detection using random forests. *Information Sciences* 278: 488–497, 2014.
59. Y. Li, Y. Liu, and H. Zhang. Cross-boundary enterprise security monitoring. In *International Conference on Computational Problem-Solving (ICCP)*, IEEE, Leshan, China, pp. 127–136, 2012.
60. A.V. Chernov, M.A. Butakova, and E.V. Karpenko. Security incident detection technique for multilevel intelligent control systems on railway transport in Russia. *23rd Telecommunications Forum TELFOR*, pp. 1–4, November 2015.

Chapter 11

Big Data Analytics for Security in Fog Computing

Shanhe Yi and Qun Li

Contents

This chapter presents a new cybersecurity domain fog computing, and discusses why big data analytics is important for fog computing as well as the security issues in fog computing. Fog computing is recently proposed as a brand new solution to support the rapid development of Internet of Things (IoT), cloud computing, and big data technologies. As an emerging computing paradigm, its concept is to extend the cloud computing paradigm to the edge of a network and provide elastic resources at the edge of Internet to enable many new applications and services. As an extension to cloud, fog computing inherits some similar security issues from cloud computing unavoidably, and additionally, it adds new complexity due to its distinct characteristics. As the fog computing is still in its infant stage, its security issues must be carefully taken care of before we can expect large adoptions from IT industrial.

11.1 Introduction

We are in the era of big data, where data sets are becoming intractable if using only traditional IT technologies due to the increasingly vast volume and complexity of data [1]. However, mining and analyzing those data are critical since the data can provide valuable insights and benefits for decision making in areas such as commercial business, IT industry biomedical research, governing and national security, and so on. Even though we understand the importance of handling big data, making it into practice is non-trivial. As a key enabler, cloud computing has been a revolutionary technology that consolidates resources (e.g., computation, memory storage, etc.) elastically to make organizations able to tackle big data problems in a "pay-as-you-go" fashion [2]. While cloud computing has been the main computing paradigm through the years, there are nontrivial challenges in the adoption of cloud computing such as unpredictable delay, lack of mobility support and location awareness, and so on. Therefore, fog computing [3] is proposed as a brand new solution to support the rapid development of the Internet of Things (IoT), cloud computing, and big data technologies. The basic idea of fog computing is to extend the cloud computing paradigm to the edge of the network, where a large scale of IoT devices facilitate the operation of compute, storage and networking services between end devices and cloud.

As an extension to cloud, fog computing unavoidably inherits some similar security issues as in cloud computing [4]. Additionally, fog computing is located at the edge of the Internet, with less protection compared to a remote cloud in data center infrastructures, which makes fog computing infrastructures and services more attractive targets. The distinct characteristics of fog computing will also add complexity to the security of fog computing. For example, the geographical distribution of fog nodes can make secure-related maintenance tasks significantly difficult and laborious. We may need better ways to track, predict, and patch security-faulty nodes. In the data domain, due to the massive scale of end devices, and the enormous volume of date generated, most data analytic tasks in fog computing are big data problems. Those tasks analyzing security-related data are of interest for enterprises and researchers to identify and defend against security threats and attacks. Instead of identifying various security threats and attacks case by case, data-driven techniques have opened a new way for security research: mining and understanding those data can improve the security of our systems. Currently, there are limited existing works [5–11] on the subject of data analytics platforms in fog computing. However, none of them are about big data analytics for fog computing security. As fog computing is still in its infant stage, the security issues must be carefully taken care of before we can expect large adoptions from the IT industry. We believe that big data analytics for fog computing security is of importance to investigate and can address the unique challenges of fog computing security.

In this chapter, we argue that big data analytics for security is a new direction to explore to enhance the security of fog computing. By surveying relevant papers, we try to understand how big data security techniques can go out of the cloud and into the fog, and answer questions like what are those big data security problems, what are the differences, and how do we solve those problems.

11.2 Background of Fog Computing

In this section, we will give a brief introduction to the definitions, features, architectures, existing implementations, and the state-of-the-art of big data analytics in fog computing.

11.2.1 Definitions

Currently, fog computing is still a buzzword, which has several definitions from various perspectives. We will discuss those definitions simply to give a comprehensive understanding on the concept of fog computing. Fog computing was introduced by Cisco with a position paper [3], which is defined as an extension of cloud computing at the edge of the Internet, to provide elastic resources to a large scale of IoT devices. Work [12] has given an integrative view of fog computing, comprehending the underlying technologies such as cloud, sensor network, peer-to-peer networks, network function virtualization (NFV), and so on. In our previous work [13], we provided a more general definition that can abstract similar concepts: "Fog computing is a geographically distributed computing architecture with a resource pool consisting of one or more ubiquitously connected heterogeneous devices (including edge devices) at the edge of the network and not exclusively seamlessly backed by cloud services, to collaboratively provide elastic computation, storage, and communication (and many other new services and tasks) in isolated environments to a large scale of clients in proximity."

11.2.2 Features

There are many features that make fog computing distinguishable from other computing paradigms such as cloud computing. Fog computing can support applications that require minimal delay such as gaming, augmented reality, and real-time video streaming processing. This is mainly because of the edge location of fog computing, which can provide rich information such as local network condition, local traffic statistics, and client-side information. Unlike the centralized cloud, fog computing is more geographically distributed in terms of resources and data. A computation node in fog computing, which provides elastic resources, is called fog node. There are a large number of heterogeneous nodes coming in different form factors, which is very different than cloud nodes. Also not like the cloud, there is a predominance of wireless access in a fog computing network. Finally, fog computing has better support for mobility because it needs to communicate directly with mobile devices.

11.2.3 Architectures and Existing Implementations

Fog computing usually has a three-layered architecture, consisting of end users, fog, and cloud, as shown in Figure 11.1 [14]. Work [13] has discussed the design goals and challenges of a standard fog computing platform. A proof-of-concept fog computing platform is built upon OpenStack. There are several existing implementations of fog computing platforms. Cloudlet [15] is a resource-rich fog node

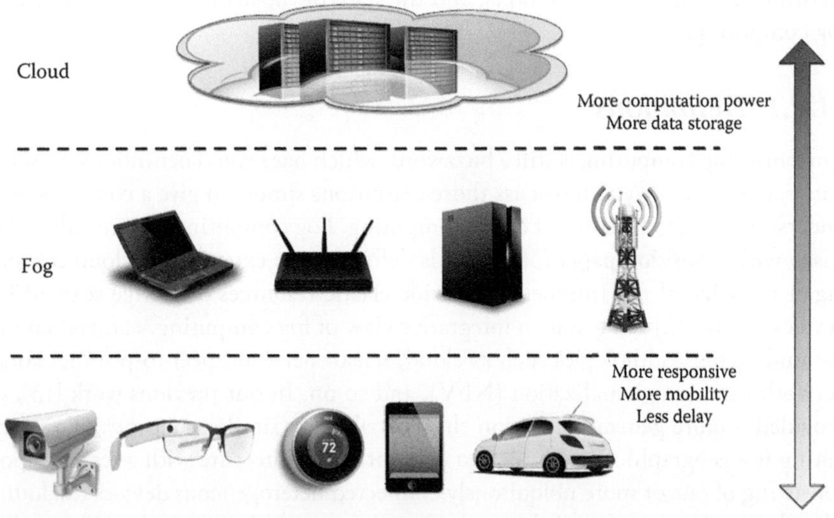

Figure 11.1 A typical conceptual architecture of user/fog/cloud. (From Yi, S., Qin, Z., Li, Q.: Security and privacy issues of fog computing: A survey. In: *Wireless Algorithms, Systems, and Applications*, pp. 685–695. Springer, 2015.)

implementation, i.e., a data center in a box, which follows the cloud computing paradigm in a more centralized manner and is built on high-volume servers. The IOx is a commercial platform, which supports developers to run scripts, compile code, and install their own operation systems [16]. Both of those two implementations use hypervisor virtualization to provide isolation. ParaDrop [17] is another fog node implementation built on wireless routers, which is suitable for lightweight tasks. Due to the limited resources on a wireless router, ParaDrop leverages containers to provide OS-level virtualization. The wireless router is an ideal fog node choice due to its ubiquity, full connectivity, and proximity to end users.

11.2.4 The State-of-the-Art of Data Analytics in Fog Computing

Since fog computing is still an emerging technique, there are limited existing works on data analytics in fog computing. Work [10] has designed a hierarchical distributed fog computing architecture for the integration of massive numbers of infrastructure components and services in the context of smart cities. GeeLytics [6] has provided a design of geo-distributed edge analytic platforms which aims at real-time stream processing both at the network edge and in the cloud. GeeLytics leverages the topology of running instances on cloud or edge to make optimized scheduling. Work [9] has proposed MigCEP to solve the operator placement and migration problem for complex event processing (CEP) in fog computing, where the mobility of users, latency, and bandwidth constraints are taken into consideration. Xu et al. [11] have implemented a message-based edge analytics platform using SDN-integrated switches as fog nodes. Yu et al. [5] have implemented FAST, a fog computing assisted distributed analytics system, with the purpose of detecting falling in real-time. CARDAP [8] is a context aware real-time data analytics platform for fog computing, which can deliver data efficiently considering the cost of energy, resources, and query processing. Other than the above data analytics platforms, a couple of fog-based applications have also been involved in multimedia data analytics including images and videos. Ha et al. [7] have designed a wearable cognitive assistant on Google Glass, which relies on Cloudlet for real-time image data processing and analytics. Zhang et al. [18] have built a wireless video surveillance system which relies on a fog server to provide real-time video analysis for tracking and surveillance in enterprise campuses, retail stores, and across smart cities. Therefore, we can easily find out that none of those existing works is about data analytics for security. Among all the existing efforts in data analytics in fog computing, none of them is related to security-related data.

11.3 When Big Data Meets Fog Computing

Big data analytics will be an indispensable component in fog computing. Interesting data analytics applications, including smart traffic light systems, smart city crowd prediction, and distributed object tracking, usually require real-time data processing and response. Fog computing as the frontier of computation can provide desirable resources to process the data, act as the controller for decision making, and upload preprocessed information for in-depth analysis to a remote cloud. To summarize the reasons why fog computing is a must for big data analytics:

- Fog computing can provide enough resources to make big data analytics possible at the edge of the network, without uploading massive amounts of data to the cloud.
- Fog computing can provide low latency responses for certain time-critical tasks. For example, it may be too late for the remote cloud to detect the malfunction of a critical machine in a certain region, which may have already brought significant economic loss to the enterprise.
- The interplay between fog and cloud can overcome several security issues in current big data analytics such as data integrity, data privacy, data provenance, and so on.
- Fog nodes can collect more information at a lower cost. The edge location enables fog nodes to collect more useful domain-specific or even more sensitive data. Processing of those data can provide insightful knowledge that can help in various decision making.

In this section, we will explain several advantages that fog computing can bring to big data handling. These benefits will fundamentally contribute to the big data analytics for security in fog computing.

Real-time big data analytics. Real-time data processing is one of the primary goals for many big data analytics applications. Phan et al. [19] have provided a case study on MapReduce job scheduling of data-intensive application in the cloud showing that handling jobs with deadlines needs improvement. As we know, big data analytics in the cloud usually cannot meet the real-time requirement due to the unpredictable delay. Unlike cloud computing, fog computing supports multi-level processing at the edge in which the event can be handled at different levels to meet various deadline requirements. The measurement in our preliminary study has shown that, compared to cloud, fog has clear advantages in delay and throughput [13].

Geo-distributed big data handling. The geo-distribution has been suggested as the fourth dimension of big data. By pushing resources to the edge, fog computing can handle a large scale of geographically distributed data. For example, many data processing tasks are essentially solving distributed optimization problems. Lubell-Doughtie et al. [20] have implemented a MapReduce-based alternating direction method of multipliers (ADMM) algorithm for distributed optimization. In those applications, fog computing can provide better services in terms of latency, cost, and scalability.

Client-side information. Fog computing can easily gather and utilize client-side information to better provide services to nearby clients. Traditional web technologies cannot adapt to user requests once the web is optimized at the server side. However, knowledge, such as local wireless network conditions or traffic statistics, can be collected at the client side or in the client's network. Work [21] has utilized an edge router as a fog node, which can easily make use of client side network conditions to optimize the web page loading dynamically. Similarly, client side detections, such as rogue AP [22], session hijacking, cross-site request forgery, and so on, can be easily integrated in fog computing to enhance security.

11.4 Big Data Analytics for Fog Computing Security

As fog computing infrastructures become critical in various applications such as Smart Home/City, e-Health, crowd sourcing, mobile applications, and so on, security-related challenges will be the main factors that impact the adoption choice of this new emerging technique. At the same time, it is not hard to infer that most security problems in the context of fog computing will have big data properties due to the massive scale of underlying IoT devices. In this section, we will mainly discuss some security issues that are significantly different with their counterparts in cloud computing and show how fog computing can leverage big data technologies to solve those security issues. We will also talk about the benefits or new opportunities that fog computing can bring to big data analytics for security.

11.4.1 Trust Management

The trust management in fog computing is very important since the service is offered to a massive scale of end devices by heterogeneous fog nodes that may belong to different organizations such as Internet service providers, cloud service providers, and even end users. This is different with cloud computing in which the service providers can be easily verified or audited by various authorities. As a potential solution for trust, a reputation-based trust model has been widely deployed in peer-to-peer [23], e-commerce [24], online social network [25], and crowd sourcing applications [26]. However, the mobility, large scale, and geo-distribution make it hard to narrow down the scope of this problem, which has to be addressed in a large scope with big data technologies. For example, a large repository of device identities, fingerprints, behavior profiles, configuration profiles, locations, and many other meta data can be constantly collected and updated, upon which the trust management can be built. Bao et al. [27] have proposed a trust management protocol that is an event-driven based occurrence of social events. However, their scheme will have scalability issues due to slow convergence in a fog deployment with a large number of devices. As the advantage of deep learning for effectively mining big data,

Zhou et al. [28] have demonstrated that a context-ware stereotypical deep learning method can achieve better robustness and an overall much higher accuracy for *a priori* trust inference.

11.4.2 Identity and Access Management

As the increasing demands of correctly resourced access in highly complex environments, identity and access management (IAM) is an important component in fog computing security for managing access control, authentication, single sign-on, digital identities, security tokens, and so on. IAM big data analytics can improve the fog computing security by finding anomalies in their IAM activities, automating access control policy generation, and so on.

Authentication. Authentication is an important security issue for fog computing since its services are provided to a massive number of end users. The authentication of a fog node is mandatory before offloading any tasks from the end device to any fog node. Stojmenovic et al. [29] have discussed the authentication and authorization techniques that can be used in fog computing. Bouzefrane et al. [30] have proposed an NFC-based authentication scheme for cloudlet. The advances in smart devices have opened new opportunities in multi-factor authentication, using various biometrics, hardware/software tokens, and so on. At the same time, big data analytics based authentication can make those procedures less abrupt and more secure. Kent et al. [31] have proposed an authentication graph to analyze the network authentication activities within an enterprise network. The authentication graph model can be easily extended to a common fog computing scenario. Freeman et al. [32] have evaluated an enterprise large-scale statistical framework that can detect suspicious login attempts. The basic idea is to classify login attempts into normal and suspicious activity based on features such as source IP, geo-location, browser configuration, and time of day.

Access control. Similar to mobile client platforms, fog nodes are designed to run applications in an isolated environment with limited privileges. How to grant access permissions becomes important in such a situation, where it should be non-disruptive, automatic, and adaptive. Also, access control is one of the important methods for many security enhancements. However, manually access control policy generation in a fog node will not be practical in the sense that a single fog node may provide services to a massive number of end devices. Policy enforcement will also be a big burden to system administrators if these tasks are not handled intelligently.

Work [33] has proposed a secure provenance-based access control in the context of cloud, which can be easily adopted in fog computing environments. Provenance is a meta data, detailing the history of the data including the source, the processing history, and so on, which can be used as the basis for attribute-based access control systems. Dsouza et al [34] have proposed a policy-based resources access management in fog computing, in which a policy-driven security management framework is designed to support collaboration and interoperability between various resources in fog computing.

11.4.3 Availability Management

As one of the triad of information security, there are plenty of security issues in fog computing availability management, such as denial-of-service (DoS) attacks, security control of APIs, and secure system upgrades.

DoS attack detection. Network flow analysis has been the primary interest of DoS attack detection [35]. Lee et al. [36] have implemented an Internet flow analysis method based on MapReduce and can improve the flow statistics computation time by 72%. One example of DoS detection using MapReduce is presented in [37]. Due to the number of connected devices in fog computing, DoS attacks are much easier to generate in such an environment and all come in very large scales. Recent advances in anomaly detection in big data environments may shed some light on DoS attack detection in IoT and fog computing. Work [38] has built on Kafka queue and Spark Streaming with two metrics, relative entropy and Pearson correlation, to dynamically detect anomalies in big data scenarios. Eagle [39] has proposed a user profile-based anomaly detection by collecting audit logs, analyzing user behavior, and predicting anomalous activities based on prior profiles. However, there are some other challenges that should be addressed in DoS attack detection in fog computing, such as predominate wireless infrastructure, massive mobility, node heterogeneity, and so on. The fog computing will also play an important role in attack mitigating and defending [40].

Secure interfaces or APIs. The availability of interfaces or APIs is key to the reliability and robustness of fog computing applications or services. Also, a unified interfacing and programming model for fog computing will ease the burden on developers to port applications to the fog computing platforms. Hong et al. [41] have proposed a high-level programming model of mobile fog for IoTs, which are large scale, geo-distributed, and latency sensitive. However, there is no discussion on security issues of those interfaces, which we believe can be strengthened by big data analytics. The abuse of insecure APIs may pose a major risk to users by allowing hackers to extract sensitive user information on a massive scale. Works [42,43] have shown how unprotected and undocumented APIs can be leveraged to support malicious attacks in mobile operating systems. Big data analytics can be used to monitor and track the usage of APIs to find abnormal usage patterns, to predict and prevent the large-scale attacks that have exploited those insecure APIs.

11.4.4 Security Information and Event Management

Security information and event management (SIEM) is a necessary IT security service in fog computing since SIEM is in charge of real-time analysis of security-related information and events, which will benefit from big data analytics in tasks such as intrusion detection, botnet detection, advanced persistent detection, and so on.

Intrusion detection. As the close distance to end users and rich resources for follow-up attacks, fog nodes will be among those preferable targets for intrusion attack. To fight against system invaders, the intrusion detection has to face the big data challenge as it is usually done by analyzing a large number of system logs or network traffic. Therefore, investigating big data techniques for intrusion detections has drawn a lot of attention from both industry and academia [44].

In the early stage, Ryan et al. [45] have shown learning user profiles could be an effective way for detecting intrusion. Lee et al. [46] have investigated a real time intrusion detection system based on data mining. In order to achieve real time performance, the computational costs of feature extraction and modeling are used in a multiple model based approach for minimal computation cost with adequate accuracy. From a more practical perspective, Sommer and Paxson [47] have indicated the difficulties of applying machine learning to intrusion detection in the "real world," large-scale, operational environments. The big data properties will make the intrusion detection system even more challenging [48]. More effort has been put into how to improve the performance of intrusion detection with big data input. Guilbault and Guha [49] have designed an experiment of an intrusion detection system using Amazon's elastic compute cloud. MIDeA [50] is a multi-parallel intrusion detection architecture tailed for high-speed networks, which combines the computation power of multiple CPUs and GPUs. Beehive [51] has proposed a scheme that can automatically extract features from dirty log data produced by all kinds of security products in a large enterprise to detect suspicious activities. By applying MapReduce, Aljarah et al. [52] have shown that the proposed intrusion detection system scales well with the sizes of data sets. Marchal et al. [53] have introduced an intrusion detection architecture which exploits scalable distributed data storage and management and is evaluated against state-of-the-art big data analysis tools such as Hadoop, Spark, Storm, and so on. Cuzzocrea et al. [54] have implemented an adaptive ensemble-based intrusion detection system to meet the requirements of distributed, cooperativeness, scalability, multi-scale network traffic analysis.

In the context of fog computing, it provides us new opportunities that fog as a shield layer can perform intrusion detection not only for the client but also for the centralized cloud. Shi et al. [55] have designed a cloudlet mesh based intrusion detection system that can identify intrusion to the remote cloud, and secure the communication channels among end devices, cloudlet, and the cloud. The distributed IDS on the cloudlet mesh can improve the detection rate since multiple IDS can collaborate in the detection. A spamming detection application on mobile social network is used as an example, in which the cloudlet mesh will try to identify the spam and only offload large sized files to the remote cloud using MapReduce filtering if the cloud mesh cannot identity whether it is spam.

Botnet detection. IoT Botnet or ThingBot is a concrete threat to current IoT and to fog computing as well in a natural course. As the fog nodes are widely deployed among switches/routers, set-top boxes, industrial controllers, embedded servers, and web cameras, it is also possible that those fog nodes are infected and become zombie nodes of the botnet. A study of Proofpoint has shown that a smart refrigerator or smart TV can be exploited to launch a spamming attack [56]. Fog nodes are of higher interest to attackers compared to IoT in terms of botnet, since they usually have rich resources, full connectivity, and a virtualization environment. Once a botnet is formed, it can be a powerful tool of attackers' own interest for network scanning, password cracking, DoS attack, spamming, click-fraud, crypt-currency mining, and so on.

While many of those detection methods are built on analyzing network traffic, they usually face the challenge of processing large amounts of traffic data. BotMiner [57] has proposed a detection framework that can identify malicious clusters after clustering on communication traffic. In order to reduce the traffic workload, flow aggregation is used to make the problem scalable. Also for computation complexity of clustering, a dimension reduction technique is employed in a two-step clustering method. BotGrep [58] has focused on detection of peer-to-peer botnets by the relative mixing rates of random walks on subgraphs, which consist of candidate P2P nodes obtained by an efficient pre-filter on a large graph. Complementary to those data reduction techniques, massive parallel processing techniques are usually used. BotGraph [59] has leveraged MapReduce framework to detect spamming bots by efficiently computing on a large user-user graph. BotCloud [60] has utilized a host dependency graph model and an adapted PageRank algorithm in a Hadoop cluster, which brings performance benefits in the average execution time for PageRank iterations. BotFinder [61] can find bots by machine learning on key features of the communication of the command-and-control (C&C). Due to the independence of features, the extraction processes can speed up with a multiprocessing library. Singh et al. [62] have built a learning-based intrusion detection system for peer-to-peer botnet attacks using Hadoop, Hive, and Mahout. As fog computing also relies on virtualization, the botnet detection should be fulfilled in virtualized environments. Hsiao et al. [63] have proposed a detection scheme that monitors guest OS and uses a learning-based method to generate guest OS behavior profiles for detection of botnet.

Advanced persistent threat. Big data analytics for security have set a new direction for advanced persistent threat (APT) attack detection. APT attacks are attacks carried out by sophisticated attackers that target specific information in high-profile companies and governments [64]. The penetration is persistent, usually over a long term and the attack methods involve different steps and different techniques. Even though there is no current evidence of its existence in fog computing, APT attacks have been found in many relevant fields of fog computing such as wireless infrastructure, hypervisor, and IoT. The advantages of utilizing big data analytics for APT detections in fog computing would rely on (1) collecting more information in a low cost due to the closer distance to users; (2) making the early stage detection much earlier by conducting detection at the edge; and (3) collaborating with the centralized cloud can create opportunities in improving the detection accuracy and reducing false positives. Existing MapReduce-based APT detection can be easily integrated into a distributed fog computing platform. Giura et al. [65]

have proposed and implemented a model for APT detection by logging all system events and computing on them using a large-scale distributed computing framework with MapReduce, which can provide near-real time detection. Kim et al. [66] have presented a secure event aggregation system over MapReduce for scalable situation analysis for APTs, which provides periodic and ad-hoc aggregation of security events and supports analytical queries.

11.4.5 Data Protection

The protection of data in fog computing has faced severe challenges in which some of them are inherited from cloud computing and some are unique in fog computing. We will briefly discuss how big data analytic techniques can improve the data protection in fog computing in terms of data audit and data leakage detection.

Data audit. Similar to cloud, a user needs to hand over control of data to the fog in order to use its services. This outsourced computation model will call for the need of data auditing in fog computing. However, in fog computing, we have to address a unique challenge of data audit, which is the geo-distribution. The geo-distribution doesn't only mean the geo-distributed resources but also the geo-distributed data due to the mobility of end users. Therefore, the provable data possession has to be deployed in a distributed manner to maximize a certain goal (e.g., minimal delay) in constraints of resources and data distribution. Zhang et al. [67] have leveraged the special features for MapReduce to automatically partition a computing job according to the security level of the data and arrange the computation across a hybrid cloud. The job can be an audit task and the arrangement of computation among fog computing can be adjusted to the available resources and data on individual fog nodes. Beside this, one important requirement for data audit is preserving data privacy; otherwise, a malicious auditee can easily forge desirable results. Zhang et al. [68] have proposed a MapReduce-based data anonymization method for the cloud platform, which can be ported to fog computing and benefit the data audit due to its MapReduce framework and privacy-preserving anonymization.

Data leakage detection. One of the potential security enhancement applications for fog computing in preserving user data privacy is to keep sensitive data on a local fog node and process them locally without uploading to any remote cloud. However, a client needs to make sure no sensitive data leakage occurs during this process while the data control is handed over to the fog. Data leakage detection (DLD) is crucial in complex systems as many computations on data are done in an outsourced manner. The user (distributor) has to supposedly trust the agents, e.g., cloud or fog computing service provider, in order to use the provided services or resources to process the data. Borders et al. [69] have proposed a scheme for quantifying information leak capacity in the outbound network traffic. Work [70] has utilized a guilt agent model to characterize the data leakage detection problem and investigated data allocation strategies and fake data injection on identifying guilty agents. Shu et al. [71] have proposed a network-based DLD detection based on a small amount of specialized digests without revealing the sensitive data. As the data volume becomes larger and larger, big data analytics are applied in DLD. Liu et al. [72] have leveraged the MapReduce framework to compute collection intersection for data leak detection. The paradigm of fog computing can be well utilized to identify and prevent the data leakage. Davies et al. [73] have designed a privacy mediator on a cloudlet-like architecture of data owner which can perform privacy data obfuscation, privacy policy enforcement, and many other privacy preserving techniques to avoid the potential leakage.

11.5 Conclusion

We have briefly introduced fog computing and its state-of-the-art in big data analytics. We envision that the big data analytics for security will be a promising technique to solve many security issues in fog computing. We have identified security issues in trust management, identity and access management, availability management, security information, and event management of fog computing. And we have surveyed existing work utilizing big data analytics for those security issues in the domain of fog computing or in relevant underlying domains.

References

1. Chen, M., Mao, S., Liu, Y.: Big data: A survey. *Mobile Networks and Applications* 19(2), 171–209 (2014).
2. Assunção, M.D., Calheiros, R.N., Bianchi, S., Netto, M.A., Buyya, R.: Big data computing and clouds: Trends and future directions. *Journal of Parallel and Distributed Computing* 79, 3–15 (2015).
3. Bonomi, F., Milito, R., Zhu, J., Addepalli, S.: Fog computing and its role in the internet of things. In: *Proceedings of the First Edition of the MCC Workshop on Mobile Cloud Computing*. pp. 13–16. ACM (2012).
4. Takabi, H., Joshi, J.B., Ahn, G.J.: Security and privacy challenges in cloud computing environments. *IEEE Security & Privacy* (6), 24–31 (2010).
5. Cao, Y., Chen, S., Hou, P., Brown, D.: Fast: A fog computing assisted distributed analytics system to monitor fall for stroke mitigation. In: *2015 IEEE International Conference on Networking, Architecture and Storage (NAS)*, pp. 2–11. IEEE (2015).
6. Cheng, B., Papageorgiou, A., Cirillo, F., Kovacs, E.: Geelytics: Geo-distributed edge analytics for large scale iot systems based on dynamic topology. In: *2015 IEEE 2nd World Forum on Internet of Things (WF-IoT)*, pp. 565–570. IEEE (2015).
7. Ha, K., Chen, Z., Hu, W., Richter, W., Pillai, P., Satyanarayanan, M.: Towards wearable cognitive assistance. In: *Proceedings of the 12th Annual International Conference on Mobile Systems, Applications, and Services*. pp. 68–81. ACM (2014).
8. Jayaraman, P.P., Gomes, J.B., Nguyen, H.L., Abdallah, Z.S., Krishnaswamy, S., Zaslavsky, A.: Scalable energy-efficient distributed data analytics for crowdsensing applications in mobile environments. *IEEE Transactions on Computational Social Systems* 2(3), 109–123 (2015).

9. Ottenwälder, B., Koldehofe, B., Rothermel, K., Ramachandran, U.: Migcep: Operator migration for mobility driven distributed complex event processing. In: *Proceedings of the 7th ACM International Conference on Distributed Event-Based Systems*. pp. 183–194. ACM (2013).
10. Tang, B., Chen, Z., Hefferman, G., Wei, T., He, H., Yang, Q.: A hierarchical distributed fog computing architecture for big data analysis in smart cities. In: *Proceedings of the ASE Big Data & Social Informatics 2015*. p. 28. ACM (2015).
11. Xu, Y., Mahendran, V., Radhakrishnan, S.: Towards sdn-based fog computing: Mqtt broker virtualization for effective and reliable delivery. In: *2016 8th International Conference on Communication Systems and Networks (COMSNETS)*. pp. 1–6. IEEE (2016).
12. Vaquero, L.M., Rodero-Merino, L.: Finding your way in the fog: Towards a comprehensive definition of fog computing. *ACM SIGCOMM Computer Communication Review* 44(5), 27–32 (2014).
13. Yi, S., Hao, Z., Qin, Z., Li, Q.: Fog computing: Platform and applications. In: *2015 Third IEEE Workshop on Hot Topics in Web Systems and Technologies (HotWeb)*, pp. 73–78. IEEE (2015).
14. Yi, S., Qin, Z., Li, Q.: Security and privacy issues of fog computing: A survey. In: *Wireless Algorithms, Systems, and Applications*, pp. 685–695. Springer (2015).
15. Satyanarayanan, M., Schuster, R., Ebling, M., Fettweis, G., Flinck, H., Joshi, K., Sabnani, K.: An open ecosystem for mobile-cloud convergence. *Communications Magazine*, IEEE 53(3), 63–70 (2015).
16. Cisco: Iox overview. https://developer.cisco.com/site/iox/ technical-overview/ (2014).
17. Willis, D.F., Dasgupta, A., Banerjee, S.: Paradrop: A multi-tenant platform for dynamically installed third party services on home gateways. In: *ACM SIGCOMM Workshop on Distributed Cloud Computing* (2014).
18. Zhang, T., Chowdhery, A., Bahl, P.V., Jamieson, K., Banerjee, S.: The design and implementation of a wireless video surveillance system. In: *Proceedings of the 21st Annual International Conference on Mobile Computing and Networking*. pp. 426–438. ACM (2015).
19. Phan, L.T., Zhang, Z., Zheng, Q., Loo, B.T., Lee, I.: An empirical analysis of scheduling techniques for real-time cloud-based data processing. In: *2011 IEEE International Conference on Service-Oriented Computing and Applications (SOCA)*, pp. 1–8. IEEE (2011).
20. Lubell-Doughtie, P., Sondag, J.: Practical distributed classification using the alternating direction method of multipliers algorithm. In: *BigData Conference*. pp. 773–776 (2013).
21. Zhu, J., Chan, D.S., Prabhu, M.S., Natarajan, P., Hu, H., Bonomi, F.: Improving web sites performance using edge servers in fog computing architecture. In: *2013 IEEE 7th International Symposium on Service Oriented System Engineering (SOSE)*, pp. 320–323. IEEE (2013).
22. Han, H., Sheng, B., Tan, C.C., Li, Q., Lu, S.: A timing-based scheme for rogue ap detection. *IEEE Transactions on Parallel and Distributed Systems*, 22(11), 1912–1925 (2011).
23. Damiani, E., di Vimercati, D.C., Paraboschi, S., Samarati, P., Violante, F.: A reputation-based approach for choosing reliable resources in peer-to-peer networks. In: *2015 IEEE International Conference on Big Data (Big Data)*, pp. 1910–1916. IEEE (2015).

24. Standifird, S.S.: Reputation and e-commerce: Ebay auctions and the asymmetrical impact of positive and negative ratings. *Journal of Management* 27(3), 279–295 (2001).
25. Hogg, T., Adamic, L.: Enhancing reputation mechanisms via online social networks. In: *Proceedings of the 5th ACM Conference on Electronic Commerce*. pp. 236–237. ACM (2004).
26. Zhang, Y., Van der Schaar, M.: Reputation-based incentive protocols in crowdsourcing applications. In: *INFOCOM, 2012 Proceedings IEEE*. pp. 2140–2148. IEEE (2012).
27. Bao, F., Chen, I.R.: Dynamic trust management for internet of things applications. In: *Proceedings of the 2012 International Workshop on Self-Aware Internet of Things*. pp. 1–6. ACM (2012).
28. Zhou, P., Gu, X., Zhang, J., Fei, M.: A priori trust inference with context-aware stereotypical deep learning. *Knowledge-Based Systems* 88, 97–106 (2015).
29. Stojmenovic, I., Wen, S., Huang, X., Luan, H.: An overview of fog computing and its security issues. *Concurrency and Computation: Practice and Experience* (2015).
30. Bouzefrane, S., Mostefa, B., Amira, F., Houacine, F., Cagnon, H.: Cloudlets authentication in nfc-based mobile computing. In: *2014 2nd IEEE International Conference on Mobile Cloud Computing, Services, and Engineering (MobileCloud)*, pp. 267–272. IEEE (2014).
31. Kent, A.D., Liebrock, L.M., Neil, J.C.: Authentication graphs: Analyzing user behavior within an enterprise network. *Computers & Security* 48, 150–166 (2015).
32. Freeman, D.M., Jain, S., Dürmuth, M., Biggio, B., Giacinto, G.: Who are you? A statistical approach to measuring user authenticity. *NDSS* (2016).
33. Bates, A., Mood, B., Valafar, M., Butler, K.: Towards secure provenance-based access control in cloud environments. In: *Proceedings of the Third ACM Conference on Data and Application Security and Privacy*. pp. 277–284. ACM (2013).
34. Dsouza, C., Ahn, G.J., Taguinod, M.: Policy-driven security management for fog computing: Preliminary framework and a case study. In: *2014 IEEE 15th International Conference on Information Reuse and Integration (IRI)*, pp. 16–23. IEEE (2014).
35. Yu, S., Zhou, W., Jia, W., Guo, S., Xiang, Y., Tang, F.: Discriminating ddos attacks from flash crowds using flow correlation coefficient. *IEEE Transactions on Parallel and Distributed Systems*, 23(6), 1073–1080 (2012).
36. Lee, Y., Kang, W., Son, H.: An internet traffic analysis method with mapreduce. In: *Network Operations and Management Symposium Workshops (NOMS Wksps), 2010 IEEE/IFIP*. pp. 357–361. IEEE (2010).
37. Lee, Y., Lee, Y.: Detecting ddos attacks with hadoop. In: *Proceedings of the ACM CoNEXT Student Workshop*. p. 7. ACM (2011).
38. Rettig, L., Khayati, M., Cudre-Mauroux, P., Piorkowski, M.: Online anomaly detection over big data streams. In: *2015 IEEE International Conference on Big Data (Big Data)*, pp. 1113–1122. IEEE (2015).
39. Gupta, C., Sinha, R., Zhang, Y.: Eagle: User profile-based anomaly detection for securing hadoop clusters. In: *2015 IEEE International Conference on Big Data (Big Data)*, pp. 1336–1343. IEEE (2015).
40. Zargar, S.T., Joshi, J., Tipper, D.: A survey of defense mechanisms against distributed denial of service (ddos) flooding attacks. *Communications Surveys & Tutorials*, IEEE 15(4), 2046–2069 (2013).

41. Hong, K., Lillethun, D., Ramachandran, U., OttenwŠlder, B., Koldehofe, B.: Mobile fog: A programming model for large-scale applications on the internet of things. In: *Proceedings of the second ACM SIGCOMM Workshop on Mobile Cloud Computing.* pp. 15–20. ACM (2013).
42. Zheng, M., Xue, H., Zhang, Y., Wei, T., Lui, J.: Enpublic apps: Security threats using ios enterprise and developer certificates. In: *Proceedings of the 10th ACM Symposium on Information, Computer and Communications Security.* pp. 463–474. ACM (2015).
43. Wang, T., Lu, K., Lu, L., Chung, S.P., Lee, W.: Jekyll on ios: When benign apps become evil. In: *Usenix Security.* 13 (2013).
44. Zuech, R., Khoshgoftaar, T.M., Wald, R.: Intrusion detection and big heterogeneous data: A survey. *Journal of Big Data* 2(1), 1–41 (2015).
45. Ryan, J., Lin, M.J., Miikkulainen, R.: Intrusion detection with neural networks. *Advances in Neural Information Processing Systems,* pp. 943–949 (1998).
46. Lee, W., Stolfo, S.J., Chan, P.K., Eskin, E., Fan, W., Miller, M., Hershkop, S., Zhang, J.: Real time data mining-based intrusion detection. In: *DARPA Information Survivability Conference & Exposition II, 2001. DISCEX'01. Proceedings.* 1, 89–100. IEEE (2001).
47. Sommer, R., Paxson, V.: Outside the closed world: On using machine learning for network intrusion detection. In: *2010 IEEE Symposium on Security and Privacy (SP),* pp. 305–316. IEEE (2010).
48. Suthaharan, S.: Big data classification: Problems and challenges in network intrusion prediction with machine learning. *ACM SIGMETRICS Performance Evaluation Review* 41(4), 70–73 (2014).
49. Guilbault, N., Guha, R.: Experiment setup for temporal distributed intrusion detection system on amazon's elastic compute cloud. In: *2009 IEEE International Conference on Intelligence and Security Informatics (ISI'09),* pp. 300–302. IEEE (2009).
50. Vasiliadis, G., Polychronakis, M., Ioannidis, S.: Midea: A multi-parallel intrusion detection architecture. In: *Proceedings of the 18th ACM Conference on Computer and Communications Security.* pp. 297–308. ACM (2011).
51. Yen, T.F., Oprea, A., Onarlioglu, K., Leetham, T., Robertson, W., Juels, A., Kirda, E.: Beehive: Large-scale log analysis for detecting suspicious activity in enterprise networks. In: *Proceedings of the 29th Annual Computer Security Applications Conference.* pp. 199–208. ACM (2013).
52. Aljarah, I., Ludwig, S.: MapReduce intrusion detection system based on a particle swarm optimization clustering algorithm. In *2013 IEEE Congress on Evolutionary Computation (CEC),* pp. 955–962. IEEE (2013).
53. Marchal, S., Jiang, X., State, R., Engel, T.: A big data architecture for large scale security monitoring. In: *2014 IEEE International Congress on Big Data (BigData Congress),* pp. 56–63. IEEE (2014).
54. Cuzzocrea, A., Folino, G., Sabatino, P.: A distributed framework for supporting adaptive ensemble-based intrusion detection. In: *2015 IEEE International Conference on Big Data (Big Data),.* pp. 1910–1916. IEEE (2015).
55. Shi, Y., Abhilash, S., Hwang, K.: Cloudlet mesh for securing mobile clouds from intrusions and network attacks. In: *2015 3rd IEEE International Conference on Mobile Cloud Computing, Services, and Engineering (MobileCloud),* pp. 109–118. IEEE (2015).
56. Proofpoint: Proofpoint uncovers internet of things (iot) cyberattack. http:// investors .proofpoint.com/releasedetail.cfm?releaseid=819799 (2014).

57. Gu, G., Perdisci, R., Zhang, J., Lee, W. et al.: Botminer: Clustering analysis of network traffic for protocol-and structure-independent botnet detection. In: *USENIX Security Symposium*. 5, 139–154 (2008).
58. Nagaraja, S., Mittal, P., Hong, C.Y., Caesar, M., Borisov, N.: Botgrep: Finding p2p bots with structured graph analysis. In: *USENIX Security Symposium*. pp. 95–110 (2010).
59. Zhao, Y., Xie, Y., Yu, F., Ke, Q., Yu, Y., Chen, Y., Gillum, E.: Botgraph: Large scale spamming botnet detection. In: *NSDI*. 9, 321–334 (2009).
60. Francois, J., Wang, S., Bronzi, W., State, R., Engel, T.: Botcloud: Detecting bot-nets using mapreduce. In: *2011 IEEE International Workshop on Information Forensics and Security (WIFS)*. pp. 1–6. IEEE (2011).
61. Tegeler, F., Fu, X., Vigna, G., Kruegel, C: Botfinder: Finding bots in network traffic without deep packet inspection. In: *Proceedings of the 8th International Conference on Emerging Networking Experiments and Technologies*. pp. 349–360. ACM (2012).
62. Singh, K., Guntuku, S.C., Thakur, A., Hota, C: Big data analytics framework for peer-to-peer botnet detection using random forests. *Information Sciences* 278, 488–497 (2014).
63. Hsiao, S.W., Chen, Y.N., Sun, Y.S., Chen, M.C.: A cooperative botnet profiling and detection in virtualized environment. In: *2013 IEEE Conference on Communications and Network Security (CNS)*, pp. 154–162. IEEE (2013).
64. Chen, P., Desmet, L., Huygens, C.: A study on advanced persistent threats. In: *Communications and Multimedia Security*. pp. 63–72. Springer (2014).
65. Giura, P., Wang, W.: Using large scale distributed computing to unveil advanced persistent threats. *Science J* 1(3), 93–105 (2012).
66. Kim, J., Moon, I., Lee, K., Suh, S.C., Kim, I.: Scalable security event aggregation for situation analysis. In: *2015 IEEE First International Conference on Big Data Computing Service and Applications (BigDataService)*, pp. 14–23. IEEE (2015).
67. Zhang, K., Zhou, X., Chen, Y., Wang, X., Ruan, Y.: Sedic: Privacy-aware data intensive computing on hybrid clouds. In: *Proceedings of the 18th ACM Conference on Computer and Communications Security*. pp. 515–526. ACM (2011).
68. Zhang, X., Yang, C, Nepal, S., Liu, C, Dou, W., Chen, J.: A mapreduce based approach of scalable multidimensional anonymization for big data privacy preservation on cloud. In: *2013 Third International Conference on Cloud and Green Computing (CGC)*, pp. 105–112. IEEE (2013).
69. Borders, K., Prakash, A.: Quantifying information leaks in outbound web traffic. In *2009 30th IEEE Symposium on Security and Privacy*, pp. 129–140. IEEE (2009).
70. Papadimitriou, P., Garcia-Molina, H.: Data leakage detection. *Knowledge and Data Engineering, IEEE Transactions on* 23(1), 51–63 (2011).
71. Shu, X., Yao, D.D.: Data leak detection as a service. In: *Security and Privacy in Communication Networks*, pp. 222–240. Springer (2012).
72. Liu, F., Shu, X., Yao, D., Butt, A.R.: Privacy-preserving scanning of big content for sensitive data exposure with mapreduce. In: *Proceedings of the 5th ACM Conference on Data and Application Security and Privacy*. pp. 195–206. ACM (2015).
73. Davies, N., Taft, N., Satyanarayanan, M., Clinch, S., Amos, B.: Privacy mediators: Helping IoT cross the chasm. In: *Proceedings of the 17th International Workshop on Mobile Computing Systems and Applications*. pp. 39–44. ACM (2016).

Chapter 12

Analyzing Deviant Socio-Technical Behaviors Using Social Network Analysis and Cyber Forensics-Based Methodologies

Samer Al-khateeb, Muhammad Hussain, and Nitin Agarwal

Contents

Online social networks (OSNs) have grown exponentially in a short period of time, and this growth has revolutionized how societies interact with each other. Many people around the world use social media on a daily basis; for example, there are about 1.3 billion registered Twitter users, with an average of 100 million daily active users, and 65 million users just in the United States [1]. In addition to Twitter, Facebook is the largest social network in the world. The social networking site comprises approximately 1.65 billion monthly active users with about 167 million daily active users in the United States and Canada who spend an average of 20 minutes of their day on Facebook [2].

12.1 Introduction

The use of social media, specifically, went from being a source of entertainment or a way to find and connect with friends or family members, no matter where they are globally, to more of a deviant usage/purpose, e.g., to conduct cybercrime, hacking, cyber terrorism, spread propaganda or misinformation, conduct cyber warfare tactics, or other similar deviant acts. For example, the Russians are spending millions of dollars to finance the Kremlin's Troll Army (legions of pro-Russia, English-speaking, Internet commenters) to promote President Vladimir Putin and his policies, and to spread disinformation about some events or disseminate a propaganda war on the Ukraine [3]. Often these acts exhibit a flash mob style behavior, i.e., a process where a group of individuals get together in cyberspace, conduct a deviant behavior, and then disappear into the anonymity of the Internet. We call such behavior deviant cyber flash mobs (DCFM) [4].

These nefarious uses of social media pose a significant threat to society, and thus require special research attention. It would be of benefit to the information assurance domain, and its respective subdomains, to conduct new research initiatives into the phenomenon of deviant behavior in OSNs especially with the vast amounts of evidentiary information that is continuously generated on different social media outlets. In this chapter, we study the following research questions:

- What strategies and tools do deviant groups, e.g., transnational crime organizations or terrorist groups, use to disseminate their propaganda? And who is responsible for disseminating it (e.g., powerful actors)?
- Can we measure an individual's interest, control, and power in the dissemination process using the theoretical constructs of collective action, thereby modeling individual motivations to participate in propaganda dissemination?
- Are botnets involved in the dissemination process and how sophisticated are these bot networks? What role do these bots play in such information maneuvers? Are there structural pattern(s) among bot networks? How can we detect them?

Seeking answers to the aforementioned research questions, we make the following contributions in this chapter:

- We develop a systematic methodology that can be followed to analyze propaganda dissemination. This methodology was obtained from several experiments we conducted on the dataset we collected for different events mentioned above.
- We identified the strategies and tools that are used by deviant groups to conduct such a deviant act, e.g., propaganda dissemination.
- We show how cyber forensics can be used to discover hidden connections between information actors and can be used to study the cross media affiliations.

The rest of the chapter is organized as follows. We provide a brief literature review in Section 12.2. Section 12.3 discusses our methodology. We discuss the two cases we have investigated (namely, Daesh or ISIS/ISIL and Novorossiya) along with the results and analysis we obtained in each case in Section 12.4. Finally, Section 12.5 summarizes the study with possible future research directions.

12.2 Literature Review

In our methodology we applied an algorithm called focal structure (FSA) which is an algorithm that was developed by Sen et al. [5] to discover a set of influential nodes in a large network. This set of nodes does not have to be strongly connected and may not be the most influential on its own but by acting together it forms a compelling power. This algorithm was tested on many real world information campaigns such as the Saudi Arabian women's *Oct26Driving* campaign on Twitter* and during the 2014 Ukraine Crisis† when President Viktor Yanukovych refused to sign a European association agreement.

Botnets/bots/or automated social actors/agents (ASAs) are not a new invention. They have been used since 1993 in the Internet relay chat (IRC), and known as Eggdrop. They used to do very simple tasks such as greeting new participants and warning them about the other users' actions [6]. Then the usage of botnets evolved over time due to their multi-functionality that can be performed and their easiness to implement. In our work we were able to identify and study the network structure (the way the network looks) of botnets in all of the aforementioned events. A similar study was conducted on the Syrian Social Bot (SSB) that was used to disseminate propaganda during the Syrian civil war in 2012 [7]. Abokhodair et al. have categorized the bots by their activity type into four categories, namely: Core

* The right to drive campaign #oct26driving (available at: http://bit.ly/1OmyCIO).

† Ukraine protests after Yanukovych EU deal rejection (available at: http://bbc.in/1qhcy6V).

bots—Generators (tweet a lot), Core bots—Short Lived (retweet a lot and were active for less than six weeks), Core bots—Long Lived (retweet a lot and were active for more than 25 weeks), and Peripheral Bots (retweeting one or more tweets generated by the core bots and the account names look like a legitimate user account name).

We have also used some cyber forensics tools and techniques to discover the hidden relationships between different blog sites. We used Maltego tool, which is an open source intelligence and forensics application. It saves a lot of time in mining and gathering of information as well as the representation of this information in an easy to understand format. In addition to that we used some cyber forensics techniques such as Google Analytics ID, which is an online analytics tool that allows a website owner to gather some statistics about their website visitors such as their browser, operating system, and country. Multiple sites can be managed under a single Google analytics account. The account has a unique identifying "UA" number, which is usually embedded in the website's code [8]. Using this code other blog sites that are managed under the same UA number can be identified. This method was reported in 2011 by *Wired*, and also was cited in the book *Open Source Intelligence Techniques* by Michael Bazzell, an FBI cyber crime expert [8,9].

12.3 Methodology

In this section, we present our methodology that we followed to obtain the results and findings mentioned in Sections 12.4.1 and 12.4.2. Figure 12.1 shows our methodology as a flowchart of operations we used in combination with the software. This is followed by a stepwise explanation of each step/component in the diagram. We used the following software in our methodology:

- **Maltego:** a cyber forensics tool that helps uncover the hidden connection between different blogs sites, available at: http://bit.ly/1OoxDCD.
- **GoogleTAGs:** for collecting data in a continuous manner, available at: http://bit.ly/1KPrRH2.
- **TAGSExplorer:** to have a live visualization of the data collected with GoogleTAGs, available at: http://bit.ly/24NmFjy.
- **Blogtrackers:** to analyze the blogs whose data we collected. The tool can be accessed via the following URL: blogtrackers.host.ualr.edu.
- **CytoScape:** an open source software platform for data visualization, available at: http://bit.ly/1VTWOow.
- **NodeXl:** to collect and analyze the data, available at: http://bit.ly/1WKA5u9.
- **Linguistic Inquiry and Word Count (LIWC):** to calculate the sentiments scores, available at: http://bit.ly/1WKAyN3.
- **IBM Watson Analytics:** to explore the dataset and get further insights, such as the nature and type of conversations, available at: http://ibm.co/214CjoD.

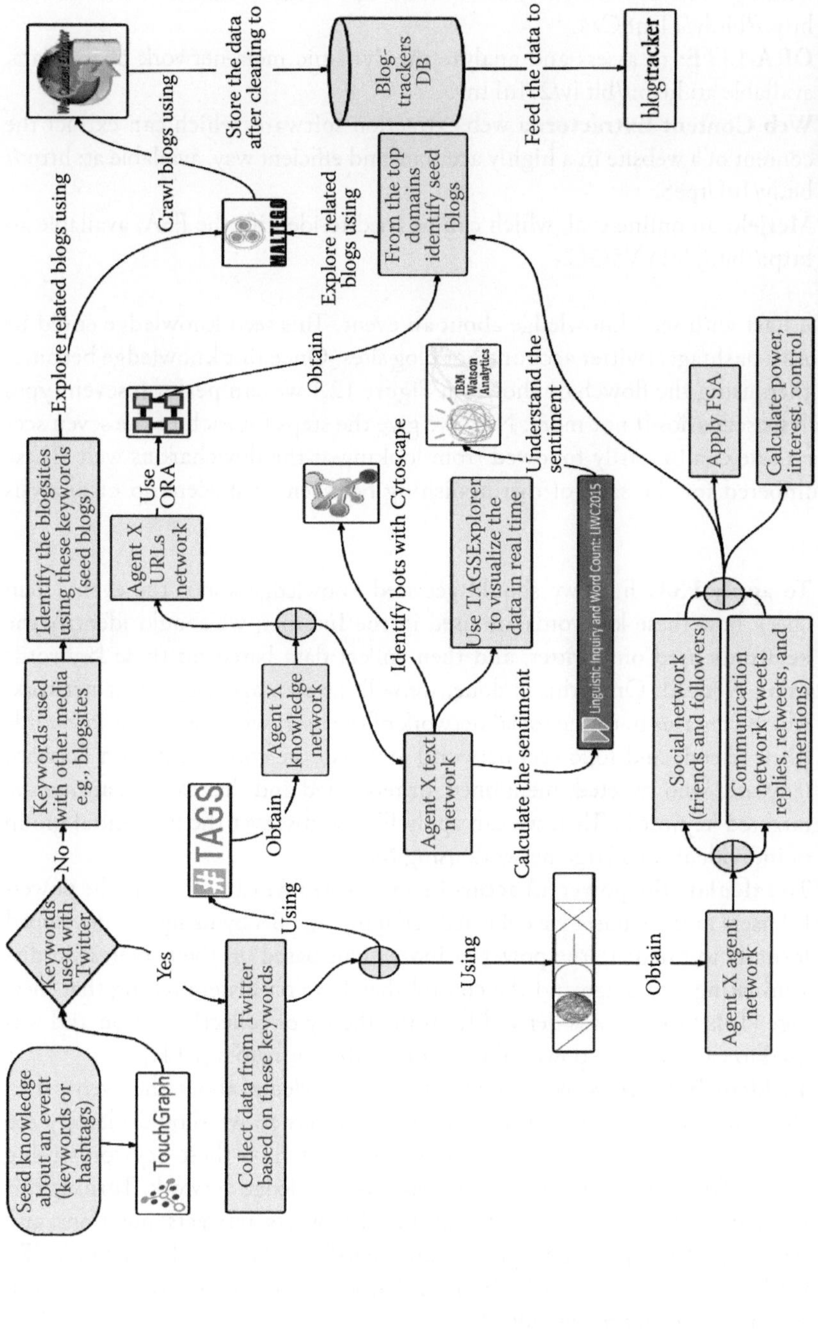

Figure 12.1 Flowchart of the methodology we followed to study the two cases.

- **TouchGraph SEO Browser:** to check the usage of a keyword or hashtag on different websites, it displays a network of connectivity (by keyword or hashtag) between websites, as reported by Google's database, available at: http://bit.ly/1Tm8Cz4.
- **ORA-LITE:** to assess and analyze the dynamic meta-network of the data, available at: http://bit.ly/27fuHnv.
- **Web Content Extractor:** a web extraction software, which can extract the content of a website in a highly accurate and efficient way, available at: http://bit.ly/1uUtpeS.
- **Merjek:** an online tool, which can be used to identify the FSA, available at: http://bit.ly/21YV5OC.

We start with seed knowledge about an event. This seed knowledge could be keywords, hashtags, twitter accounts, or blog sites. Once this knowledge becomes clear, then using the flowchart shown in Figure 12.1 we can perform seven types of analysis/scenarios if not more. Next we give the steps for each of the seven scenarios; these can be easily followed from looking at the flowchart as well. These are numbered for the sake of distinguishing between each scenario or analysis type:

1. **To apply FSA:** first, we should get seed knowledge about the event, then check how these keywords are used in the Internet; we should identify the keywords used on Twitter, and then collect data based on these keywords using NodeXl. Once this is done, we will have an agent-by-agent network, which contains both the social network of the users who used these keywords (their friends and followers network) and also the communication network (any user who tweeted, mentioned, or retweeted and the text containing the targeted keyword). Then we can apply FSA to discover the influential group of individuals in a large network using Merjek.
2. **To calculate the powerful actors in a network:** we can calculate the powerful users in the dataset we collected for applying FSA by using our developed formula to calculate the power of individuals based on their interest in disseminating a message and the control they have on disseminating that message. This formula was derived from the theory of collective action and was used to calculate the power of ISIL top 10 disseminators [10,11].
3. **To identify botnets:** we should get seed knowledge about the event, then check how these keywords are used in the Internet; we should identify the keywords used on Twitter, then collect data based on these keywords using GoogleTAGs. Then we will get an agent-by-knowledge network. Turning this into a network of agent-by-text (text includes tweets, retweets, mentions, and replies) and using CytoScape we can identify botnets in the network. We used this method to identify botnets that were working to disseminate ISIL beheading video propaganda [4].

4. **Understanding the sentiments:** we can use the same network mentioned in the previous step to understand the sentiments of the public about a specific event, e.g., how does the public feel about an issue or what kind of narrative is being pushed in the propaganda? This can be done by using LIWC to calculate the score of the sentiments of the text, and then use IBM Watson Analytics to ask questions of interest, and then find an answer to it.
5. **Have a live visualization of the data:** on the same data collected in Step 3 we can use TAGSExplorer to continuously collect data and have a live visualization of the Twitter feed of users talking about the event.
6. **Using Maltego to discover related blogs sites:** anytime we have a seed blog or a Twitter handle we can use Maltego to discover the other blogs that are owned by the same person or managed by the same unique identifying "UA" number. We can also find blogs from the Twitter handle or vice versa to study the cross media affiliation using Maltego.
7. **Blog analysis using Blogtrackers:** once we identify the blogs of interest we can crawl their data using a web content extractor tool to extract the content of the blog's site and then clean the data and feed it to the Blogtrackers tool for further analysis.

12.4 Case Studies

12.4.1 DAESH or ISIS/ISIL Case Study: Motivation, Evolution, and Findings

12.4.1.1 Exploring the Network of the Top Disseminators of ISIL

Our interest in studying the Islamic State's (also known as ISIL, ISIS, or Daesh) behavior on social media started with a study we conducted on the network of the top 10 disseminators of ISIL on social media [11] that were released by the International Center for Study of Radicalization and Political Violence (ICSR) in September 2014 [12]. In Carter et al.'s study, they interviewed the disseminators and recruiters of ISIL on social media and published their identities. In our work, we crawled those recruiter's friends' and followers' network (in August 2014) and then applied our developed framework to identify the powerful actors in that network. *Powerful actors* are individuals who assert a lot of control on the dissemination of a message and possess a great interest in disseminating them [10,11]. We found out that the top disseminator nodes are not only the most central nodes (most connected) but they also constitute a focal structure, meaning the top disseminators are coordinating with each other. They are coordinating in disseminating ISIS propaganda, forming a powerful campaign organization network. Figure 12.2(a) and (b) show two tweets as samples of the tweets we collected from the ISIL network containing propaganda as well as a message to the their followers. We did a

(a) (b)

Figure 12.2 This figure shows a sample of the tweets we collected from the Daesh/ISIL network containing propaganda and messages to their followers. (a) Propaganda tweeted by one of the top 10 disseminators we have in our datasets. (b) Tweet containing a message to the followers of that account.

follow-up on the accounts we collected in their network and found out that some of these accounts were suspended by Twitter, others were attacked by Anonymous* (a hacking group), while the owners of other accounts were physically captured by law enforcement. Therefore, we decided to recrawl the network on February 2015 (six months later) to find out how the suspensions and cyber attacks affected the overall network. We found that ISIL increased its recruiting activities to almost double. Also, we found out some accounts were mostly used/owned by more than one individual, e.g., the owner of *@shamiwitness* was captured by law enforcement but the account was still active and attracting more people as we recrawled the network. Figure 12.3 shows the old and new network after recrawling it by six months, where red nodes represent the nodes that still exist, white nodes are the nodes suspended by Twitter, and blue nodes are the new ones added. The big 10 nodes represent the top 10 disseminators of ISIL as identified by ICSR.

Since very few users share their location on Twitter, we tried to infer the location of those Twitter accounts using the time zone they follow which is available for most users we collected (see Figure 12.4). Figure 12.4 shows the top 10 disseminators marked in orange while the rest of their friends and followers are marked in green. We zoomed-in on two of the top 10 disseminators *@Shamiwitness* bottom left and *@Ash_shawqi* bottom right. We found out that many users do not follow the time zone where they actually live in which indicates that they are either using proxy servers to hide their physical location or they are responsible for disseminating messages to audiences in different time zones than the one they follow. For example, *@Shamiwitness* follows Central Africa time zone but he was captured in

* Anonymous "Hacktivists" strike a blow against ISIS (Available at: http://bit.ly/1vzrTSQ).

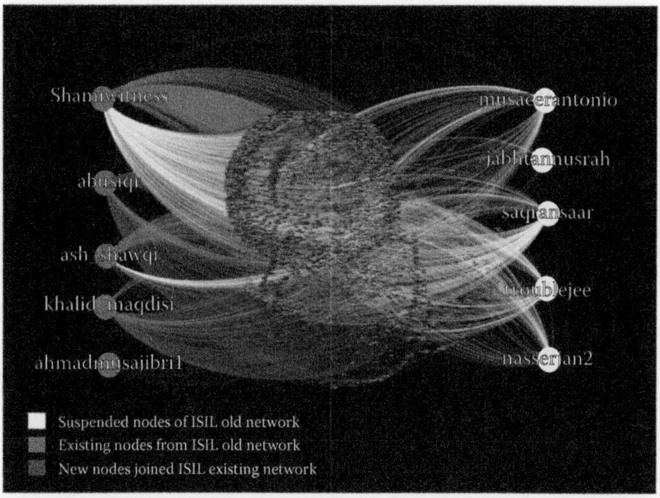

Figure 12.3 A total of 16,539 nodes and 21,878 edges (the friends/followers of ISIL's top 10 disseminators/powerful actors.

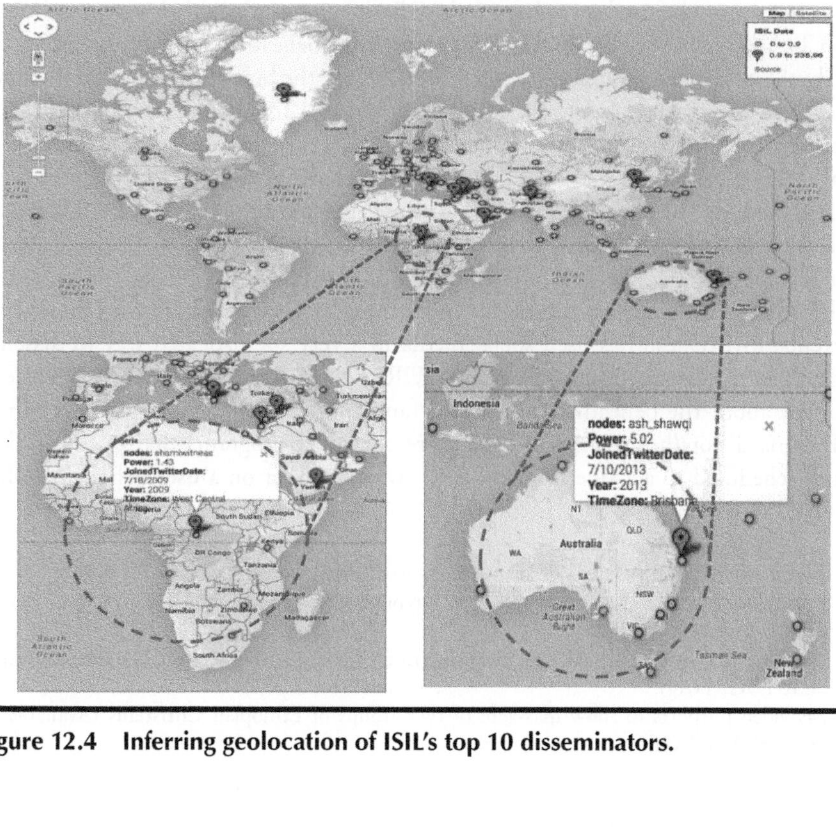

Figure 12.4 Inferring geolocation of ISIL's top 10 disseminators.

Bangalore, India.* We also found out that some accounts changed their identity after we recrawled the network, e.g., the account *@Ash_shawqi*: On the time of data collection this account had 5,990 tweets, 3,867 followers, and follows 279 users. His time zone is Brisbane, Australia. Six months later this account looks totally different. First, he wiped his old tweets and friends/followers (has just three tweets and one follower). Second, his profile language changed from Arabic to Russian. Third, he shared his location as in "Москва" which means "Moscow" in English. Finally, he used to describe himself as a member of Ahlu-Sunnah Wal Jama'ah (Platform of Tawhid and Jihad) but six months later his description changed into Russian language "Помощь должна совершаться не против воли того, кому помогает," which is translated using the Google translation service to English as "Aid should not be committed against the will of the one who helps."

12.4.1.2 Beheading of Innocent People by ISIL

In 2015, the so-called Islamic State or Daesh started releasing videos on social media where they depicted gruesome beheadings of innocent people and accusing them of being unbelievers or traitors in an attempt to spread horror among the minority religious in the Middle East and capture the attention of the media. We crawled the communication network (tweets, retweets, replies, and mentions) of the Twitter users who used some keywords or hashtags specific in their communication on Twitter to three beheading events, namely: the beheadings of Egyptian Copts in Libya† (on February 15, 2015) [see Figure 12.5(a)], the beheading of an Arab-Israeli "spy" in Syria‡ (on March 10, 2015) [see Figure 12.5(b)], and the beheading of Ethiopian Christians in Libya§ (on April 19, 2015) [see Figure 12.5(c)]. This resulted in three datasets with a total of 80,685 texts including: 22,580 tweets, 8,295 mentions, and 49,810 retweets. These texts were generated by 47,148 Twitter users with the majority of them setting their language to English (67% of total users), Arabic in second place (17% of total users), French in third place (5% of total users), while the other 11% represents users who speak other languages [4]. During these three events, ISIL/Daesh has used social media in a very sophisticated way to disseminate their propaganda (messages have a URL to an image/YouTube video, or news article about the beheadings) to a large audience in a very short period of time. They used bots/botnets/ASAs, which are computer programs that can be tasked and scheduled to act like humans, e.g., tweet, retweet on a user behalf [4]. They

* Shami witness arrest rattles ISIS' cages on Twitter (Available: http://bit.ly/1Ty7um0).

† ISIS video appears to show beheadings of Egyptian Coptic Christians in Libya (Available at: http://cnn.it/1vO9CkA).

‡ ISIL executes an Israeli Arab after accusing him of being an Israeli spy (Available at: http://bit.ly/1DGRHAg).

§ Isis video purports to show massacre of two groups of Ethiopian Christians (Available at: http://bit.ly/1yJX8fp).

(a) (b) (c)

Figure 12.5 This figure shows a screenshot for each of the beheadings of innocent people executed by ISIL/Daesh. (a) The beheading of Egyptian Copts in Libya by ISIL on February 15, 2015. (b) The beheading of the Arab-Israeli "spy" in Syria by ISIL on March 10, 2015. (c) The beheading of the Ethiopian Christians in Libya by ISIL on April 19, 2015.

have used some of the very effective information maneuvers to disseminate their messages such as:

- Misdirection, where the bot tweets unrelated news that is happening somewhere else but mentions a hashtag related to the beheading crises.
- Hashtag-latching, when strategically associating unrelated but popular or trending hashtags to target a broader, or in some cases a very specific, audience (e.g., using the #WorldCup and then including a URL of a beheading video).
- Smoke screening, when the bot would mention something about ISIL but not necessarily related to the beheading (similar techniques have been used in the SSB to raise awareness of the Syrian civil war [7]).
- Thread-jacking, the change of topic in a "thread" of discussion in an open forum (e.g., using a hashtag of #ISIL but the tweet has a link to a shopping website).

We also observed that once the news released about the event many people talk about it and try to disseminate it to their friends/followers but two days later the activity started to decline (people know about the event already either by social media or some other means). We also intersected the datasets we collected about ISIL (the one mentioned in Section 12.4.1.1 and the three datasets mentioned in Section 12.4.1.2) to identify the common nodes in an attempt to find the new disseminators' network. We found out a lot of common nodes between datasets, which means those common users possess greater interest in disseminating the propaganda of ISIL/Daesh. Table 12.1 shows the number of common nodes resulting from the intersection (∩) between ISIL datasets that we collected. The symbol (∩) we use in the table is the mathematical intersection of two sets, i.e., the intersection between two sets, set "X" and set "Y" is the set "Z" which contains the unique elements from both set "X" and set "Y" [13].

Table 12.1 The Number of Common Nodes between the Datasets We Collected

Dataset Names	*# of Nodes*
Beheading of Coptic's ∩ beheading of Arab Israeli	265
Beheading of Coptic's ∩ beheading of Ethiopians	753
Beheading of Ethiopians ∩ beheading of Arab Israeli	339
Dataset of top 10 disseminators ∩ beheading of Arab Israeli	126
Dataset of top 10 disseminators ∩ beheading of Ethiopians	83
Dataset of top 10 disseminators ∩ beheading of Coptic's	61
Beheading of Coptic's ∩ beheading of Arab Israeli ∩ beheading of Ethiopians	68

Note: These common nodes have a great interest in disseminating ISIL's propaganda and might be the new disseminators of ISIL propaganda.

12.4.2 Novorossiya Case Study: Motivation, Evolution, and Findings

In this case study we studied the influence operations in Novorossiya. We followed a similar approach to that we followed in the ISIL case study, but here we added the cyber forensics aspect to reveal hidden connections between different organizing groups and to study the cross media affiliation of individuals and groups.

We started by studying the case of the Crimean water crisis* when the Russians invaded the Crimean peninsula on March 16, 2014. This crisis was met with international discontent and a sense of Russian imperialism to expand their reign of power. The United Nations as well as the NATO Secretary General condemned this expansion of Russian sphere of influence. Pro-Russian media propagandized that the closing of a main irrigation canal in April by Ukrainian authorities caused starvation in the peninsula and the death of many crops like rice, corn, and wheat. The pro-Russian media further emphasized that this has caused a humanitarian crisis, which was followed by grievances and requests for help. Many on-the-ground reports on developing conflicts and problems are reported in a variety of open source platforms including blogs, websites, Twitter, Facebook, and other open source channels such as YouTube. During this crisis, bots were used to effectively disseminate thousands of messages in relation to the Crimean water crisis. We collected data for the period between April 29, 2014 8:40:32 PM and July 21, 2014 10:40:06 PM UTC from Twitter using keywords related to this crisis and we wanted to investigate the tactical information maneuvers, especially the role of botnets in propaganda dissemination

* Aid Elusive, Crimea farms face hurdles (available at: http://nyti.ms/1UOpzlg).

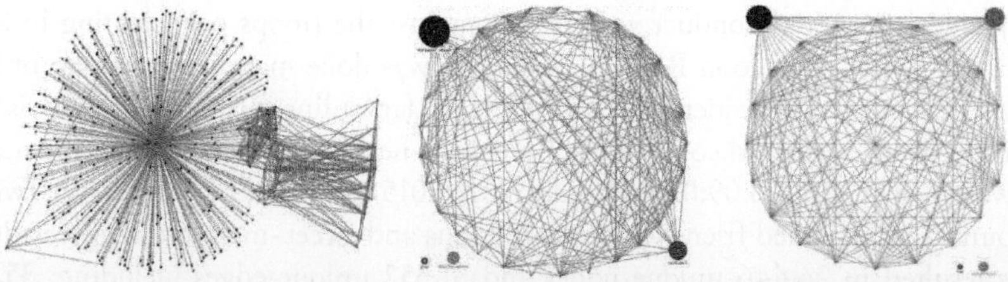

Figure 12.6 Naive botnets observed during the Crimean water crisis (2014). Mutual reciprocity and extremely closely knit behaviors were observed.

campaigns. This resulted in collection of 1,361 unique tweets, 588 unique Twitter users, and 118,601 relations/edges between the Twitter users. There are four basic types of relations in the Twitter data, namely, follows, mentions, replies, and tweets. We found out that these bots had a central account that is responsible for giving the propaganda to them and they work to disseminate these propaganda messages. By closely examining their network, as depicted in Figure 12.6, we found out that they have a mutually reciprocated relationship, suggesting the principles of "Follow Me and I Follow You" (FMIFY) and "I Follow You, Follow Me" (IFYFM) in practice—a well-known practice by Twitter spammers for link farming or quickly gaining followers [14–16]. The bots in this case were considered simple bots, which means if you find one you find others. While in the following case explained next we found more sophisticated bots, which were harder to discover.

After the study of the Crimean water crisis, we studied the propaganda projected against two military exercises conducted by U.S. forces and NATO, namely the Dragoon Ride Exercise* and the Trident Juncture Exercise† (TRJE 2015). In the Dragoon Ride Exercise, a march of U.S. soldiers were sent on a mission as part of Operation Atlantic Resolve and began Operation Dragoon Ride (in March 21, 2015) to exercise the unit's maintenance and leadership capabilities and demonstrate the freedom of movement that exists within NATO. That march covered more than 1,100 miles and across five international borders including Estonia, Latvia, Lithuania, Poland, and the Czech Republic. The Trident Juncture Exercise, which involved 36,000 personnel from more than 30 nations, took place throughout Belgium, Germany, the Netherlands, Norway, Spain, Portugal, Italy, Canada, the Mediterranean Sea, and the Atlantic Ocean to demonstrate NATO's capability and capacity to meet the present and future security challenges.

There was a lot of propaganda projected during these two military exercises. In addition to that, some of the local residents from the participating countries did not like those exercises. There were calls for civil unrest and a lot of propaganda asking

---

* Operation Atlantic Resolve exercises begin in Eastern Europe (available at: http://1.usa.gov/1rDSxcb, Last accessed: June 12, 2016).

† Trident Juncture 2015 (available at: http://bit.ly/1OdqxpG, last accessed: June 12, 2016).

people to protest and conduct violent acts against the troops participating in both exercises. For the Dragoon Ride Exercise, this was done mainly by a group of botnets. These botnets were identified using Scraawl (an online social media analysis tool available at www.scraawl.com). We collected the network of these bots in the period between May 8, 2015 8:09:02 PM and June 3, 2015 11:27:31 PM UTC of 73 Twitter accounts that included friend–follower relations and tweet–mention–reply relations. This resulted in 24,446 unique nodes and 31,352 unique edges including: 35,197 friends and followers edges, 14,428 tweet edges, 358 mention edges, and 75 reply edges. We studied their network structure in an attempt to understand how they operate and compare how different they are from the Crimean water crisis bots. As depicted in Figure 12.7, we found out the bots network here is not as simple as the one in the Crimean water crisis. Bots here do not follow the principles of "Follow Me and I Follow You" (FMIFY) and "I Follow You, Follow Me" (IFYFM) but the identification of these bots has been challenging because the bots here are also coordinating. This behavior is more pronounced in the communication network (retweet + mention + reply). Meaning, if we look at the friends–followers network we don't see much coordination (unlike the Crimean water crisis simple bots). While looking at the communication network it does reflect coordination, and that too is observed by applying a very sophisticated network structure analysis algorithm, i.e., our FSA approach [5].

In the Trident Juncture Exercise, we did an empirical study of the anti-OTAN and anti-TRJE 2015 cyber propaganda campaigns organized on Twitter and the blogosphere. Domain experts identified six groups that propagated their messages on social media inviting people to act against NATO and TRJE 2015. We identified their blog sites as well as their Twitter handles using Google search and cyber forensics techniques. Then we collected their Twitter network for the period of August 3, 2014 4:51:47 PM UTC to September 12, 2015 3:22:24 AM UTC. This

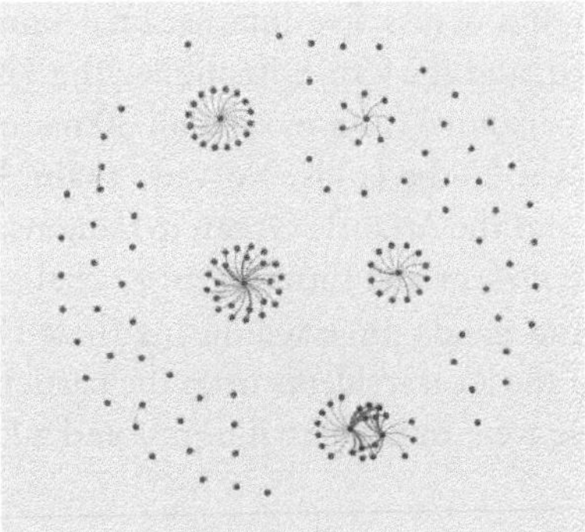

Figure 12.7 Coordination among Dragoon Ride (2015) bots discovered on examining the communication network. Social network does not exhibit any coordination.

resulted in 10,805 friends–followers, 68 replies, 654 tweets, 1,365 mentions, 9,129 total unique nodes, and 10,824 total unique edges.

Then we used cyber forensics tools (Maltego: an open source intelligence and forensics application. It saves a lot of time in mining and gathering of information as well as the representation of this information in an easy to understand format [see Figure 12.8]) and cyber forensics techniques, such as tracking Google Analytics ID, which is an online analytics tool that allows a website owner to gather some statistics about their website visitors such as their browser, operating system, and country. As depicted in Figure 12.8, multiple sites can be managed under a single Google analytics account. Using the techniques in [8] and [9], we were able to uncover the hidden relations between different blog sites and also to study the cross media affiliation of different groups.

After identifying these blogs, we crawled them and fed their data to our in-house developed Blogtrackers tool, where further analysis on the blogs level as well as blogger level can be conducted. Using Blogtrackers we were able to see the spike of activity of blogs (number of blog posts) just before the Trident Juncture Exercise (see Figure 12.9). We were also able to identify the most influential posts [17] that happened to have a lot of propaganda and a clear call for civil unrest against NATO forces (see Figure 12.10).

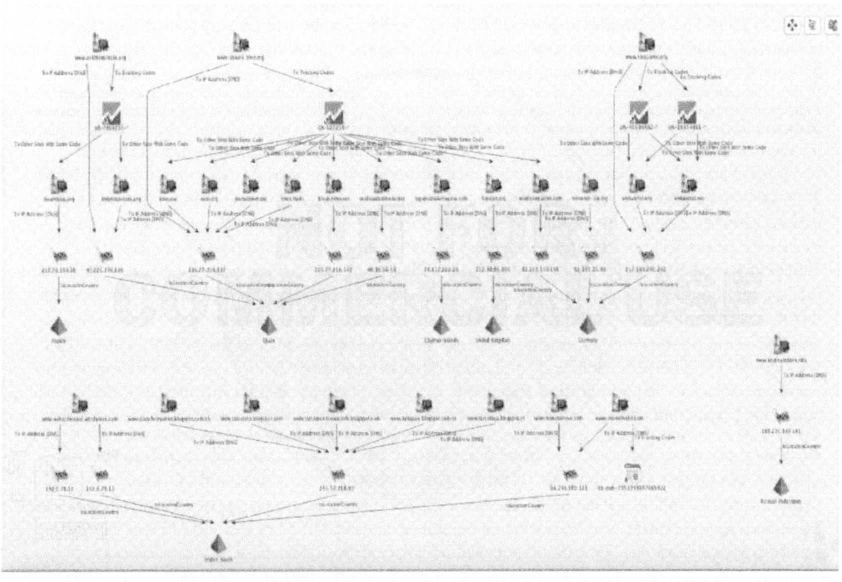

Figure 12.8 Finding related websites, IP addresses, and locations of websites using the Maltego tool and the unique identifier (Google Analytics ID).

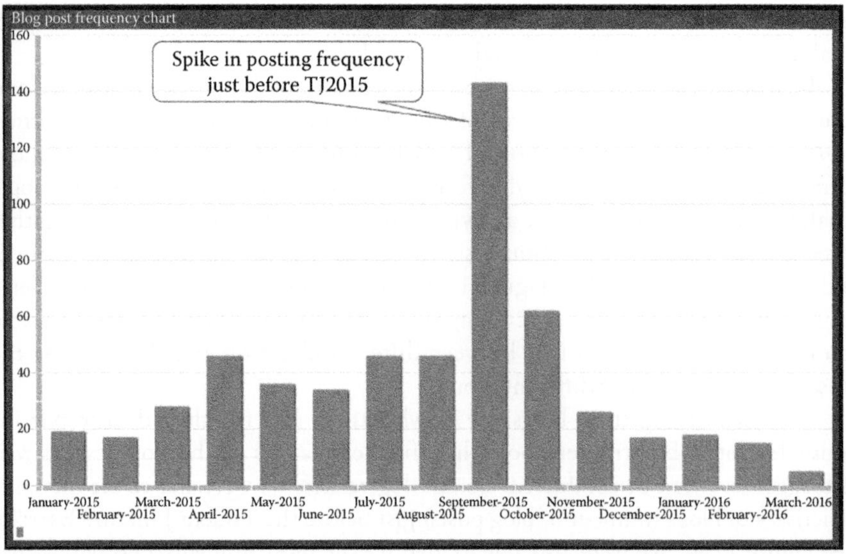

Figure 12.9 This shows the spike in blogs posting activity just before the Trident Juncture Exercise.

camp program: TODAY October 11, 2015 **EVENT Antimilitarist** TO 18 IN CAGLIARI. CONCENTRATION PIAZZA D'ARMI. THE **CAMP IS LOCATED IN THE FORMER QUARRY OF MONTE URPINU (NEAR THE URBAN GARDENS)** VIA RAFFA GARZIA. For visitors REMAINS THE APPOINTMENT this morning on October 9, UP TO 11 IN PIAZZA DEL CARMINE. **Friday, October 9: From 9 to 11 reception in the square of the carmine** - the opening of the camp in the former quarry at Monte Urpinu- afternoon initiatives in the city '21.00 dinner - Assembly of the camp Saturday, October 10 18:00 meeting on the prospects for anti-militarist struggle and against the trident juncture - PRESENTATION oF THE NEW CALENDAR oF EXERCISES iN SARDINIA following dinner Sunday, October 11 Morning conclusive Assembly Afternoon parade The program potra 'vary due to weather issues, because of the cops or contingency. **PORT TENT, SLEEPING BAG, FLAT AND SERVERS.** THE LOCATION OF THE CAMP WILL 'PUBLISHED TOMORROW MORNING, THEN Meet RECEPTION !! **CAMPING Antimilitarist FIGHT - AROUND CAGLIARI 9-10-11 October 2015** Out of the mobilization against the Capo Frasca polygon of 13 September 2014, **initiatives and actions directed against the military presence in Sardinia** have multiplied and diversified to try to jam the mechanism of the war. **Cuts of networks, slowing the means and blocking exercises have taken the "necessary serenity" to the conduct of military activities.** Thanks to its experience and in the wake of the procession of 11 June 2015 in Decimomannu, as No Bases Network here or elsewhere we decided to **call for the second weekend of October an anti-militarist struggle camping.** These three days they want to continue and refine the forms of struggle practiced until now, with the aim of sabotaging the military and everything revolves around us. For this **we would like active participation and contribution by all and all,** then it can be a starting point for a reproducibility of the practices in their contexts and territories. **The campground also wants to act as a springboard for international mobilization, called for the second half of October, against the exercise Trident Juncture 2015.** With this exercise, NATO intends to test its intervention force in the short term, to prepare for the increasingly Possible conflict on Middle East fronts, North African and Russian. 36000 men, hundreds of vehicles, aircraft and ships will fire in Sardinia, Sicily, Spain and Portugal. **For this exercise, the largest since 2002, NATO once again a tribute in terms of pollution, resource exploitation and militarization of the territories to train for war.** As it has been for the exercises of Aries brigade, the brigade of Aosta and STAREX, **we can not make ourselves complicit in all of this, do not let them rest assured.** Proposal mobilization against the Trident DOWNLOAD INFORMATION MEMORANDUM ON TRIDENT Juncture 2015 46

Figure 12.10 This shows the most influential post, which has a clear call for civil unrest against the NATO forces.

12.5 Conclusion and Future Work

In conclusion, with the rapid advancement of technology, people are more connected than ever before. Internet and social media boosted the speed of information diffusion tremendously across the globe. Thus, disseminating propaganda or misinformation about events, i.e., conducting deviant acts, becomes convenient, effective, and fast. Deviant groups can nowadays coordinate cyber campaigns in order to achieve strategic goals, influence mass thinking, and steer behaviors or perspectives about an event in a very sophisticated way (hard to discover) and yet easy to be done. In this chapter, we provided two important and detailed case studies, namely Daesh (ISIS: Islamic State in Iraq and Syria/ISIS/ISIL) and Novorossiya. We analyzed the situational awareness of the real world information environment in and around those events by employing computational social network analysis and cyber forensics informed methodologies to study information competitors who seek to take the initiative and the strategic message away from the main event in order to further their own agenda. We showed the methodology we followed and the results we obtained from each case study. The research gave many interesting findings that are mentioned above and was of great benefit to NATO and U.S. forces participating in both exercises on the ground.

Acknowledgments

This research is supported in part by grants from the U.S. Office of Naval Research (ONR) (award numbers: N000141010091, N000141410489, N000141612016, and N000141612412), U.S. Navy Small Business Technology Transfer (STTR) program (award number: N00014-15-P-1187), U.S. Army Research Office (ARO) (award number: W911NF1610189), and the Jerry L. Maulden/Entergy Fund at the University of Arkansas at Little Rock. The researchers gratefully acknowledge the support. Any opinions, findings, and conclusions or recommendations expressed in this material are those of the authors and do not necessarily reflect the views of the funding organization.

References

1. Smith, Craig. 2016. By The Numbers: 170+ Amazing Twitter Statistics. *DMR (Digital Marketing Ramblings)*. April 30. http://bit.ly/1bSfjNi.
2. Smith, Craig. 2016. By The Numbers: 200 Surprising Facebook Statistics (April 2016). *DMR (Digital Marketing Ramblings)*. June 1. http://bit.ly/1qVayhl.
3. Sindelar, Daisy. 2014. The Kremlin's Troll Army: Moscow Is Financing Legions of pro-Russia Internet Commenters. But How Much Do They Matter? *The Atlantic*, August. http://www.theatlantic.com/international/archive/2014/08/the-kremlins-troll-army/375932/.
4. Al-khateeb, Samer, and Nitin Agarwal. 2015. Examining Botnet Behaviors for Propaganda Dissemination: A Case Study of ISIL's Beheading Videos-Based Propaganda. In *Data Mining Workshop (ICDMW), 2015 IEEE International Conference on*, 51–57. IEEE.

5. Sen, Fatih, Rolf Wigand, Nitin Agarwal, Serpil Yuce, and Rafal Kasprzyk. 2016. Focal Structures Analysis: Identifying Influential Sets of Individuals in a Social Network. *Social Networks Analysis and Mining* 6: 1–22. doi:10.1007/s13278-016-0319-z.
6. Rodríguez-Gómez, Rafael A., Gabriel Maciá-Fernández, and Pedro García-Teodoro. 2013. Survey and Taxonomy of Botnet Research through Life-Cycle. *ACM Computing Surveys (CSUR)* 4(4): 45.
7. Abokhodair, Norah, Daisy Yoo, and David W. McDonald. 2015. Dissecting a Social Botnet: Growth, Content and Influence in Twitter. In *Proceedings of the 18th ACM Conference on Computer Supported Cooperative Work & Social Computing*, 839–51. ACM. http://dl.acm.org/citation.cfm?id=2675208.
8. Alexander, Lawrence. 2015. Open-Source Information Reveals Pro-Kremlin Web Campaign. News Website. *Global Voices*. July 13. https://globalvoices.org/2015/07/13/open-source-information-reveals-pro-kremlin-web-campaign/.
9. Bazzell, Michael. 2014. Open Source Intelligence Techniques: Resources for Searching and Analyzing Online Information. 4th ed. CCI Publishing. https://inteltechniques.com/book1.html.
10. Al-khateeb, Samer, and Nitin Agarwal. 2014. Developing a Conceptual Framework for Modeling Deviant Cyber Flash Mob: A Socio-Computational Approach Leveraging Hypergraph Constructs. *The Journal of Digital Forensics, Security and Law: JDFSL* 9 (2): 113.
11. Al-khateeb, Samer, and Nitin Agarwal. 2015. Analyzing Deviant Cyber Flash Mobs of ISIL on Twitter. In *Social Computing, Behavioral-Cultural Modeling, and Prediction*, 251–57. Springer.
12. Carter, Joseph A., Shiraz Maher, and Peter R. Neumann. 2014. #Greenbirds: Measuring Importance and Influence in Syrian Foreign Fighter Networks. The International Center for the Study of Radicalization and Political Violence (ICSR). http://icsr.info/wp-content/uploads/2014/04/ICSR-Report-Greenbirds-Measuring-Importance-and-Infleunce-in-Syrian-Foreign-Fighter-Networks.pdf.
13. DeHaan, Mike. 2012. Introducing Math Symbols for Union and Intersection. *Decoded Science*. July 26. http://www.decodedscience.org/introducing-math-symbols-union-intersection/16364.
14. Al-khateeb, Samer, and Nitin Agarwal. 2016. Understanding Strategic Information Manoeuvres in Network Media to Advance Cyber Operations: A Case Study Analysing pro-Russian Separatists' Cyber Information Operations in Crimean Water Crisis. *Journal on Baltic Security* 2(1): 6–17.
15. Ghosh, Saptarshi, Bimal Viswanath, Farshad Kooti, Naveen Kumar Sharma, Gautam Korlam, Fabricio Benevenuto, Niloy Ganguly, and Krishna Phani Gummadi. 2012. Understanding and Combating Link Farming in the Twitter Social Network. In *Proceedings of the 21st International Conference on World Wide Web*, 61–70. ACM. http://dl.acm.org/citation.cfm?id=2187846.
16. Labatut, Vincent, Nicolas Dugue, and Anthony Perez. 2014. Identifying the Community Roles of Social Capitalists in the Twitter Network. In *The 2014 IEEE/ACM International Conference on Advances in Social Networks Analysis and Mining*, China. doi:10.1109/ASONAM.2014.6921612.
17. Agarwal, Nitin, Huan Liu, Lei Tang, and Philip S. Yu. 2012. Modeling Blogger Influence in a Community. *Social Network Analysis and Mining* 2(2): 139–62.

III

TOOLS AND DATASETS FOR CYBERSECURITY

Chapter 13

Security Tools

Matthew Matchen

Contents

When people are prepared to apply cybersecurity ideas and theory to practical application in the real world, they equip themselves with tools to better enable the successful outcome of their efforts. However, choosing the right tools has always been a challenge.

The focus of this chapter is to identify functional areas in which cybersecurity tools are available and to list examples in each area to demonstrate how tools are better suited to provide insight in one area over the other. In particular, we discuss boundary tools, network monitoring tools, memory protection tools, memory forensics tools, and password management tools. Our discussion is guided by NIST's cybersecurity framework with the intent to provide clear guidance and standards on protecting U.S. critical infrastructure but is applicable to all aspects of cybersecurity. We also discuss how traditional cybersecurity tools such as network monitoring, firewall, or antivirus tools can be implemented to work with big and higher velocity data.

13.1 Introduction

When people are prepared to apply cybersecurity ideas and theory to practical application in the real world, they equip themselves with tools to better enable the successful outcome of their efforts. But do they choose the right tools? Are these tools multipurpose or oriented toward a more specific function? Even if tools are multipurpose, should they still be used in a dedicated capacity or should usage be split between different objectives? The cybersecurity markets are flooded with advertisements, research, and accredited professionals all competing for attention and time in an effort to increase adoption of various tools that further revenue, research grants, and personal objectives. How, then, can someone choose the right tools?

The focus of this chapter is to identify functional areas in which cybersecurity tools are available and to list examples in each area to demonstrate how tools are better suited to provide insight in one area over the other. This chapter is by no means an exhaustive list and serves as a starting point in cybersecurity toolkit development. Our first phase in developing this toolkit is to determine functional areas of cybersecurity. Thankfully there are already a plethora of functional models, but a core challenge is attempting to map cybersecurity functions in a standardized and simplified approach. In 2014, the United States National Institute of Standards and Technology published the first version of the cybersecurity framework for improving critical infrastructure. In this context, the myriad of cybersecurity facets is condensed into five functions labeled the *Framework Core** as depicted in Table 13.1.

Each core component has categories that better define specific needs, and out of the categories available, these appear to be the most relevant under which we can discuss practical cybersecurity tools as shown in Table 13.2.

Table 13.1 NIST's Cybersecurity Framework Core*

Identify	Protect	Detect	Respond	Recover

Source: http://www.nist.gov/cyberframework/upload/cybersecurity-framework-021214.pdf.

* http://www.nist.gov/cyberframework/upload/cybersecurity-framework-021214.pdf

Table 13.2 NIST Cybersecurity Framework Core with Categories

Identify	*Protect*	*Detect*	*Respond*	*Recover*
Asset management	Access control	Anomalies and events	Response planning	Recovery planning
Business environment	Awareness and training	Security continuous monitoring	Communications	Improvements
Governance	Data security	Detection processes	Analysis	Communications
Risk assessment	Information protection processes and procedures		Mitigation	
Risk management strategy	Maintenance		Improvements	
	Protective technology			

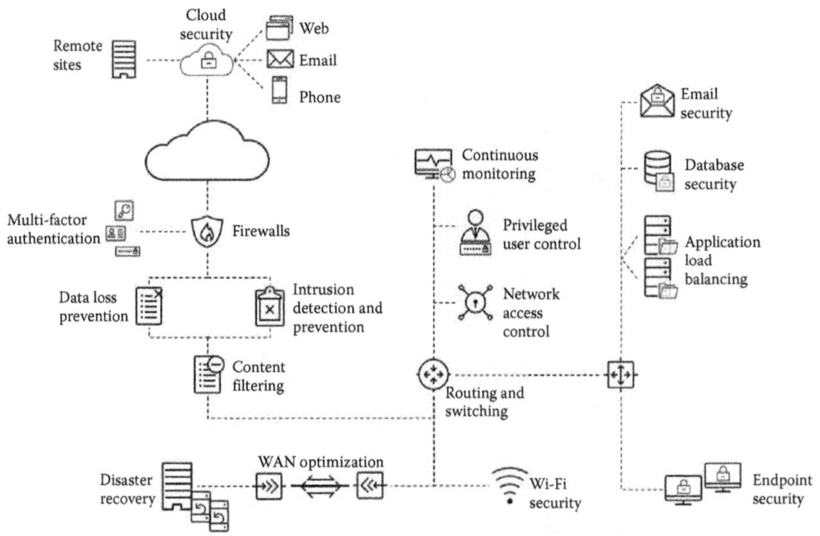

Figure 13.1 Visual example of an enterprise cybersecurity footprint.

13.2 Defining Areas of Personal Cybersecurity

NIST published the cybersecurity framework with the intent to provide clear guidance and standards on protecting U.S. critical infrastructure, but the foundation of the framework is built on cybersecurity knowledge many have come to recognize through certifications such as CompTIA Security+, EC-Council Certified Ethical Hacker, and ISC^2 Certified Information Systems Security Professional. In addition, NIST collected input from cybersecurity experts within the U.S. government as well as commercial organizations and individual subject matter experts. Government agencies and even commercial organizations look to NIST's cybersecurity framework and the concepts therein when considering which tools they incorporate into their cybersecurity toolkits. Even when downsizing the scale of that approach, several areas remain applicable to implementing and maintaining a strong cybersecurity profile on a personal level. For example, an enterprise security footprint can be visualized in Figure 13.1.

Combining areas of cybersecurity that overlap between what NIST defines and what cybersecurity professionals need to protect on their home networks seems to provide toolset categories that apply to both realms.

13.3 Tools for Big Data Analytics

It is hard to define a clear boundary between big data analytics and traditional cybersecurity tools. On the one hand, traditional cybersecurity tools such as network monitoring, firewall, or antivirus tools can be implemented to work with big and higher velocity data. In this case, these tools take advantage of load balancing, parallel data ingestion, distributed data stores, or other scalable services designed for cloud computing. From this point of view, the challenge is to use the appropriate software or service to make the application more scalable. For example, one can run various copies of a popular network monitoring tool, namely Wireshark, using a scalable framework such as a Kafka/Storm combination, and assign each copy to monitor different segments of the network. In this example, Wireshark becomes a "big data tool" not because it is implemented with scalability in mind but by taking advantage of big data software. In another example, a tool that performs a simple machine learning operation such as classification or clustering can be implemented using a scalable programming framework such as MapReduce or Spark and hence becomes a big data analytics tool.

On the other hand, big data analytics tools can also be realized as tools that apply practical and scalable machine learning and artificial intelligence for cybersecurity. Note that these tools are beyond running a simple application or an algorithm but are deployed and specialized to solve complex cybersecurity problems, generally at the enterprise level. Three examples of these tools are IBM Cognitive Security – Watson for Cyber Security,* Teradata Cyber Security,† and Sqrrl Enterprise.‡ For the purposes of this book, we will not delve into these applications and refer the reader to their respective manuals.

In both cases, big data is in the eye of the beholder. Even relatively straightforward tasks such as recording network packets can be unfeasible at large scales. Hence, it is more beneficial to pick and choose tools that are more suited for the scale of the cybersecurity problem at hand. Big data tools also come with an overhead such as computation and maintenance, and they might not be the most efficient solution at smaller scales. We recommend the readers to learn and experience the basic analytical tools first, and then move into more advanced tools. Therefore, we first start with studying boundary tools as the first line of defense. Note that the outputs of these tools (e.g., logs of blocked traffic) can also be used to support data analytics.

13.4 Boundary Tools

Similar to how barriers control access in the physical realm, the logical barriers provided by firewalls enforce boundary separation to help define, at a minimum, a "trusted" zone and an "untrusted" zone. Most people think of "trusted" and "untrusted" as being the LAN and the WAN, but they could also be network segment A and network segment B, both residing in IP space not accessible from the Internet. In an enterprise network, big firewall names include companies like Palo Alto, Check Point, Cisco, and Juniper.

* http://www-03.ibm.com/security/cognitive/
† http://www.teradata.com/solutions-and-industries/cyber-security-analytics
‡ https://sqrrl.com/

13.4.1 Firewalls

Procuring an appliance from one of the companies above to act as a firewall in a home network is cost-prohibitive for most, but the need to protect devices connected in the home from attack and compromise remains. Thankfully, if a home is Internet-connected, Internet service providers provide basic firewall functionality when provisioning one of their routers or cable modems. It is at this ISP-provided firewall we review our first practical cybersecurity tool, because in the absence of any other means, it is useful to understand what firewall capabilities are available.

13.4.1.1 ISP Firewalls

In this example, we'll review the Actiontec MI424WR-F router provided by Verizon and what firewall settings are available. Regardless of what hardware ISPs provide, most have similar settings just arranged in a different way. In Figure 13.2, we show Verizon router's main display. When logging in, the dashboard presents a heads-up display of sorts to show whether the Internet is detected, what Internet public IP address is provisioned, connected devices in the home, and shortcuts to other configuration areas.

Many people may take this display for granted, but the list of connected devices is an important visibility factor and falls under the *Identify* component of the NIST cybersecurity framework core. In this example, the Actiontec device is not providing any Wi-Fi services, which is why the device connection types are only Ethernet

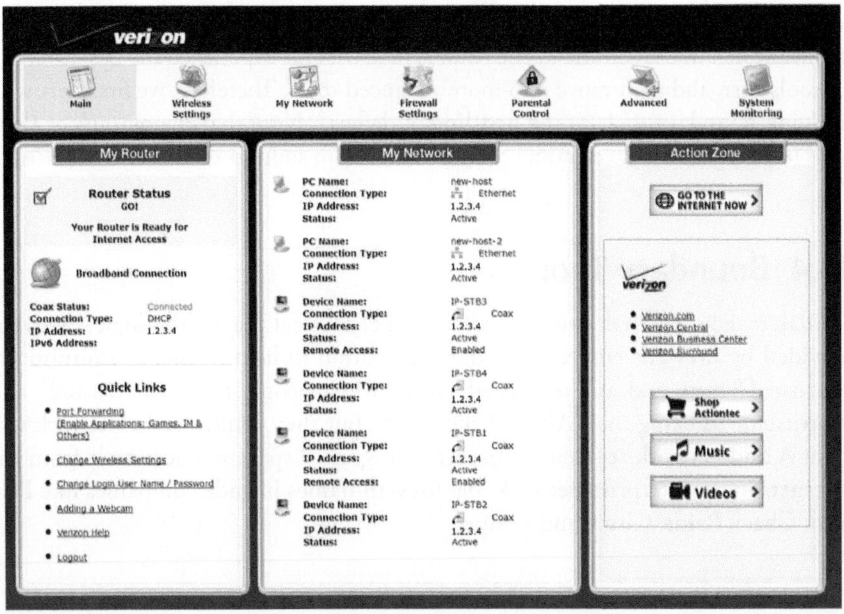

Figure 13.2 Verizon router: main display.

and Coax. Wireless security settings are standard across devices with the Internet providing a multitude of examples and recommendations of how the Wi-Fi settings should be set, but explanations of the firewall settings are much less common.

A review of the firewall settings shows many of the same basic protection controls present in the Actiontec that are also present in enterprise-class firewalls. These controls map the *Protect* component of the NIST cybersecurity framework. For ease of deployment and configuration, ISPs choose an initial operating mode that accounts for most home user access to the Internet without causing issues so that the ISP technician assigned to the installation can deploy and leave quickly without getting stuck in troubleshooting.

Notice that in Figure 13.3, all outbound traffic is accepted. Unlike the home-based firewall configuration, in a popular enterprise firewall such as Palo Alto, the configuration is not pre-staged for rapid deployment and must be built from scratch. Defining a policy on the Palo Alto similar to what the Verizon router provides would look similar to Figure 13.4. Comparing the two figures, many menu options reflect the same configuration setting concepts overall but are implemented in different ways. For instance, the Access Control and Advanced Filtering options on the Verizon router equate to setting Security policy rules in the Palo Alto firewall, whose policy view can be seen in Figure 13.4. Benefits that firewall vendors such as Palo Alto and others provide build on top of the core firewall configuration elements to include capabilities such as SSL/TLS decryption, URL content filtering, and application signature recognition, to name only a few.

Firewall best practices advise to deny by default, and only permit by exception, and to do so for both inbound *and* outbound policies. However, to block all outbound traffic and only permit by exception means each Internet-outbound request

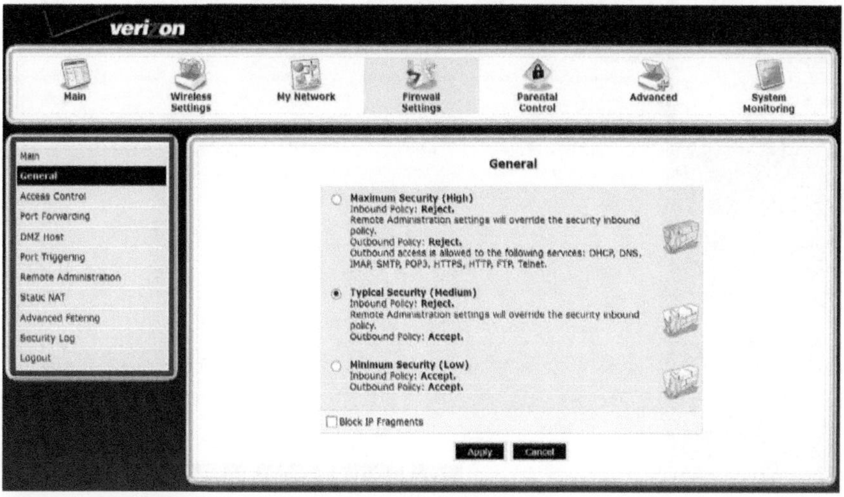

Figure 13.3 Verizon router, firewall settings.

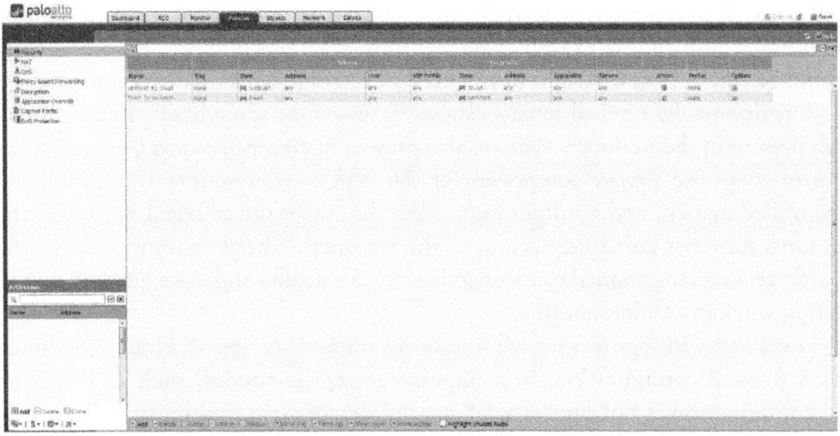

Figure 13.4 Palo Alto firewall, policy view.

must be reviewed to determine if it should be permitted. That approach delays service implementation and can be difficult to deploy without a strategic implementation plan, which is why many home networks and even small- to medium-sized businesses have firewall policies allowing all outbound traffic. A sample of rules required in the Verizon router firewall policies if choosing to reject all outbound traffic unless otherwise defined is depicted in Figure 13.5.

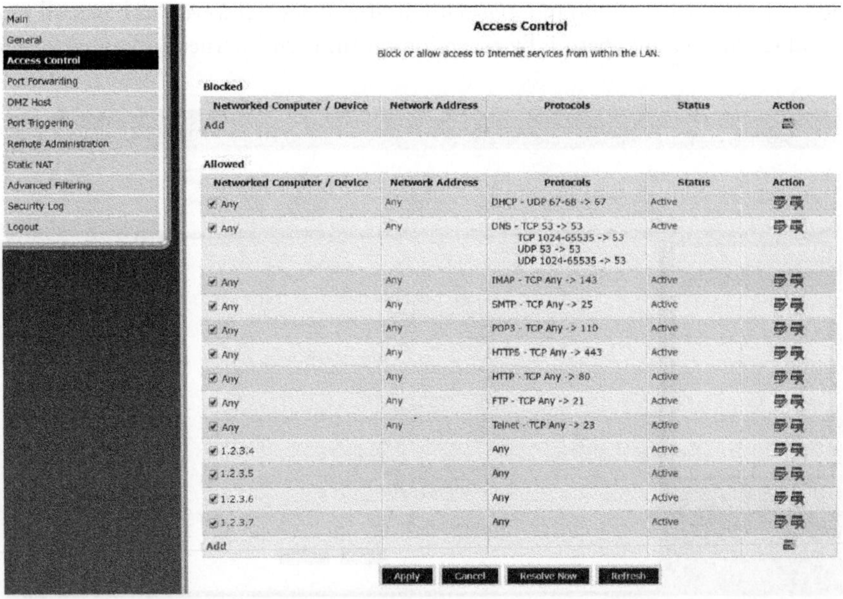

Figure 13.5 Verizon router strict ruleset.

It is worth taking the time to explore the router provided by the ISP to determine what granularity of control can be implemented in the firewall area, because in some cases desired capabilities or features are absent. People who travel often may need access to home network resources while on the road, and the most secure method for remote access is an encrypted tunnel established using a virtual private network (VPN) connection. Typically, ISP-provided routers do not provide VPN services on the device itself, but setting up a VPN connection to a home network is a common enough use case that there is a myriad of choices available.

13.4.1.2 Home Firewalls

One VPN implementation option is to purchase a router from a different vendor such as Asus or Netgear, in which the device purchased would market VPN capability as a feature. For instance, on the ASUS RT-AC68U setting up a VPN is in the advanced settings area and provides VPN server choices between PPTP and OpenVPN. The OpenVPN settings view can be seen in Figure 13.6.

Instead of choosing one device over the other, both devices could be used to isolate functions as well as provide defense-in-depth. An example of isolating

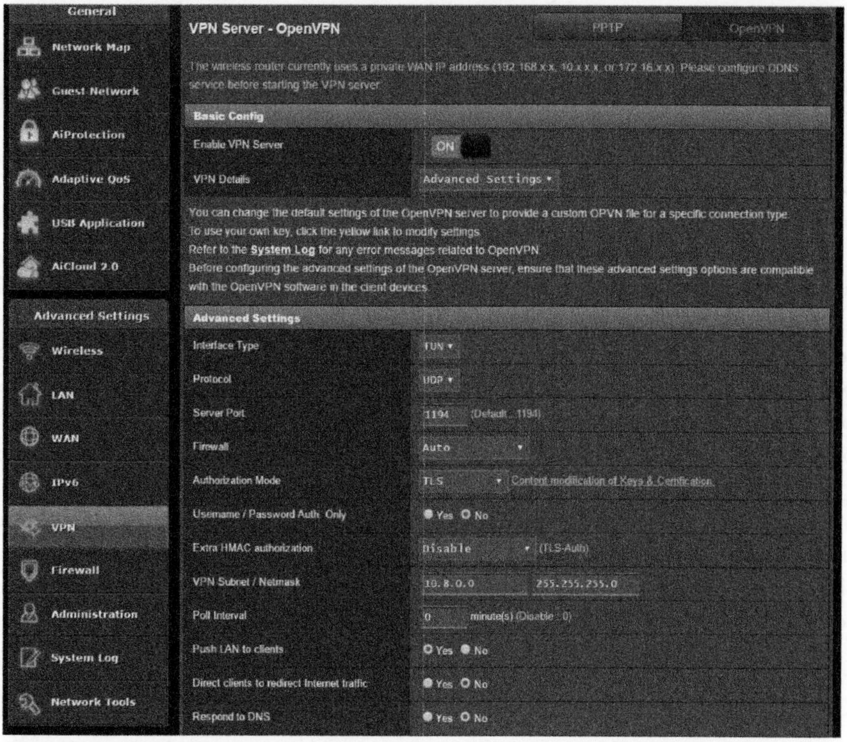

Figure 13.6 Asus RT68U OpenVPN settings.

functions would be to disable the wireless completed on the ISP router, so that the Asus router provides Wi-Fi. For defense-in-depth, the Asus router can firewall off its Ethernet connection to the ISP router so that if the ISP router becomes compromised, then the Asus is the next layer of defense an attacker would have to overcome. For even more network boundary security, another firewall can be layered in the home network path and instead of purchasing another hardware device, some software-based firewalls are available that are also free.

13.4.1.3 Free Software Firewalls

A recent trend in cybersecurity companies that sell products is to provide a free offering for home users. In the firewall market two examples are Sophos and Comodo and although they both offer software-based firewalls, the "form-factor" for each is different. The offering from Sophos is marketed as a unified threat management (UTM) firewall and is deployed as a virtual appliance.* Installation requires a virtual environment such as a VMware ESX host for applied use, but for testing VMware, Player can be used. Sophos distributes the UTM virtual appliance in the form of a *.iso* file, which can be mounted in VMware Player as a live CD from which to boot. After booting the image and setting networking information, the Sophos UTM virtual machine can be accessed via the network.

For home users and even businesses that want to pay for the licensed version, the Sophos UTM is a fully featured product that provides several cybersecurity options. Settings displayed in Figure 13.7 depict this instance being used as an HTML5 SSL-VPN, with VPN rules set to establish a closed VPN tunnel so Internet access is routed through the VPN connection, and firewall rules to set boundaries on what internal networks connected VPN clients are permitted to access.

The difference between the Sophos UTM and Comodo firewalls is that Comodo offers a software installation package for its firewall instead of a full virtual appliance. An easier way to think of them is a network-based firewall (Sophos) compared to a system-based firewall (Comodo). Comodo has more than firewall functions built into its software package. It also includes a host intrusion prevention (HIPS) component, antivirus, sandboxing, and content filtering. An example of the HIPS preventing execution of a batch file from a malicious binary is shown in Figure 13.8.

Comodo HIPS also looks for known registry key manipulation and will both alert and log instances of malicious registry key manipulation. Alerts provide the user a similar screen to the one in Figure 13.8, providing choices of how to treat the situation. Once the user confirms the choice, the event is logged. A representative set of Comodo HIPS logged events can be seen in Figure 13.9.

---

* https://www.sophos.com/en-us/products/free-tools/sophos-utm-home-edition.aspx#

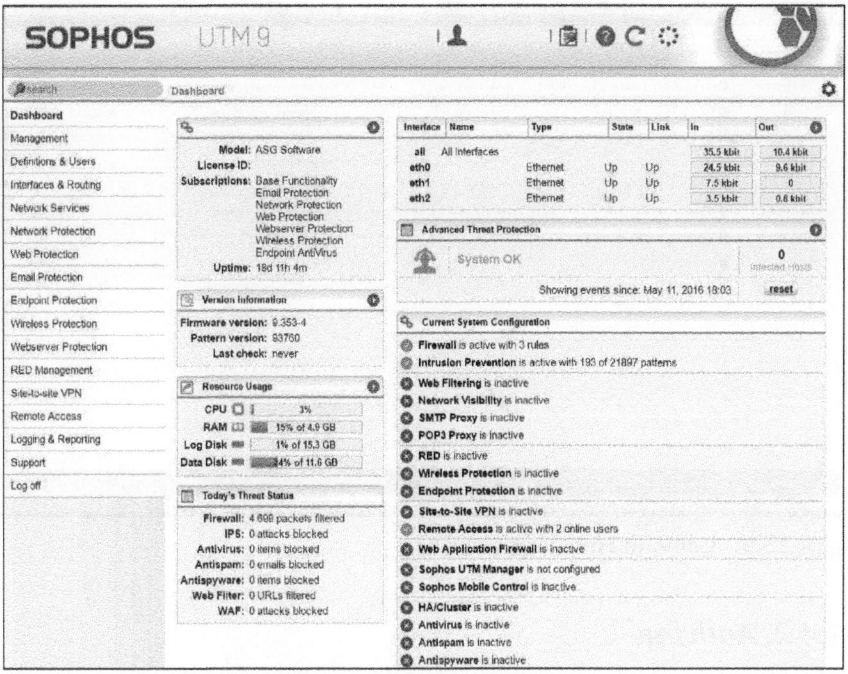

Figure 13.7 Sophos UTM management dashboard.

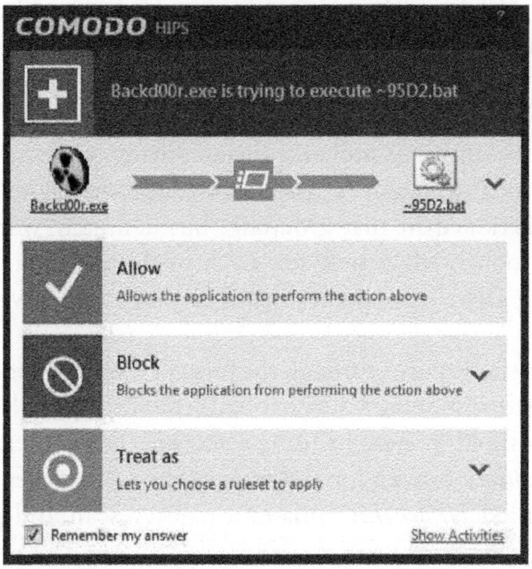

Figure 13.8 Comodo HIPS preventing malware launch of batch script.

Figure 13.9 Comodo HIPS logged events.

13.4.2 Antivirus

Currently almost dismissed from serious consideration as an element of cybersecurity defense, antivirus software is less and less a standalone piece of software and more often built into another software solution as a subcomponent. Perhaps not considered by some as crucial a part of defense as it once was, antivirus is still beneficial to assist in preventing script kiddies or other malicious actors using known malware payloads. Cybersecurity vendors seem to have recognized to protect individual machines requires more than pattern matching, and through the other capabilities layered on top, the new up and coming phrase to describe what antivirus protection is enveloped under is "Endpoint Protection."

Big players in the antivirus tool area include many names already popularized such as TrendMicro, Intel Security (McAfee), Kaspersky, Symantec, and Sophos. One not often mentioned in that grouping, but definitely worth mentioning as another antivirus tool, is MalwareBytes. Each of these companies provides some sort of free offering as well as enhanced paid versions for software providing antivirus protection.

TrendMicro offers antivirus through the form of their free tool called *HouseCall*, which markets a feature looking for system vulnerabilities as well.* For the malware that entrench a foothold in systems using a rootkit, TrendMicro also offers a free tool called *RootkitBuster* to scan for and remove them.† Another free tool provided by TrendMicro called *HijackThis* initiates a registry scan and generates a report

* http://housecall.trendmicro.com/

† http://free.antivirus.com/us/rootkit-buster/index.html

where the findings include files commonly manipulated by both good software and malware. It may not be as popular of a tool because it requires manual analysis of the findings to determine if the item found should be ignored and marked as normal behavior or if the item should be deleted. A practical approach to using this tool would be to run in as soon as a system is purchased so all known software can be flagged as "good" so that baseline will be available the next time *HijackThis* is used.

Intel Security (McAfee) provides their *Security Scan Plus* tool free and it is often seen bundled with other installation packages such as Adobe Reader and Flash as an extra option.* Most of the other free tools offered by McAfee are either built for single-purpose use or they are legacy and more oriented toward older operating systems.† A similar tool to *Security Scan Plus* from Intel Security is offered by Kaspersky under the name *Security Scan*. When comparing the two, it seems the name provides an exact idea of what these tools do, which is scan. At the end of the scan, a report is presented with either a system's clean bill of health or malware findings with a link to purchase the full software so that malware can actually be removed. Kaspersky does provide a *Virus Removal* tool, but the description is vague. It may be similar to some of the single-purpose tools Intel Security provides. Like Intel Security, Kaspersky offers other free tools which appear to be supplemental to overall cybersecurity, but it appears these tools are relevant to systems currently in use.‡

Symantec provides free antivirus tools in the form of specific malware removal and crimeware removal. Malware removal offered is targeted toward specific instances of malware, rather than scanning an entire system.§

Sophos offers antivirus protection in the form of a product called *Sophos Home*, emulating a trend in Managed Security Services where a cloud-based dashboard presents a management interface through which administrators remotely monitor computers for observed threats and apply security policies. Security functions capable of being leveraged through Sophos Home include antivirus as well as content filtering, and can be deployed for free in up to 10 personal devices. Currently, only Windows and Mac are supported. Sophos Home dashboard view is shown in Figure 13.10.

Antivirus scans can be initiated remotely as well as on the devices itself by the user. From the dashboard, policies for web content filtering can be set to provide or block access or when chosen, provide a warning page to advertise a caution message to the user before they can proceed. Without making a more granular selection, by default if content filtering is selected it will prevent devices with the Sophos Home agent installed from accessing sites known by Sophos to contain malware.

---

* http://home.mcafee.com/downloads/free-virus-scan
† http://www.mcafee.com/us/downloads/free-tools/index.aspx
‡ http://free.kaspersky.com/us
§ https://www.symantec.com/security_response/removaltools.jsp

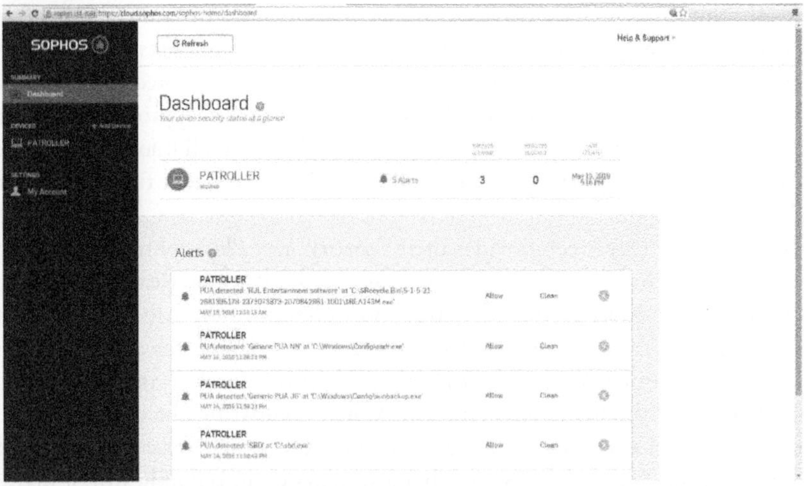

Figure 13.10 Sophos home, dashboard view.

The Sophos Home dashboard must be used to initially deploy the agent, but then deployed users can initiate scans and get alerted locally on the installed device. This local view is shown in Figure 13.11.

The added aspects to antivirus monitoring include the free remote management for multiple devices and content filtering. It should be mentioned here that

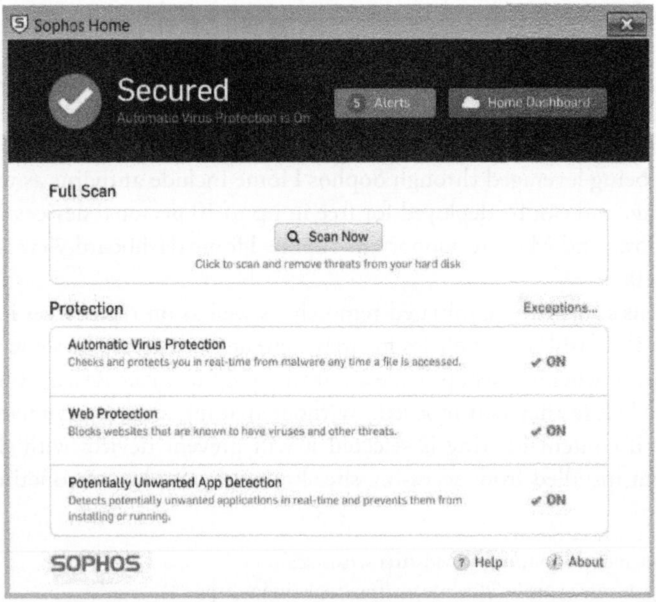

Figure 13.11 Sophos home, local device view.

Comodo also has free remote management for multiple devices, but the service offerings are slightly different with one example being remote patch management. Comparing these additional free services beyond antivirus will be left to the reader to exercise.

13.4.3 Content Filtering

Jumping right into web content filtering, first it is worth discussing the two strategies applied through free content filtering products: DNS and proxying. Controls based on DNS requests are leveraged by setting DNS server settings on devices or by provisioning the DNS server through DHCP settings so that each device receives the DNS settings automatically as they connect to the network. When these devices receive provisioning pointing DNS queries to servers providing protection, any time a DNS query is received asking for a site belonging to a prohibited category, the DNS response provides an IP address directing the device to initiate a request staged to provide the device a path to a page instructing the user that the request is blocked due to content filtering. A benefit to DNS-based content filtering is that by setting the DNS content filter servers on the DHCP server, all machines receiving DNS settings can be centrally provisioned. Controls based on proxying are typically device-isolated, meaning that the software applying the content filtering control is installed on each device. Instead of using DNS to review the intended destination, the proxy software sees the request before the device transmits any outbound data and can query its content filter database and/or cloud component to receive a category response and apply policy. An advantage to this approach is that the full request can be inspected, rather than just the DNS hostname queries.

To illustrate the two approaches, an example could be an ecommerce website called "shopthissiteforthingstobuy.com" recently compromised by a bad actor and now presents a malware payload to unsuspecting website visitors. The malware payload URL is accessed during the loading of the webpage footer content as an image link from the ecommerce domain referenced in the CSS of each page being loaded. If a DNS-based content filtering solution believes the website hostname is categorized correctly, then the possibility of payload delivery is high. Once the DNS-based content filtering solution becomes aware of the malware from the ecommerce site, then the entire site would be blocked. A DNS-based content-filter workflow is depicted in Figure 13.12.

From the perspective of the proxy content filtering solution, the payload is only delivered via a specific URL and if each URL is inspected individually, only the URL called during the loading of the footer would be blocked while the rest of the page is displayed, which is shown in Figure 13.13.

Free solutions for each approach are available, with OpenDNS* (recently acquired by Cisco) providing DNS-based content filtering and Blue Coat providing

* https://www.opendns.com/

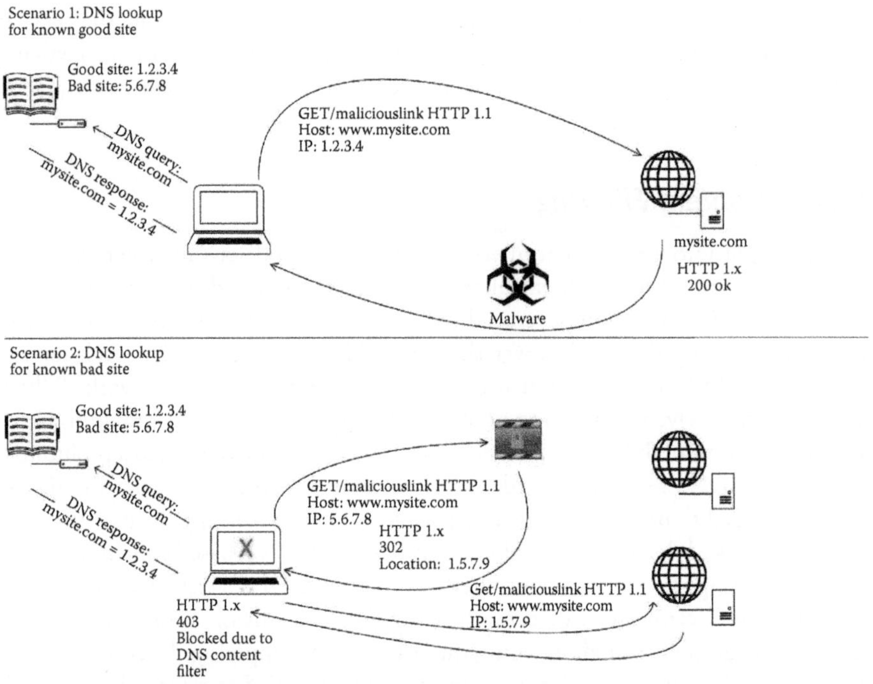

Figure 13.12 DNS-based content filter workflow.

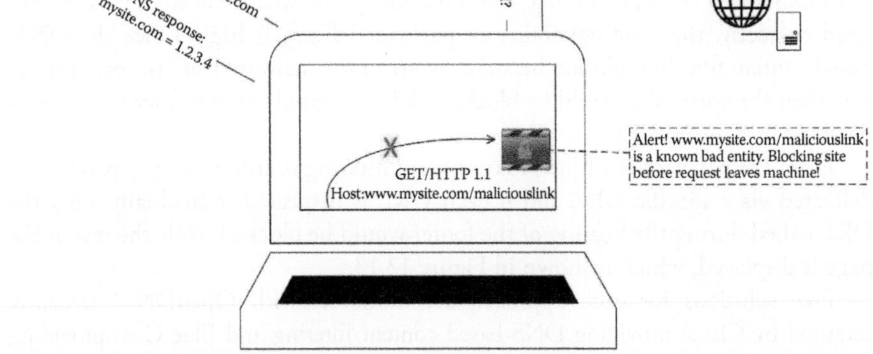

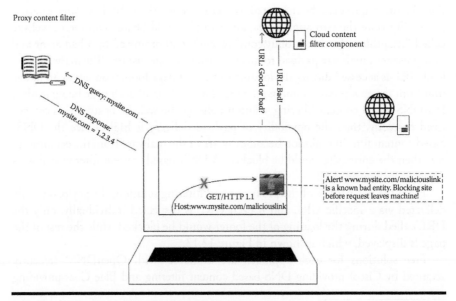

Figure 13.13 Proxy agent content filtering.

Table 13.3 Free Content Filter Solution Comparison

Solution	*Central Control*	*Granular Control*	*Vendor*
DNS	Yes	No	OpenDNS.com
Proxy	No	Yes	Blue Coat

proxy content filtering through their K9 Web Protection* software. The free content filter solution comparison is summarized in Table 13.3.

13.5 Network Monitoring Tools

In the previous section, discussion focused on boundary tools typically seen as part of an enterprise boundary protection solution suite. Supplementing the protection and enforcement aspects of cybersecurity are the tools used to inspect network traffic. Rules applied in protection and enforcement tools provide boundaries; threat actors are typically aware of basic boundaries applied by the tools focused on those areas and so will attempt to mask activity inside what appears to be authorized network traffic. Cybersecurity professionals are aware that threat actors know this as well, and have applied network monitoring tools to inspect traffic as it ingresses and egresses the network and/or device to provide on-demand granular inspection. Free tools providing such network inspection capability include Wireshark, NetWitness, Netminer, and TCPView.

Ample information is already present through other resources discussing Wireshark,† as it is by far the most popular free network traffic analysis tool. To provide a sample though, many cybersecurity certifications and classes discuss port scans, but often not many have actually seen what a port scan looks like when viewed through a packet capture.

Figure 13.14 contains the captured traffic of a port scan. Packets 934 and 935 reveal an open port (1099), whereas all others in the view show the "victim" machine being scanned sending reset [RST] packets to the "attacker" machine. In many scanning tools, Packets 934 and 934 simply appear as "Port 1099: Open," and this packet capture reveals the mechanism by which the scanning tool determined the port was indeed available. From a different perspective, this also reveals how noisy scanning tools can be since there is no delay from the time the "attacker" machine receives the RST packet to the time the next SYN packet is sent looking for the next port according to the scanning logic used.

* http://www1.k9webprotection.com/

† https://www.wireshark.org/

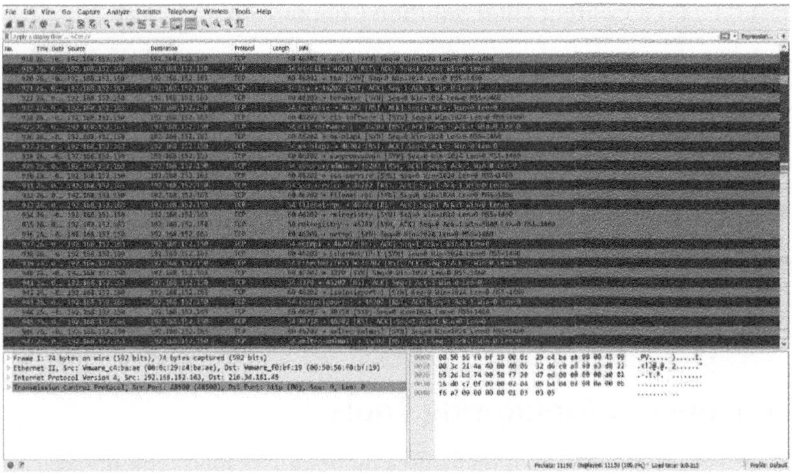

Figure 13.14 Wireshark port scan display.

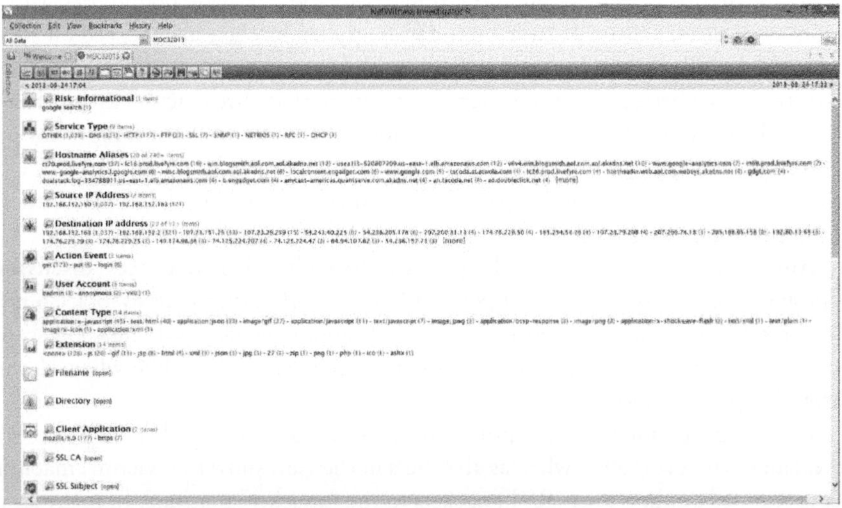

Figure 13.15 NetWitness analyst initial view.

NetWitness* operates differently than Wireshark in that it seems more oriented toward looking at a packet capture analysis instance in terms of case management. To begin analysis packet captures have to be imported into collections, after which the capture is parsed through to define easy investigative starting points from which analysts can drill down. The NetWitness view of the same packet capture depicted in Figure 13.14 is shown in Figure 13.15.

* https://register.netwitness.com/register.php

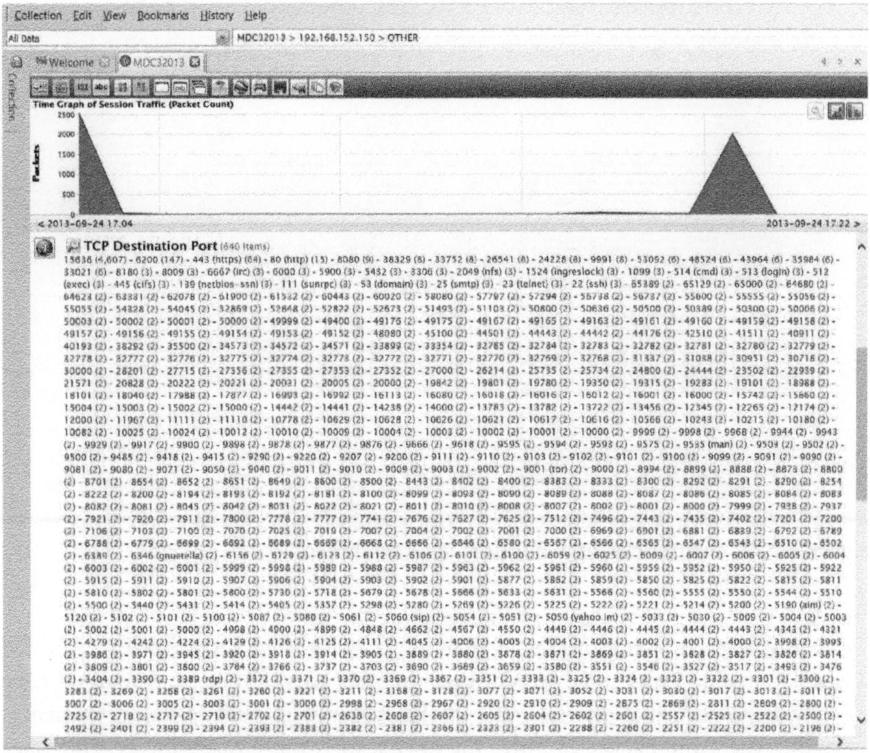

Figure 13.16 NetWitness port scan view.

If the same attacker IP address is chosen from the packet capture as the starting point, the view changes (see Figure 13.16 for this view). Notice that certain information is parsed out immediately such as observed actions (login, get), observed user accounts (badmin, anonymous, vxu), and observed file extensions (.zip). While this presents interesting information parsed out in readily clickable filters, the port scan isn't visible in the same way. Only by selecting the source or destination could I then look at what TCP ports were used, and once sorted by session, "Other" provided 640 entries.

While most of those entries only displayed packet count indicators of one packet, port 21 showed 21 packets. Once a path is drilled down to its most interesting "leaf" node, clicking on the number of packets brings up a session view wherein if the service is recognized then only the plaintext translation of bytes to ASCII is represented in a request/response breakdown. For unrecognized traffic, the raw bytes are displayed for review in the same request/response breakdown. Between the two, it seems that Wireshark is best for a "from the ground up" view, while NetWitness provides a "top down" view.

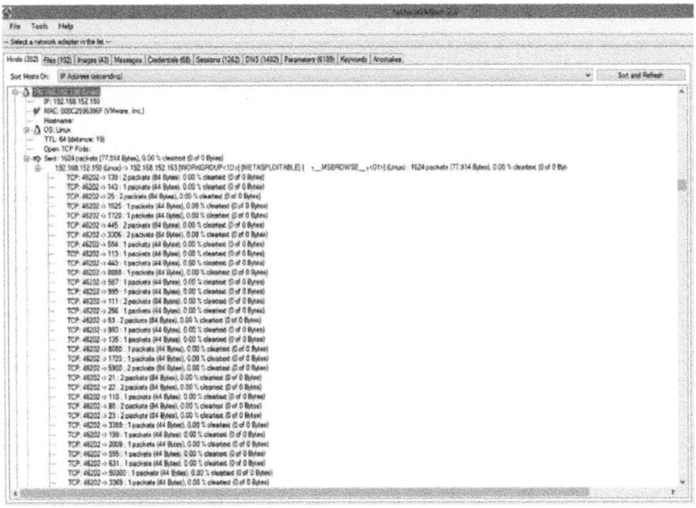

Figure 13.17 NetworkMiner 2.0 port scan evidence.

A tool that provides another viewpoint altogether is NetworkMiner,* which is similar in one aspect to NetWitness, attempts to save network analysts time by extracting information from the packet capture in easy-to-navigate menus. Sampling the same packet capture, the port scan is more easily discernable once the "attacker" IP address information is expanded. This port scan evidence can be observed in Figure 13.17.

Looking at the parsed results, NetworkMiner displays the "attacker" machine using the same port to send multiple connection attempts to the "victim" machine on various ports. Clicking through the tabs at the top displays automatically parsed information related to the topic chosen, including: files, images, messages, credentials, sessions, DNS, command parameters, and anomalies. Keywords can be prepopulated in hex format for NetworkMiner to have as filters when the packet capture is first loaded.

Up to this point, these network analysis tools are all system-independent in the sense that they can review network traffic captured in a packet capture format from any network segment from any organization. TCPView is different from the rest in that it is used on Windows systems to view current network connection states (see Figure 13.18) including the process spawning the connection. This free tool can be a great supplement to the network traffic analysis tools above if in the network analysis workflow a Windows system is identified to have generated suspicious network traffic. Instead of immediately removing the network connection from that system and assuming it can be quarantined into a forensic investigative LAN

* http://www.netresec.com/?page=NetworkMiner

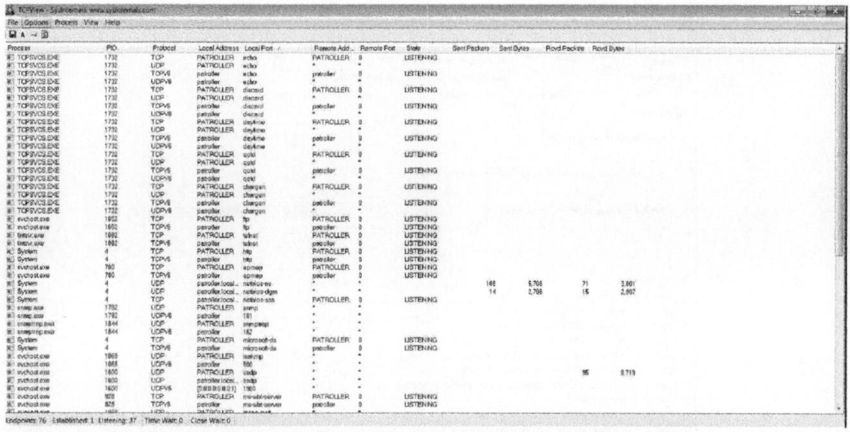

Figure 13.18 TCPView displaying current network connection states.

segment, then TCPView could be loaded to observe what processes are generating the suspect outbound traffic.

Using TCPView can validate suspicion if mysterious network traffic is observed from an upstream device, as well as audit behavior of newly installed applications. Occasionally applications will install using settings that spawn network listeners, and unless users are aware those connection vectors exist or if the post-install configuration is altered so the process avoids enabling that functionality, the machine can have those ports open indefinitely.

13.6 Memory Protection Tools

In the world of Windows, Microsoft's free Enhanced Mitigation Experience Toolkit (EMET)* is one of the best defenses applied to Windows memory protection available. When installed, the EMET administrator must choose which applications will receive memory protection as well as what types of protection. Almost every aspect of deploying EMET is a manual process because if not applied carefully and correctly it is very possible to break application functionality. In the example in Figure 13.19, Firefox is manually configured to be protected by EMET.

In Linux, a popular free memory protection tool is grsecurity.† However, to use grsecurity requires installing it as a kernel patch, and interested installers should follow whatever distro is the selected target to determine how to install a kernel patch. Once installed, grsecurity provides many of the memory protection options EMET does but reflected toward a Linux system.

* https://technet.microsoft.com/en-us/security/jj653751

† https://grsecurity.net/

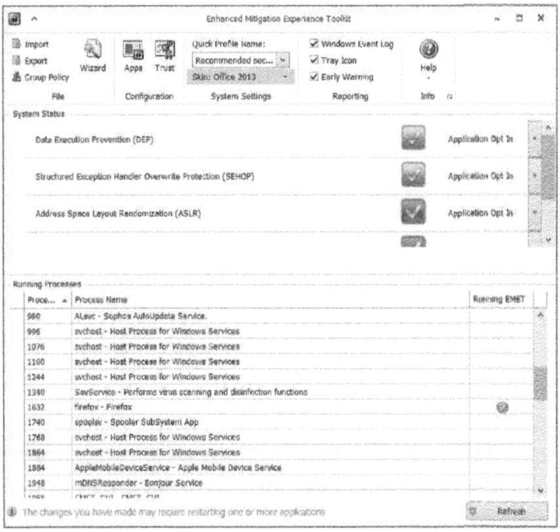

Figure 13.19 **Microsoft enhanced mitigation experience toolkit.**

13.7 Memory Forensics Tools

In the event a system becomes compromised (or as many would say now, when), it may prove useful to analyze a memory image from an infected machine. Three of the most popular free tools for this purpose are Volatility, Rekall, and Redline. Prior to analysis, a system memory dump must be taken, and a quick search will reveal several free tools to do so.

Many cheat sheets are available for Volatility* and several blog posts are available describing its use, not to mention a 900-page book *The Art of Memory Forensics*, so suffice it to say that it is covered in much more detail elsewhere. For a simple view into what it can reveal, Figure 13.20 contains the output of the processes observed when the memory dump was taken on a target machine.

Rekall† is another memory forensics analysis tool that uses plugins similar to Volatility through which information targeted to a specific goal can be extracted. In Figure 13.21, instead of looking at processes via methods that help uncover rootkits, this output views processes and parent processes to determine how child processes were spawned.

Redline‡ is a Windows-only based tool from Mandiant (Fireeye) that can analyze memory dumps as well. Be prepared though, for it is much more time-intensive to generate analysis output than Volatility or Rekall. Once a memory image is loaded, Redline

* http://www.volatilityfoundation.org/
† http://www.rekall-forensic.com/
‡ https://www.fireeye.com/services/freeware/redline.html

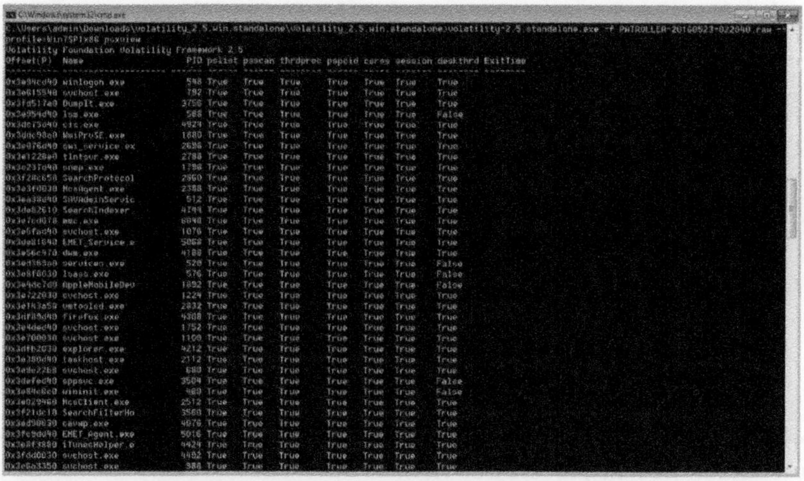

Figure 13.20 Volatility output of running processes.

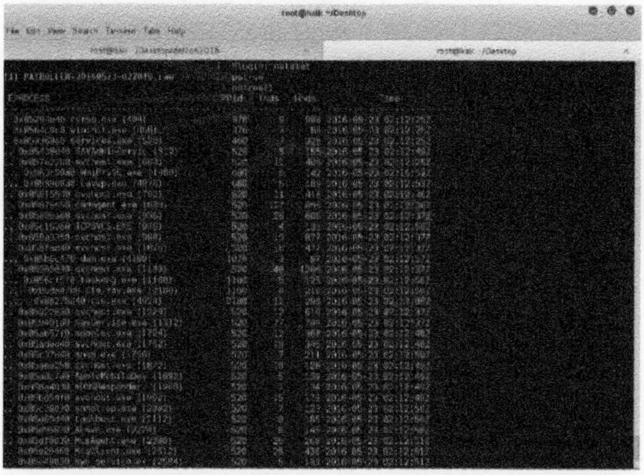

Figure 13.21 Rekall output of process tree plugin.

will run it through analysis and provide choices from an investigative starting viewpoint to guide users into the most likely prominent area to investigate first. A workflow view similar to the process tree output provided by Rekall is provided in Figure 13.22.

Each memory analysis tool has its own strengths, and should be exercised by the reader to determine useful strengths with respect to each individual's workflow.

13.8 Password Management

Probably one of the most practical cybersecurity tools is using a password management tool. Tools providing password management essentially enable users to store

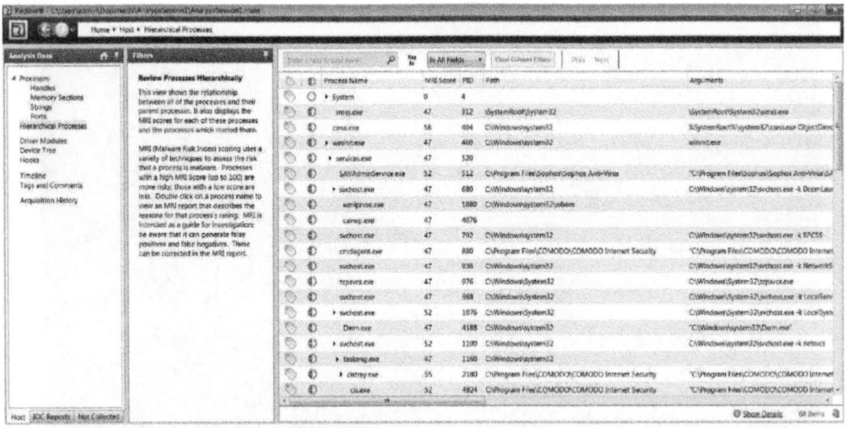

Figure 13.22 Redline process tree view.

all passwords into a single vault, which itself can be encrypted and secured with two-factor authentication. Examples in this category include LastPass, DashLane, and KeePass. All three provide the capability to be used on various operating systems, web browsers, and devices. The biggest benefit in using a password management tool is the ability to generate secure passwords that are random and

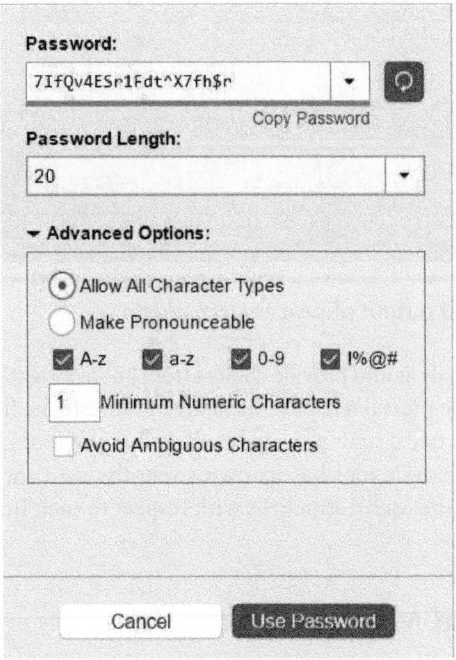

Figure 13.23 LastPass secure password generator.

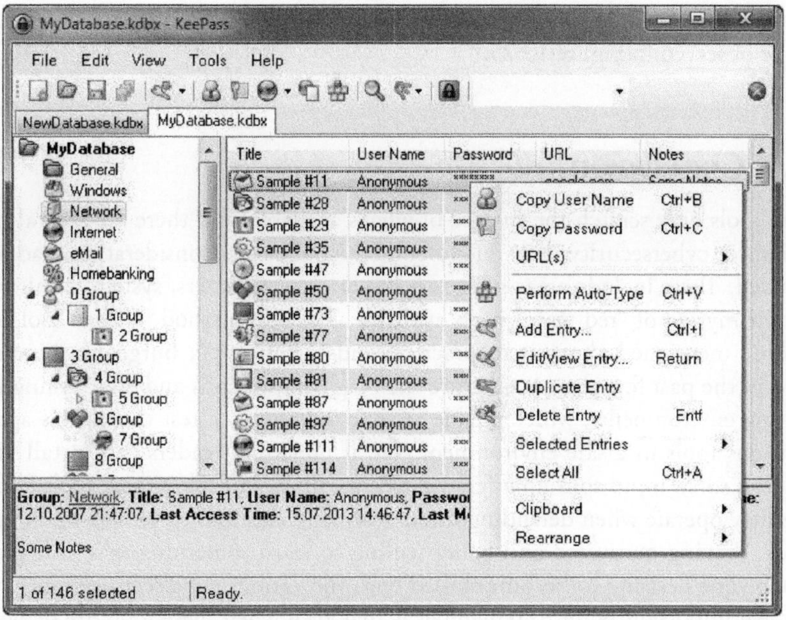

Figure 13.24 KeePass database view.

meet complex password security requirements to ensure password cracking will be difficult at best. A view of LastPass secure password generation is provided in Figure 13.23.

KeePass can be installed into web browsers similar to LastPass and Dashlane, but at first install it provides a view into a password database stored on the local system as depicted in Figure 13.24.

To alleviate concern about storing all passwords in a single location, each respective password management application provides strong protections against unauthorized attempts to recover the stored passwords. Enabling two-factor authentication in addition to the password vault encryption is the best method of ensuring that even if the company were to become compromised, passwords would be unrecoverable without the two-factor token. Google has adopted two-factor authentication in

Figure 13.25 Google two-factor authentication.

many of its services, and a representative view of Google's two-factor authentication can be observed in Figure 13.25.

13.9 Conclusion

These tools only scratch the surface of what's available, and there are several more sections of cybersecurity that, due to content conciseness consideration, had to be excluded. These include areas such as best practices analyzers, system monitoring, and the myriad of "red team" tools available. The best method to learn tools such as those mentioned above is to practice, and fortunately a burgeoning industry trend in the past few years is Capture the Flag competitions and establishing legal hacking environments, which enable anyone interested to test these tools against malicious tools in a safe environment. Or, if preferred, readers can install virtualization software to spin up a few virtual machines to deploy these tools and see how they operate when defending under normal conditions as well as when under attack. Staying motivated and being willing to learn something new will greatly help anyone desiring to become skilled with the various cybersecurity tools available. An important point to remember is that even when these tools are deployed, it is vital to understand as much as possible how to configure them and understand their intended purpose. Tools can only automate so much, and it's up to humans to fill in the remaining cybersecurity gap.

Chapter 14

Data and Research Initiatives for Cybersecurity Analysis

Julia Deng and Onur Savas

Contents

Big data based cybersecurity analytics is a data-centric approach. Its ultimate goal is to utilize available technology solutions to make sense of the wealth of relevant cyber data and turn it into actionable insights that can be used to improve the current practices of network operators and administrators. At its core is data. As in other fields, however, obtaining access to and curating data has always been challenging. This chapter aims at introducing relevant data sources for cybersecurity analysis, such as benchmark datasets for cybersecurity evaluation and testing, and certain research repositories where real world cybersecurity datasets, tools, models, and methodologies can be found to support research and development among cybersecurity researchers. In addition, some insights are added for the future directions on data sharing for big data based cybersecurity analysis.

14.1 Cybersecurity Data Sources

The datasets can be categorized by where they are collected from (e.g., network vs. host), which layer they are collected from (e.g., application layer vs. network layer), or how they are collected (e.g., network routers vs. system kernel). Instead of reinventing a wheel, we would like to follow the categorization presented in [1], and list cybersecurity datasets from the *Operating System*, *Network Traffic*, and *Applications*.

14.1.1 Datasets from the Operating System

An operating system (OS) is a system software that manages computer hardware and software resources and provides common services for computer programs. All computer programs require an operating system to function. OS has both volatile and non-volatile memory. Volatile memory, contrary to non-volatile memory, is computer memory that requires power to maintain the stored information; it retains its contents while powered on but when the power is interrupted the stored data is lost very rapidly or immediately. Examples of volatile memory include RAM while examples of non-volatile data include hard drive, CD, USB storage, and memory cards. Non-volatile memory is typically used for long-term persistent storage. Operating systems store and use many files in the non-volatile memory.

These files are invaluable sources as datasets for network forensics and cybersecurity applications.

Configuration files: Configuration files or config files configure the parameters and initial settings for some computer programs. They are used for user applications, server processes, and operating system settings. Some of the important configuration files that are of great interest for analysis are as follows.

- **File system:** File system mounting and unmounting records, modules that are currently loaded by the system, and configuration for copy, create directory, format, and so on operations.
- **System administration:** Group and user account management, superuser (or root) access privileges, package installation, and password management are some examples of system administration.
- **Networking:** Configuration for the wireless and wired networking interfaces, routing tables, gateways and networks that can be accessed by the current network(s), distributed file system access, and networking protocols information.
- **System commands:** System commands are commands that make the system work in harmony. Some examples include login, the commands that provide interaction between a user and the computer (e.g., bash in Linux), and boot commands.
- **Daemons:** Daemons are programs that run in noninteractive mode, or in other words, run in the background. Most of them run as services and are mostly related to the networking area. Some examples include FTP and Web servers, MySQL server, and timing servers.
- **User programs:** There are also many "user" programs that are not part of the kernel. They include configurations about how the program runs. For example, the character set they use, the time-zone, or the UI coloring preferences.

Logs: Log files contain events that are logged by the operating system components. These events are often predetermined by the operating system itself. System log files may contain information about device changes, device drivers, system changes, events, operations, and more while a data service log file records log events for each server request that runs a data service. Some examples of OS log files are as follows.

- **System events:** Each OS maintains several system logs that help administrators of the system by informing them of important events. The events

are written into a log file, which can record a variety of events, including system error messages, system startups, and system shutdowns.
  - **Application and service events:** Application and service events include operational actions performed by applications and services, such as startup, restart, and shutdown, application failures, and major application configuration changes.
  - **Command history:** Command history allows administrators to see a listing of the commands previously run under user and group accounts.
  - **File system access:** File access data records inserts, writes, reads, and deletes to the file system. The file system can be networked. The file access can be through processes or services.
- **Application files:** Applications files include executables, shell scripts, configuration files, log files, history files, libraries, application policies, user customization, and multimedia.
- **Data files:** Data files are the primary source for storing information for applications. Text files, document processing files, spreadsheets, databases, postscript and PDFs, and multimedia files are all examples of data files.
- **Swap files:** Operating systems use swap files as a file to provide space for programs that have been transferred from the processer's memory. They are generally temporary files and are deleted once the need is over.
- **Temporary files:** The temporary files that are needed for installation, or can be used to recover lost data if the program or computer is abnormally halted.
- **Volatile datasets:** Operating systems use RAM as a form of computer data storage which stores frequently used program instructions to increase the general speed of a system. RAM allows data items to be read or written in almost the same amount of time irrespective of the physical location of data inside the memory. Some important examples of RAM datasets are as follows.
  - **Network configuration:** Networking is a dynamic process. Hence, some of the network configuration is determined on the fly and stored in the RAM.
  - **Network connections:** With the availability of the wireless connections such as 4G, LTE, Wi-Fi, and Bluetooth, and the number of online services an operating system makes use of, it is very common to use various network interface configurations.
  - **Running processes:** A process is an instance of a computer program that is being executed. In addition, a process can have multiple threads, and a process can be launched by another process (e.g., by using "fork" in Linux). Identifying the running processes is beneficial for identifying programs that should be disabled or removed.
  - **Open files:** A program or a service generally opens many files during its execution. For example, a document or a spreadsheet is kept open while being edited. It is beneficial to keep track of open files, and restrict access to certain ones for system stability and security.

14.1.2 Datasets from Network Traffic

Data from network traffic can be used to detect network-based attack, spread of malicious programs, as well as network management. Almost all modern operating systems use the TCP/IP communication stack, which is composed of four major layers (if the physical layer is also included, then five major layers). The first layer is the Application Layer, which sends and receives data for applications such as hypertext transfer protocol (HTTP), file transfer protocol (FTP), or simple mail transfer protocol (SNMP). The Transport Layer provides end-to-end or host-to-host communication services for applications within a layered architecture of network components and protocols. This layer provides services such as connection-oriented data stream support, reliability, flow control, and multiplexing. The Network Layer is responsible for packet forwarding including routing through intermediate routers. Internet protocol (IP) is the de facto Network Layer protocol. The fourth layer is the Data Link Layer, which transfers data between adjacent network nodes in a wide area network (WAN) or between nodes on the same local area network (LAN) segment. Ethernet is the most commonly used Data Link Layer.

The following two datasets from these layers are of great interest for cybersecurity analytics:

NetFlow data: By default, traffic flow records in NetFlow can be exported to a user-specified monitoring station using UDP packets, if one of the following conditions occurs:

- The transport protocol indicates that the connection is completed (TCP FIN); there is a small delay to allow for the completion of the FIN acknowledgment handshaking;
- Traffic inactivity exceeds 15 seconds;
- For flows that remain continuously active, flow cache entries expire every 30 minutes to ensure periodic reporting of active flows.

Every single UDP datagram contains one flow header and 30 flow records. Each flow record is made up of several fields, including source/destination IP address, next hop address, input and output interface number, number of packets, total bytes, source/destination port, protocol, type of service (ToS), source/destination autonomous system (AS) number, and TCP flags (Cumulative OR of TCP flags). Note that the NetFlow record represents the packets in an aggregated format. Each line does not represent the information of a packet. Instead, each line represents the information of all packets in a flow (which is defined as a series of packets sent from a source IP address to a destination IP address over a period of time).

SNMP data: SNMP is an "Internet-standard protocol for managing devices on IP networks." As a component of the Internet Protocol Suite, SNMP consists of a set of standards for network management, including an application layer protocol, a database schema, and a set of data objects. Supported by typical network devices (e.g., routers, switches, servers, workstations, printers, modem racks, etc.), SNMP is widely used in network management systems to monitor network-attached devices for conditions that warrant administrative attention. SNMP exposes management data in the form of variables on the managed systems, which describe the system configuration. These variables can then be queried (and sometimes set) by managing applications. Typical management data includes operational status information, performance data, and other metrics specific to the function of a particular device. SNMP provides a flexible and practical method to retrieve information about the behavior of a device, without resorting to proprietary vendor software and drivers.

SNMP is an application layer protocol used to monitor network-attached devices. SNMP works as the *manager/agent* model. The manager and agent use a management information base (MIB) and a relatively small set of commands to exchange information. The MIB is organized in a tree structure with individual variables, represented as leaves on the branches. A long numeric tag or object identifier (OID) is used to distinguish each variable uniquely in the MIB and in SNMP messages.

14.1.3 Datasets from the Application Layer

Applications such as browsers, document processing software, e-mail, and computer games as well as services such as web servers and databases, use and create data. From an analytics point of view, collecting, examining, and analyzing this application data provides a great opportunity. In this section, we study what datasets can be collected from the application layer and have potential to further enhance big data analytics.

E-mail: E-mail is still widely used to exchange messages. E-mail is an asynchronous form of communication where the sender and recipient do not have to be online, as opposed to online messaging. In addition to the content of the e-mail, which might include attachments such as spreadsheets or images, e-mail metadata is a useful source of data and can be mined to provide insights into network forensics. The metadata is stored in the message header. The sender, and the recipient(s) of the message, which can include carbon-copied (CC'ed) or blind-carbon-copied (BCC'ed), are required fields. In addition, other metadata such as message identification number, type of e-mail client, routing information, and message content type is also available in the header.

Web usage: Web usage data contains information about user browsing data and metadata, and web server logs. For example, using browser metadata, the information about browser types, sites visited, cookies stored by websites, type of operating system or device used for web access, and interactions made with the web sites and/or browser can be retrieved. Web server logs contain information about the requests, including client IP address, request date/time, page requested, HTTP code, bytes served, user agent, and referrer.

Instant messaging and chats: Chats and instant messaging provide an environment for participants of the chat to share text, audio, and video among each other. This can be achieved either via peer-to-peer or using a server/client architecture. Chat and instant messaging logs contain information about files shared between the participants, the audio and video connection metadata, and other application specific metadata.

File sharing: File sharing can be achieved via peer-to-peer or client/server architecture. Traditionally, file sharing clients, e.g., FTP, use the server by initiating connections to it, authenticating to it (if required), reviewing the list of available files (if needed), and then transferring files to or from the server. Under peer-to-peer file sharing, the file sharing applications typically have a central server that gives clients information on where other clients are located, but the server does not participate in the transmission of files or file information.

14.2 Benchmark Datasets

A common practice in the cybersecurity community is to use benchmark datasets for the evaluation of cybersecurity algorithms and systems. For this purpose, cybersecurity researchers and analysts have been seeking methods to effectively curate benchmark datasets [2–9]. In the following we review several benchmark datasets widely accepted by the community, and their limitations.

14.2.1 DARPA KDD Cup Dataset

14.2.1.1 Website

https://www.ll.mit.edu/ideval/data/

14.2.1.2 Short Description

The DARPA KDD dataset [2,3] is the first stand corpora for evaluation of computer network intrusion detection systems. It was constructed and published by the Cyber Systems and Technology Group (formerly the DARPA Intrusion Detection Evaluation Group) of MIT Lincoln Laboratory in 1998, 1999, and 2000. This dataset was later criticized for issues associated with the artificial injection of normal and attack traffic data types into the generated datasets. The key problems with this approach are that they do not reflect real-world network traffic data, contain irregularities in the dataset such as the absence of false positives, are outdated for effective intrusion detection system (IDS) evaluation of modern networks both in terms of attack types and network infrastructure, and lack actual attack data records.

The KDD Cup 1999 dataset was created by processing the tcpdump portions of the 1998 DARPA IDS evaluation dataset [10]. The network traffic records were generated through simulations performed on a military networking environment that consisted of normal background traffic and attack traffic data records and where the two types are merged together in a simulated environment. Despite this, the dataset has been widely used as a benchmark IDS dataset; however, it has now become outdated as its network traffic of attacks and normal users cannot reflect real-world traffic patterns in modern computer networks.

14.2.2 CDX 2009 Dataset

14.2.2.1 Website

http://www.usma.edu/crc/sitepages/datasets.aspx

14.2.2.2 Short Description

The CDX 2009 dataset [4,5] was established through Cyber Defense Exercise (CDX) 2009 in an attempt to provide users of the dataset with a means to correlate IP addresses found in the PCAP files with the IP addresses to hosts on the internal USMA (United States Military Academy) network. It includes *3 days Snort Intrusion Detection Logs, 3 days Domain Name Service Logs,* and *24 hour Web Server Logs.* This dataset demonstrates that network warfare competitions can be utilized to generate modern-day labeled datasets with real-word attacks and normal uses. This data has been used as a benchmark dataset. However, it has also become kind of outdated as it could not provide enough volume and diversity of traffic normally seen in production networks.

14.2.3 UNB ISCX 2012

14.2.3.1 Website

http://www.unb.ca/research/iscx/dataset/iscx-IDS-dataset.html

14.2.3.2 Short Description

The UNB ISCX 2012 dataset [6,7], generated by the University of New Brunswick, represents dynamically generated data which reflects network traffic and intrusions. This dataset is collected using a real-time testbed that generates real traffic (e.g., HTTP, SMTP, SSH, IMAP, POP3, and FTP) to mimic users' behavior. It also incorporates various multistage attack scenarios for malicious traffic. It is built on the concept of profiles that include the details of intrusions. It uses two profiles—α and β—during the generation of the datasets. α profiles are constructed using the knowledge of specific attacks and β profiles are built using the filtered traffic traces. Normal background traffic is provided by executing user-profiles that were synthetically generated at random synchronized times creating profile-based user behaviors. This dataset represents a good sampling of the most widely used datasets by the research community; however, it still lacks realistic Internet background noise and the overall normal traffic is not comparable to a real live network.

14.3 Research Repositories and Data Collection Sites

Several research repositories [11–13] have been built to share real world cybersecurity datasets, tools, models, and methodologies, in order to support research and development among cybersecurity researchers, technology developers, and policymakers in academia, industry, and the government. In addition, there are some public repositories or data collection websites [14–16], maintained by an individual or a private company or university, which are freely available on the Internet. Those websites provide rich data sources for cybersecurity researchers. We realize it is impossible to list all the available data repositories and data collection sites. In the following we only list some examples, and suggest that readers visit various sites to find relevant data fitting their needs.

14.3.1 IMPACT (The Information Marketplace for Policy and Analysis of Cyber-Risk & Trust)

14.3.1.1 Website

https://www.dhs.gov/csd-impact

14.3.1.2 Short Description

IMPACT has been established and is funded by the U.S. Department of Homeland Security (DHS) Science and Technology Directorate (S&T) Cyber Security Division (CSD). Its predecessor program is Protected Repository for the Defense of Infrastructure Against Cyber Threats (PREDICT). IMPACT provides current network operational data to researchers in a secure and controlled manner, that respects the security, privacy, and legal and economic concerns of Internet users and network operators. Three key capabilities offered by IMPACT are

1. A Web-based portal that catalogs current computer network and operational data, and handles data requests.

2. Secure access to multiple sources of data collected on the Internet. It provides standardized policies and procedures to connect researchers with a federation of providers and hosts, and a central interface and process to discover and access tools to analyze and/or use data from within and outside of IMPACT. It provides vetted data source provenance and mediated access entitlement, so sensitive data is shared with legitimate researchers.
3. Facilitates data sharing among IMPACT participants for the purpose of developing new models, technologies, and products, thereby increasing cyber security capabilities. It provides feedback mechanisms among providers, hosts, researchers, and domain experts to improve and optimize data, tools, analytics, and collective knowledge.

IMPACT continually adds new data that is responsive to cyber risk management (e.g., attacks and measurements) to provide the R&D community with timely, high-value information to enhance research innovation and quality.

14.3.1.3 Example Datasets

- *Application Layer Security Data*: The scan data of the HTTPS ecosystem includes regular and continuing scans of the HTTPS Ecosystem from 2012 and 2013, including parsed and raw X.509 certificates, temporal state of scanned hosts, and the raw ZMap output of scans on port 443. The dataset contains approximately 43 million unique certificates from 108 million hosts collected via 100+ scans. The total size of the dataset is 120 GB.
- *BGP Routing Data*: A BGP route hijacking incident dataset includes BGP control-plane data (i.e., route updates) that captures several route hijacking incidents. This dataset can be used for evaluating algorithms that aim to detect route miscreant behavior or for evaluating the effects of such activity (e.g., how far these updates propagated in the Internet). The total size of the dataset is 170 MB.
- *IDS and Firewall Data*: Firewall/IDS logs dataset includes logs submitted by over 1700 networks (5 full Class B networks, over 45 full Class C networks, and many smaller subnetworks). The logs provide a condensed summary obtained from various firewall and IDS platforms including BlackIce Defender, CISCO PIX Firewalls, ZoneAlarm, Linux IPchains, Portsentry, and Snort. The total size of the dataset is 2 GB.
- *Sinkhole Data*: Client connection data from a Flashback sinkhole includes the IPv4 address of the connecting client (bot), and the number of attempted connections from that IP address in a minute. Number of attempted connections was measured by the number of TCP SYN/ACK packets sent to clients as Step 2 of the TCP three-way handshake. The total size of the dataset is 225 MB.
- *Synthetically Generated Data*: Packet captures from the 2016 National Collegiate Cyber Defense Competition (nccdc.org). NCCDC is a multi-day competition that specifically focuses on the operational aspects of managing and protecting

an existing commercial network infrastructure. Teams of undergraduate and graduate students are provided with a fully functional (but insecure) small business network they must secure, maintain, and defend against a live Red Team. Teams must also respond to business tasks called "injects" throughout the competition. The total size of the dataset is 1900 GB.

- *Traffic Flow Data*: DNS AMPL DDOS DEC2015 is a real-world distributed denial of service (DDoS) attack captured at Merit's border router in SFPOP. It is a reflection and amplification DDoS attack that is mostly based on the DNS protocol. The attack appears within ft-v05.2015-07-22.140000-0400. The attack victim should appear under 204.38.0.0/21.
- *Scalable Network Monitoring Program Traffic*: Netflow data that captures the large NTP DDoS attacks during the early months of 2014. The total size of the dataset is 1.5 GB.

14.3.2 CAIDA (The Center for Applied Internet Data Analysis)

14.3.2.1 Website

http://www.caida.org/data/

14.3.2.2 Short Description

CAIDA is an analysis and research group based at the University of California, San Diego's Supercomputer Center. CAIDA promotes data sharing, provides a privacy sensitive data sharing framework that employs technical and policy means to balance individual privacy, security, and legal concerns against the needs of government researchers and scientists for access to data in an attempt to address the inevitable conflict between data privacy and science. It maintains servers that allow researchers to download data via secure login and encrypted transfer protocols.

CAIDA aims to (1) provide collection, curation, analysis, visualization, and dissemination of sets of the best available Internet data, (2) provide macroscopic insight into the behavior of Internet infrastructure worldwide, (3) improve the integrity of the field of Internet science, (4) improve the integrity of operational Internet measurement and management, and (5) inform science, technology, and communications public policies.

14.3.2.3 Example Datasets

- *DDoS Attack 2007*: One hour of anonymized traffic traces from a DDoS attack on August 4, 2007. This type of denial-of-service attack attempts to block access to the targeted server by consuming computing resources on the server and by consuming all of the bandwidth of the network connecting the server to the Internet. The total size of the dataset is 5.3 GB (compressed; 21 GB uncompressed).

- *The CAIDA UCSD IPv6 DNS Names Dataset*: DNS names are useful for obtaining additional information about routers and hosts making up the Internet topology. For example, DNS names of routers often encode the link type (backbone vs. access), link capacity, point of presence (PoP), and geographic location. This dataset is collected from CAIDA's large-scale traceroute-based measurements running on the Archipelago (Ark) measurement infrastructure.
- *The Dataset on the Witty Worm*: This dataset contains information useful for studying the spread of the Witty worm. The dataset is divided into two portions: a publicly available set of files that contains summarized information that does not individually identify infected computers, and a restricted-access set of files that does contain more sensitive information, including packet traces containing complete IP and UDP headers and partial payload received from hosts spreading the Witty worm.
- *Internet Traces 2014 Dataset*: This dataset contains anonymized passive traffic traces from CAIDA's equinix-chicago and equinix-sanjose monitors on high-speed Internet backbone links. This data is useful for research on the characteristics of Internet traffic, including application breakdown, security events, topological distribution, and flow volume and duration.

14.3.3 Publicly Available PCAP Repository Collections—netresec.com

14.3.3.1 Website

http://www.netresec.com/?page=PcapFiles

14.3.3.2 Short Description

This site, maintained by an independent software vendor, provides a list of public packet capture repositories, which are freely available on the Internet. It provides the PCAP datasets in the following categories:

- Cyber Defense Exercises (CDX): This category includes network traffic from exercises and competitions, such as CDX and red-team/blue-team competitions.
- Capture the Flag Competitions (CTF): PCAP files from CTF competitions and challenges.
- Malware Traffic: Captured malware traffic from honeypots, sandboxes, or real world intrusions.
- Network Forensics: Network forensics training, challenges, and contests.
- SCADA/ICS Network Captures

- Packet Injection Attacks/Man-on-the-Side Attacks
- Uncategorized PCAP Repositories
- Single PCAP files

14.3.3.3 Example Datasets

- Dataset under CDX
  - MACCDC—PCAPs from National CyberWatch Mid-Atlantic Collegiate Cyber Defense Competition. The MACCDC is a unique experience for college and university students to test their cybersecurity knowledge and skills in a competitive environment. The MACCDC 2012 data set is generated from the MACCDC 2012 competition. It includes everything from scanning/recon through exploitation, as well as some c99 shell traffic. Roughly it has 22694356 total connections. http://www.netresec.com/?page=MACCDC
  - ISTS—PCAPs from The Information Security Talent Search. http://www.netresec.com/?page=ISTS
  - Captures from the "2009 Inter-Service Academy Cyber Defense Competition" served by Information Technology Operations Center (ITOC), United States Military Academy. https://www.itoc.usma.edu/research/dataset/
- Dataset under CTF
  - DEFCON Capture the Flag Contest traces (from DEF CON 8, 10 and 11). http://cctf.shmoo.com/
  - DEFCON 17 Capture the Flag Contest traces
    - http://ddtek.biz/dc17.html
    - https://media.defcon.org/torrent/DEF CON 17 CTF.torrent (torrent)
    - https://media.defcon.org/dc-17/DEFCON 17 Hacking Conference—Capture the Flag complete packet capture.rar (direct download)
- Malware Traffic
  - Contagio Malware Dump: Collection of PCAP files categorized as APT, Crime or Metasplot.
  - Malware analysis blog that shares malware as well as PCAP files. http://malware-traffic-analysis.net/
  - GTISK PANDA Malrec—PCAP files from malware samples run in PANDA. http://panda.gtisc.gatech.edu/malrec/
  - Stratosphere IPS—PCAP and Argus datasets with malware traffic. https://stratosphereips.org/category/dataset.html
  - Regin malware PCAP files. http://laredo-13.mit.edu/~brendan/regin/pcap/
  - Ponmocup malware/trojan (a.k.a. Milicenso) PCAP. https://download.netresec.com/pcap/ponmocup/vm-2.pcap

- Network Forensics
  - Hands-on Network Forensics—Training PCAP dataset from FIRST 2015. https://www.first.org/_assets/conf2015/networkforensics_virtualbox.zip (VirtualBox VM), 4.4 GB PCAP with malware, client- and server-side attacks as well as "normal" Internet traffic.
  - Forensic Challenge 14—"Weird Python" (The Honeynet Project). http://honeynet.org/node/1220
- SCADA/ICS Network Captures
  - 4SICS ICS Lab PCAP files—360 MB of PCAP files from the ICS village at 4SICS. http://www.netresec.com/?page=PCAP4SICS
  - Compilation of ICS PCAP files indexed by protocol (by Jason Smith). https://github.com/automayt/ICS-pcap
  - DigitalBond S4x15 ICS Village CTF PCAPs. http://www.digitalbond.com/s4/s4x15-week/s4x15-ics-village/
- Packet Injection Attacks/Man-on-the-Side Attacks
  - PCAP files from research by Gabi Nakibly et al. [17] http://www.cs.technion.ac.il/~gnakibly/TCPInjections/samples.zip
  - Packet injection against id1.cn, released by Fox-IT at BroCon 2015. https://github.com/fox-it/quantuminsert/blob/master/presentations/brocon2015/pcaps/id1.cn-inject.pcap
  - Packet injection against www.02995.com, doing a redirect to www.hao123.com. https://www.netresec.com/files/hao123-com_packet-injection.pcap

14.3.4 Publicly Available Repository Collections—SecRepo.com

14.3.4.1 Website

http://www.secrepo.com/

14.3.4.2 Short Description

This site, maintained by Mike Sconzo, provides a list of security related data in the categories of network, malware, system, and others. This data is shared under a Creative Commons Attribution 4.0 International License. It also provides a collection of links to other third-party data repositories. It is a rich data source for cybersecurity researchers. Here we only list some examples.

14.3.4.3 Example Datasets

- Network
  - Bro logs generated from various Threatglass samples, Exploit kits, benign traffic, and unlabeled data. 6663 samples available.

- Snort logs generated from various Threatglass samples, Exploit kits, benign traffic, and unlabeled data. Two datasets, 5 MB and 9 MB.

■ Malware
- Static information about Zeus binaries—Static information (JSON) of about 8 k samples from ZeuS Tracker.
- Static information about APT1 binaries—Static information (JSON) of APT1 samples from VirusShare.

■ System
- Squid Access Log—Combined from several sources (24 MB compressed, ~200 MB uncompressed).
- Honeypot data—Data from various honeypots (Amun and Glastopf) used for various BSides presentations posted below. Approx 213 k entries, JSON format.

■ Other
- Security Data Analysis Labs, Connection Log—(522 MB compressed, 3 GB uncompressed) ~22 million flow events.

■ Third-Party Data Repository Links
- Network
    - Internet-Wide Scan Data Repository (https://scans.io/)—Various types of scan data (License Info: Unknown)
    - Detecting Malicious URLs (http://sysnet.ucsd.edu/projects/url/)—An anonymized 120-day subset of our ICML-09 data set (470 MB and 234 MB), consisting of about 2.4 million URLs (examples) and 3.2 million features. (License Info: Unknown)
    - OpenDNS public domain lists (https://github.com/opendns/public-domain-lists)—A random sample of 10,000 domain names all over the globe that are receiving queries, sorted by popularity. (License Info: Public Domain)
    - Malware URLs (http://malware-traffic-analysis.net/)—Updated daily list of domains and URLs associated with malware. (License Info: Disclaimer posted in link)
    - Information Security Centre of Excellence (ISCX) (http://www.unb.ca/research/iscx/dataset/index.html)—Data related to Botnets and Android Botnets. (License Info: Unknown)
    - Industrial Control System Security (https://github.com/hslatman/awesome-industrial-control-system-security)—Data related to SCADA Security. (License Info: Apache License 2.0 [site], Data: various)
- Malware
    - The Malware Capture Facility Project (http://mcfp.weebly.com/)—Published long-runs of malware including network information. The Malware Capture Facility Project is an effort from the Czech Technical University ATG Group for capturing, analyzing, and publishing real and long-lived malware traffic. (License Info: Unknown)

    - Project Bluesmote (http://bluesmote.com/)—Syrian Bluecoat Proxy Logs. This data was recovered from public FTP servers in Syria over a period of six weeks in late 2011. The logs are from Blue Coat SG-9000 filtering proxies (aka "deep packet inspection") installed by Syrian ISPs and used to censor and surveil the Internet. The data set is ~55 GB in total compressed, and almost 1/2 TB uncompressed. (License Info: Public Domain)
    - Drebin Dataset (https://www.sec.cs.tu-bs.de/~danarp/drebin/index.html)—Android malware. The dataset contains 5,560 applications from 179 different malware families. The samples have been collected in the period of August 2010 to October 2012. (License Info: Listed on site)
- System
    - Website Classification (http://data.webarchive.org.uk/opendata/ukwa.ds.1/classification/)—(License Info: Public Domain, info on site)
    - Public Security Log Sharing Site (http://data.webarchive.org.uk/opendata/ukwa.ds.1/classification/)—This site contains various free shareable log samples from various systems, security and network devices, applications, and so on. The logs are collected from real systems; some contain evidence of compromise and other malicious activity. (License Info: Public, site source)
    - CERT Insider Threat Tools (https://www.cert.org/insider-threat/tools/index.cfm)—A collection of synthetic insider threat test datasets, including both synthetic background data and data from synthetic malicious actors. (License Info: Unknown)
- Threat Feeds
    - ISP Abuse Email Feed—Feed showing IOCs from various abuse reports (other feeds also on the site) (License Info: Unknown)
    - Malware Domain List (https://www.malwaredomainlist.com/mdl.php)—Labeled malicious domains and IPs (License Info: Unknown)
    - CRDF Threat Center (https://threatcenter.crdf.fr/)—List of new threats detected by CRDF Anti Malware. (License Info: Open Usage)
    - abuse.ch trackers (https://www.abuse.ch/)—Trackers for ransomeware, ZeuS, SSL Blacklist, SpyEye, Palevo, and Feodo (License Info: Unknown)

14.4 Future Directions on Data Sharing

As we have discussed thus far, many large and rich cybersecurity datasets are generated due to the recent advances in computers, mobile devices, Internet-of-Things, and computing paradigms. However, access to them and identifying a suitable dataset is not an easy task, which clearly hinders cybersecurity progress. In addition, the data is now so overwhelming and multidimensional that no single lab/organization can possibly completely analyze it. There is an increasing need for sharing the data sources to support the design and develop cybersecurity tools, models, and methodology.

Several research initiatives and data sharing repositories have been established, aiming to provide an open but standardized way to share the cybersecurity resources among cyber security researchers, technology developers, and policymakers in academia, industry, and the government. There are also many public repositories or data collection websites, maintained by an individual or a private company or university, which are freely available on the Internet.

It is worth noting that the current practice of data sharing still does not completely fulfill the increasing need, due to the following reasons:

- There is *no well-established method to protect the data access right*. Mostly, the current practice is to provide open access to the community, which is not practical as data original owners (generator or original collector) with certain contexts need to specify the access condition. In particular, the contributing lab/researchers should be able to determine when—and to what extent—the data is made available, and the conditions under which it can be used (e.g., who, what organization, when, etc.).
- There is *no established mechanism to monitor and track the usage of data*. There is no established mechanism to provide credit for sharing data and, conversely, in competitive situations, shared data could even be used unfairly by reviewers in confidential paper reviews.
- There are *many data formats and there is no standard for metadata*. Annotated metadata is often obsolete but is very important.
- There is *no internal connection among these tools*. In the cybersecurity community, there are different groups of researchers and experts, and various users have different focus and expectations for data sharing. Over the last decade, the amount of openly available and shared cybersecurity data has increased substantially. However, lack of internal connections among these tools limits their wide adoptions.
- There is *no easy way to share and access*. Some existing systems require many lengthy steps (create accounts, fill forms, wait for approval, upload data via ftp, sharing services, or shipping a hard drive, etc.) to share data, which may significantly reduce their engagement. Some systems provide only limited access to certain users, which again significantly impacts its adoption.
- *Lack of sufficient benchmark data and benchmark analytics tools for cybersecurity evaluation and testing*. It is the common practice in the cybersecurity community to use benchmark datasets for the evaluation of cybersecurity algorithms and systems. It was found that the state-of-the-art cybersecurity benchmark datasets (e.g., KDD, UNM) are no longer reliable because their datasets cannot meet the expectations of current advances in computer technology.

Benchmark tools and metrics also help cybersecurity analysts take a qualitative approach to the capabilities of their cybersecurity infrastructure and methodology. The community is looking for new benchmark data and benchmark analytics tools for cybersecurity evaluation and testing.

In short, data sharing is a complex task with many challenges. It needs to be done properly. If it is done correctly, everyone involved benefits from the collective intelligence. Otherwise, it may mislead participants or create a learning opportunity for our adversaries.

The ultimate goal of cybersecurity analysis is to utilize available technology solutions to make sense of the wealth of relevant cyber data, turning it into actionable insights that can be used to improve the current practices of network operators and administrators. In other words, cybersecurity analysis is really dealing with the issue of how to effectively extract useful information from cyber data and use that information to provide informed decisions to network operators or administrators. With more and more shared datasets, a more standardized way of sharing, and more advanced data analysis tools, we expect that the current practice of cybersecurity analysis can be significantly improved in the near future.

References

1. Kent, K. et al. Guide to integrating forensic techniques into incident response, NIST Special Publication 800-86.
2. KDD cup data, https://www.ll.mit.edu/ideval/data/1999data.html.
3. McHugh, J. Testing intrusion detection systems: A critique of the 1998 and 1999 DARPA intrusion detection system evaluations as performed by Lincoln Laboratory, *ACM Transactions on Information and System Security*, 3(4): 262–294, 2000.
4. CDX 2009 dataset, http://www.usma.edu/crc/SitePages/DataSets.aspx.
5. Sangster, B., O'Connor, T. J., Cook, T., Fanelli, R., Dean, E., Morrell, C., and Conti, G. J. Toward instrumenting network warfare competitions to generate labeled datasets, in *CSET* 2009.
6. UNB ISCX 2012 dataset, http://www.unb.ca/research/iscx/dataset/iscx-IDS-dataset.html.
7. Bhuyan, M. H., Bhattacharyya, D. K., and Kalita, J. K. Towards generating real-life datasets for network intrusion detection, *International Journal of Network Security*, 17(6): 683–701, Nov. 2015.
8. Zuech, R., Khoshgoftaar, T. M., Seliya, N., Najafabadi, M. M., and Kemp, C. New intrusion detection benchmarking system, *Proceedings of the Twenty-Eighth International Florida Artificial Intelligence Research Society Conference*, 2015.
9. Abubakar, A. I., Chiroma, H., and Muaz, S. A. A review of the advances in cyber security benchmark datasets for evaluating data-driven based intrusion detection systems, *Proceedings of the 2015 International Conference on Soft Computing and Software Engineering (SCSE'15)*.

10. Tavallaee, M., Bagheri, E., Lu, W., Ghorbani, A. A detailed analysis of the KDD CUP 99 Data Set. In *Proceedings of the 2009 IEEE Symposium on Computational Intelligence in Security and Defense Applications (CISDA 2009)*, 2009.
11. https://www.dhs.gov/csd-impact.
12. https://www.caida.org/data/.
13. https://catalog.data.gov/dataset?tags=cybersecurity.
14. http://www.netresec.com/?page=PcapFiles.
15. http://www.secrepo.com/.
16. http://www-personal.umich.edu/~mejn/netdata/.
17. Nakibly, G. et al. Website-targeted false content injection by network operators. https://arxiv.org/abs/1602.07128, 2016.

Index

A

B

E

F

G

U

V

W

X

Z